Queenship and Power

Series Editors

Charles Beem
University of North Carolina, Pembroke
Pembroke, NC, USA

Carole Levin
University of Nebraska-Lincoln
Lincoln, NE, USA

This series focuses on works specializing in gender analysis, women's studies, literary interpretation, and cultural, political, constitutional, and diplomatic history. It aims to broaden our understanding of the strategies that queens—both consorts and regnants, as well as female regents—pursued in order to wield political power within the structures of male–dominant societies. The works describe queenship in Europe as well as many other parts of the world, including East Asia, Sub-Saharan Africa, and Islamic civilization.

More information about this series at
http://www.springer.com/series/14523

William B. Robison
Editor

History, Fiction, and *The Tudors*

Sex, Politics, Power, and Artistic License
in the Showtime Television Series

Editor
William B. Robison
Southeastern Louisiana University
Hammond, Louisiana, USA

Queenship and Power
ISBN 978-1-137-43881-2   ISBN 978-1-137-43883-6 (eBook)
DOI 10.1057/978-1-137-43883-6

Library of Congress Control Number: 2016946224

© The Editor(s) (if applicable) and The Author(s) 2016
This work is subject to copyright. All rights are solely and exclusively licensed by the Publisher, whether the whole or part of the material is concerned, specifically the rights of translation, reprinting, reuse of illustrations, recitation, broadcasting, reproduction on microfilms or in any other physical way, and transmission or information storage and retrieval, electronic adaptation, computer software, or by similar or dissimilar methodology now known or hereafter developed.
The use of general descriptive names, registered names, trademarks, service marks, etc. in this publication does not imply, even in the absence of a specific statement, that such names are exempt from the relevant protective laws and regulations and therefore free for general use.
The publisher, the authors and the editors are safe to assume that the advice and information in this book are believed to be true and accurate at the date of publication. Neither the publisher nor the authors or the editors give a warranty, express or implied, with respect to the material contained herein or for any errors or omissions that may have been made.

Cover image © Photos 12 / Alamy Stock Photo

Printed on acid-free paper

This Palgrave Macmillan imprint is published by Springer Nature
The registered company is Nature America Inc.
The registered company address is 1 New York Plaza, New York, NY 10004, U.S.A.

ACKNOWLEDGMENTS

An editor incurs a lot of debts. Mine begin with Sue Parrill, with whom I coauthored *The Tudors on Film and Television* and whose knowledge and insight have been a positive influence on my work with this new project. I certainly must acknowledge the kind encouragement I have received from Susan Doran and Thomas Freeman, editors of the exemplary collection, *Tudors and Stuarts on Film: Historical Perspectives*, and the numerous opportunities Tom has given me to participate with a brilliant array of scholars in roundtable discussions of the Tudors on film at meetings of the Sixteenth Century Society and Conference. I am grateful for the opportunity to participate in a 2010 Folger Shakespeare Library workshop, "Reassessing Henry VIII," where *The Tudors* was a frequent topic of fruitful discussion. Kristin Purdy and Michelle Smith at Palgrave Macmillan have been extraordinarily helpful and patient. I have benefited hugely from the friendship and support of Karen Fontenot, Dean of the College of Arts, Humanities, and Social Sciences at Southeastern Louisiana University. I have enjoyed hours of discussion about Tudor films with my colleagues and friends, Charles Elliott, Barbara Forrest, and Harry Laver. I have learned a great deal from the students in my special topics classes on history and film. I am especially proud that three of my former students—Keith Altazin, Caroline Armbruster, and Samantha Perez—have chapters in this volume. They and the other contributors—Tom Betteridge, Susan Bordo, Elizabeth Furdell, Maria Hayward, Robin Hermann, Megan Hickerson, Krista Kesselring, Carole Levin, Estelle

Paranque, Carlie Pendleton, Glenn Richardson, Victor Stater, Tania String, Anne Throckmorton, Retha Warnicke, and Kristen Walton—have done such outstanding work that my job as editor has been an easy one. My greatest thanks, as always, go to my wife Bibbet, my son Matt and his wife Sara, and my daughters Zoë and Molly.

Contents

1 Introduction 1
  William B. Robison

2 Henry VIII in *The Tudors*: Romantic Renaissance
  Warrior or Soap Opera Playboy? 27
  William B. Robison

3 Catherine of Aragon in *The Tudors*: Dark Hair, Devotion,
  and Dignity in Despair 59
  William B. Robison

4 *The Tudors*, Natalie Dormer, and Our "Default"
  Anne Boleyn 77
  Susan Bordo

5 The Last Four Queens of Henry VIII in *The Tudors* 97
  Retha M. Wanicke

6 The Significance of the King's Children in *The Tudors* 115
  Carole Levin and Estelle Paranque

7	The King's Sister(s), Mistresses, Bastard(s), and "Uncle" in *The Tudors* Kristen P. Walton	127
8	The King's In-Laws in *The Tudors* Anne Throckmorton	139
9	The King's Friends in *The Tudors* Victor L. Stater	153
10	Postmodern and Conservative: The King's Ministers in *The Tudors* Robin Hermann	167
11	A Cardboard Crown: Kingship in *The Tudors* Glenn Richardson	179
12	*The Tudors* and the Tudor Court: Know Your Symptom Thomas Betteridge	195
13	"The Dyer's Hands Are Always Stained": Religion and the Clergy in *The Tudors* Caroline Armbruster	209
14	Fact, Fiction, and Fantasy: Conspiracy and Rebellion in *The Tudors* Keith Altazin	223
15	Crime, Punishment, and Violence in *The Tudors* Krista J. Kesselring	235
16	Humanism and Humanitarianism in *The Tudors* Samantha Perez	249

17	All That Glitters is (Fool's) Gold: Depictions of Court Entertainment in *The Tudors* *Carlie Pendleton*	265
18	Holbein and the Artistic Mise-en-Scène of *The Tudors* *Tatiana C. String*	281
19	Fashionable Fiction: The Significance of Costumes in *The Tudors* *Maria Hayward*	293
20	Putting Women in Their Place: Gender, Sex, and Rape in *The Tudors* *Megan L. Hickerson*	307
21	Incomplete Prescription: Maladies and Medicine in *The Tudors* *Elizabeth Lane Furdell*	329

Index 343

ADDITIONAL PRAISE FOR *HISTORY, FICTION, AND THE TUDORS*

"*History, Fiction, and The Tudors: Sex, Politics, Power, and Artistic License in the Showtime Television Series* is an insightful, remarkably balanced, and highly readable contribution to the scholarly conversation about how history is repurposed and repackaged for popular entertainment, specifically television."

– Carolyn Colbert, Visiting Assistant Professor of English, Memorial University of Newfoundland, and contributor to *Henry VIII and History*

"As a guide to the historical errors and distortions of the popular television series *The Tudors*, this book is unequalled in the breadth and depth of its coverage. Twenty expert contributors in twenty chapters examine in detail both what *The Tudors* got right and the many places where the real history was distorted or ignored. C. L. R. James, the great Caribbean historian, wrote, 'There is no drama like the drama of history.' It is a dictum that the contributors appreciate and the makers of *The Tudors* are shown to have clearly neglected."

– Ronald H. Fritze, Dean of the College of Arts and Sciences and Professor of History, Athens State University, and editor of *Historical Dictionary of Tudor England*

"With a Henrician appetite for accuracy, these twenty essays examine all aspects of *The Tudors*: the persons who ruled; the places they romped; and their political, theological, and intellectual beliefs. Ideal for classroom use, these scholarly, accessible analyses of writing history and making fiction offer a clear, careful, and wide-ranging blend of fact and theory to guide students, scholars, theater and television professionals, and series fans to a more informed view of the Tudors."

– Catherine Loomis, Professor of English and Women's Studies, University of New Orleans, President of the Queen Elizabeth I Society, and author of *The Death of Elizabeth I: Remembering and Reconstructing the Virgin Queen*

"For better or worse, Showtime's *The Tudors* will define the way a generation of global television viewers visualizes and thinks about Henry VIII and his court. But what should we think about *The Tudors*? In this admirably wide-ranging volume William Robison and an international team of scholars of Tudor history carefully evaluate the series' strengths and weaknesses, its insights and moments of apparent madness. This is a comprehensive guide to *The Tudors* as both history lesson and popular cultural phenomenon."

– Greg Walker, Regius Professor of Rhetoric and English Literature, University of Edinburgh, and author of *The Private Life of Henry VIII: A British Film Guide*

List of Contributors

Keith Altazin teaches history at University High School, Baton Rouge and currently is revising his doctoral dissertation, "The Northern Clergy and the Pilgrimage of Grace" (Louisiana State University, 2011) for publication.

Caroline Armbruster is a PhD candidate in History at Louisiana State University, where she is writing about religion and gender.

Thomas Betteridge is Professor of English Literature and Drama at Oxford Brookes University. He is the author of *Writing Faith: Literature, Religion, and Politics in the Works of Thomas More* (2010), *Shakespearean Fantasy and Politics* (2005), *Literature and Politics in the English Reformation* (2004), and *Tudor Histories of the English Reformation 1530–1583* (1999); editor of *Borders and Travelers in Early Modern Europe* (2007), *Sodomy in Early Modern Europe* (2002); and coeditor with Thomas S. Freeman of *Henry VIII and History* (2012), coeditor with Greg Walker of *The Oxford Handbook to Tudor Drama* (2012), and coeditor with Anne Riehl of *Tudor Court Culture* (2010).

Susan Bordo is Professor of Gender and Women's Studies and holder of Otis Singletary Chair in the Humanities of the University of Kentucky. She is the author of *The Creation of Anne Boleyn: A New Look at England's Most Notorious Queen* (2013), *The Male Body: A New Look at Men in Public and Private* (2000), *Feminist Reinterpretations of Rene Descartes* (1999), *Twilight Zones: The Hidden Life of Cultural Images from Plato to O.J.* (1997), and *The Flight to Objectivity: Essays on Cartesianism and Culture* (1987); coauthor with Leslie Heywood of *Unbearable Weight: Feminism, Western Culture, and the Body* (2004); coeditor with Alison M. Jaggar of *Gender/Body/Knowledge: Feminist Reconstructions of Being and Knowing* (1989); and host of "The Creation of Anne Boleyn" blog.

Elizabeth Lane Furdell is retired Professor of History at the University of North Florida. She is the author of *Fatal Thirst: Diabetes in Britain Until Insulin* (2009), *Publishing and Medicine in Early Modern England* (2002), *The Royal Doctors: Medical Personnel at the Tudor and Stuart Courts* (2001), and *James Welwood: Physician to the Glorious Revolution* (1998); and editor of *Textual Healing: Essays on Medieval and Early Modern Medicine* (2005).

Maria Hayward is Professor of Early Modern History at the University of Southampton. She is the author of *Rich Apparel: Clothing and the Law in Henry VIII's England* (2009) and *Dress at the Court of Henry VIII* (2007); editor of *The Great Wardrobe Accounts of Henry VII and Henry VIII* (2012), *The 1542 Inventory of Whitehall: The Palace and Its Keeper* (2006); coeditor (with Elizabeth Kramer) of *Textiles and Text: Re-establishing the Link Between Archival and Object-based Research* (2007) and (with Frances Lennard) of *Tapestry Conservation: Principles and Practice* (2005).

Robin Hermann is Associate Professor of History at the University of Louisiana at Lafayette and author of "Money and Empire: The Failure of the Royal African Company," in Daniel Carey and Christopher Finlay, editors, *The Empire of Credit: The Financial Revolution in the British Atlantic World* and "Empire Builders and Mushroom Gentlemen: The Meanings of Money in Colonial Nigeria," in *The International Journal of African History*.

Megan L Hickerson is Associate Professor of History at Henderson State University and author of *Making Women Martyrs in Tudor England* (Palgrave Macmillan, 2005).

Krista J. Kesselring is Professor of History and Associate Academic Dean at Dalhousie University. She is the author of *Mercy and Authority in the Tudor State* (2003) and *The Northern Rebellion of 1569: Faith, Politics, and Protest in Elizabethan England* (Palgrave Macmillan, 2007); and coeditor with Tim Stretton, of *Married Women and the Law: Coverture in England and the Common Law World* (2013).

Carole Levin is Willa Cather Professor of History and Director of the Medieval and Renaissance Studies Program at the University of Nebraska. She is the coeditor with Charles Beem of Palgrave Macmillan's "Queenship and Power" series; and author of *Dreaming the English Renaissance: Politics and Desire in Court and Culture* (Palgrave Macmillan, 2008), *The Reign of Elizabeth I* (Palgrave Macmillan, 2002), and *The Heart and Stomach of a King: Elizabeth I and the Politics of Sex and Power* (1994); coauthor with John Watkins of *Shakespeare's Foreign Worlds: National and Transnational Identities in the Elizabethan Age* (2009); and editor of *Encyclopedia of Women in the Renaissance* (2007), *High and Mighty Queens of Early Modern England: Realities and Representations* (Palgrave 2003), and *Elizabeth I: Always Her Own Free Woman* (2003).

Estelle Paranque is a PhD candidate in History at University College London.

Carlie Pendleton is a PhD candidate in History at Oxford University.

Samantha Perez is a PhD candidate in History at Tulane University, an Instructor of History at Southeastern Louisiana University, and author of *The Isleños of Louisiana: On the Water's Edge* (2011).

Glenn Richardson is Reader in Early Modern History and Academic Director of History and Philosophy at St. Mary's University College. He is the author of *Renaissance Monarchy: The Reigns of Henry VIII, Francis I, and Charles V* (2002) and *The Field of the Cloth of Gold* (2013); editor of *The Contending Kingdoms: England and France 1420–1700* (2008); and coeditor with Susan Doran of *Tudor England and Its Neighbours* (Palgrave Macmillan, 2005).

William B. Robison is Professor of History and Head of the Department of History and Political Science; coauthor with Sue Parrill of *The Tudors on Film and Television* (2013) and host of the associated website www.tudorsonfilm.com; coeditor with Ronald H. Fritze of the *Historical Dictionary of Stuart England* (1996) and *Historical Dictionary of Late Medieval England* (2002); and director of the film *Louisiana During World War II*.

Victor L. Stater is Professor of History and Chair of the Department of History at Louisiana State University and author of *Duke Hamilton Is Dead: A Story of Aristocratic Life and Death in Stuart Britain* (1999), *Noble Rule: Stuart Lord Lieutenancy and the Transformation of English Politics* (1994), and *A Political History of Tudor and Stuart England: A Sourcebook* (2002).

Tatiana String is Associate Professor of Art at the University of North Carolina at Chapel Hill, author of *Art and Communication in the Reign of Henry VIII* (2008), and coeditor with Marcus Bull of *Tudorism: Historical Imagination and the Appropriation of the Sixteenth Century* (2012).

Anne Throckmorton is Assistant Professor of History at Randolph-Macon College.

Kristen P. Walton is Professor of History at Salisbury University and the author of *Catholic Queen, Protestant Patriarchy: Mary Queen of Scots and the Politics of Gender and Religion* (Palgrave Macmillan, 2007) and a forthcoming biography of Margaret Tudor.

Retha M. Warnicke is Professor of History at Arizona State University and author of *Wicked Women of Tudor England: Queens, Aristocrats, Commoners* (Palgrave Macmillan, 2012), *Mary Queen of Scots* (2006), *The Marrying of Anne of Cleves: Royal Protocol in Early Modern England* (2000), *The Rise and Fall of Anne Boleyn: Family Politics at the Court of Henry VIII* (1989), *Women of the English Renaissance and Reformation* (1983), and *William Lambarde, Elizabethan Antiquary 1536–1601* (1973).

CHAPTER 1

Introduction

William B. Robison

"You think you know a story, but you only know how it ends. To get to the heart of the story, you have to go back to the beginning." Thus does a voiceover by Jonathan Rhys Meyers as Henry VIII introduce each of the thirty-eight episodes of Showtime's *The Tudors*. His statement is one with which historians can only agree. Regrettably, its apparent promise of concern for historical accuracy is one on which four seasons and thirty-five hours of the hugely popular cable television series largely fail to deliver. More revealing of what is to come is that the first episode starts not in 1509, the real beginning of Henry's reign, but c. 1518 with the well-staged but fictitious assassination of Henry's nonexistent uncle, followed in rapid succession by the king being "inconsolable," angrily calling for war with France, and gleefully having sex with Bessie Blount, all within a few minutes both on-screen and in the storyline. From there the anachronisms, time compression, distortions, and outright inventions multiply, mingling with occasional moments of historicity and culminating with Henry agreeing with Thomas More and Thomas Wolsey's proposal to create something that sounds like the League of Nations.[1]

W.B. Robison (✉)
Department of History and Political Science, Southeastern Louisiana University, Hammond, LA, USA

This initial episode reveals a fundamental identity crisis that pervades the entire series. Is it supposed to be a serious historical drama, a clever deconstruction of traditional history, an artsy exercise in sociopolitical criticism, a period soap opera, or the world's longest piece of soft-core pornography? Is its target audience well-read history buffs, the hip intelligentsia, the demographic drawn to "chick flicks," or fans who like some semblance of a plot with their gratuitous sex and violence? That one can perhaps answer "all of the above" to both questions does not really clarify matters. Creator and writer Michael Hirst's response to criticism of the series has been similarly ambivalent. On one hand, he has said that his goal was entertainment rather than historical accuracy, which is fair enough—he is in the entertainment business. On the other hand, it is clear that he wants to be taken seriously in commenting about history even if not for recounting it literally. For example, he has said that his goal was to challenge the traditional views of Henry and the English Reformation. Further, he admits that there was too much emphasis on sex in the first two seasons, but that did not prevent his creating a bevy of fictitious sexual encounters in the third and fourth. Beyond that, he has made the all-too-frequent mistake of assuming that he can "improve" an already exciting story.[2]

Nevertheless, *The Tudors* is a genuine cultural phenomenon, one that historians of early modern England can hardly afford to ignore. It is by far the longest filmic event ever to deal with the Tudor dynasty. Filmed in Ireland for the Showtime premium cable television channel in the USA, it also appeared on BBC2 in the UK, CBC Television in Canada, and TV3 in Ireland, is now in syndication on other networks, is being distributed by Sony Pictures Television International, has been released through various digital outlets, and is available all over the world on DVD and Blu-ray, both as individual seasons and in a boxed set. It has won forty-one television awards and been nominated for sixty-five more, many of its stars have become international celebrities, it has its own rather sophisticated website, where one can buy a variety of series-related merchandise, and it has spawned fan sites, fan clubs, and fan fiction, as well as keeping Tudor blogs abuzz with commentary. Although the show has drawn fire from some television critics, others have had a largely positive reaction, while viewers have made it one of the highest rated programs in Showtime's history.[3]

The popular appeal of *The Tudors* poses both a dilemma and an opportunity to historians. Many have reacted with amusement, dismay, hostility, and/or cynical resignation to its extremely casual relationship with historicity. But despite its many inaccuracies, the plot lines are often dramatic and engaging, the actors are generally good, the production values are high, and the series does certain things well, for example, its depiction of court pageantry and sport. All this makes the story seem plausible, gives it an "authentic" look, and renders it as likely to mold popular opinion about Henry and his era in the twenty-first century as Alexander Korda's *The Private Life of Henry VIII* (1933) did in the twentieth century. Historians cannot afford simply to disdain and dismiss the show; rather, they have a responsibility to engage constructively the inaccuracies in *The Tudors* (and other films) unless history is to concede the field to fiction.[4]

However, historians can also take advantage of the popularity of *The Tudors*. In terms of scholarship, it provides abundant material for students of the emerging field of "Tudorism," which Marcus Bull and Tatiana String describe as "the post-Tudor mobilization of any and all representations, images, associations, artefacts, spaces, and cultural scripts that either have or are supposed to have their roots in the Tudor era." *The Tudors* already has been the subject of scholarly articles and presentations at professional conferences, in many of which contributors to this volume have participated. Moreover, historical films like *The Tudors* can serve a practical purpose, for discussing them in the classroom and the public forum—as well as scholarly publications—can encourage interest in real history, stimulate critical thinking, and reinforce memory. With proper guidance, students and others can be remarkably adept at comparing films with works of history and ferreting out errors. The extraordinary popularity of *The Tudors* makes it particularly useful in this regard. Therefore, rather than merely bemoaning its manifold flaws, it behooves historians to expose its errors while exploiting its Tudorist appeal.[5]

English filmmaker Michael Hirst is no stranger to the Tudor period or to controversy about his history-based projects, having written the screenplays for Shekhar Kapur's feature films *Elizabeth* (1998) and *Elizabeth: The Golden Age* (2007). Most of the directors for *The Tudors*—Jon Amiel, Ciaran Donnelly, Brian Kirk, Alison Maclean, Colm McCarthy, Charles McDougall, Jeremy Podeswa, Steve Shill, Dearbhla Walsh—have worked in both film and television, and some have collaborated with Hirst and/or worked on other historically themed shows, as have cinematographer Ousama Rawi, editors Lisa Grootenboer and Wendy Hallam Martin, score composer Trevor Morris, and costume designer Joan Bergin.[6]

The star of *The Tudors*, Jonathan Rhys Meyers, is an odd choice to play Henry VIII, to whom he bears absolutely no physical resemblance and whose colossal ambition, conflicting impulses, gargantuan appetites, and outsized emotions he often struggles to convey. On-screen more than anyone except the king is Henry Cavill as Charles Brandon and, after him, Anthony Brophy as imperial ambassador Eustace Chapuys, both decidedly ahistorical but nonetheless engaging. Several characters who were major players in the political and religious struggles of the 1530s and 1540s and who thus should appear in all four seasons arrive late or depart without explanation: Henry Czerny, a lightweight amalgamation of the 2nd and 3rd Dukes of Norfolk, the latter of whom should have a major role throughout Henry's reign but vanishes at the end of Season One; Hans Matheson, who portrays Archbishop Thomas Cranmer with insufficient gravitas in Season Two and then is gone; Simon Ward, a rather one-dimensional Catholic fanatic as Stephen Gardiner, who does not show up until Season Three; and Alan Van Sprang, a remarkably unpleasant Francis Bryan who mysteriously appears at the beginning of Season Three and disappears at the end.

Seasons One and Two are distinctly better than Three and Four, in part because Maria Doyle Kennedy and Natalie Dormer's strong performances as Henry's longest-lasting and most interesting wives, Catherine of Aragon and Anne Boleyn. Neither Anita Briem or Annabelle Wallis, Jane Seymour in Seasons Two and Three, respectively, measures up; Joss Stone is able but miscast as the supposedly ugly Anne of Cleves; Tamzin Merchant's adolescent appearance and behavior as Catherine Howard make her frequent nude scenes seem like child pornography; and Joely Richardson, though very good, has a fairly limited role as Catherine Parr. The first two seasons also feature stronger supporting actors, notably Sam Neill as the most fully realized on-screen Wolsey ever; Jeremy Northam, who emerges from the shadow of Paul Scofield (*A Man for All Seasons*) as Thomas More; Nick Dunning, splendidly slimy as Thomas Boleyn; and James Frain as a more complex Thomas Cromwell than the paper villain usually seen on film. The major characters in Seasons Three and Four are less compelling, for example, Max Brown and Andrew McNair as Edward and Thomas Seymour, respectively; Emma Hamilton as Anne Stanhope; Rod Hallett as Richard Rich; Frank McCusker as Risley (Thomas Wriothesley); Torrance Coombs as Thomas Culpeper; and David O'Hara as the Earl of Surrey. A notable exception is Sarah Bolger, who plays Princess Mary with considerable subtlety as she evolves from a sad, neglected teenaged girl into the bitter young woman who later burned nearly 300 heretics.

Season One's main attraction is the breakup of Henry's first marriage to Catherine of Aragon and perpetually hot pursuit of Anne Boleyn, whose family urge her to replace her sister Mary in the king's bed but who refuses to yield, even if in a dream sequence she urges him, "Seduce me." Other story lines include Wolsey's efforts to obtain a divorce for the king and the papal crown for himself; a failed plot by the Duke of Buckingham (Steve Waddington) to seize the throne; the birth of the royal bastard Henry Fitzroy (Zak Jenciragic) to Elizabeth Blount (Ruta Gedmintas), his ennoblement as Duke of Richmond, and eventual death; alternating plans for war against and alliances with Francis I of France (Emmanuel Leconte) and Emperor Charles V (Sebastian Armesto), including marriage proposals for Princess Mary and much pageantry; completely invented marriages by Henry's sister Margaret (Gabrielle Anwar) to the king of Portugal and then Brandon; Henry's pamphlet war with Martin Luther; More's estrangement from the king and nascent persecution of Lutherans; Cromwell's premature arrival; royal temper tantrums; and lots of sex; all culminating with Wolsey's fictitious suicide.

Marital politics continue to dominate Season Two, with Henry getting his divorce and marrying Anne, who gives him a daughter Elizabeth but no son, encourages his affair with Madge Shelton (Laura Jane Laughlin) to forestall other rivals but is gradually supplanted by Jane Seymour anyway, and is arrested and convicted on charges of adultery trumped up by Cromwell. Also, Henry breaks with a Roman Catholic Church anachronistically led by Pope Paul III (Peter O'Toole); Cranmer rises to prominence as Anne encourages religious reform; the Boleyns secretly try to poison Bishop John Fisher (Bosco Hogan), whose cook Richard Rouse (Gary Murphy) is boiled alive for the offense; More and Fisher are executed for refusing to take the Oath of Allegiance to Henry; Catherine is exiled from court, separated from Princess Mary, and stoically declines and expires; Mary is declared illegitimate and forced to serve her younger sister, later declared a bastard herself; Anne dies after a dramatic speech from the scaffold; and Henry gluttonously devours a swan, which is clearly a symbol for his deceased second bride.

It is the triangle of Henry, Catherine, and Anne that gives the first two seasons dramatic tension, and once both women die, the series loses energy. Season Three (eight episodes instead of the usual ten) introduces a new Jane Seymour, who reconciles Henry with his daughters, unsuccessfully appeals for mercy to the rebels in the Pilgrimage of Grace, and dies after giving birth to Prince Edward, which leads to a bizarre episode in which the king goes into seclusion (and apparently mad) with only his fool Will Somers (David Bradley) for company. Meanwhile, Brandon savagely suppresses the Pilgrimage of Grace (a role that in reality belonged to Norfolk), and Henry has a fling with the fictitious Lady Ursula Misseldon (Charlotte Salt), who also sleeps with Bryan when he is not having sex with Anne Stanhope or on the continent trying to assassinate Reginald Pole (Mark Hildreth). Cromwell, with the assistance of artist Hans Holbein (Peter Gaynor), engineers the king's marriage to Anne of Cleves, the failure of which leads Cromwell to the scaffold and Henry to the bed of the nymphet Catherine Howard. Princess Mary has a brief flirtation with Philip of Bavaria (Collin O'Donoghue), but his Protestantism and rapid departure put a sad end to that.

Season Four witnesses Henry's marriage to the incredibly silly Catherine Howard, whose past affair with Francis Dereham (Allen Leech) and current one with Thomas Culpeper lead to divorce and beheading for her, heartbreak for the presumably aging king (who does not look older), and an unexpected royal marriage for Catherine Parr, the wife of Lord Latimer (Michael Elwyn) and the unofficial fiancé (pending her husband's death) of Thomas Seymour. It also includes the king's highly improbable bedding of the recently rejected Anne of Cleves. The Seymours' feud over politics and social status with Surrey and over religion with Gardiner, who relentlessly pursues Protestants, including Anne Askew (Emma Stansfield) and the queen. Seeking to recover his youth on the battlefield, Henry successfully besieges Boulogne at an enormous cost in lives and money, and Brandon has an affair with the imaginary Brigitte Rousselot (Selma Brook). Gardiner's intrigues against Catherine and plot to put Mary on the throne get him imprisoned in the Tower, while Surrey's ambition for the crown leads to his execution. While Holbein paints Henry's famous portrait, the ghosts of the king's first three wives appear in succession and berate him for his poor treatment of them and their children. Henry sends his family away, and the series ends with him examining his new portrait and then turning to leave the room. His death is not shown.

Unfortunately, while *The Tudors* is visually appealing and features some good performances, no amount of beauty or good acting can rescue it from Hirst having drastically rewritten history without any real justification for doing so. One expects a certain amount of invented dialogue and "stage business" in even the most accurate of historical dramas, but such things as amalgamating Henry's two sisters into one, having Margaret marry and murder the King of Portugal (she did neither) and then wed

Brandon (whom her missing sister Mary married) mangles history to no apparent dramatic purpose. The plethora of similar inaccuracies throughout the series belies Hirst's claim that it was "85 % accurate." However, Hirst does enjoy some support among scholars. Ramona Wray seeks to explain the many historical inaccuracies in *The Tudors* not as anomaly or error but as indicative of "a process now recognized as a characteristic of quality television—a 'complex seeing.'" In other words, it is rife with clever inside jokes. Wray's observation might make sense with a film like *Shakespeare in Love*, which consistently engages in clever self-mockery, but it gives Hirst more credit than his record—with *Elizabeth*, *Elizabeth: The Golden Age*, and *The Tudors*—seems to deserve. However, Wray is not alone. Jerome de Groot also sees it as an extended example of postmodern playfulness.

Still, a major element of *The Tudors*' appeal is not so much intellectual subtlety but lots of good-looking men and women, brightly (if inaccurately) costumed and frequently naked, with the more or less constant prospect during moments of non-erotic activity that they will be naked again soon. As Ginia Bellafante observed in her *New York Times* review of Season Two, "If *The Tudors* fails to live up to the great long-form dramas cable television has produced, it is not simply because it refuses the visceral messiness of a *Rome* or a *Deadwood*... but more significantly because it radically reduces the era's thematic conflicts to simplistic struggles over personal and erotic power." Or as Tim Dowling noted in *The Guardian* in 2009, "Almost everyone in *The Tudors* is young, thin and beautiful. Not only is this a little unlikely, it can also make it hard to tell them apart."

All that said, the goal of this volume is not merely to do a "hatchet job" on *The Tudors* but to assess it as a work of art, as a representation of history, as a reflection of modern and perhaps postmodern concerns, and as a potential tool for teaching. While the contributors express strong criticism where we believe it justified, we also express appreciation for what the series does well. Moreover, we do not all agree in our assessments of the series, and we hope that our disagreements will be as interesting and useful to readers as our agreements.

Chapter 2: "Henry VIII in *The Tudors*: Romantic Renaissance Warrior or Soap Opera Playboy?" is twice as long as the others not as the result of editorial self-indulgence but because it also incorporates warfare and diplomacy. Henry's legacy and his place in historical memory—both real and imagined—occupy all contributors to this volume; Henry is the main character, whose depiction in Hirst's script and by Meyers on-screen sets the tone for the entire series; and *The Tudors*' central problem is the way it portrays the king's personal life, England's domestic politics, Henrician foreign policy, and the international ramifications of the break with Rome and the English Reformation. The historical Henry remains controversial, and filmmakers genuinely concerned with historicity must address his complex personality and the myriad motives for his often unpredictable actions; his abundant talents, powerful intellect, and extensive learning, as well as his boisterous behavior; the real reasons for his ardent pursuit of both love and war; if, when, and why he changed from a young Renaissance humanist prince into a brutal tyrant; whether he made his own policy or followed the lead of ministers like Wolsey, Cromwell, and Cranmer; to what extent he abandoned traditional Catholic doctrine and embraced reform after the break with Rome; and other issues.

It might be difficult for a typical two-hour film to address adequately and accurately all these aspects of a reign lasting almost four decades, but it certainly should be possible for a thirty-five-hour television series to do so. Yet, if Hirst's script occasionally pays lip service to such a goal, it fails to pursue it in a sustained and nuanced manner and is frequently ahistorical. From start to finish, *The Tudors* is characterized by tensions between actual history and inexplicable fictional deviations, between the complex Henry and Meyers' one-dimensional character, between traditional filmic tropes and Hirst's self-conscious new paradigm, between the filmmakers' desire to be taken seriously and the temptation to pander to viewers with sex and sensationalism, between the capricious and cruel but charismatic king of reality and the merely capricious and cruel incarnation on-screen, between the romantic Renaissance warrior and the soap opera playboy.

If Chap. 2 criticizes the series for eschewing historical accuracy and departing from filmic tradition to depict Henry in ways that are troubling, Chap. 3: "Catherine of Aragon in *The Tudors*: Dark Hair, Devotion, and Dignity in Despair," credits it for breaking with the typical on-screen treatment of Catherine, who almost always suffers badly in comparison with Anne Boleyn. Though Catherine was the daughter of two powerful and successful regnant monarchs, Ferdinand of Aragon and Isabella of Castile, was an intelligent, learned, politically skillful, and deeply religious woman, and was married to Henry longer than his other five wives put together, film and television often concentrate on her later years, make her appear old and shrewish, and downplay her intellect, learning, and religion. *The Tudors*—while not entirely free of these tendencies—gives Catherine far more time on-screen, covers a greater portion of her life than any production except *The Six Wives of Henry VIII* (1970), and treats her religious devotion more seriously than any save *Anne of the Thousand Days* (1969). True, it ignores her early years in England as Prince Arthur's wife and widow, the happy phase of her marriage to Henry (foreshortened in the series by Anne's early arrival), her intellectual parity with the king, and her accomplishments as queen, notably as regent during Henry's absence in France in 1513, and at times it makes her too much a victim. It also, like every other filmic depiction except *Six Wives*, makes her brunette rather than blonde. However, Hirst offers a more fully developed Catherine who is not just a bit player in the story, and Maria Doyle Kennedy gives her depth, displays a genuine range of emotions, and invests her with real dignity. Therefore, despite its problems, *The Tudors* offers at least a partial corrective to popular views of Catherine.

Similarly, Susan Bordo argues in Chap. 4: "*The Tudors*, Natalie Dormer, and Our 'Default' Anne," that Dormer's Anne is superior to the default version derived from Eustace Chapuys and Catholic polemicist Nicholas Sander, described by Paul Friedmann in *Anne Boleyn* (1884) as "incredibly vain, ambitious, unscrupulous, coarse, fierce, and relentless," and still found in modern scholarship like David Starkey's *Six Wives: The Queens of Henry VIII* (2004) and fiction such as Philippa Gregory's *The Other Boleyn Girl* (2001) and Hilary Mantel's *Wolf Hall* (2009) and *Bring Up the Bodies* (2012). The real Anne, though fond of a good time, encountered evangelical thought at the French court, became an avid student of scripture, assisted importation of English Bibles, gave Henry copies of Simon Fish's *Supplication of the Beggars* and William Tyndale's *Obedience of the Christian Man*, sought to convert monasteries to educational purposes, and was the patron of such evangelicals as Thomas Cranmer, William Barlow, William Bill, Edward Foxe, Thomas Goodrich, Hugh Latimer, Matthew Parker, and Nicholas Shaxton, and reformist scholars at Cambridge. The filmic Anne appears on-screen more often than any other wife, usually in some variation of the default version, which gives scant attention to her intellect, learning, and zeal for reform. Emphasis on romance typically takes the story farther from documented history, for though Henry's love letters survive, their amorous activity on camera is the fruit of scriptwriters' imagination. Initially *The Tudors* offered little improvement, for Hirst scripted Anne as a one-dimensional sex object in Season One, where her sexuality overpowers other aspects of her character, especially after the signature "Seduce me" scene. However, Dormer, a student of history bothered by this mischaracterization, persuaded him to pay more attentionto Anne's faith and intellect in Season Two, where—though it comes amid a welter of factual errors and inventions—her character increasingly reflects the queen's real convictions.

If *The Tudors* offers clearer understanding of Catherine of Aragon and Anne Boleyn even in the absence of accurate narrative, that is not the case with their successors, as Retha Warnicke demonstrates in Chap. 5: "The Last Four Queens of Henry VIII in *The Tudors*." They are less well represented in contemporary sources and modern scholarship, get less attention on film, and are less familiar to viewers, which can tempt filmmakers to treat them as a blank slate. Jane Seymour was likely quiet and religiously conservative but remains enigmatic, and on-screen she has been everything from a ruthless schemer to a virtual nun. In *The Tudors* she is a bit of both, for in Season Two Anita Briem's Jane is on the verge of becoming Henry's mistress, while in Season Three Annabelle Wallis' Jane is his devoutly Catholic wife. The conventional wisdom is that Anne of Cleves was ugly, though film makers often prefer to make her funny. In *The Tudors* she is neither, for its account of her marriage is persistently grim, and there never has been a more epic failure to cast a homely Anne than with Joss Stone. Though Hirst draws upon historical sources for her dialogue, he forfeits the credit by having her sleep with Henry after his remarriage. Warnicke aptly describes the youthful Tamzin Merchant's Catherine Howard as an early modern Lolita, though Vladimir Nabokov's adolescent heroine is less silly. Conversely, Joely Richardson is a compellingly mature Catherine Parr, and Hirst notes her intellect and Protestant activism, though he fabricates some details, for example, making Hugh Latimer her chaplain.

The series exhibits more sensitivity with Henry's progeny, as Carole Levin and Estelle Paranque show in Chap. 6: "The Significance of the King's Children in *The Tudors*." Mary was a tragic figure who has never been the primary subject of a serious film in English, though she figures briefly as a child in movies about Henry and Edward VI and as the bad old queen in those about Lady Jane Grey and Elizabeth. Thus, her status as a major character in *The Tudors* is a significant departure. Perhaps, because it never exploits her for sexual content (save for Francis Bryan's pointlessly vulgar joke about cunnilingus at her expense and an occasional wistful kiss), it deals with her psychological development with considerable subtlety, and Sarah Bolger does a fine job in the role of the adolescent and young adult princess—the gradual emergence of her determination to wipe out heresy is especially effective. Bláthnaid McKeown is also good as the younger, oft-betrothed Mary. Elizabeth is the queen of Tudor film stars, but her childhood prior to Henry's death has received little attention on-screen. Kate Duggan and Claire Macaulay have only bit parts in *The Tudors* as the toddler and child Elizabeth, respectively, but Laoise Murray accurately portrays the adolescent princess as a budding intellectual, politically astute, and cautiously circumspect, though Hirst has her make prophetic remarks about her then improbable future reign. Edward, except for his well-known fictitious role in the many versions of *The Prince and the Pauper*, mostly appears on film as a sickly boy who is nearly kidnapped by his uncle Thomas Seymour and/or dies of tuberculosis. In fact, he was not only intelligent and devout but also, contrary to popular belief, vigorous and healthy—much like his father—until he became ill at sixteen. *The Tudors* shows little of this, employing Eoin Murtagh primarily for the cuteness factor, as it does with Zak Jenciragic as Henry Fitzroy, who appears long enough to be made Duke of Richmond and then dies tragically and much earlier than in reality. On the whole, *The Tudors* does better with Henry's daughters than his sons, though—to be fair—Mary and Elizabeth were around for much longer during the period the series covers.

In Chap. 7: "The King's Sister(s), Mistresses, Bastard(s), and 'Uncle' in *The Tudors*," Kristen Walton addresses some of Hirst's oddest dramatic decisions. The first is opening the series with the fictitious assassination of Henry's nonexistent uncle and ambassador (Sean Pertwee) in the ducal palace of Urbino by agents of Francis I of France. In reality, Henry's only paternal uncle, Jasper Tudor, died in 1495, and any living brother of his mother—Elizabeth of York, daughter of Edward IV—would have been king himself. Even stranger is the amalgamation of Henry's two sisters into one—Margaret—and the invented plotline in which she marries and murders the King of Portugal (Joseph Kelly) before wedding Brandon. The real Margaret's marriages to James IV, the Earl of Angus, and Lord Methven had important consequences, as did her sister Mary's to Louis XII of France and Brandon, but none of that is apparent in *The Tudors*. The portrayal of Elizabeth Blount is broadly correct, but the chronology of her relationship with Henry is scrambled. The king's affair with Mary Boleyn (Perdita Weeks), which lasted four or five years, appears to be reduced to a few days or weeks in *The Tudors*, and there is no mention of her first husband William Carey or their children, sometimes alleged to be Henry's, though he never acknowledged them as he did Henry Fitzroy. Finally, Henry's affair with Madge Shelton may be a case of mistaken identity, as his mistress appears to have been her sister Mary; however, *The Tudors* adds considerable embroidery to the erroneous tradition. Combined with Anne Boleyn's arrival seven or eight years early and the substantial compression of time associated with Henry's courtship of her and pursuit of a divorce, the result is a highly inaccurate picture of Henry's personal and family life in the 1520s and early 1530s.

Henry had as problematic a collection of in-laws as anyone has ever had. Many were important in their own right, but because *The Tudors* focuses so much on marital politics, their role is greater, and inaccuracies loom larger, as Anne Throckmorton reveals in Chap. 8: "The King's In-Laws in *The Tudors*." Hirst recycles an erroneous trope found in many films, whereby Thomas Boleyn and Norfolk try to put first Mary and then Anne Boleyn in the king's bed to cultivate royal favor. In reality, both were important courtiers from the start of Henry's reign, and Anne came to the king's attention, later and without their assistance or insistence, as one of Catherine of Aragon's ladies-in-waiting. *The Tudors* gives Boleyn his longest on-screen outing by far, but Hirst assigns Dunning too much to do in the role—though he correctly serves as a diplomat, he also informs on Buckingham, pays cook Richard Rouse (Gary Murphy) to poison Fisher, and indulges in other fictitious skullduggery before abandoning his children Anne and George (Padraic Delaney) to their fates. George follows his usual path to the scaffold, but Hirst invents a homosexual relationship between him and Mark Smeaton (David Alpay), the musician executed for alleged adultery with Anne. Henry Czerny's Norfolk is miscast, unconvincing, and—as in other films—a combination of the 2nd and 3rd Dukes. He disappears after Season One, though the real 3rd Duke lived until 1554, joined Gardiner in advocating conservative religious policy, helped destroy Cromwell, promoted Henry's marriage to his niece Catherine Howard, and was imprisoned when his son, the Earl of Surrey, was charged with treason—all developments featured in *The Tudors* but minus Norfolk. His mother, the Dowager Duchess (Barbara Brennan), seems to be running a brothel, whence Catherine is fetched for Henry's carnal pleasure. Surrey suddenly appears at the beginning of Season Four, is introduced to Henry as though they were strangers, is much older than he should be, and is the implacable enemy of the Seymours, with whom he was quite friendly at the time. There is a huge amount of nonsense about the Seymours, the worst example being that Edward's wife Anne Stanhope, quite loyal in reality, sleeps with Bryan, Surrey, and her brother-in-law Thomas, who fathers her nonexistent son.

Henry surrounded himself with boon companions and had close relationships with his ministers, so "king's friends" is a broad category that might even include Will Somers, who joins the king in seclusion and lunacy after Jane Seymour's death on *The Tudors*. In Chap. 9: "The King's Friends in *The Tudors*," Victor Stater focuses on five of the most important: Charles Brandon, Francis Bryan, William Compton, Henry Norris, and Thomas Wyatt. Anthony Knivert, one of a raucous group of friends in Season One, is a fictional character based on Sir Thomas Knyvett, who died in 1512, before *The Tudors* begins. Early in his reign, Henry's companions included not only Knyvett but also Brandon, Bryan, Compton, and Norris, and *The Tudors* at least gets their unruly behavior right, but not much else. Brandon's life is fabricated from beginning to end, though particularly noteworthy are his marriage to the wrong sister of the king (Margaret instead of Mary), his role in suppressing the Pilgrimage of Grace (instead of Norfolk), his fictitious affairs, his conversations with Lord Darcy's ghost, and his appearance, for Cavill looks no more like the Brandon than Meyers does Henry. Bryan does not show up until Season Three (c. 1536), and though he correctly has an eye patch and really may have been involved in a plan to assassinate Reginald Pole, almost everything else he does on-screen is the product of Hirst's imagination. Before *The Tudors* allows Compton, correctly, to die during an outbreak of sweating sickness in 1528, it gives him an entirely gratuitous homosexual relationship with composer Thomas Tallis, who in reality did not arrive at court until the 1540s and was happily married (on the show he does redirect his amorous intentions to women after Compton's death). Norris gets Henry's permission to marry the king's mistress Madge Shelton, which historically he considered but did not conclude; however, he was executed for his alleged sexual relationship with Anne Boleyn, as he is on the show. Wyatt frequently figures in Seasons One and Two, but his poetry is largely used to hint at his unproven amorous relationship with Anne Boleyn.

James Frain as Thomas Cromwell, Sam Neill as Thomas Wolsey, and Jeremy Northam as Thomas More give three of the best performances on *The Tudors*, though they do so in highly fictionalized roles. In Chap.10: "Postmodern and Conservative: The King's Ministers in *The Tudors*," Robin Hermann argues that despite adopting a putatively postmodern approach to Henry's reign, Hirst actually ends up presenting a conservative interpretation of history in which only great men like Henry VIII are agents of change (a view more resonant of Thomas Carlyle than Jacques Derrida). Neill's Wolsey is intelligent, subtle, worldly, ambitious, yet sincerely dedicated to peace, justice, and the welfare of his young royal protégé. Regrettably, Hirst has him interact with imaginary churchmen as well as the real Cardinal Campeggio and gives him a great many ridiculous things to say and do, culminating with cutting his own throat on camera. Northam, as More, not only compares favorably to Paul Scofield but is in one respect an improvement, revealing a fanatical hatred for heretics, even if he burns the wrong one—Simon Fish, who died of natural causes. But Hirst succumbs to presentism when Henry, Wolsey, and More discuss plans for a 1518 Treaty of London that Woodrow Wilson might have drafted. Frain's Cromwell is too thin and too early, serving as Henry's secretary while Wolsey is still in power (he entered royal service only in 1530 or 1531). However, he is a more complex Cromwell than in most on-screen depictions, demonstrating his Lutheran sympathies, reacting with horror to Rouse's execution by boiling, and mingling love for his family with his own Machiavellian cruelty. In *The Tudors*, as in *A Man for All Seasons* and to some extent real life, Richard Rich is a key villain in More's martyrdom and a fairly unpleasant character thereafter. Richard Pace (Matt Ryan) is the subject of an ahistorical intrigue wherein Wolsey accuses him of treason and sends him to the Tower, where he goes mad. Risley (Thomas Wriothesley) is not particularly well developed, but the series does get right the general trajectory of his career, wherein he went from being Cromwell's associate to becoming a persecutor of Protestants.

Though *The Tudors* does not address the issue of kingship per se, its main character is a king who frequently interacts with other kings and their emissaries, which is bound to give viewers certain notions of what being an early sixteenth-century king was like. However, as Glenn Richardson shows in Chap. 11: "A Cardboard Crown: Kingship in *The Tudors*," Hirst shows little understanding of early modern kingship. The "King of Portugal" (never identified by name) appears only long enough for the completely fictitious segment in which Henry's sister Margaret marries and murders him; therefore, he does not figure much in shaping viewers' perceptions, save perhaps to create the impression that kings had really dirty feet. However, Charles V and Francis I are more real and substantial characters, and as with Meyers' Henry VIII, casting creates some problems. Armesto's Charles is unintentionally reminiscent of Mandy Patinkin's overtly comedic turn as Iñigo Montoya in *The Princess Bride* (1987), while Leconte's Francis may embody more French stereotypes than any on-screen character since Pepe le Pew. The problem this poses for suspension of disbelief increases exponentially when either actor shares the screen with Meyers. Glimpses of Henry, Charles, and Francis "being kings" in *The Tudors* are sporadic. The monarchs are rarely seen at war except for Henry's 1544 foray into France, and the comparatively svelte Meyers is a far cry from the morbidly obese man the king had become by that time. There are more scenes featuring the pageantry of royal diplomatic meetings, notably the Field of the Cloth of Gold. Perhaps the best are those that show Henry "practicing" for war and proving his manliness by jousting. There are also numerous scenes in which he dispenses royal patronage. On the whole, however, *The Tudors* gives the impression that being king was a great deal of fun—especially with regard to sex—the sustained revelry being interrupted only occasionally by pain and fear and seldom by the tedium of work. What it does not adequately convey is the extent to which kings of this era were—and were expected to be—"Renaissance men" capable of doing virtually everything well. Viewers see little of Henry the humanist, the linguist, and the musician, and when he has a completely fictional encounter with Marguerite of Navarre—sister of Francis I, wife of Henri II of Navarre, and one of the great literary figures of the age—he does not engage her in intellectual discourse, which would have been the likely result of such a meeting; rather, he seduces her.

In recent years, Tudor historians (e.g., G.R. Elton, David Loades, David Starkey) have demonstrated that the court was as important a venue for politics as parliament or the royal council. In Chap. 12: "*The Tudors* and the Tudor Court: Know Your Symptom," Thomas Betteridge offers a fascinating description of how *The Tudors* depicts the court, the role of court politics in Anne of Boleyn's fall, and the way Thomas Wyatt presents the court in his poetry. Access to the king was crucial for obtaining royal favor or for advancing a particular agenda, and those who served in the king's privy chamber were well placed to do both. The court was where the king displayed his majesty to its fullest, where much royal policy was conceived, and where the dangerous but irresistible game of courtly love never stopped. Court factionalism lay behind many of the political ups and downs of the period, as Eric Ives has demonstrated in Anne's case. Overall, *The Tudors* succeeds in demonstrating that every act and event at court, however great or small, had political significance and that a courtier's greater proximity to the king—desirable in and of itself for any man (or woman) on the make—carried with it an increased risk of the unpredictable king's displeasure and of treachery from one's fellow courtiers. What it does not do is to give much indication of how the court actually functioned on a daily basis. Most scenes "at court" are set pieces involving political scheming, conflict between Henry and some unfortunate target of the royal wrath, or the prelude to a new bout of erotic activity. It is telling that the character credited merely as "Chamberlain" (actor Guy Carleton)—who appears in more episodes that anyone save Henry, Brandon, and Chapuys—is never mentioned by name, though the Lord Chamberlain of the Household was one of the most important court officials. In fact, there is no explicit indication that this is not instead the Lord Great Chamberlain, one of the major officers of state, though that is unlikely. In either case, multiple individuals held the two offices during Henry's reign, whereas "Chamberlain" is the same man from beginning to end of the series. There are some scenes involving meetings of the privy council, though collectively they imply that the normal condition of that body was conflict rather than cooperation and the rather dull business of routine administration. But the series ignores the crucial political role of the privy chamber. Moreover, because so many important courtiers come and go as characters in the series, the court is almost always missing key players.

Religion and the clergy are often center stage in *The Tudors*, but that is not to say that the series does much to elucidate the role of either, as Caroline Armbruster confirms in Chap. 13: "'The Dyer's Hands Are Always Stained': Religion and the Clergy in *The Tudors*." The script brings up but does not adequately explain the polemical battle between Henry and Luther over the seven sacraments, Wolsey's alleged desire to be pope, More's abhorrence of Protestantism, Cromwell and the Boleyn family's commitment to reform, Gardiner's opposition to "heresy," the persecution of Anne Askew, the plot against Catherine Parr, and various pieces of church-related legislation. It is abundantly clear that Catholics and Protestants disagree, often violently, but except for the papacy and the divorce, it is not clear what divides them. As with other subjects, much of the treatment of religious history is inaccurate. For example, the dissolution of the monasteries led to confiscation of monastic property and its conversion to other uses, not to the wanton vandalism and brutalization of monks that the series depicts. Furthermore, Cranmer's disappearance at the end of Season Two eliminates from the story the great struggle over doctrine that he carried on against Gardiner for the last decade of Henry's reign. *The Tudors* does convey the grandeur of the early sixteenth-century liturgy and the religiosity of such characters as Catherine of Aragon and Thomas More, but more often it emphasizes the venality of the clergy, and it is guilty of a great deal of dime-store iconoclasm. If Hirst sought to challenge the positive view that Englishmen have of the English Reformation, his account is so muddled that it is difficult to tell what is being undermined. As with the films *Elizabeth* and *Elizabeth: The Golden of Age*, both of which he scripted, religion is often employed either to demonstrate the brutality of fanatics or to put modern-sounding platitudes about liberty and toleration in the mouths of sixteenth-century characters. Moreover, whereas historians like Eamon Duffy and Christopher Haigh have countered the providential Protestant view of the Reformation by seeking to rehabilitate English Catholicism, Hirst brings to *The Tudors* the same anti-Catholic sentiment found in the Elizabeth movies. Finally, the series only haphazardly engages the powerful, if somewhat narcissistic, devotion of Henry himself.

In Chap. 14: "Fact, Fiction, and Fantasy: Conspiracy and Rebellion in *The Tudors*," Keith Altazin analyzes the depiction of conspiracy (real, imagined, and invented) and rebellion. Conspiracy is a subject particularly prone to inspire flights of fantasy. *The Tudors* has Buckingham continuously baiting the king, plotting with Norfolk and Boleyn (the latter of whom reports all this to Henry), raising an army and accepting their homage, and dying in cowardly fashion on the scaffold, for none of which there is any evidence. Equally unfounded are scenes in which Brandon, acting on the king's behalf, warns Norfolk to find Buckingham guilty and in which Wolsey reacts with surprise to the verdict, which in reality he engineered. Pope Paul III's "plot" for William Brereton to murder Anne Boleyn is made up out of whole cloth. The series does not have to invent the Pilgrimage of Grace, the most dangerous rebellion faced by Henry VIII (or any of the Tudor monarchs) or the king's duplicity in dealing with the rebels; however, it takes enormous liberties with other facts of that uprising. For example, it has John Constable urge Robert Aske to lead the insurrection and makes him an ardent supporter, when in reality he opposed the rebellion, joined under duress, and later sat on the commission that judged the rebels at Hull. Norfolk, who suppressed the rising, is missing in action, and Brandon does the king's dirty work instead. On the other hand, the horrors of royal retribution against Aske and the other rebels are all too real. The series is perhaps right in suggesting that Henry prosecuted Margaret Pole, Countess of Salisbury, and her son Henry, Lord Montague primarily because of his hatred of the countess' son Reginald. However, it departs from the evidence in several respects, making Edward Seymour (instead of William Fitzwilliam, Earl of Southampton) the principal investigator of the alleged Pole conspiracy, having Bryan discover in the countess' possession a royal banner of the Plantagenets and another bearing the Five Wounds of Christ (the symbol of the Pilgrimage), and including a heart-rending but entirely imaginary scene in which Montague's son Henry, a small boy, is led away to execution. Curiously, in dealing with the affair of the Poles, the series makes no mention of Lord Montague's brother, Sir Geoffrey, whose behavior did much to implicate his family. Nor does it reference the conspiracy involving Henry Courtenay, Marquess of Exeter, and Sir Nicholas Carew, who had links to the Poles—Exeter and Montague actually were executed at the same time. In addition, Montague was executed in 1539 and Lady Margaret not until 1541, but in the series they die at about the same time. Montague's son Henry was arrested and imprisoned in the Tower but was not executed; he died there of unknown causes in 1542.

Crime—street fights, rape, murder, conspiracy, treason, and more—is a major element of *The Tudors*, as is cruel, dehumanizing, and gory punishment. Added to the criminal and judicial violence are frequent brutalities to women, ruthless repression of the powerless, and the bloody mayhem of battle. Sad to say, none of this is far-fetched with regard to the Tudor period, as Krista Kesselring demonstrates in Chap. 15: "Crime, Punishment, and Violence in *The Tudors*," though the relentlessness with which violence occurs on-screen is, like the nonstop sex and political backstabbing, rather gratuitous. Moreover, as with everything else in the series, it entails a great deal of invention and factual error. The violence shown in conjunction with the dissolution of the monasteries is fictitious, as are the assassination of Henry's "uncle," Margaret's murder of the Portuguese king, Edward Seymour's torture of John Constable, and (possibly) Culpeper's rape of the park keeper's wife. Of course there is no way to actually show burnings, beheadings, and torture on-screen without it being fairly unpleasant. However, the makers of *The Tudors* seem to glory in violent spectacle, for example, depicting the boiling alive of Richard Rouse in a hugely oversized caldron and prolonging the scene more than necessary to convey what occurs. Largely missing is any exposition of criminal law, the courts, or judicial and law enforcement officials. Henrician justice was sometimes arbitrary, as it was with Fisher, More, Anne Boleyn, Catherine Howard, and various rebels and heretics in reality and is on-screen in *The Tudors*. More often, though, the common law courts (King's Bench, Common Pleas, Exchequer) and ecclesiastical courts followed fairly strict procedure, while the conciliar courts (Chancery, Requests, Star Chamber) offered alternative equity proceedings for those who were poor, confronted "overmighty" opponents, or became bogged down in the common law courts. Moreover, if violence and crime were common, they were not routine. Finally, one of the striking things about the Tudors is how often they resisted the temptation to violent retribution against rebels and other troublemakers.

The Tudors begins hopefully for those interested in Renaissance humanism (or Christian humanism, as it was often called). In Episode One Henry has a long discussion with More about his desire to rule according to humanistic principles, and he brings up the subject again when considering Wolsey's proposal for a universal peace treaty. Thereafter, however, the series only occasionally references humanism and never really explains it. In large part, as Samantha Perez shows in Chap. 16: "Humanism and Humanitarianism in *The Tudors*," this is because it confuses humanism and humanitarianism and fails to understand either. It gives little attention to the humanist education of Catherine of Aragon, Anne Boleyn, and Catherine Parr, or of such characters as Stephen Gardiner, Richard Pace, and Reginald Pole. On the other hand, Henry and More have an unlikely conversation comparing Machiavelli's *The Prince* (which circulated only in manuscript until its publication in 1532) and More's own *Utopia* (published 1516). Reflecting upon the former, Henry ponders whether it is better to be feared or loved, but there is no explication of More's famous work. Likewise ignored are the humanist underpinnings of Henry's polemical battle with Luther, with the script concentrating instead on their viciousness and vulgarity. Henry's real-life friend Desiderius Erasmus never makes an appearance, nor does the English humanist John Colet. But poetry does—in Henry's dream, Anne urges him to seduce her with words, to write poetry for her. Wyatt recites poetry to fellow courtier and Bryan does likewise with his lover. Surrey writes poetry and translates classic literature, though otherwise his character is so boorish that it is difficult to accept his on-screen manifestation as a sensitive literary figure. As previously noted, Marguerite of Navarre is simply another imaginary sexual conquest for Henry. On the whole, then, the series pay lip service to humanism and literature but fails to explore either in any depth.

In Chap. 17: "All That Glitters Is (Fool's) Gold: The Depiction of Court Entertainment in *The Tudors*," Carlie Pendleton examines the use of court entertainments, both indoors (dancing, drama, music, and the like) and outdoors (jousting), to create a plausible (if not necessarily accurate) Tudor court. On the whole, this is one of the better features of *The Tudors*. Lavish entertainments were of major importance at the Tudor court, and

Henry was a consummate jouster, an accomplished musician, profoundly vain about his dancing and his well-turned calves, and almost boyishly fond of play-acting. There is no shortage of jousting in *The Tudors*, and it is done well except for the presence in the lists of imaginary combatants like the "Earl of Dorchester" and the "Earl of Newcastle." The script pays due attention to the associated rituals of courtly love, for example, Henry and his courtiers carry on their lances the "favors" of the present objects of their affection, though in the king's case that usually signifies more than the Platonic love normally associated with such gallantry. There is also pageantry aplenty, particularly when Henry visits France for the Field of the Cloth of Gold or receives Charles V and other foreign dignitaries. The dancing, feasting, masques, plays, and other entertainments are realistic enough, as are the celebration of Christmas and the exchange of New Year's gifts. However, the king's weddings are rather more spectacular than they were in reality—typically they occurred in private with only a handful of family and friends in attendance. There is also plenty of music, though not as much by Henry as there should be. But court musicians are the subjects of some pretty bald-faced fictions. Mark Smeaton flirts far more with Anne Boleyn than is probable and has a homosexual affair with her brother. Thomas Tallis is an anachronistic presence in the 1520s and 1530s, and he also is depicted, without evidence, as bisexual.

In Chap. 18: "Holbein and the Artistic *Mise-en-Scène* of *The Tudors*," Tatiana String examines the use of art to create a plausible (if not necessarily accurate) Tudor court. Art in all its manifestations was an extremely important feature of court life everywhere in sixteenth-century Europe and played a critical role in creating a sense of majesty around the person of the king. To grasp its importance for Henry's reign, one need only consider his famous portrait by Hans Holbein, which took on iconic status even in the sixteenth century and has maintained it down to the present. *The Tudors* uses Holbein's creation of that painting and Henry's contemplation of the finished piece to great dramatic effect in the final episode, though it indulges in abundant fantasy and fiction to do so. Holbein, who died in 1543—over three years before Henry—completed his most famous painting of Henry in 1537, not as the king was dying. Moreover, it was not a stand-alone portrait but part of the Whitehall Mural that also included Henry VII, Elizabeth of York, and Jane Seymour. And it seems a fairly safe bet that the ghosts of Henry's first three wives did not appear to him while Holbein was at work. Holbein figures, realistically enough, elsewhere in the series, designing artwork for Anne Boleyn's coronation, creating a gift for her to give to Henry, and painting the supposedly too-flattering portrait of Anne of Cleves during the negotiations for the king's fourth marriage. But while painting an imaginary portrait of the king's imaginary mistress Lady Ursula, he gets into an imaginary fight with her imaginary fiancé Tavistock, who then has an imaginary confrontation with the king. Henry also references Holbein painting Henry VII, which he did not do during the latter's life; in fact, his only painting of the first Tudor king was in the Whitehall Mural.

In Chap. 19: "Fashionable Fiction: The Significance of the Costumes in *The Tudors*," Maria Hayward examines the use of costuming to create a plausible (if not necessarily accurate) Tudor court. Films about *The Tudors* are not known for accurately clothing characters, though the BBC series *The Six Wives of Henry VIII* (1970), *Elizabeth R* (1971), and *Shadow of the Tower* (1972) are notable exceptions. However, Jean Bergin, costume designer for *The Tudors*, admits that she was less interested in accuracy than in making a strong visual impression. That she has certainly accomplished, winning Emmy Awards for costuming in 2007 and 2008. If not accurate, the apparel worn by Henry and others is certainly memorable. In addition, because it does not look "modern," it perhaps appears "plausibly contemporary" to viewers unfamiliar with Tudor portraiture and sixteenth-century fashion, thus contributing to the illusion of authenticity. One does not have to be an authority on Tudor apparel to perceive the most obvious problem with costuming, which is that Meyers' attire often makes him look more like a circus performer or jester than a regal monarch, further exacerbating the challenges to suspension of belief that stem from his physique, performance, and scripted behavior and dialogue. However, other problems are subtler. For example, *The Tudors* is rather notorious for fully exposing the bodies of its female characters in a manner not entirely consistent with sixteenth-century notions of modesty, but also problematic in that regard is that they frequently appear without any head covering, which a Tudor-era woman would have been most unlikely to do. Also, to the extent that they draw upon Tudor examples at all, the costumes owe much more to Elizabethan fashions than to those of the Henrician period. Lest this seem like quibbling over trivia, it is critical to recall the importance the English monarchy placed upon sumptuary laws, which strictly regulated what the various social classes could and could not wear.

In Chap. 20: "Putting Women in Their Place: Gender, Sex, and Rape in *The Tudors*," Megan Hickerson examines the use (or overuse) of sex as a plot device and the depiction of sex, sexuality, and gender roles in Hirst's script and the performances by actors in pertinent roles. Critics have likened *The Tudors*, without much exaggeration, to soft-core pornography. On the other hand, there is little doubt that sex sells, and it certainly helped to market *The Tudors* to viewers of both genders. Of course, much of it is sheer fantasy. Both male and female characters who appear nude on-screen are perfectly proportioned, remarkably clean, have good teeth, and do not seem bothered by the cold when naked, while the women have no body hair. Apparently, no one has an unpleasant aroma except Anne of Cleves, whose "evil smells" disenchant Henry, and the king himself, the odor of whose ulcer his fourth wife finds disgusting (evidently this either gets better or Catherine Howard has no sense of smell). Further, while it might be unfair to doubt the creativity of amorous sixteenth-century couples, one would never guess from *The Tudors* that the *Kama Sutra* was not translated into English until the nineteenth century (at least the conclusion of the series at 1547 spared the world from *Fifty Shades of Lady Jane Grey*). There is also a misogynist element to the series. The poster for Season One is revealing. Henry is seated, looking either seductively powerful or constipated—it is hard to tell. Behind him one can see the prominent cleavage of five women but nothing above the neck, suggesting perhaps that what is in their heads is not important. Hirst invents several sexual partners for Henry but none for any of the female characters. Female characters are naked more often than male ones. No one ever seems to pay for violent acts against women; for example, Culpeper gets away with rape and suffers execution only because he trifles with the king's wife. In one episode, Henry (improbably) selects a woman for his evening's entertainment as casually as one might buy a piece of fruit. But even more pervasive a problem is the gratuitous nature of much of the on-screen sex, perhaps most egregiously the conversion of faithful Anne Stanhope into a wanton slut. Also inexplicable is the decision to turn several historically heterosexual figures into homosexual characters. Though Hirst perhaps intended this as a nod to gay rights and tolerance, there is much about these characters that tends to reinforce unfavorable stereotypes about homosexuality.

In Chap. 21: "Incomplete Prescription: Maladies and Medicine in *The Tudors*," Elizabeth Lane Furdell analyzes the depiction of maladies and medicine. Henry's morbid fear of illness and the prevalence of disease, injury, and death in Tudor England make this chapter very pertinent.

Moreover, *The Tudors* effectively depicts the mixture of alchemy, astrology, herb-lore, magic, mumbo-jumbo, and practical surgical skills that the practice of "medicine" comprised in the early sixteenth century, as well as the king's own obsession with his health. The same can be said of its treatment of the panic induced by the sweating sickness—in 1528 for example—though Hirst does rather unscientifically resurrect Dr. Thomas Linacre, who died in 1524, to treat William Compton four years later and has him exhibit precocious knowledge of contagion, warning Mistress Hastings (Compton's common-law wife) that she must burn his bedding, clothing, and so on to avoid infection. Henry's famously ulcerated leg is a recurrent element in the story even if his morbid obesity in later life is not. Not surprisingly, given Henry's difficulties in obtaining a male heir, the series also does a good job of illustrating the horrors of childbirth in the early modern era. The death of thousands of soldiers of the flux (dysentery) at the siege of Boulogne is also realistic. All that said, viewers would benefit from further contextualization of the elements of sixteenth-century medical practice that appear in the series. For example, some explanation of humoral theory is required to understand the purpose of bloodletting. Similarly, it is helpful to know how early modern practitioners conceived the interaction of the humors (choler, melancholy, phlegm, blood), the elements (earth, water, air, fire), associated physical properties (cold, heat, dryness, moisture), astrological influences (the position and behavior of sun, moon, stars, planets, comets, etc.), alchemical practice (a blend of nascent science and pseudo-science), magic (universally accepted as real and likewise a blend of science and superstition), the work of apothecaries (whose sometimes efficacious herbal preparations were frequently mixed with expensive and presumably tasty but useless doses of spices and wine), and the quite literal belief in the role of diabolical forces (notably the idea that monstrous births were the work of the Devil). Also critical is that in the Tudor period university-trained physicians studied the classical *trivium* (grammar, logic, rhetoric) and *quadrivium* (arithmetic, geometry, music, astronomy), but not anatomy, physiology, pharmacology, and other elements of modern medicine, and seldom performed "hands-on" activities such as bloodletting and surgery. These tasks they left to barber-surgeons, who had considerably more practical knowledge.

Notes

1. For a detailed synopsis and critique of each episode of *The Tudors*, see Sue Parrill and William B. Robison, *The Tudors on Film and Television* (Jefferson, NC: McFarland, 2013), 247–290.
2. Susan Bordo, *The Creation of Anne Boleyn: A New Look at England's Most Notorious Queen* (Houghton Mifflin, 2013); see also http://thecreationofanneboleyn.wordpress.com/.
3. For a full list of awards, see http://www.imdb.com/title/tt0758790/awards; the official website is http://www.sho.com/sho/the-tudors/home; for links to ratings and reviews by season and interviews with Hirst and others, see http://www.tudorsonfilm.com/about-the-films/.
4. David Starkey has been particularly livid about *The Tudors*, but he has not been alone in criticizing the series, for example, http://www.telegraph.co.uk/news/celebritynews/3210142/BBC-period-drama-The-Tudors-is-gratuitously-awful-says-Dr-David-Starkey.html; for a rather less critical view, see Tracy Borman, "The Truth Behind the Tudors," *History Extra*, August 28, 2009, www.historyextra.com/feature/truth-behind-%E2%80%98-tudors%E2%80%99; on the influence of Korda's film, see Greg Walker, *The Private Life of Henry VIII: A British Film Guide* (London: I.B. Tauris, 2003) and Thomas S. Freeman, "A Tyrant for All Seasons: Henry VIII on Film," in Susan Doran and Thomas S. Freeman, eds., *Tudors and Stuarts on Film: Historical Perspectives* (New York: Palgrave Macmillan, 2009), 30–45; for the view that historians should ignore films about history—contrary to the opinion expressed here—see David Herlihy, "Am I A Camera? Other Reflections on Film and History," *American Historical Review* 93 (1988).
5. "Tudorism" is analogous to the field of medieval studies known as "medievalism," per Marcus Bull and Tatiana String, eds., *Tudorism: Historical Imagination and the Appropriation of the Sixteenth Century* (Oxford: Oxford University Press, 2011), 1; the book includes a chapter by Jerome de Groote entitled "Slashing History: *The Tudors*,"; see also Ramona Wray, "Henry's Desperate Housewives: *The Tudors*, the Politics of Historiography and the Beautiful Body of Jonathan Rhys Meyers," in Gregory M. Semenza, ed., *The English Renaissance in Popular Culture: An Age for All Time* (New York: Palgrave Macmillan, 2010), 25–42; Basil Glynn, "The Conquests of Henry VIII: Masculinity, Sex and the National Past in The Tudors," in Basil Glynn, James Aston, and Beth Johnson, eds., *Television, Sex and Society: Analyzing Contemporary Representations* (New York and London: Continuum, 2012), 157–74; Christopher J. Ferguson, "Positive Female Role-Models Eliminate Negative Effects of Sexually Violent Media," *Journal of Communication* 62 (2012): 888–899; the series was the subject of much discussion at a Folger Shakespeare Library conference on

"Reassessing Henry VIII," in November 2010, roundtables at the Sixteenth Century Society and Conference on "Henry VIII in Popular Culture," in 2011 and "Cutting-Edge Drama: Assessing Showtime's *The Tudors*," in 2012, and a panel at the latter on "Screening Two Wives of Henry VIII: Catherine of Aragon and Anne Boleyn on Film," which collectively involved twelve of the contributors to this volume, several more than once; on the utility of teaching with film, see Eric Josef Carlson, "Teaching Elizabeth Tudor with Movies," *Sixteenth Century Journal* 38(2) (2007): 419–428.

6. Hirst also wrote the screenplay for *1906* (2012), a film about the San Francisco earthquake; created and wrote all episodes of *Camelot* (Starz 2011); was executive producer for *The Borgias* (Showtime, 2011); and is the creator and executive producer of *Vikings* (History Channel, 2013); see http://www.imdb.com/name/nm0386694/; http://unitedagents.co.uk/michael-hirst#profile-4; http://www.broadcastnow.co.uk/michael-hirst-the-tudors/5001701.article; Amiel worked on *The Borgias* 2012; Donnelly *Camelot* 2011, *Titanic: Blood and Steel* 2012, *Vikings* 2013; Kirk *Game of Thrones* 2011; Podeswa *Camelot* 2011, *The Borgias* 2011; Shill *Rome* 2005–2007, *Ben Hur* 2010; Walsh *The Irish Empire* 2000, *The Borgias* 2011; Rawi *Zulu Dawn* 1979, *Ben Hur* 2010, *The Borgias* 2011; Grootenboer *The Borgias* 2011–2012; Martin *Camelot* 2011, *The Borgias* 2011–2012; Morris *Pillars of the Earth* 2010, *Immortals* 2011, *The Borgias* 2011–2012; Bergin *Camelot* 2011; for further information on each, see IMDb.

CHAPTER 2

Henry VIII in *The Tudors*: Romantic Renaissance Warrior or Soap Opera Playboy?

William B. Robison

Henry VIII is both the main character and the central problem of *The Tudors*.[1] While creator/writer Michael Hirst's selection of Jonathan Rhys Meyers to portray Henry may appeal to a young audience, it is awkward otherwise. Meyers looks nothing like Henry. His spare physique inhibits discerning viewers from suspending disbelief and leads to unintentional comedy, notably when he wrestles with Francis I (Emmanuel Leconte), who is a full head taller. In early episodes Meyers' youth is an advantage; however, he never ages significantly save for a sparse beard and an unconvincing grayish tint to his hair, and he remains thin, unlike the morbidly obese older Henry, because he refused to wear a fat suit. As for acting, his only concessions to the king's advancing years are an occasional limp and his inexplicable adoption in Season Four of a choked Scots accent. Meyers is not a bad actor, but he is miscast, Henry mischaracterized, and the history of his reign often misrepresented. Nor does Meyers compare favorably with stronger cast members, notably Maria Doyle Kennedy as Catherine of Aragon, Natalie Dormer as Anne Boleyn, Sam Neill as Wolsey, and Jeremy Northam as More, all gone by the end of Season Two. Without the dramatic tension

---

W.B. Robison (✉)
Department of History and Political Science, Southeastern Louisiana University, Hammond, LA, USA

© The Editor(s) (if applicable) and The Author(s) 2016
W.B. Robison (ed.), *History, Fiction, and* The Tudors,
Queenship and Power, DOI 10.1057/978-1-137-43883-6_2

between Catherine and Anne and with an overall weaker cast and script, Seasons Three and Four are less engaging, and this affects Meyers' Henry. Overall, his portrayal is a significant departure from traditional representations, yet *The Tudors* is so popular that Meyers' hip but diminutive monarch could become the new popular image of Henry.[2]

Another problem is costumer Joan Bergin's decision to eschew authenticity in favor of apparel that is eye-catching. True, this will bother viewers familiar with Henrician clothing more than others, for it is no more distracting than staging Shakespeare in modern dress. However, Henry stands out for the wrong reason. Ideally his garments should emphasize his regal nature, but some are outlandish enough to resemble those of a circus performer or, with a cap and bells added, a court jester. In film clips of Emil Jannings, Charles Laughton, Robert Shaw, Richard Burton, Keith Michell, Ray Winstone, or other actors who have portrayed the king, it is obvious from their costumes and beards that they are supposed to be Henry VIII, even if they do not perfectly match his portraits. Meyers looks like the soccer player from *Bend It Like Beckham* dressed for a Renaissance Fair.[3]

If Meyers is a shrunken Henry, Hirst's scripts reduce the larger-than-life Renaissance man of history to a one-dimensional soap opera playboy. While both admit that *The Tudors* is indeed a soap opera and that theirs is not the historical Henry, they want critics and historians to take the series seriously. Yet their Henry is less at home at the Tudor court than he might have been in daytime drama, where abusive, surly, adolescent narcissists are irresistible to beautiful but shallow female victims. All their Henry cares about is sex and power, in pursuit of which politics is merely a tool, not a divinely appointed calling. Except for a few throwaway lines about humanism, he is not the multilingual, talented, learned intellectual of reality. Little indicates his deep (if troubled) faith and interest in Christian theology aside from a few shots of him praying, an angry outburst at Martin Luther's profane response to his *Assertio Septem Sacramentorum*, and the absurd idea that he rewrote the Lord's Prayer and Ten Commandments. Their Henry almost never dances, plays no music except a snatch of "Greensleeves" (which he did not write), and patronizes only composer Thomas Tallis (at court twenty-five years early and unaccountably bisexual) and painter Hans Holbein for portraits of sex (a nude of the fictional Ursula Misseldon) or power (his famed portrait of Henry taken out of context). He bullies rather than reasoning with clergymen, diplomats, ministers, and parliament. Finally, he is unlikeable, little resembling the charming, charismatic king—surrounded by boon companions and scholars—that the real Henry was until the mid-1530s, and his personality never alters, as the real Henry's did.[4]

An especially glaring omission from *The Tudors* is Henry's role as a warrior. True, he participates in peacetime substitutes for battle, but he often jousts against fictitious opponents, and while he talks about hunting, viewers rarely see him doing it. However, he does not fight. The series skips his first decade as king and thus his early war in France, where in 1513 he and the English army chased the French from the field in the Battle of the Spurs (Guinegate) and captured Therouanne and Tournai. During the siege of Boulogne in 1544, he is in better physical shape than the historical Henry, who was so fat he had to be hoisted onto his horse; however, on-screen he does nothing but observe. His army and navy do not fight much either. Though Henry shows off his ships to Charles V, there are no maritime battles. When Charles Brandon, Duke of Suffolk (Henry Cavill), suppresses the Pilgrimage of Grace in Season Two—taking the role of Thomas Howard, 3rd Duke of Norfolk (Henry Czerny, who leaves after Season One)—viewers see mostly the aftermath of combat. As for Scotland, Flodden occurred in 1513, before the series begins, Solway Moss (1542) receives minimal attention, and there is no account of the Rough Wooing (1543–1551), Henry's attempt to force marriage between Prince Edward and Mary, Queen of Scots. Despite declaring he will win fame by emulating Henry V, victor of the Battle of Agincourt (1415), Henry VIII does little to follow in his hero's footsteps.[5]

The series pays more attention to diplomacy but makes a hash of chronology. Brandon, the only character besides Henry in every episode, is both warrior and diplomat, performing tasks he really carried out and many that are invented or the work of others. Imperial ambassador Eustace Chapuys (Anthony Brophy) appears in twenty-five episodes but is only the most ubiquitous of many diplomats. Wolsey, who dominates nonromantic plot lines in Season One, and Cromwell, who does likewise in Season Two, engage heavily in diplomacy, as do Thomas Boleyn (Nick Dunning), More, and Thomas Wyatt (Jamie Thomas King). Stephen Gardiner (Simon Ward) emerges as a major diplomat in the last two seasons, as do Francis Bryan (Alan van Sprang) in Season Three and Henry Howard, Earl of Surrey (David O'Hara), in Season Four. Viewers cannot miss the rivalry among the young monarchs Henry, Francis I, and Charles V; international implications of England's break with Rome; recurrent threats from Scotland; use of royal marriage as a diplomatic tool; duplicity of diplomats; and fluidity of alliances. However, the devil is in the details, which the series frequently gets wrong.[6]

The conclusion of *The Tudors* in 2010 capped a century of Henry VIII on film. The first Tudor film, *The Execution of Mary, Queen of Scots*, appeared in 1895, but the first to feature Henry was in 1909, followed by cinematic epics, mini-series, television movies, documentaries, cartoons, and spoofs, spanning a broad range of artistic quality and historical accuracy. Tudor films typically privilege royal romance, focusing especially on Henry and his wives, Elizabeth I and her suitors, and Mary, Queen of Scots' tragic marriages. Most Henrician films concentrate on the king–queen–mistress love triangle of Henry, Catherine of Aragon, and Anne Boleyn, though some feature other wives, and the king is in most versions of *The Prince and the Pauper*. Additionally, because filmmakers sometimes do research by watching earlier cinematic Henries rather than studying the original, fictional tropes reappear in film after film. Yet, enough of the real Henry remains to make his fictitious representations plausible and to allow suspension of disbelief, rendering filmic Henries highly problematic for historians concerned about historicity. The many on-screen portrayals range from brilliant to ludicrous to just plain awful, but in almost every case before *The Tudors*, the king on-screen reflects three interlinked Tudorist influences.[7]

First, Holbein created an image of Henry that has influenced perceptions for 500 years—the massive, confident-looking fellow with broad shoulders, wide stance, elaborate regalia, assertive codpiece, and hand resting on his dagger. Second, stage productions of William Shakespeare and John Fletcher's *The Famous History of the Life of King Henry the Eight* created a behavioral stereotype to match, incorporating the Holbein image and well-documented, if frequently exaggerated, elements of Bluff King Hal's personality into a Falstaff-like character with gargantuan appetites and outsized emotions.[8] Third, silent films took their cue from theater, often using actors who had portrayed Henry onstage. In the best one, *Anna Boleyn* (1920), Emil Jannings' Henry is attired like Holbein's king, alternately leers and rages, and enjoys carousing with courtiers.[9] In the first talking Tudor film, *The Private Life of Henry VIII* (1933), Charles Laughton draws on Jannings' example while striking the Holbein pose, mixing comedy, gravity, and pathos—buffoonish, imperious, or pitiable— and solidifies the perception of Henry as a jolly, gluttonous lecher. He reprised the role, less funny but even more bombastic, in *Young Bess* in 1953. In the intervening two decades, he left his mark on others; thus, since *Private Life*, almost every filmic Henry has been part Holbein, part Shakespeare, and part Jannings and Laughton.[10]

As Tom Freeman notes, a new wave of Tudor films began in the 1950s, inspired by two plays, Maxwell Anderson's *Anne of the Thousand Days* (1948) and Robert Bolt's *A Man for All Seasons* (1954), though the traditional film Henry is still on-screen. In Fred Zinneman's award-winning 1966 film of *A Man for All Seasons* (with Paul Scofield as Thomas More), Robert Shaw's Henry alternates between jolly Laughton-esque exuberance and furious Shakespearean rage amid considerable Holbein-informed swagger. Charlton Heston's 1988 television film of the stage play is more faithful to the original; thus, Martin Chamberlain is less flamboyant, though still Holbein-esque. Anderson's play appeared in abbreviated form as *The Trial of Anne Boleyn* on the 1952 debut of Alastair Cooke's *Omnibus*, starring a traditional-looking Rex Harrison. In 1969, Charles Jarrott directed the outstanding film version of *Anne of the Thousand Days* with a liberated Anne played by Genevieve Bujold and a lust-driven Henry portrayed by Richard Burton, who as usual really plays himself, though viewers can see his predecessors' influence.[11] *The Six Wives of Henry VIII*, a 1970 BBC series directed by Naomi Capon and John Glenister, is the first to include all the wives and show the transition from the little-known young, athletic Henry to the more familiar elderly, obese man he became. Keith Michell, as the king, is still the only actor to age convincingly. Visually, it is a remarkable piece of Tudorism, with many shots based on period art. Michell reprised his role in the 1972 movie *Henry VIII and His Six Wives* and the 1996 BBC mini-series *The Prince and the Pauper*. After *Six Wives* came a hiatus in major movies, though Henry appeared in other versions of Mark Twain's novel, Shakespearean revivals, comic spoofs, minor productions, and even a pornographic film.[12]

The twenty-first century finds Henry in vogue again, with both comic and serious films, all of which—except *The Tudors*—preserve elements of the traditional filmic king. In Granada Television's *Henry VIII* (2003), director Pete Travis tried to make the king as crude, boorish, and ruthless as mobster Tony Soprano in what he calls "*The Godfather* in tights," but Ray Winstone looks like Henry and exhibits Laughton-esque behavior even if he keeps his working-class accent and plays a harder, more vulnerable king who rages, is wantonly cruel, but weeps over stillborn children and the demise of marriages. There are two versions of *The Other Boleyn Girl*, a BBC television movie, with Jodhi May as Anne and Jared Harris as Henry (2003) and a feature film with Natalie Portman as Anne and Eric

Bana as a Henry who looks right but acts poorly while striding around boldly, looking manly and determined. In *The Twisted Tale of Bloody Mary* (2008), an amateurish, anti-Protestant independent film, Jason Sharp is a conventional Henry.[13]

Meyers' Henry in *The Tudors* is thus a radical departure from a century of film tradition, though it is important to keep this in perspective. First, Holbein's portrait is not a photograph nor is it entirely Holbein, for a 1698 fire destroyed the original Whitehall Mural he painted in 1537, with only copies surviving. A propaganda piece, the image depicts an oversized Henry and three persons then dead—Henry VII, Elizabeth of York, and Jane Seymour. To whatever extent it is realistic, it captures only a moment and is but one in a long string of portraits from Henry as chubby toddler to the beardless youth who took the throne in 1509 to the handsome bearded athlete of the 1510s and 1520s to the increasingly obese king of the 1530s and 1540s. The problem with Meyers' Henry is not that he starts out young but that he is too short, has dark hair instead of red, and never grows a proper Henrician beard, gains weight, or shows any realistic sign of aging, while failing to portray the king in all his complexity. Second, Fletcher and Shakespeare's *Henry VIII* is not scholarly biography but historical drama written for the stage, featuring a fictionalized king and also functioning as pro-Tudor propaganda. Third, previous films about Henry are not documentaries but rather historical fiction, and many are as inaccurate as *The Tudors*, though even documentary reenactments resort to Holbein's image and sometimes contain errors. It is the scale of *The Tudors* and its popularity that make it a special case.[14]

Season One begins with French agents assassinating Henry's imaginary uncle in Urbino, then shifts to Whitehall Palace, where the king is "mad with grief, inconsolable," but recovers quickly, for after denouncing Francis for fictional "just causes of war," he announces, "Now I can go play," and has sex with Bessie Blount (Ruta Gedmintas). There is a lot more sex in this and subsequent episodes, but the war never materializes. Henry accepts More and Wolsey's proposal for a Wilsonian perpetual peace with collective security and pan-European institutions, apparently forgiving Francis, who evidently has abandoned his own bellicose intentions. In reality, Wolsey secured international agreement to universal peace in the 1518 Treaty of London, but the 1519 imperial election undermined it, with Charles I of Spain being elected Holy Roman Emperor as Charles V over Francis and Henry. The 1520 Field of the Cloth of Gold was part of a new diplomatic dance in which Henry and Francis professed undying brotherhood while Wolsey left to secretly discuss an anti-French alliance with Charles. Visually the Anglo-French summit captures the pageantry of such occasions but otherwise is largely inaccurate. Henry did swear not to shave until the meeting but did not ride alone to meet Francis in the Val d'Or or have a violent tantrum after losing at wrestling. There is jousting aplenty in *The Tudors* but none in France despite its real prominence. The script downplays Queens Catherine and Claude; instead, Francis brags about making Mary Boleyn his "English mare," and Henry begins an affair with her.[15]

A manufactured storyline has Edward Stafford, 3rd Duke of Buckingham (Steven Waddington) executed for a failed coup. The duke pointlessly insults Henry at every opportunity, and Henry goads Buckingham, instigating a bet that leads Brandon to seduce his daughter Anna (Anna Brewster), refusing his demand for justice after the duke catches them, and taunting him when he offers a New Year's gift. Buckingham tries to involve Norfolk and Thomas Boleyn and gathers an army of retainers, but Henry lures him into a trap and has Brandon intimidate Norfolk, who presides at the trial, to ensure he is found guilty. Wolsey, who tries to mitigate the duke's punishment, is shocked at the trial's outcome, and Buckingham dies in cowardly fashion. None of this happened in reality. Though the Plantagenet Buckingham foolishly speculated about the succession, he hatched no plot, it was Wolsey who sought to convict him, and he died bravely.[16]

Another ahistorical plotline involves Henry's sister Margaret (Gabrielle Anwar), whom Hirst amalgamates with younger sibling Mary into a single character. Henry forces her to marry an elderly King of Portugal (Joseph Kelly). Brandon escorts her to the wedding, they end up in bed en route, Margaret murders her new husband and marries Brandon without Henry's permission, and the king banishes and threatens to execute both. After he eventually forgives them, Brandon is unfaithful, Margaret dies of consumption, and Henry is furious again but forgives him once more. This is complete invention. In 1503 Margaret married James IV of Scotland, who was killed at Flodden in 1513; in 1514 she married Archibald Douglas, 6th Earl of Angus, whom she divorced in 1527; and in 1528 she married Henry Stewart, 1st Lord Methven, living until 1541. Mary reluctantly married the elderly Louis XII of France in 1514 and after his death in 1515 married Brandon (already Duke of Suffolk), which did anger Henry. The real Margaret was the grandmother of both Mary, Queen of Scots, and her second husband, Henry Stuart, Lord Darnley, while Mary was the grandmother of Jane, Catherine, and Mary Grey.[17]

The series soon establishes that Henry is a sex-crazed misogynist nonetheless irresistible to women, for after the first of his many unpleasant exchanges with Catherine, she invites him to visit her bedchamber, and arriving to discover she is at prayer, he has sex with her maid. The script also compresses and distorts his romantic activities c. 1518–1525. His affair with Bessie Blount was real, as was Henry Fitzroy, the illegitimate son she bore in 1519. But Mary Boleyn (Perdita Weeks) becomes his mistress earlier than in reality, and he discards her even more quickly, though their relationship probably lasted from 1521 to 1525. Her exit allows Anne's early arrival at court as Henry prematurely expresses doubts about his marriage to Catherine. As in *The Other Boleyn Girl*, Anne is her father and Norfolk's pawn in a scheme that makes the king a dupe, as if neither Henry nor Anne exercised real agency in their relationship. On-screen their courtship begins with a well-staged masked pageant during which Henry "rescues" Anne from a castle where she and other Virtues are prisoners of the Vices. In a dream sequence, Anne instructs Henry, "Seduce me," and subsequently he sends her jewels, writes her letters (using language from real correspondence), and secretly meets and kisses her. Playing hard to get, Anne writes that he frightens her but sends him a locket with her portrait, declines to be his "one true mistress" but sends him a model ship carrying a damsel in distress, and engages in heavy petting but not sex. When Catherine finds them together, the king heartlessly refuses to send Anne away. But pursuit of Anne does not prevent him from fictitiously taking pleasure elsewhere, notably in a ludicrous sequence in which he seduces Francis' sister, Marguerite of Navarre (Sara James).[18]

Meanwhile, there is diplomatic activity on several fronts. Mendoza (Declan Conlon) and Chapuys arrive in England sometime c. 1521–1525 to prepare for a visit Charles V actually made in 1520, though Mendoza was not imperial ambassador until 1526–1529 and Chapuys until 1529–1545. Later, Henry and Catherine welcome Charles, the king shows off the ship *Mary Rose* and talks of conquering France. Wolsey proposes betrothal of the emperor and Princess Mary to the envoys, who promise to support him for the papacy, a subplot perhaps based on A.F. Pollard's discredited notion that the cardinal's diplomacy reflected his desire to be pope. More accurately, the Anglo-Imperial alliance falls apart after Charles defeats and captures Francis at the Battle of Pavia (1525), marries Isabel of Portugal, and releases the French king without consulting Henry. On-screen there quickly follows the sack of Rome, which was actually in 1527. This made Pope Clement VII the emperor's prisoner and, though Hirst's script does not explain it, created an insurmountable obstacle for Henry's attempt to divorce Charles' aunt.[19]

Subsequently, Henry, more desperate for a male heir after he nearly dies vaulting a ditch, creates Henry Fitzroy (Zak Jenciragic) as Earl of Nottingham and Duke of Richmond and Somerset, which he actually did in 1525; however, his bastard son did not supersede Mary as Wolsey tells Catherine, nor did he die soon after, living until 1536. Wolsey convenes an ecclesiastical court to investigate the marriage and revives the idea of a French match for Mary, whom Henry banishes to Ludlow, telling Catherine they are not legally married. The king sends Wolsey to France, where he fails to assemble the cardinals to rule on the divorce. Cromwell—who appears early—informs Henry that Clement has escaped, and the king sends William Knight (Brian de Salvo) to him with two documents erroneously described as bulls, one allowing him to marry Anne despite the impediment of his relationship with her sister and the other permitting bigamous marriage, an idea that originated with Clement. Wolsey intercepts Knight and is implausibly surprised. Returning to reality, he comes home with gifts from Francis to Henry but with no solution to the King's Great Matter. He sends Gardiner and Edward Foxe (Philip Desmeules) to meet Clement (Ian McElhinney) at Orvieto and advises them, if all else fails, to threaten that the king will circumvent the Holy See. When they try this, the pope laughs and states that he will send Cardinal Campeggio (John Kavanagh) to England as his legate.[20]

When the sweating sickness of 1528 strikes on-screen, many people succumb, while Dr. Thomas Linacre (Clive Geraghty)—who died in 1524—is miraculously resurrected and demonstrates precociously modern knowledge of contagion. Henry resorts to his own traditional remedies but does take the doctor's unscientific advice that exercise prevents the disease by producing natural sweat. The epidemic highlights tension within the royal love triangle. The king prays with Catherine, sends her to Ludlow, and dispatches Anne to Hever, where she nearly dies. Henry locks himself away, succumbs to hypochondria, and is haunted by morbid dreams. When the threat subsides, Henry appears holding Catherine's hand, then embracing Anne at Hever. Henry and Catherine pose for an imaginary portrait, and he angers Anne by contending that for now he must continue sharing the queen table and bed, as he actually did. Wolsey unrealistically threatens Campeggio with annihilation of papal authority and spread of Lutheranism in England, and the two cardinals propose that Catherine enter a nunnery, but she will have none of it, even after Archbishop William Warham (Eamon Rohan) and Bishop Cuthbert Tunstall (Gordon Sterne) try persuading her and Henry threatens to prevent her seeing Mary. When Anne suggests Wolsey is not doing his best, Henry sends Brandon to question Francis about the cardinal and less accurately dispatches Cromwell to Rome to threaten the pope.[21]

Campeggio and Wolsey open the legatine court at Blackfriars, Catherine pleads with the king, leaves when he is unmoved, and refuses to return, as in reality. The king encounters resistance from Bishop John Fisher (Bosco Hogan), More fails to obstruct Franco-Imperial peace, and Campeggio prorogues the court on secret instructions from Clement. Anne tells Henry he is both emperor and pope—actually Cromwell's idea—and gives him William Tyndale's *Obedience of a Christian Man*, which he reads approvingly. Henry deprives Wolsey of office, charging him with violating the Statute of Praemunire. After the season finale begins, for no apparent reason, with Henry masturbating, he complains to the council about being deceived, tells the newly arrived Chapuys that Luther was right except about the sacraments, and declares that he will reform the church. Cromwell—rather than Gardiner and Foxe—relates Cranmer's suggestion to canvas European theological faculties about the divorce. More accurately, Henry makes Thomas Boleyn Earl of Wiltshire and Lord Privy Seal and George (Padraic Delaney) Lord Rochford, but gives Hampton Court to Anne, which did not happen. Henry regrets dismissing Wolsey, complains to his councilors about unrest and lack of funds, and orders More to summon parliament. But he has Wolsey arrested for corresponding with the emperor and pope, and—in a ridiculous development—the cardinal commits suicide. Out riding, Henry and Anne begin having sex, but she stops him, and he stalks away angry.[22]

Season One gives only sporadic, superficial attention to the Reformation. Aside from instances already noted, it touches on Henry's theological dispute with Martin Luther, Cromwell consorts with Lutherans, and More tells his daughter Margaret (Gemma Reeves)—anticipating Karl Marx by over three centuries—"There is a specter haunting Europe," though it is not communism but the Lutheranism that inspired the German Peasants Revolt of 1524–1525. He says it is necessary to purge such sickness with fire, and after Henry compels him to become Lord Chancellor, he burns several heretics, as in reality, but on-screen this includes Simon Fish, author of *Supplication of the Beggars*, who actually died of natural causes.[23]

Season Two is still primarily about sex and power but—thanks to Natalie Dormer's insistence—pays more attention to Anne's role in the Reformation. In fact, it opens with Henry and Anne praying. However, there is no shortage of inaccuracies and inventions. Paul III (Peter O'Toole) becomes pope in 1529 rather than 1534 and instigates a bogus plot whereby William Brereton tries to assassinate Anne, Cromwell introduces Cranmer to Henry three years after they actually met, Henry makes Cromwell Lord Chancellor in 1533 rather than Lord Privy Seal in 1536 and "vice-regent" instead of vicegerent for ecclesiastical affair, the king takes Bess Webbe (Katie McGrath) from her husband William (Damien Kearney) for sex, the court sees John Bale's *King John* two or three years before the playwright wrote it in 1538, Cromwell proposes Thomas Boleyn as "Lord Protector" when Henry is knocked unconscious in a joust, and after Henry makes Anne pregnant a third time, Boleyn tells her in explicable blasphemy, "Think that I am the angel come down to tell you that you carry the Christ child in your belly." On the other hand, the plot addresses important legislation—the pardon of the clergy (1531) who acknowledged Henry as Supreme Head of the Church "in so far as the law of Christ allows" (set in parliament rather than convocation) and the Acts of Annates (1532), for the Submission of the Clergy (1533), in Restraint of Appeals (1533), of Succession (1534), of Supremacy (1534), and of Treason (1534). It gets right Henry's appointment of George Boleyn to deal with Warham and Fisher, the king's discovery that the clergy are "only half our subjects," Anne's encouragement of Bible-reading among her ladies, the fraudulent holy blood of Hailes Abbey, and the *Valor Ecclesiasticus*.[24]

Henry continues mistreating Catherine and Mary and increasingly does likewise to Anne; indeed, the series might be subtitled (with apologies to Susan Forward) "kings who hate women and the women who love them." When Anne complains that Catherine is still making the king's shirts, he is rude to both. He refuses to accompany Catherine to visit Mary when she is ill and later keeps them apart altogether, banishes her to the More in Hertfordshire and denies her visitors, refuses a cup she sends at Christmas, and demands that she return the royal jewels and stop using the title of queen. At first he lavishes attention on Anne, making her Marquess of Pembroke. They have sex in France in 1532 (likely it was on their return), Anne gets pregnant, they marry, and she is crowned in 1533. When Elizabeth is born, he is visibly disappointed but reassures Anne, "You and I are both young, and by God's grace, boys will follow." All this is fairly accurate, but Henry also begins a fling with the fictitious

Eleanor Luke, real infidelities apparently being insufficient to maintain his credentials as a soap opera philanderer.[25]

By the next Christmas Anne is pregnant again, but the king dances with Eleanor, George tells Anne they are lovers, and she has the fictitious mistress accused of fictitious theft and removed from court, causing a fictitious tiff with Henry. Following her father's advice that the king must have the right mistress while she is with child, she arranges for Madge Shelton to assume that role (actually Henry may have had an affair with her sister Mary Shelton in 1535). It is hard to say who is more sordid, the king or Thomas Boleyn. When Anne miscarries, the king offers little sympathy. Anne worries, as she did in reality, about the threat that Catherine and Mary pose but also implausibly flirts with Smeaton in front of Henry. Unable to persuade him to share her bed, she complains about his extramarital amours, and he accurately retorts, "You must shut your eyes and endure as your betters have done before" and "I can drag you down as quickly as I have raised you." He tells her Francis, the emperor, and the pope think Elizabeth a bastard and Anne not his rightful wife, blames her for his decision to execute More, and warns her to leave diplomacy to him. Not long after he visits Anne's chamber for rough sex, he is at Wolf Hall and meets Jane Seymour (Anita Briem), who actually had been at court since 1529.[26]

In a poignant sequence, Catherine's death is intercut with scenes of Henry reading her last letter and experiencing genuine grief. But Anne rejoices and reveals she is pregnant again. Henry jousts while wearing Jane's favors and is knocked unconscious, which really happened, after which Anne finds him kissing her, which did not. When Anne miscarries, Henry rages, "You have lost my boy," they quarrel, and he tells Cromwell he has been seduced by witchcraft and wants a new wife. The doctors tell Henry the fetus was deformed (there is no evidence of this), Anne angrily confronts Jane, and her ladies jump to false conclusions about her relationship to Henry Norris (Stephen Hogan), Smeaton, and her brother George. Anne threatens Cromwell when he disagrees about using monastic wealth to support education, and she unwisely tells George's wife—née Jane Parker, now Lady Rochford (Joanne King)—"The king cannot satisfy a woman. He has neither the skill nor the virility." When Brandon reports Anne's alleged adultery, Henry appoints a commission of oyer and terminer that interrogates her women and arrests George Boleyn, Brereton, Norris, Smeaton, and Wyatt, but not two men missing from the cast: Francis Weston, who was executed, or Richard Page, who was released.

They also arrest Thomas Boleyn, which did not happen—he cooperated with Henry. In a truly cringe-worthy scene, Henry spills his sorrows to Brandon and then weeps in his lap. Even more problematic, Anne's alleged lovers are executed without his advance knowledge or approval.[27]

Much of Season Two's diplomacy concerns the divorce, the international consequences of the break with Rome and the deaths of Fisher, More, and Catherine, the balancing of France and the Empire, and the fruitless pursuit of marriages for Mary and Elizabeth. Henry's persecution of More and Fisher converts an admired diplomat into a diplomatic issue, an obstructionist bishop into a cardinal, and both into Catholic martyrs. The series might have made more of Chapuys and Fisher's intrigues against Henry, but it accurately depicts Paul III's brinkmanship in sending the imprisoned Fisher a cardinal's hat in 1535. Fisher and More's execution arouses international indignation and causes Henry regret, as it did historically. Paul III condemns their "murder," and Chapuys toasts them in a tavern, where he hears that Anne has "devil's teats." Meanwhile, Henry tells Charles via Chapuys he will do as he pleases about marriage, presents Anne to Francis (whose wife and sister refuse to meet her), and agrees to a joint crusade, a commonplace bit of armchair bellicosity when rulers were deep in their cups.[28]

Though Francis refuses to recognize his marriage, Henry proposes betrothing Elizabeth to Francis' son Charles, Duke of Angouleme, invites the Admiral of France Philippe Chabot (Philippe de Grossouvre) to England, but ominously assigns the pro-imperial Brandon to handle his visit over Anne's suggestion that her father do so. Chabot is cold to Anne, Henry and Brandon fictitiously flirt with his niece Germaine (Sorcha Callaghan), and he befriends Chapuys, tells Henry the marriage is impossible because Catholics do not accept Elizabeth's legitimacy, offers the marriage of the Dauphin to Mary, and threatens that otherwise the Dauphin will marry Charles' daughter, leaving England isolated. Angry, Henry turns back to the empire, applauds the emperor's capture of Tunis (1535), and has Cromwell discuss renewing Anglo-Imperial friendship with the envoy, who replies that Charles will persuade the pope to withdraw Henry's excommunication and support his marriage if he will make Mary his heir. Later, Cromwell tells Chapuys that Anne is the only obstacle to legitimizing Mary, she warns the French ambassador (Jonathan Ryan) that she is lost if Elizabeth is not betrothed to the Dauphin (not Angouleme), Cromwell raises with Chapuys the prospect of Henry remarrying, Boleyn tells Anne to give up the French alliance, he and George try to make amends with Chapuys, Anne insults the French ambassador, and Henry excludes the Boleyns from an audience with Chapuys. However, when the envoy suggests that God wants a female succession, Henry flies into a rage and demands imperial recognition. However, what Anne gets from France is an executioner.[29]

Dormer is at her best in Season Two's finale as Anne shifts from hysteria to despair to calm resolution in the Tower, prepares for death in scenes intercut with Jane happily preparing to meet Henry (reminiscent of *Private Life*), and makes peace with God aided by Cranmer. Her compelling execution scene compares favorably to those in other films. Henry, irritable and self-centered as usual, is angry about the delay in the French swordsman's arrival, orders Cromwell to have Anne executed with an axe, threatens to send him the scaffold as well, and then relents before heading to Wolf Hall to announce his marriage to Jane. Finally, in an effective but disturbing gambit, Henry periodically watches two swans swimming in a pond, which clearly symbolize the king and Anne. After her execution, servants bring present a large dish to the king, alone at table. The cover is removed to reveal one of the swans. Henry breaks it open and begins to eat with his hands, gravy dripping down his chin.[30]

Season Three, only eight episodes, has a new Jane (Annabelle Wallis), Cranmer vanishes like Norfolk before him, and Francis Bryan (Alan Van Sprang) arrives late, though in reality he was one of the young king's minions. Among the usual inventions and distortions, Henry denies Elizabeth is his child and refuses to pay for her clothes, enjoys the favors of the imaginary Lady Ursula Misseldon (Charlotte Salt), and has to settle an imaginary quarrel between her imaginary fiancé Sir Robert Tavistock (Danny Seward) and Holbein. On-screen, Gardiner marries Henry and Jane in a crowded Chapel Royal, though he really was in Europe at the time, and they wed privately in the Queen's Closet at Whitehall. A swan adorns the table at the wedding feast. However, marriage does not impede Henry's sexual activity with Ursula, and the new queen says that he must do as he will while women must honor and obey. Henry's poor health allows Ursula to play slutty nurse, and Jane even asks her to care for him if she dies in childbirth. Whatever old ideas Hirst seeks to undermine, they apparently do not include male chauvinism. Jane's faith is uncertain, but a priest gives her Catherine's crucifix, and at Christmas 1536 she, Henry, and Mary attend church with a traditional candlelit procession. However, when she tries to persuade him to restore the abbeys, he warns her not to meddle. Soon she is pregnant, has a difficult labor but a healthy son,

Henry is overjoyed—blessing Prince Edward in the name of God, the Virgin Mary, and St. George—and then she dies, leaving him distraught. Less realistically, a mad Henry goes into seclusion with only his fool for company, while disorder reigns in the kingdom.[31]

Hirst conflates the Lincolnshire Rising of 1536 and the Pilgrimage of Grace of 1536–1537, attributing both in part to Henry destroying monasteries, which his agents merely confiscated. He also alters the roles of important participants, for example, Henry appoints Brandon rather than Norfolk to suppress the rebellion. Still, he gets rebel demands right—restoration of abbeys and traditional holidays, an end to heresy, replacement of Cranmer and Cromwell by nobleman—and accurately depicts the rumors about taxes, Aske's initial reluctance to oppose Henry, and the rebel emblem, the Five Wounds of Christ. Henry quells the Lincolnshire rising with threats and talks of pardons, promises Yorkshire rebels a parliament in York, entertains Aske at court over Christmas, and promises to pardon others but reneges. When the king orders Brandon to deny clemency to rebels who refuse the oath, he and Cromwell object, but Henry asserts that rebellion is a sin and the latter's low birth makes him unfit to comment. The revival of the rebellion in 1537 departs almost completely from accuracy, except that Henry has Aske hanged in chains for treason.[32]

Rebellion suppressed, Henry announces he will restrict evangelical excess and impose religious unity. Later, he "authors" the Six Articles, a conservative reaction to the more reformist Ten Articles of 1536, which *The Tudors* never mentions. Of course, he did not write either, though he approved both, and the Six Articles did not appear until 1539. However, the script describes the articles correctly except in making hanging, drawing, and quartering the penalty for denying the sacrament of confession. This is also the point at which he supposedly rewrites the Lord's Prayer and the Ten Commandments. When Gardiner reports evangelicals are preaching against the articles, including Cromwell's friend John Lambert, Henry has the latter burned. But the missing Cranmer and Norfolk are not allied with Cromwell and Gardiner, respectively, so the struggle over religion is neither as accurate nor as a dramatic as it might have been.[33]

The chronology of diplomacy, much of it concerning the break with Rome, marriages, and Mary, is muddled. Charles congratulates Henry on his marriage, and Mary writes asking her father's forgiveness, which he refuses; however, Chapuys urges Jane to reconcile them. Henry has Bryan, Season Three's all-purpose bad guy, present Mary with articles accepting the royal supremacy and the illegitimacy of her parents' marriage and her birth, but she refuses to sign, and Bryan threatens her with treason, though in reality he supported her restoration. When Jane urges Henry not to proceed against Mary, he warns her not to discuss such matters. Chapuys urges Mary to sign and make a protestation apart (secretly foreswear before witnesses), as Henry and the emperor are on the verge of an alliance, and she does so. Jane persuades Henry to meet Mary, and they reconcile, but in a gratuitously adolescent scene, Bryan—acting on the king's orders to investigate her innocence—quizzes the princess about her knowledge of oral sex.[34]

Meanwhile, another papal plot against Henry is afoot that—though not made of whole cloth—radically alters chronology. An elderly Cardinal von Waldburg (Max von Sydow) urges Reginald Pole (Mark Hildreth) to return to England and challenge the king. Later he adds that the pope wants him to write a pamphlet in English denouncing Henry, will send him as legate to France and the Netherlands to persuade Francis and Charles to support English rebels, and simply hands Pole a red cardinal's hat. In reality, Waldburg, born in 1514, actually was in his 20s and did not become a cardinal until 1544, while Pole became a cardinal in 1536 and legate in 1537, wrote *Defence of the Unity of the Church* in 1536 in response to the king's request for his opinion, published it in 1539 in Latin as *Pro ecclesiasticae unitatis defensione*, and did not go home until 1554. Pole meets Mendoza in the "Spanish" Netherlands to discuss overthrowing Henry in favor of Mary. Henry sends Bryan to persuade Francis to hand over Pole or to kidnap him, which they did consider. Bryan and Thomas Seymour (Andrew McNair) meet the fictional Lord Talleyrand (Jean-David Beroard) and fictionally pursue Pole in Italy.[35]

This fails, so Henry arrests and executes Pole's mother Lady Margaret, Countess of Salisbury (Kate O'Toole), brother Henry Lord Montague (Jake Maskall), and nephew Henry (Daniel Rhattigan-Walsh) for treason. Bryan finds banners with the Plantagenet emblem and the Five Wounds of Christ among the countess' possessions, though in reality two officials not featured in the cast—William Fitzwilliam, Earl of Southampton, and Thomas Goodrich, Bishop of Ely—found a tunic supposedly indicating Pole's intention of marrying Mary. The real story is one of unwarranted cruelty, but *The Tudors* makes it worse by having Brandon arrest the family while they are praying, having Edward Seymour take each to the executioner, ignoring Pole's brother Sir Geoffrey, whose behavior implicated the family, and omitting the conspiracy of Henry Courtenay, Marquess of Exeter and Sir Nicholas Carew, who had links to the Poles. Exeter and Montague were executed in 1539, Lady

Margaret in 1541, and young Henry died in the Tower. After the executions, Henry declares, "There you are, Cardinal Pole, now eat your heart."[36]

Meanwhile, marital diplomacy continues. Chapuys proposes marrying Mary to Portugal's heir Don Luis, apparently forgetting the unfortunate business with Margaret. After Jane's death, Henry tells the French ambassador, presumably Castillon, he is interested in a French bride, especially Marie de Guise, but she is promised to James V of Scotland, so Francis proposes a double marriage of his son Henri to Mary and Henry to one of Marie's sisters. Henry complains in implausibly modern slang that the French "want to mess me around," and Charles suggests Christina, Duchess of Milan. Henry has John Hutton (Roger Ashton-Griffiths) investigate, and Cromwell orders him to visit Cleves to learn more about Amelia (Roxana Klein) and Anne (Joss Stone), sisters of Duke William (Paul Ronan). Hutton writes favorably about all three, and Henry says he has heard that Anne is no great beauty, which Hutton actually said. Cromwell urges a Cleves marriage as a means to ally with the "Protestant League," presumably the Schmalkaldic League, of which Cleves was not actually a member. Henry sends Holbein to paint Christina, but she comments—as she famously did—"If I had two heads, one would be at his majesty's service," adding that she will only marry Henry if Charles V commands it.[37]

Cromwell tells Henry about Francis' cousins, Anne of Lavenne and Marie de Vendome, and the king suggests that Francis assemble several potential brides at Calais, where he can examine them. Castillon says this is impossible, leading to a nasty exchange of threats. The king sends Hutton and Richard Beard (Wesley Murphy) to Cleves to propose Henry's marriage to Anne and Mary's to the duke's son and request access to the Protestant League, the right to recruit 100 cannoneers, and permission to meet Anne and have Holbein paint her portrait. William initially refuses the last, accusing them of treating his court as a "meat market." Subsequently, though, he allows Hutton to meet both sisters—who are veiled—and changes his mind about Holbein, whom Cromwell instructs to make Anne look good—a familiar story based on no hard evidence.[38]

Henry prepares for a possible invasion by Charles and Francis, now allied by the Treaty of Toledo (1539) and urged on by the pope, though it never comes. Cromwell again argues for a Protestant alliance, the portrait arrives, and William demands that Henry come to Cleves, says Anne is promised to the Duke of Lorraine's son, and declares that his country is not a brothel. A fleet of sixty-eight imperial ships appears off the coast but turns out to be bound for Spain, and Chapuys soon reports that Charles has broken his treaty with France because of Francis' alliance with the Turks. He also offers Christina's hand, but Henry sends him away in a rage. Beard and Hutton (actually Nicholas Wotton) return to Cleves and tell William that Henry will forfeit Anne's dowry, and the wedding is set. Henry sends Brandon to escort Anne to England, and he teaches her to play cards while waiting for favorable weather—actually Southampton did this. When she arrives, the king decides to surprise her, is disappointed at her appearance, observes, "I like her not," and complains that she looks like "a Flanders mare." This strains credibility, for Joss Stone as Anne is quite attractive, and Bishop Gilbert Burnet invented the "mare" story in the seventeenth century. In any case, Cromwell tells Henry that there is no way out, as Charles and Francis have renewed their alliance and even William might pose a military threat. The king then slams Cromwell against a wall, which did not happen, and declares that if it were not to satisfy the world, he would do this "for no earthly thing," which he did say.[39]

The wedding is grim, with Henry glowering throughout and Anne looking confused. That night they play cards (a trope that originated with *The Private Life of Henry VIII*), and Henry is unable to consummate the marriage. The next day he tells Cromwell, "She is nothing fair and she has evil smells about her, and I know she is no maid because of the looseness of her breasts and other tokens, so I had neither the will nor the courage to prove the rest. I have no appetite for unpleasant airs. I left her as good a maid as I found her." *The Tudors* addresses speculation about why Henry was unable or unwilling to have sex with Anne by having him tell his doctor he is not impotent, having recently had two nocturnal emissions. It also calls attention to the irony of this situation by having Anne complain about the stinking ulcer on Henry's leg. Later, Lady Bryan concludes that Anne is still a virgin and advises her that she must "put his member inside you and stir it," but she demurs, saying she has all the attention from Henry she wants, though she apprehensively asks whether he will kill her if she cannot please him. All this leads to a second scene with Henry masturbating (unsuccessfully this time), which is really two too many.[40]

In the season finale, France and the Empire are again at odds, Henry concludes that he does not need Cleves, and the marriage is annulled on the grounds that Anne was precontracted. Less accurately, Anne instigates an unsuccessful courtship of Mary by the Lutheran Philip of Bavaria (Collin O'Donoghue), actually underway when she arrived in England. In an even greater departure from history, Brandon asks Bryan to find a diversion for the king, and he visits the Dowager Duchess of Norfolk (Barbara Brennan) at Lambeth Palace, which seems very much like a brothel, and selects Catherine Howard (Tamzin Merchant), who is described as the Duke of Norfolk's "distant relative" and comes across as a wanton halfwit. In fact, she was the daughter of Norfolk's brother Lord Edmund Howard and was one of Anne's ladies-in-waiting. But Henry is smitten, accurately enough. He makes Anne his "sister," provides her with land and income, has Cromwell arrested and executed, and begins a new courtship. Viewers are treated to another round of sex and nudity; in fact, the season ends with him watching Catherine naked on a swing. Here Meyers' refusal to get older on-screen minimizes the gap in Henry and Catherine's ages, for while Meyers (thirty-two in 2009) and Merchant (then twenty-two) are ten years apart, Henry (forty-nine in 1540) was much older than Catherine (probably seventeen).[41]

Season Four covers Henry's last seven years, though neither he nor most other characters age much. Conversely, Surrey—Norfolk's son, a famed poet, and a new character—appears middle aged, though he was twenty-three or twenty-four in 1540, and the script makes him Catherine Howard's uncle rather than cousin. There are other problems. Henry introduces Lady Bryan, Edward, and Elizabeth to Catherine as though they are strangers and later does the same with Anne of Cleves and Catherine, though the latter had been one of Anne's ladies. He again shows remarkable—if manufactured—ignorance about his own policy, asking who is being kept prisoner in the Tower, and orders the execution of Lord Dacre, Lord Bray, Lord Lisle, and Sir John Neville, only the first of whom died in reality. When Henry makes Surrey a Knight of the Garter, Edward Seymour has to explain the Order to him, and Surrey reacts with contempt, which is ludicrous, given that his father, grandfather, and great-grandfather (1st, 2nd, and 3rd Duke of Norfolk, respectively) all had been members of England's highest chivalric order and that one of his character traits in the series is contempt for lesser men. Chapuys also makes the nonsensical claim that Prince Edward's succession is in doubt because his mother was never crowned. Henry and Catherine Howard have lots of sex, though he tires of her immaturity, visits Anne of Cleves, and improbably has sex with her. Catherine has sex with Thomas Culpeper (Torrance Coombs), just as she used to with Francis Dereham (Allen Leech), Henry Manox, and apparently Joan Bulmer (Catherine Steadman). Henry and

Catherine Parr (Joely Richardson), who looks and behaves like an adult, have no sex, and the king no imaginary mistresses, but Brandon has the fictitious Brigitte Rousselot (Selma Brook) when not talking to ghosts of his victims from Season Three, Surrey has an invented affair with Anne Stanhope, and Culpeper with Lady Rochford.[42]

The investigation of Catherine's infidelity and resulting executions is remarkably error-ridden and tasteless. Henry learns about it from an anonymous letter rather than Cranmer, orders Edward Seymour to investigate, though in reality it was Norfolk, Southampton, the Marquess of Winchester, Sir Thomas Audley, Cranmer, and Thomas Wriothesley ("Risley" in the show, played by Frank McCusker), and Gardiner instead of Cranmer tells the king about Catherine's agitated state and delivers his offer of pardon if she confesses. Henry blames Brandon and Seymour for introducing Catherine to him, though they did no such thing (Bryan, no longer in the series, escapes his share of the nonexistent blame). Henry has parliament pass a bill allowing Lady Rochford's execution despite her insanity, which did not happen, though she and Catherine were condemned by an act of attainder rather than a court trial. One gets little sense of Henry's grief, unlike with Keith Michell in *Six Wives* and Ray Winstone in *Henry VIII*. Rather, a drunken Henry lets ladies sit on the throne in scenes intercut with Catherine practicing at the executioner's block, once while completely naked. When Lady Rochford dies, Catherine urinates on herself, though really she died first. Where her turn comes, she inaccurately declares, "I die a queen but I would rather die the wife of Culpeper" and "Life is very beautiful."[43]

Henry is not alone for long. At Christmas, Catherine Parr comes to court to dispel Henry's suspicion that her ailing husband, Lord Latimer (Stephen Russell), is a traitor, and courtship blossoms. Henry sends rival Thomas Seymour on a "permanent" embassy to the Netherlands that really lasted three months (April–July 1543) and deputes Edward Seymour and Risley to offer his hand when Latimer dies. As usual, the wedding is larger on-screen, where Gardiner marries them in church before a large congregation, than in reality, where the ceremony took place in the Queen's Closet at Hampton Court with eighteen people present. Because of their age, the king's children play a larger role in Season Four, and in his relationships with them, Meyers' Henry is at his most human. He is kinder to Mary, praises Elizabeth, and is concerned about Edward's health, and Catherine persuades him to invite them to court more often.[44]

England's religious trajectory remains uncertain, as in reality. Cromwell's fall in 1540 removed a major advocate for reform, which Cranmer's absence from the cast accentuates. Season Four begins with Henry having Catholics and Lutherans burned on the same day and with 500 heretics in the Tower, though he later pardons them. But when Henry makes a treaty with Charles in 1542, Gardiner tells Risley it is time to hunt down Lutherans and evangelicals, including those close to the king. Henry allows him to arrest the Chapel Royal's master of choristers John Marbeck, the organist Robert Testwood, and singing man Edmund Harman, though it really was Marbeck, Testwood (a chorister), Henry Filmer, and Anthony Peerson—Harman was the king's barber. Gardiner interrogates Testwood under torture, questions Risley about Catherine Parr's beliefs, and tells Rich that Henry is "cherishing a serpent in his bosom." She appoints Hugh Latimer, whom Gardiner supposedly has dismissed from his bishopric, as her chaplain and tells him she will use her position to advance the Reformation, though it was Henry who removed Latimer as Bishop of Worcester in 1539, and he never was Catherine's chaplain. Gardiner temporarily convinces Henry that Catherine is a heretic, pursues the queen and her ladies, and arrests, tortures, interrogates, and eventually burns Anne Askew. Catherine barely escapes by throwing herself on the king's mercy, in accord with traditional accounts, though Tom Freeman has questioned whether Gardiner was really behind a plot against the queen.[45]

On the diplomatic front, Henry welcomes both Chapuys and French Ambassador Charles de Marillac (Lothaire Bluteau) and introduces them to Catherine Howard. Henry expresses sympathy for the Dauphin's recent death to Marillac, who in turn delivers Francis' proposal that Mary wed the new heir, Prince Henri (later Henri II, who married Catherine de Medici). But subsequently—and for no apparent reason—the king sends Surrey and Thomas Seymour for an imaginary show of force before Ardres, and Francis sues for peace. Later, he warns Marillac that Francis would be foolish to invade England because he believes it is divided over religion, and the ambassador assures him the French king is his friend. Eventually, Chapuys offers Henry an alliance with Charles, who is fighting both France and the Turks, promising that he will regain Aquitaine. Marillac counters that Charles breaks promises, offers payment of Henry's overdue French pension, and argues the Anglo-French alliance has maintained the balance of power in Europe for a decade. But Henry makes a secret treaty with Charles and plans to invade France.[46]

Henry appoints Brandon commander, Thomas Seymour Admiral of the Fleet, and Surrey Marshal of the Field, though John Dudley, Viscount Lisle was Lord High Admiral (Seymour became an admiral later) and Surrey was Marshall of the Army at Montreuil, not at Boulogne. In a bogus subplot, Henry suspects Edward Seymour of opposing the war. Charles sends the Duke of Najera (Fabio Tassone) to further preparations, antagonizing Marillac. Brandon trains soldiers for a "new" kind of war with guns. Henry, impatient for battle and unrealistically svelte and healthy despite references to his ulcer bursting, insists on a shorter timetable for departure. The episodes on the Boulogne campaign devote considerable attention to two completely fictitious characters, Harry Hurst and Richard Leland, who add little to the story. In France it rains a lot, food is short, and an epidemic erupts. Henry, eager to capture Boulogne before Charles takes Luxembourg and Saint-Denis, rushes the mining operation of artist/engineer Girolamo de Treviso, who dies in a cave-in, though he actually was killed by cannon fire. Henry spends a lot of time in pain, observing from a tower, and irrationally raging at others as things go badly. After much ado, Boulogne surrenders, and Henry goes home, leaving Surrey in charge (in reality it was Lisle). Chapuys reveals that Charles has made a separate peace with France, announces he is leaving, and soon after dies, though he really lived until 1556.[47]

The series does no better with Scotland. Though it gives a fairly accurate account of Henry's visit to the North to meet James V, his failure to appear, and Henry's resulting fury, Hirst invents a retaliatory attack against Scotland. Henry later "orders" James to end his alliances with France and the papacy and, when he refuses, sends an army led by Surrey, who defeats the Scots at Solway Moss, a battle actually won by Thomas, Lord Wharton. When reporting the victory, Henry says James died the same day his daughter Mary was born; in fact, the battle occurred on November 24, 1542, Mary's birth December 8, and her father's death December 14. Edward Seymour refers to the "Regent Queen of Scotland" negotiating marriage between Mary and Prince Edward, though James Hamilton, 2nd Earl of Arran was regent 1544–1554, and Marie of Guise (Mary's mother) was regent—not regent queen—from 1554–1560. Henry says Mary soon will be Queen of Scots, a title held the minute her father died. However, the Treaty of Greenwich (1543) did provide for such a marriage, though the Scots reneged in favor of a French match.[48]

The final episode opens with a slow-motion sequence of a galloping white horse with a voiceover by Henry: "When we compare the present life of man on earth with that time of which we have no knowledge, it seems to me like the swift flight of a single sparrow through a banqueting hall on a winter's day. After a few moments of comfort, he vanishes from sight into the wintry world from which he came. Even so, man appears on earth for a little while, but of what went before this life or what will follow, we know nothing." This is a paraphrase of the Venerable Bede's account of Paulinus of York converting Edwin of Northumbria to Christianity in the seventh century. Brandon, who died in 1545, is still around on-screen. In a fabricated subplot, Mary attempts to subvert Edward's succession. Henry again changes diplomatic horses, breaks with Charles, and proposes a new treaty with Francis that founders on the latter's death. Gardiner's plot against Catherine comes to naught, she and the king become "perfect friends," and he fictitiously banishes Gardiner. Henry commissions a portrait by Holbein, referring to a nonexistent portrait of Henry VII and acting as though this will be the first time Holbein has painted him. The first painting Holbein produces depicts the king as old and sick, so he insists on another that features the pose in the Whitehall Mural. As Holbein works, Henry sees the ghosts of Catherine of Aragon, Anne Boleyn, and Jane Seymour, who chastise him for his poor treatment of them and their children. He sends Catherine Parr and his children away and makes imaginary plans for Seymour to be Lord Protector. After having a dream in which a knight with a skull face shadows him, he stands before the second portrait amid flashbacks to various earlier scenes, and a series of captions sketch the succession of his three children. He does not die on-screen.[49]

It remains to be seen if Meyers' Henry will replace the Holbein-Shakespeare-Laughton composite that preceded him. He already has competition from Damian Lewis of *Wolf Hall* (2015), which seems to have more aesthetic cachet despite being just as inaccurate as *The Tudors* but has not achieved the popularity of the latter. If Meyers does become the new archetype of Henry in popular culture, it hardly will be an improvement. True, *The Tudors* does portray him as a young, vigorous man, as the real king certainly was until the mid-1530s, but so does *Six Wives*, and that series has him age realistically. Meyers has fans, not a few of whom openly admit that they find him attractive enough to excuse the errors in the series and the flaws in his portrayal of Henry. But those problems are not limited to factual errors. It has been suggested that Laughton's Henry and the many subsequent Henries he influenced were so bombastic and at times buffoonish that they led viewers not only to discount the real Henry's intellect and talents but also to ignore his manifest cruelty and brutality.

It is quite possible that many viewers of *The Tudors* excuse Meyers' Henry not because he is funny or over the top but because he is sexy. The difficulty is that while *The Tudors* still downplays Henry's intellect and talent, it regularly displays his cruelty, not only on climactic occasions like the executions of Fisher, More, Anne Boleyn, and Catherine Howard or the burning of heretics but also as a routine aspect of his day-to-day relationships with others, in his profoundly abusive, exploitive, and misogynist relationships with his wives and mistresses, and in his unmitigated narcissism. If possible, the series makes Meyers' Henry—unlike his Laughton-esque predecessors—worse than the real king. He is less a romantic than a Lothario, seldom the Renaissance man that he should be, and hardly ever a warrior. He is much more the shallow soap opera playboy. That many viewers still find him appealing is perhaps the most troubling aspect of the phenomenon that is *The Tudors*.[50]

Notes

1. One could cite hundreds of works on Henrician England in documenting where *The Tudors* departs from historicity, but practicality and limitations on space preclude that. Short scholarly biographical essays for most of the historical figures who appear as characters in the series can be found in H.C.G. Matthew and Brian Harrison, eds., *Oxford Dictionary of National Biography* (Oxford: Oxford University Press, 2004), available online at http://www.oxforddnb.com/. J.J. Scarisbrick, *Henry VIII* (New Haven: Yale University Press, 1997), first published in 1968, remains the standard biography; on his wives, see David Starkey, *Six Wives: The Queens of Henry VIII* (Vintage, 2004); on his two great rivals, R.J. Knecht, *Francis I* (Cambridge: Cambridge University Press, 192), and William S. Maltby, *The Reign of Charles V* (New York: Palgrave Macmillan, 2002); other relevant works are cited where appropriate.
2. For Meyers' refusal to wear a fat suit, see Susan Bordo, *The Creation of Anne Boleyn: A New Look at England's Most Notorious Queen* (Boston: Houghton Mifflin, 2013), 202.
3. For more on costuming, see Maria Hayward, Chapter 18: "Fashionable Fiction: The Significance of the Costumes in *The Tudors*," in this volume, and her *Dress at the Court of King Henry VIII* (Leeds: Maney Publishing, 2007) and *Rich Apparel: Clothing and the Law in Henry VIII's England* (Farnham: Ashgate, 2009).
4. For examples of Hirst and Meyers' comments, see Bordo, *The Creation of Anne Boleyn*, Chapter 11.

5. Among many useful works on Henrician warfare are Charles Cruickshank, *Army Royal: Henry VIII's Invasion of France, 1513* (Oxford: Oxford University Press, 1969); George Goodwin, *Fatal Rivalry: Flodden 1513: Henry VIII, James IV, and the Decisive Battle for Renaissance Britain* (New York: W.W. Norton, 2013); Steven Gunn, David Grummitt, and Hans Cools, *War, State, and Society in England and the Netherlands, 1477–1559* (Oxford: Oxford University Press, 2008); R.W. Hoyle, *The Pilgrimage of Grace and the Politics of the 1530s* (Oxford: Oxford University Press, 2003); David Loades, *The Tudor Navy: An Administrative, Political, and Military History* (Aldershot: Scolar Press, 1992); and Gervase Phillips, *The Anglo-Scots Wars, 1513–1550: A Military History* (Woodbridge, Suffolk: Boydell Press, 1991).
6. On diplomacy in general, see David Potter, "Foreign Policy," in Diarmaid MacCulloch, ed., *The Reign of Henry VIII: Politics, Policy, and Piety* (New York: Palgrave Macmillan, 1995), 101–134, and Glenn Richardson, *Renaissance Monarchy: The Reigns of Henry VIII, Francis I, and Charles V* (London: Hodder Education Publishers, 2002); for the major players here, see also Susan Brigden, *Thomas Wyatt: The Heart's Forest* (London: Faber & Faber, 2012); Jessie Childs, *Henry VIII's Last Victim: The Life and Times of Henry Howard, Earl of Surrey* (New York: Thomas Dunne Books, 2007); Steven Gunn, *Charles Brandon: Henry VIII's Closest Friend* (Stroud, Gloucestershire, Amberley, 2015); Peter Gwyn, *The King's Cardinal: The Rise and Fall of Thomas Wolsey* (London: Barrie & Jenkins, 1990); Lauren Mackay, *Inside the Tudor Court: Henry VIII and His Six Wives Through the Writings of the Spanish Ambassador Eustache Chapuys* (Stroud, Gloucestershire: Amberley Press, 2014); Richard Marius, *Thomas More: A Biography* (New York: Alfred A. Knopf, 1984); Glyn Redworth, *In Defence of the Church Catholic, The Life of Stephen Gardiner* (Oxford: Basil Blackwell, 1990); and John Schofield, *The Rise and Fall of Thomas Cromwell: Henry VIII's Most Faithful Servant* (Stroud, Gloucestershire: The History Press, 2011).
7. The term "film" includes television productions; see Parrill and William B. Robison, *The Tudors on Film and Television* (Jefferson, NC: McFarland, 2013), 4–6 and for filmographic details for all films cited here through 2012, passim; for those after 2012, see the updates at www.tudorsonfilm. com; Thomas S. Freeman, "A Tyrant for All Seasons: Henry VIII on Film," in Susan Doran and Thomas S. Freeman, eds., *Tudors and Stuarts on Film: Historical Perspectives* (Palgrave Macmillan, 2009), 30–45; the recycling of tropes and the substitution of plausibility for historicity are the subject of "Why Isn't Anne of Cleves Ugly? Female Beauty, Film, and Suspension of Disbelief from The Private Life of Henry VIII to The Tudors," a paper I presented to the Sixteenth Century Studies Conference

in 2011 and am revising for publication; Tatiana String and Marcus Bull, eds., *Tudorism: Historical Imagination and the Appropriation of the Sixteenth Century* (Oxford University Press, 2011), 1, defines Tudorism as "the post-Tudor mobilization of any and all representations, images, associations, artefacts, spaces, and cultural scripts that either have or are supposed to have their roots in the Tudor era."

8. Oskar Bätschmann and Pascal Griener, *Hans Holbein*, 2nd ed. (London: Reaktion Books, 2014); Tatiana String, *Art and Communication in the Reign of Henry VIII* (Aldershot: Ashgate, 2008), "Myth and Memory in Representations of Henry VIII, 1509-2009," in String and Bull, *Tudorism*, 201–221, and "Projecting Masculinity: Henry VIII's Codpiece," in Mark Rankin, Christopher Highly, and John N. King, eds., *Henry VIII and His Afterlives: Literature, Politics, and Art* (Cambridge University Press, 2009), 143–159; Barbara Mowat, "*Henry VIII*: A Modern Perspective," in William Shakespeare, *Henry VIII*, Folger Shakespeare Library, eds. Barbara Mowat and Paula Werstine (New York: Simon & Schuster, 2007), 253–269; Freeman, "A Tyrant for All Seasons," 30–45; Robison and Parrill, *Tudors on Film and Television*, 181–182.

9. Lost are *The Prince of the Pauper* (1909) with Charles Ogle; *Henry VIII and Catherine Howard* (1910); *Henry VIII* (1911) with Arthur Bourchier, who resembles Holbein's Henry in a surviving still photograph, shakespeare.berkeley.edu/gallery2/main.php?g2_itemId=16924; *Anne Boleyn* (1912); and *A Tudor Princess* (1913), with Robert Brower, who also favors Holbein's image in *The Kinetogram*, 9 (3) (December 15, 1913): 12. Other silent Holbein-esque Henries are August Volny (probably) in *Anne Boleyn* (1911); Tefft Johnson, a lecherous, predatory voyeur who spies on Anne as she is changing clothes in *Cardinal Wolsey* (1912); Max Maxudian, who presides over "the court of Henry VIII, when the liberties of England lay prostrate at the feet of the Merrie Monarch—and Pleasure ruled supreme," in *Anne de Boleyn* (1913), a partial version of which survives as Library of Congress FRA 3515; Robert Broderick *The Prince and the Pauper* (1915); Albert Schreiber, who eschews the usual buffoonery in *Prinz und Bettelknabe* (1920); Lyn Harding in *When Knighthood was in Flower* (1922); and Shep Kemp in *Hampton Court Palace* (1926).

10. Technically, the comedy *Don't Play Bridge with Your Wife* (1933), with Richard Cramer as the king, preceded *Private Life*, which concentrates on the last four wives and introduces the recurrent trope of Henry and Anne of Cleves playing cards on their wedding night; for more on the film, see Greg Walker, *The Private Life of Henry VIII: British Film Guide* (I.B. Tauris, 2003); Laughton's portrayal influenced A.S. Bryan's "Little King" in *The Bride of Frankenstein* (1935); Frank Cellier in *Tudor Rose* (1936) Montague Love in *The Prince and the Pauper* 1937), Alexandre Rignault in *Francis I*

(1937), the cartoon Henry in Looney Tunes' *Book Revue* (1946), Arthur Young in *The Rose Without a Thorn* (1947) and Basil Sydney (1952) in another version of the same, Ramond Rollett in *The Trial of Andy Fothergill* (1951), Rafael Luis Calvo in *Catalina de Inglaterra* (1951), James Justice in *The Sword and the Rose* (1953), Paul Rogers in *The White Falcon* (1956), Douglas Campbell in *The Prince and the Pauper* (1957), and Rogers again in *The Prince and the Pauper* (1962), and the cartoon Henry in "Mr Peabody's Improbable History," on *The Bullwinkle Show*, Episode 87 (1962).

11. As Freeman, "A Tyrant for all Seasons," 33–35, notes, the plays owe much to three books that emphasize Henry's brutality—Francis Hackett, *Henry the Eighth* (New York: Horace Liveright, 1929); Martin Hume, *The Wives of Henry VIII* (London: E. Nash, 1905), and R.W. Chambers, *Thomas More* (London: Jonathan Cape, 1935). Bolt adapted his radio play for BBC television with Noël Johnson as Henry in 1957, and a longer version appeared on Australian television in 1964. Anderson's play took two decades to make it from stage to big screen because of frank talk about adultery, bastards, and incest. Rex Harrison played Henry onstage; Lily Palmer, his real wife at the time, played Anne on *Omnibus*. See also Glenn Richardson, "The 'Sexual Everyman?' Henry VIII in Maxwell Anderson's Anne of the Thousand Days," and Ruth Ahnert, "Drama King: The Portrayal of Henry VIII in Robert Bolt's *A Man for All Seasons*," in Thomas Betteridge and Thomas Freeman, eds., *Henry VIII and History* (Ashgate, 2012), 195–206, 207–222; Peter Marshall, "Saints and Cinemas: 'A Man for All Season,' and Glenn Richardson, 'Anne of the Thousand Days'," in Doran and Freeman, ed., *Tudors and Stuarts on Film*, 46–59, 60–74.

12. Additional Henries in *The Prince and the Pauper* include Manoel da Nobrega (1972), Ronald Radd (1976), Charlton Heston (*Crossed Swords*, 1977), Alan Bates (2000), and a plethora of cartoon versions and modern takeoffs; Shakespeare's *Henry VIII* features John Stride (1979) and Philippe Rouillon (1991); spoofs include Jack Fife in *I Dream of Jeannie*, "The Girl Who Never Had a Birthday," (1966), Terry Jones in *The Complete and Utter History of Britain* (1969), Ronald Long in *Bewitched*, "How Not to Lose Your Head to Henry VIII," (1971), Sid James in *Carry On Henry* (1971), Rusty Goffe in *U.F.O.* (1993), Martyn Ellis in *Julia Jekyll and Harriet Hyde* (1998), and Brian Blessed in *The Complete and Utter History of Everything* (1999); less well-known Henries include Michel de Ré in *Marie Tudor* (French TV, 1966), Anthony Paul in *The Golden Age* (1967), Jan Werich in *King and Women* (Czech TV, 1967), Jean Le Poulain in *La jument du roi* (1973), Jonathan Adams in *It Could Happen to You* (1977), Javier Loyola in *La segunda señora Tudor* (1977),

Ken Sharrock in *Agony* (1981), Keith Barron in *God's Outlaw* (1986), Frank Patton in *Beauty and the Beast: Masques* (1987), Billy Riddoch in *Border Warfare* (1990), and Michael Hofland in *Relic Hunter: The Royal Ring* (2001); the porn flick is *The Undercover Scandals of Henry VIII a/k/a Royal Flesh* (1970) with Steve Vincent; and there are various filmed performances of Donizetti's opera, *Anna Bolena*.

13. Comic or offbeat indications of Henry's renewed popularity are *The Simpsons*, "Margical History Tour," (2004) with Homer as Henry; *Tudor Rose* (2008); *Henry 8.0* (2009) with Brian Blessed; *Love Across Time* (2010) with Ron Schneider, and segments of *Horrible Histories* called "The Terrible Tudors." Among serious movies, *Henry VIII* deals with all six wives but passes quickly over Catherine of Aragon, Anne of Cleves, and Catherine Parr, focuses on the king's efforts to father a son, gives viewers little sense that Henry was a highly educated Renaissance man, and largely ignores the Reformation, though it includes the Pilgrimage of Grace; both versions of *The Other Boleyn Girl*, based on a Philippa Gregory novel that casts history to the winds for no advantage in plot development, are rife with howlers.

14. Henry's portraits are online at www.luminarium.org/renlit/henry8face.htm; Tatiana C. String, *Art and Communication in the Reign of Henry VIII* (Aldershot: Ashgate, 2008), 5–6, 49–52, 69–78; Derek Wilson, "Was Hans Holbein's Henry VIII the Best of Propaganda Ever?" *The Telegraph*, 7 December 2015, www.telegraph.co.uk/news/uknews/5206727/Was-Hans-Holbeins-Henry-VIII-the-best-piece-of-propaganda-ever.html; Peter Saccio, *Shakespeare's English Kings: History, Chronicle, and Drama*, 2nd ed. (Oxford: Oxford University Press, 2000), Chapter IX; Freeman, "A Tyrant for All Seasons," 30–45; Parrill and Robison, Tudors on Film and Television, 4–6, and for individual films, *passim*.

15. *The Tudors*, Episodes 1:1–1:2; Gwynn, *The King's Cardinal*, Chapter 3; Glenn Richardson, *The Field of the Cloth of Gold* (New Haven: Yale University Press, 2014); Eric Ives, *The Life and Death of Anne Boleyn* (Oxford: Blackwell Publishing, 2004).

16. *The Tudors*, Episodes 1:1–1:2; Barbara J. Harris, *Edward Stafford, Third Duke of Buckingham, 1478–1528* (Palo Alto: Stanford University Press, 1986); Carol Rawcliffe, *The Staffords, Earls of Stafford and Dukes of Buckingham: 1394–1521* (Cambridge: Cambridge University Press, 1978).

17. *The Tudors*, Episodes 1:3–1:6, 1:9; Maria Perry, *The Sisters of Henry VIII: The Tumultuous Lives of Margaret of Scotland and Mary of France* (New York: St. Martin's Press, 1999).

18. *The Tudors*, Episodes 1:1–1:6; Beverley A. Murphy, *Bastard Prince: Henry VIII's Lost Son* (Stroud, Gloucestershire: Sutton Publishing, 2001); Patricia Francis Cholakian and Rouben C. Cholakian, *Marguerite de Navarre*

(1492–1549): Mother of the Renaissance (Columbia: Columbia University Press, 2005).
19. *The Tudors*, Episodes 1:3–1:6; the Mendoza in the series is Íñigo López de Mendoza y Zúñiga.
20. *The Tudors*, Episodes 1:3–1:6; Redworth, *In Defence of the Church Catholic*, Part 1; Scarisbrick, *Henry VIII*, 159–161, 198–240; Cromwell first appears as Henry's secretary in Episode 1:4, and the king and Wolsey make extensive use of him for the remainder of Season One, though during this period he was unknown to anyone at court save the cardinal.
21. *The Tudors*, Episode 1:7–1:8; Paul Slack, *The Impact of Plague in Tudor and Stuart England* (London: Routledge & Kegan Paul, 1985); Guy Thwaites, Mark Taviner, and Vanya Gant, "The English Sweating Sickness," *The New England Journal of Medicine* 336 (1997): 580–582.
22. *The Tudors*, Episodes 1:9–1:10; Gwyn, *The King's Cardinal*, Chapters 12–13; Scarisbrick, *Henry VIII*, Chapter 8, and "Fisher, Reform, and the Reformation Crisis," in Brendan Bradshaw and Eamon Duffy, eds., *Humanism, Reform, and the Reformation: The Career of Bishop John Fisher* (Cambridge: Cambridge University Press), 155–168; Eric Ives, *The Life and Death of Anne Boleyn* (Oxford: Blackwell Publishing, 2004), Chapter 9.
23. *The Tudors*, Episodes 1:3–1:4, 1:7, 1:10; on Henry and Luther, Scarisbrick, *Henry VIII*, 110–117; on More's persecution of heretics, see J.A. Guy, *The Public Career of Thomas More* (Brighton: Harvester Press, 1980); on Henry and the Reformation, G.W. Bernard, *The King's Reformation: Henry VIII and the Remaking of the English Church* (New Haven: Yale University Press, 2005); A.G. Dickens, *The English Reformation*, 2nd ed. (University Park: Penn State University Press, 1989); Christopher Haigh, *English Reformations: Religion, Politics, and Society Under the Tudors* (Oxford: Oxford University Press, 1993); Richard Rex, *Henry VIII and the English Reformation*, 2nd ed. (New York: Palgrave Macmillan, 2006).
24. *The Tudors*, Season Two, *passim*; Bordo, *The Creation of Anne Boleyn*, Chapter 11; Ives, *The Life and Death of Anne Boleyn*, Chapter 18; Stanford E. Lehmberg, *The Reformation Parliament 1529–1536* (Cambridge: Cambridge University Press, 1970).
25. *The Tudors*, Episodes 2:1–2:3; on Catherine, see Julia Fox, *Sister Queens: The Noble, Tragic Lives of Katherine of Aragon and Juana, Queen of Castile* (New York: Ballantine Books, 2012); Giles Tremlett, *Catherine of Aragon: The Spanish Queen of Henry VIII* (London: Walker Books, 2010); Patrick Williams, *Catherine of Aragon* (Stroud, Gloucestershire: Amberley Publishing, 2013); on Anne, Ives, *The Life and Death of Anne Boleyn*, Chapter 12.

26. *The Tudors*, Episodes 2:4–2:7; Ives, *The Life and Death of Anne Boleyn*, Chapters 20–21.
27. *The Tudors*, Episodes 2:8–2:9; Ives, *The Life and Death of Anne Boleyn*, Chapter 22; for the idea that Anne actually was guilty, see G.W. Bernard, *Anne Boleyn: Fatal Attractions* (New Haven: Yale University Press, 2010); for the view that there was a homosexual connection among the accused, Retha Warnicke, *The Rise and Fall of Anne Boleyn* (Cambridge: Cambridge University Press, 1989).
28. *The Tudors*, Episodes 2:1–2:5; Scarisbrick, *Henry VIII*, Chapter 8; see also Diarmaid MacCulloch, *Thomas Cranmer: A Life* (New Haven: Yale University Press, 1996).
29. *The Tudors*, Episodes 2:4, 2:6, 2:8, 2:10; Ives, *The Life and Death of Anne Boleyn*, Chapter 13.
30. *The Tudors*, Episode 2:10; Ives, *The Life and Death of Anne Boleyn*, Chapter 23.
31. *The Tudors*, Episodes 3:1–3:5; on Jane, see David Loades, *Jane Seymour: Henry VIII's Favourite Wife* (Stroud, Gloucestershire: Amberley, 2013).
32. *The Tudors*, Episodes 3:1–3:4; Hoyle, *The Pilgrimage of Grace*.
33. *The Tudors*, Episodes 3:5–3:6; Bernard, *The King's Reformation*, Chapter 6, especially 492–505.
34. *The Tudors*, Episodes 3:1–3:2; on Mary's youth, David Loades, *Mary Tudor* (Stroud, Gloucestershire: Amberley, 2011), Chapters 1–4.
35. *The Tudors*, Episodes 3:1–3:2, 3:4–3:5; Thomas F. Mayer, *Reginald Pole: Prince and Prophet* (Cambridge: Cambridge University Press, 2000).
36. *The Tudors*, Episode 3:6; Hazel Pierce, *Margaret Pole, Countess of Salisbury, 1473–1541: Loyalty, Lineage, and Leadership* (Cardiff: University of Wales Press, 2009).
37. *The Tudors*, Episodes 3:4, 3:6; Scarisbrick, *Henry VIII*, Chapter 11.
38. *The Tudors*, Episodes 3:7; Retha Warnicke, *The Marrying of Anne of Cleves: Royal Protocol in Early Modern England* (Cambridge University Press, 2000).
39. Ibid.
40. Ibid.
41. *The Tudors*, Episode 3:8; on Catherine Howard, see Lacey Baldwin Smith, *Catherine Howard*, rprt. (Stroud, Gloucestershire: Amberley, 2010).
42. *The Tudors*, Episodes 4:1–4:5; Scarisbrick, *Henry VIII*, Chapters 13–14.
43. *The Tudors*, Episodes 4:5; Smith, *Catherine Howard*.
44. *The Tudors*, Episodes 4:6–4:7. Susan E. James, *Catherine Parr: Henry's Last Love* (Stroud: Gloucestershire: History Press, 2009); Linda Porter, *Katherine the Queen: The Remarkable Life of Katherine Parr, the Last Wife of Henry VIII* (New York: St. Martin's Press, 2010).

45. *The Tudors*, Episodes 4:1, 4:6–4:7, 4:9–4:10; Thomas S. Freeman, "One Survived: The Account Katherine Parr in Foxe's 'Book of Martyrs,'" in Tom Betteridge and Suzannah Lipscomb, eds., *Henry VIII and His Court* (Aldershot: Ashgate), 235–252.
46. *The Tudors*, Episodes 4:1, 4:4, 4:6; Scarisbrick, *Henry VIII*, Chapter 13.
47. *The Tudors*, Episodes 4:7–4:9; Scarisbrick, *Henry VIII*, Chapter 13.
48. *The Tudors*, Episodes 4:4, 4:6, Scarisbrick, *Henry VIII*, Chapter 13.
49. *The Tudors*, Episode 4:10; Bede, *A History of the English Church and People* (Harmondsworth: Penguin Books, 1955), 127; Scarisbrick, *Henry VIII*, Chapter 14.
50. Many female participants in my history and film courses (and not a few older adults and professional colleagues) have informed me in no uncertain terms that they do not care whether *The Tudors* is accurate or not, as long as it features abundant images of Meyers and Henry Cavill. That male participants have made similar remarks about various women in the cast is perhaps less surprising. In any case, *The Tudors* apparently offers an equal opportunity to observe "beautiful bodies," to borrow Ramona Wray's term for Meyers. Happily, other participants of both genders do care about the series' accuracy. What has been most striking about such classes, however, is the ability and willingness of students—regardless of such distractions—to compare *The Tudors* to reading assignments drawn from serious scholarship and identify inaccuracies, inconsistencies, and logical contradictions in the series. There is hope.

CHAPTER 3

Catherine of Aragon in *The Tudors*: Dark Hair, Devotion, and Dignity in Despair

William B. Robison

Catherine of Aragon was a strawberry blonde. That is one of many things *The Tudors* gets wrong, for Maria Doyle Kennedy, who portrays Catherine in Seasons One and Two, has dark hair. Ironically, Showtime executives wanted to make Natalie Dormer's character, the brunette Anne Boleyn, a blonde, and they were chagrined when she dyed her naturally flaxen hair a darker hue after her initial audition. Perhaps this is because blondes reputedly have more fun—Anne certainly has a better time than Catherine for most of the first two seasons of *The Tudors*. More generally, series creator and writer Michael Hirst is often carelessly inattentive to details or—as more favorable commentators claim—willfully ignores them from a sense of postmodern playfulness.[1] In any case, *The Tudors* is not alone with regard to Catherine, who has appeared on-screen as a blonde only once—played by Annette Crosbie—in the BBC mini-series, *The Six Wives of Henry VIII* (1970). Otherwise, she is dark-haired, like Kennedy, Irene Papas in *Anne of the Thousand Days* (1969), and Joanne Whalley in *Wolf Hall* (2015), though early in the latter show Cardinal Thomas Wolsey

---

W.B. Robison (✉)
Department of History and Political Science, Southeastern Louisiana University, Hammond, LA, USA

(Jonathan Pryce) mentions to Thomas Cromwell (Mark Rylance) that the young Catherine had red hair.[2]

More importantly, though, there are things about Catherine that *The Tudors* gets right. One is her devotion—to Henry VIII, their daughter Mary (Sarah Bolger), her nephew Charles V (Sebastian Armesto), the English people, the Roman Catholic Church, and God. Another is her dignity in despair as her husband of twenty years repudiates, abandons, and then actively persecutes her while separating her from Mary and apostatizing—as Catherine sees it—from the true faith. This is significant, for *The Tudors* offers by far the most extensive filmic depiction of Catherine and one of the few—along with *Anne of the Thousand Days* and *Six Wives*—to present her in a positive light.[3]

In fact, compared to her rival Anne Boleyn—who appears in more films and is usually the star—Catherine gets short shrift on-screen, even though she was married to the king longer than his subsequent five wives put together. Anne is beautiful, clever, sexy, and dies quickly and tragically, still in the bloom of youth and the victim of judicial murder. Catherine typically appears on-screen in her last decade, when Henry abandons her, and is faded, dull, prudish, and a shrew, a pathetic elderly martyr to neglect who dies slowly, alone, and unloved. Silent films treat Anne more favorably than her predecessor, and one (*Anne de Boleyn*, 1913) informs viewers: "Queen Catherine takes little part in the gaities [sic] of Henry's court—finding her happiness in good deeds," that is, she is philanthropic but dull. The first sound film about Henry's reign, *The Private Life of Henry VIII* (1933), omits her from the cast altogether and begins with the observation: "Henry VIII had six wives. Catherine of Aragon was the first but her story is of no particular interest—she was a respectable woman. So Henry divorced her. He then married Anne Boleyn. This marriage also was a failure—but not for the same reason." Again, Catherine is "respectable" but boring—and implicitly a failure. Subsequent films that do include Catherine are seldom less unflattering.[4]

Furthermore, though Henry's quest to divorce Catherine helped spawn the English Reformation, films pay little attention to the role of religion in the King's Great Matter and, in the devout Spanish Catholic Catherine's case, often portray it in a negative light, depicting her as a stubborn adherent of the old, superstitious faith, lacking the intellectual spark of her husband and his English Protestant mistress, while ignoring her extensive humanist education. One might expect films based on Robert Bolt's play, *A Man for All Seasons*, to note Thomas More's support for Catherine and acknowledge their similarities regarding faith and Christian humanism, but she is not even a character in them. By contrast, *The Tudors*—rife with howlers and hardly on a par aesthetically with Fred Zinneman's 1966 award-winning film—nevertheless repeatedly depicts More's involvement with Catherine.[5] It also offers a more well-rounded picture of the queen than *Henry VIII and His Six Wives* (1972), which portrays Catherine (Frances Cuka) as long-suffering, stubborn, and inclined to mortification of the flesh; Shakespeare's *Henry VIII* (1979), which offers the queen (Claire Bloom) more pity than respect; Granada Television's *Henry VIII* (2003), which ignores her learning, though Catherine (Assumpta Serna) prays to St. Casilda of Toledo for a son, plans a pilgrimage to Our Lady of Walsingham, and wears the obligatory hair shirt; both versions of *The Other Boleyn Girl* (2003, 2008), which leave Catherine (Yolanda Vazquez, Ana Torrent) undeveloped; and *Wolf Hall* (2015), which gives her only a minor role.[6]

As numerous biographers demonstrate, such portrayals are a disservice to Catherine. Her parents—Ferdinand of Aragon and Isabella of Castile—insured that she received an exemplary education from the Dominican reformer Pascual de Ampudia and the Italian humanists Alessandro and Antonio Gerladini. Her intelligence and knowledge won praise from Erasmus and Jean Luis Vives; she was the intellectual match of her Renaissance-man husband and proved a capable political leader during their first decade-and-a-half of marriage; she was a great patron of the church (especially the Observant Franciscans), the universities at Oxford and Cambridge, and such scholars as John Leland, Thomas Linacre, Richard Pace, and Thomas Wyatt; and in 1523 she brought Vives to England and commissioned his *De institutione foeminae Christianae* (*The Education of Christian Women*), though there is no film or television show—*The Tudors* or any other—that takes full account of this aspect of her life. Otherwise, she was neither credulous nor superstitious, supported reform from within the church (though she abhorred Protestantism), and displayed a profound inner-directed piety. Though she showed ascetic tendencies from early on that might have influenced her behavior after Henry initiated divorce proceedings in 1527, it also took enormous courage and a well-grounded faith to resist the might of the king as she did.[7]

Oddly enough, the first sympathetic portrayal of Catherine is Charles Jarrot's *Anne of the Thousand Days*, an outstanding film—based on Maxwell Anderson's 1948 play—that focuses primarily on the romance between Henry and Anne. Released in 1969, three years after Zinneman's

A Man for All Seasons, it did not receive the critical acclaim or the awards lavished upon the latter, but it is just as good, if not better. It holds up well today and does less damage to history than the cinematic sanctification of Thomas More. Richard Burton is an acceptable Henry, and—appropriately for a film released during the peak of second-wave feminism—Bujold's Anne is a strong, liberated woman, though the screenplay fails to emphasize her faith and learning. Catherine actually fares better in terms of historicity, even though the film begins c. 1527, she is a secondary character, and her limited time on-screen allows for no exposition of her education and patronage. Irene Papas gives her considerable depth, and she also is a strong woman. Despite her austere black clothing—in sharp contrast to Anne's brightly colored dresses—Catherine is not dour; in fact, at one point she admonishes one of her ladies, who is performing a sad tune on the lute, to play something cheerful. Naturally, Catherine experiences considerable woe as the story progresses, but the film makes clear that she draws strength from her faith. She wears a large crucifix and has a private altar in her chamber. When Henry asserts that they have been living in sin, she replies that her conscience is clear and affirms that she never consummated her previous marriage to the king's brother Arthur. Regarding Princess Mary (Nicola Pagett), she defiantly declares to Henry: "Neither you nor the pope can make my child a bastard," a line implicitly recognizing that Catherine was no unthinking minion of the papacy. Later, she refuses to recognize the authority of the legatine court—Cardinals Campeggio (Marne Maitland) and Wolsey (Anthony Quayle)—to examine the validity of her marriage, proclaiming, "To God I commit my cause." It is Papas' Catherine whom Kennedy's in *The Tudors* most resembles. Both experienced actresses, they powerfully convey her devotion and dignity in despair, giving her a greater presence in the story and providing viewers with a genuine sense of her strength and character rather than a demeaning and dismissive caricature. *Anne of the Thousand Days* and especially *The Tudors* contain ahistorical elements; however, as several contributors to this volume note, even fictionalized accounts of historical events can contain elements of "truth," and both Papas and Kennedy bring us closer to the real Catherine.[8]

The Six Wives of Henry VIII, which appeared in 1970, offers the only depiction of a young, beautiful, intelligent, and learned Catherine—one with whom Keith Michell's Henry is completely smitten—though it concentrates on her early years in England and the period after her estrangement from the king, skipping the period between the death of their infant son (Henry, Duke of Cornwall) in 1511 and the king's decision to seek a divorce in 1527. Early on, Henry praises her learning, and later her ladies describe her as "devout" and "cheerful and uncomplaining." But though she once appears silently praying, there is little overt reference to her faith. While Henry speaks learnedly about religion himself, it does not figure in his discussion on their wedding night of his plans for a "golden age." When years later he presents Catherine with his argument from Leviticus that their marriage is invalid, she weeps hysterically but does not argue with his interpretation. Subsequently, she defends the sanctity of her marriage to Cardinal Campeggio, but only on the grounds that her first marriage to Arthur was never consummated. When Campeggio urges her to enter a nunnery, she declares that she has no calling to the "religious" life, an accurate reflection of her refusal to give up marriage for monasticism. Though she angrily and courageously defends herself against Henry and Wolsey, she does not do so on scriptural or theological grounds. The closest she comes to a statement of faith is at her brief appearance before the legatine court, when she tells Henry that if he will not hear her, she will appeal to God, and later when she worries that the king is "endangering his immortal soul." The episode's final verdict is that Catherine followed "conscience and love." However, like *A Man for All Seasons* does with More, it gives Catherine's "conscience" a rather generic meaning rather than one clearly rooted in faith. Crosbie as Catherine is also more of a victim—at times nearly a damsel in distress—than Papas or Kennedy.[9]

In sum, prior to *The Tudors*, there are only two favorable depictions of Catherine, only one addresses her early years and neither the period 1511–1527, and one emphasizes her faith and the other her learning. This has two implications for *The Tudors*. First, Catherine's favorable characterization and extended presence are a welcome change from the norm. Second, though, it is regrettable that the series does not actually "go back to the beginning" as it claims. Catherine was born in 1485, came to England to marry Arthur in 1501, was widowed in 1502, married Henry in 1509, and was frequently pregnant between then and 1518. By beginning c. 1518, *The Tudors* eliminates thirty-three years of her life, seventeen in England, nine of marriage and queenship, and much potential dramatic material. While it might be impractical to go back as far as her youth or widowhood, beginning with Henry's accession and marriage in 1509 would have served both historicity and narrative integrity, as well as providing context for Catherine's grief and incredulity at the king's demand for a divorce. In addition, by introducing Anne prematurely

c. 1518–1520, the series significantly warps the timeline from then until Catherine's death in 1536. Furthermore, it distorts the age differential among the royal love triangle—in 1518, Henry was twenty-seven, Catherine thirty-two, and Anne seventeen, but when *The Tudors* began, Jonathan Rhys Meyers was thirty, Maria Doyle Kennedy forty-three, and Natalie Dormer twenty-five.[10]

During their first decade of marriage, Catherine and Henry were extremely close, both personally and politically. The king was enchanted with his new bride, as one might expect of any barely postadolescent male with a slightly older, attractive, intelligent, cultured, and—with her Mediterranean heritage—rather exotic woman. One thing *The Tudors* omits by not including this phase of their relationship is the extent to which they shared in court revels. Indeed, as Glenn Richardson points out in his chapter on "Kingship," the series neglects Henry's obsession with dancing, a form of entertainment he and Catherine shared when young. The royal couple also had a common enthusiasm for Christian humanism and enjoyed the company of Erasmus, More, and other humanist thinkers, though—as Samantha Perez notes in her chapter—*The Tudors* pays only lip service to humanism. Furthermore, prior to his decision to seek a divorce, the king was as devoted to the Catholic Church as Catherine; in fact, until the mid-1520s Henry probably had a better relationship with Rome than any English monarch since William the Conqueror.

The Tudors also avoids Catherine's pregnancies, of which there reportedly were at least six between 1509 and 1518. Following a stillborn daughter in 1510, she gave birth in 1511 to Henry, Duke of Cornwall, which led to great rejoicing by both parents and the national at large until his death less than two months later. As Carole Levin and Estelle Paranque note in their chapter on the king's children, one of the series' most poignant scenes (Episode 1:5) has Henry mourning the (anachronistic) death of his illegitimate son, Henry Fitzroy (Zak Jenciragic), which shows how powerful might have been a similar depiction of his and Catherine's reaction to the loss of their son. Catherine had another son who died in infancy in 1513 and possibly one who was stillborn in 1514. Her only surviving child, Mary, came in 1516, after which another daughter died as an infant in 1518. Again, the birth of Mary—a healthy daughter but not the hoped-for male heir—was no less bittersweet for Henry and Catherine than that of Elizabeth was for the king and Anne in 1533, but *The Tudors* includes only the latter (Episode 2:3). Fortunately, the series does better at portraying Mary's relationship to her parents and five stepmothers, her ongoing role in marital diplomacy, her maturation, and the development of her bitter hatred of Protestants.

Early on, Catherine also exercised considerable political authority. She served as an intermediary between her husband and her father, Ferdinand of Aragon, until the latter's death in 1516, and though it is unclear how much she influenced English foreign policy, Spanish ambassadors could ill afford to incur her displeasure, as Don Gutierre Gómez de Fuensalida and Don Luis Caroz both discovered. In 1513, Henry campaigned in France, defeating Louis XII's forces at the Battle of the Spurs (Guinegate) and capturing Therouanne and Tournai. This would have made a dramatic addition to *The Tudors*, as does the account of the regency of Catherine Parr (Joely Richardson) during the 1544 Boulogne campaign in Season Four (Episodes 4:7–4:8), for it would have showcased not only the young king's military prowess but also the role Catherine of Aragon played as governor of the realm and captain-general in his absence. Given her own council and the power to make appointments and levy troops, she stayed in touch with the royal entourage in France by corresponding with Wolsey. In August, Henry's brother-in-law, James IV of Scotland, invaded northern England, and Catherine proved herself as ruthless as her warrior mother, Isabella. Though Thomas Howard, Earl of Surrey (later 2nd Duke of Norfolk), defeated the Scots at Flodden, the queen was headed northward with a second army when news of his victory arrived. Moreover, she wanted to send the corpse of the Scots king, slain in the battle, as a trophy to Henry until councilors persuaded her to settle for sending just his bloodstained coat. *The Tudors* does include Henry's peaceful return to France, accompanied by Catherine, for the Field of the Cloth of Gold in 1520, but downplays her role and—among other inaccuracies—uses the occasion for him to begin an affair with Mary Boleyn (Perdita Weeks).

Once *The Tudors* does begin Catherine's story, it takes her religious devotion seriously, and Kennedy gives her more *gravitas* than almost all of the other characters—only Sam Neill's Wolsey, Jeremy Northam's More, and Dormer's Anne are comparable. In the series, as in reality, it is often hard—and it might be artificial—to disentangle politics, religion, and personal feelings with Catherine and other characters, for example, the intrigues Eustace Chapuys (Anthony Brophy) conducts on her behalf, the mutual hostility between the queen and Wolsey, and the support More gives her. However, certain moments highlight her political acumen, her skill at diplomatic intrigue, her faith, and her emotions. In addition, having cast the unlikely Meyers as Henry to ensure that the king is sexually attractive to viewers, Hirst for some reason does almost nothing to make him an appealing character otherwise. The king comes off as a misogynistic jerk rather than the charming Bluff King Hal, and whether Hirst intended this or not, the scenes Catherine share with Meyers' Henry always present her as the more admirable of the two.[11]

Catherine first appears in Episode 1:1, not long after Henry has a sexual romp with Bessie Blount. As the royal couple dine and discuss Princess Mary and Charles V, Henry is rude and patronizing, and when the queen warns him against placing too much trust in Wolsey, he reacts angrily. Here Catherine is a bit too much the victim, for despite the king's threats, she invites him to visit her bedchamber that night. However, anyone expecting a scene with marital sex will be disappointed. In a simultaneously clever and off-putting bit of symbolism, the king—while preparing himself for his wife's bed—bites sloppily into a pomegranate, which was Catherine's badge. However, when he arrives at her bedroom, she is praying in her chapel, so—appropriately for this sex-drenched drama—he romps with her maid instead. Later, Catherine laments to a group of servants—including Bessie—that Wolsey has dismissed her Spanish ladies and that she is unable to bear a living son, Henry anachronistically expresses doubts in the confessional about the legitimacy of his marriage, and the queen tells him she dislikes the beard he has sworn not to shave until his meeting with Francis I (Emmanuel Leconte).[12]

In Episode 1:2, Catherine plays only a decorative role at the Field of the Cloth of Gold, and the two kings' chivalrous interplay inaccurately excludes their wives, though Catherine and Claude share a moment of anxiety at their husbands' ill-considered wrestling match. The chronologically jumbled storyline intermingles this diplomatic summit in 1520, the execution of Edward Stafford, 3rd Duke of Buckingham (Steven Waddington) in 1521, and Henry Fitzroy's birth in 1519, at the king's public celebration of which Catherine offers a sad, silent toast. Later, she prays to Our Lady of Walsingham for a son. By the end, Henry has bedded and discarded Mary Boleyn in a matter of days (as opposed to a three- or four-year affair in reality), and Anne has arrived at court, where early in Episode 1:3 she meets the king while performing in a pageant and becomes one of the queen's ladies-in-waiting. At table, Catherine assures Henry that she never consummated her marriage to Arthur, and he kisses her before abruptly departing and randomly selecting a girl for yet another sexual tryst. The queen actually enjoys herself when Charles V visits England, but she also shares with him her suspicion that Henry plans to divorce her just before the dream sequence in which Anne advises the besotted king, "Seduce me."[13]

In Episode 1:4, Henry and Catherine attend mass together, though Anne's presence there generates predictable tension. Then, implausibly adding insult to injury for Catherine, the king—ahistorically—seduces Francis I's sister, Marguerite of Navarre. Later at a joust, More and Wolsey discuss the problem Catherine's popularity poses for Henry's quest for a divorce, and the queen gives a secret message for Charles V to a courier who has arrived to report the emperor's victory at Pavia (1525). Subsequently, Catherine complains to Henry that Wolsey is opening her mail, which he promises to stop; the royal couple watch courtiers dancing (rather than participating) while Anne flirts with the king with her eyes; and Henry tells Wolsey that God is punishing him for marrying Catherine and orders him to procure a divorce. All of this dramatically telescopes events. In Episode 1:5, Catherine has to endure a ceremony—for once in the right year, 1525—where the king ennobles Henry Fitzroy as Earl of Salisbury and Duke of Richmond and Somerset, after which Wolsey incorrectly informs her that the king's bastard supersedes Mary in the succession, she learns that Charles V has broken his betrothal to the princess by marrying Isabella of Portugal (which actually occurred in 1526), and Wolsey announces that Henry plans to give Mary her own household at Ludlow. Occasionally, viewers get to see Catherine's devotion without any sexual by-products, as in this episode when Catherine observes the ritual of creeping to the cross at Lambeth and distributes alms to the poor. Rather sadly, she is praying when Henry comes to announce that their marriage is invalid. Later, Wolsey reveals that Catherine is writing to Charles V, the king disingenuously tells More that he will happily live with Catherine if the pope is right about the validity of their marriage, the queen comes close to confronting Anne but refrains, and Henry dances with Anne while she watches.[14]

In Episode 1:6, the tension within the royal love triangle increases. Catherine again contacts Charles via Mendoza (Declan Conlon), warns Anne that she will not take Henry away from her, everyone at court—including a reluctant Anne—does obeisance to the queen, Catherine finds Henry and Anne together and walks out after he refuses to dismiss the younger woman, and she calls Anne an "expensive whore" after seeing her wearing a necklace the king gave her. In Episode 1:7, Catherine receives via the Spanish ambassador a coded reply from Charles promising his support. She also enjoys a temporary reconciliation of sorts with Henry, for during an outbreak of sweating sickness (apparently in 1528), they and Mary pray together, he sends Catherine and their daughter to Ludlow for their safety, and the queen suggests to him that he is more afraid of the sweat than he is infatuated with Anne. But later, after a brief shot of Henry holding Catherine's hand, he goes to Hever and embraces the newly recovered Anne.

Episode 1:8 opens improbably with Henry and Catherine posing for a painting, though the king also tells Anne that for appearances' sake he must continue sharing Catherine's bed and table. But the pressure on Catherine increases, and so does her resolve in resisting. Campeggio fails to convince her to enter a nunnery, and she witheringly admonishes Wolsey for suggesting the same. She argues with Henry about the validity of their marriage, and when Campeggio hears her confession, she denies having sex with Arthur. She is unintimidated when Warham and Tunstall tell her about plots against Henry and Campeggio and warn that she and Mary would be suspects, rejects their attempts to persuade her to become a nun, and is unmoved even when Henry joins her in bed and threatens to keep her away from Mary.

In a very dramatic and realistic scene, when the legatine court begins its proceedings at Blackfriars, Catherine falls on her knees before Henry and begs for justice, and when he is unresponsive, she departs, never to return to the premises. Thus, Episode 1:9 opens with the legatine court seeking to determine in Catherine's absence whether she and Arthur consummated their marriage. Anthony Willoughby (Michael Patric) reports hearing the late Prince of Wales say the morning after his wedding, "Last night I was in the midst of Spain," and "Masters, it's a good pastime to have a wife." Wolsey also claims to have bloodstained sheets from the marital bed, though why these should have been preserved for nearly two decades is a mystery. Later, Catherine prays as Wolsey and Thomas Cromwell (James Frain)—already anachronistically at court—wait to see her. When Wolsey informs her that Henry wants to know why she is not at court and commands that she surrender the matter of their marriage into his hands lest the court condemn her, she disingenuously replies, "I am but a poor woman, lacking in wit and understanding." Less accurately, she also accuses Wolsey of opposing her because Charles V prevented his becoming pope. Later, Henry warns that if the legatine court fails him, he will denounce the pope as a heretic and marry as he pleases. But Mendoza reveals to her that Campeggio has secret instructions from the pope to move the trial to Rome, that Charles V is working on her behalf, and that he is leaving England and will be replaced by Eustace Chapuys, whom she soon meets. She tells him that Wolsey has lost favor and advises that he seek out Thomas Boleyn (Nick Dunning), the Duke of Norfolk (Henry Czerny), and Charles Brandon (Henry Cavill), but warns him that all three are her mortal enemies.

In Episode 1:10, Henry—in one of his sporadic and inconsistent moments of on-screen kindness—visits Catherine after hearing that she is unwell. She brings up the agents he has sent abroad to canvas the universities for opinion in support of the divorce and claims that she can do the same and find more supporters than he will among the learned. Meanwhile, Chapuys urges her not to give up hope and later brings her a letter from Wolsey offering to create a rapprochement between them, Charles V, and Clement VII, and to secure a papal bull ordering Henry to abandon Anne, return to Catherine, and reinstate the Cardinal. Subsequently, Chapuys tells Catherine he can no longer serve the emperor at the English court because of the hatred there for all that is sacred, and she asks him to tell Charles not to use force against England. Wolsey's help never materializes, for—in one of the series' most absurd deviations from history—he commits suicide by cutting his own throat.

Season Two opens in 1532 with Henry and Anne kneeling in a London church, intercut with shots of Catherine and More praying. In another instance based in reality, Anne observes a servant taking linen to Catherine to make shirts for Henry and has a furious argument with Henry, who subsequently tells Catherine to stop doing so. Despite such rebuffs, however, the queen continues to profess her love for the king. When she tells him that Mary is unwell and suggests that they visit her, he responds that she should go alone and stay, to which she replies that she will not leave him for Mary or anyone else. But she is hardly prepared to surrender. When Brandon delivers a message from Henry asking her to be sensible and drop her suit, promising to deal fairly with her, she refuses. Still she faces further tribulations, some of which occur earlier on-screen than in reality. After she sadly watches Henry and Anne depart the court together, Cromwell delivers the king's demands that she take up residence at the More in Hertfordshire (which actually occurred in 1531) and return the royal jewels, though she refuses the latter. Still, she receives encouragement from those who watch her depart, and she sends a messenger to Henry, wishing him farewell and asking about his health (which infuriates him).

From this point, Catherine's role gradually diminishes and her fortune declines. At Christmas, in Episode 2:2, Mark Smeaton (David Alpay) comments on the lack of mirth at court, Thomas Wyatt (Jamie Thomas King) answers that everything is different because Catherine and her ladies are absent, and Henry bluntly refuses to accept a cup she has sent him as a gift. Wyatt then (inaccurately) goes to the More and delivers a new demand that she return the jewels. In Episode 2:3, Brandon reluctantly delivers Henry's commands that Catherine is not to return to court, must use the title of princess dowager of Wales rather than queen, will have to cut her expenses as the king will no longer pay them, and may not see Mary. Here she movingly observes that if she had to choose between extreme happiness and sorrow, she would choose the latter because the former makes you forget God, but in the latter He is always with you. Brandon departs, and Catherine declares to Elizabeth Darrell (Krystin Pellerin) that she will always call herself queen. Henry denies Chapuys access to Catherine and forbids Mary (via Thomas Boleyn) to write to her mother, while More is only able to see her by obtaining permission from Cromwell. Still she will not give into Henry's demand that she stop calling herself queen. In Episode 2:4, Henry rejects Chapuys' appeal that he allow Catherine to nurse the ailing Mary, claiming they will conspire against him. In Episode 2:5 he criticizes More for supporting and visiting Catherine, and she informs Chapuys that Thomas Boleyn and others have threatened her in an attempt to make her take the Oath of Supremacy. Finally, in a very moving scene in Episode 2:7, Catherine receives the last rites, declares her last will and testament, and writes to Henry, intercut with shots of him reading her letter. She dies, and he weeps. However, she makes one more appearance, in Episode 4:10, when as a phantasm she tells a hallucinating Henry she has come to check on her daughter, complains of his treatment of her, and disappears.

In Season Two, Catherine's faith underlies her stoic response to Anne's increasing prominence at court and her own banishment, separation from Mary, refusal to renounce the title of Queen or take the Oath of Supremacy, and final illness. Susan Bordo reports that Natalie Dormer persuaded Michael Hirst to give Anne Boleyn more intellectual heft in the second season, and though her sexuality overpowers other aspects of her character, her faith comes up a lot. Thus, she and Catherine are worthy adversaries. Without Catherine and Anne—who dies in Episode 2:10—*The Tudors* loses much of its dramatic tension and energy in Seasons Three and Four, and the quality of the episodes—even as historical fiction—

deteriorates. Hirst has to resort to imaginary sex objects like Lady Ursula Misseldon and Brigitte Rousselot, phony love affairs involving Anne Stanhope, and Charles Brandon talking to ghosts.[15]

Since *The Tudors* concluded its run in 2010, there has been only one major English-language production to include a filmic depiction of Catherine of Aragon, who has a fairly minor role in *Wolf Hall*. In that mini-series, in which Cromwell is the hero and his opponents appear in an unfavorable light, Catherine reverts to being a rather cranky victim (and, inexplicably, Mary seems to be afflicted in some way).[16] Thus, it remains the case that most films handle Catherine's faith, intellect, and fate very imperfectly. There may even be reason to ask whether they do more harm by ignoring religion completely or by offering an error-ridden account within a warped perspective. In the end, of course, the goal of filmmakers is not didactic but to entertain audiences and generate profits. As that is unlikely to change, it behooves historians to expose the errors of films about the ever-popular Tudors while exploiting their appeal. In the case of Catherine, long denied her just desserts in film, there is even greater reason for doing so. A good place to start is with Irene Papas' portrayal in *Anne of the Thousand Days*, Annette Crosbie's in *Six Wives*, and especially Maria Doyle Kennedy's in *The Tudors*. At the same time, however, Kennedy's strong portrayal of the queen and Hirst's unusually judicious scripting of her role make Catherine stand out as one of the few characters in the series who convey some measure of historical "truth" rather than undermining the historicity of its narrative; thus, they are a poignant reminder of how much better *The Tudors* could have been.

Notes

1. Juan de Flandes' portrait (c. 1496), generally considered to be of the 11-year-old Catherine, shows her with reddish-blonde hair. The identification of Catherine as the blonde-haired subject of the portrait (c. 1502) by Michael Sittow (c. 1469–1525) in the Kunsthistorisches Museum in Vienna is controversial. For an extensive summary and analysis of all four seasons of *The Tudors*, see Sue Parrill and William B. Robison, *The Tudors on Film and Television* (Jefferson, NC: McFarland, 2013), 247–290; for Dormer's dye dilemma, see Susan Bordo, *The Creation of Anne Boleyn: A New Look at England's Most Notorious Queen* (Boston: Houghton Mifflin Harcourt, 2013), 204–205; Ramona Wray makes some intriguing arguments but perhaps gives Hirst more credit for postmodern cleverness than he deserves in "Henry's Desperate Housewives: *The Tudors*, the Politics of

Historiography, and the Beautiful Body of Jonathan Rhys Meyers," in Greg Colón Semenza, ed., *The English Renaissance in Popular Culture: An Age for All Time* (New York: Palgrave Macmillan, 2010), 25–42, and "The Network King: Recreating Henry VIII for a Global Television Audience," in Mark Thornton Burnett and Adrian Street, eds., *Filming and Performing Renaissance History* (New York: Palgrave Macmillan, 2011), 16–32, as does Jerome de Groot in "Slashing History: The Tudors," in Tatiana C. String and Marcus Bull, eds., *Tudorism: Historical Imagination and the Appropriation of the Sixteenth Century* (Oxford: Oxford University Press, 2011), 243–260.

2. None of the actresses named here is Spanish: Papas was born in Greece as Irene Lelekou in 1926, was briefly married to Alkis Papas from 1947 to 1951, and appeared in almost a hundred films and television shows between 1948 and 2003, www.imdb.com/name/nm0660327; Crosbie was born in Scotland in 1934, began acting on-screen in 1959, and won a BAFTA TV Award as Best Actress for *Six Wives* (1971), www.imdb.com/name/nm0188950/; Kennedy was born in Ireland, began acting in 1991, and won a Gemini Award (2008) and two IFTA Awards (2008, 2009) as Best Supporting Actress for *The Tudors*, www.imdb.com/name/nm0448204/; Whalley was born in England in 1962 and began acting in 1975, www.imdb.com/name/nm0000695/. Papas had a lengthy recording career, Kennedy has been singing longer than she has been acting, Crosbie sang in *The Slipper and the Rose* (1976), and Whalley recorded with Cindy and the Saffrons. The raven-haired Papas has a distinctly Mediterranean complexion and most nearly fits the stereotype of how Spanish women supposedly look, if not Catherine of Aragon's actual appearance. Wolsey discusses Catherine's hair in *Wolf Hall* (2015, Blu-Ray/DVD: PBS, 2015), www.imdb.com/title/tt3556920/, Episode 1:1.

3. The classic biography is Garrett Mattingly, *Catherine of Aragon* (Boston: Little, Brown and Company, 1941); for more recent scholarship, see C.S.L. Davies and John Edwards, "Katherine (1485–1536)," *Oxford Dictionary of National Biography* (Oxford University Press, 2004); online edn, May 2011 [http://www.oxforddnb.com/view/article/4891, accessed 7 November 2015]; Julia Fox, *Sister Queens: The Noble, Tragic Lives of Katherine of Aragon and Juana, Queen of Castile* (New York: Ballantine Books, 2012); Giles Tremlett, *Catherine of Aragon: The Spanish Queen of Henry VIII* (London: Walker Books, 2010); Patrick Williams, *Catherine of Aragon* (Stroud, Gloucestershire: Amberley Publishing, 2013); see also Antonia Fraser, *The Wives of Henry VIII* (New York: Knopf, 1992); David Starkey, *Six Wives: The Queens of Henry VIII* (New York: Harper Collins, 2003).

4. *Anne de Boleyn* (1913), Library of Congress FRA 3515, is the only extant copy that I have found; *The Private Life of Henry VIII* (1933, DVD: Allied Artists Entertainment, 2003), www.imdb.com/title/tt0024473/; see also Greg Walker, *The Private Life of Henry VIII: A British Film Guide* (London: I.B. Tauris, 2003); Parrill and Robison, *The Tudors on Film and Television*, 16–17, 181–182.
5. Robert Bolt, *A Man for All Seasons* (New York: Samuel French, 1960); the film versions are as follows: (BBC 1957), www.imdb.com/title/tt1667059/; (Australian television 1964), www.imdb.com/title/tt0374856/; (Zinneman's feature film 1966, DVD: Columbia/Sony, 2005), www.imdb.com/title/tt0060665/; (American and British television 1988, VHS: Agamemnon/Turner, 1988); on film's general neglect of religion in portrayals of Tudor royal women, see William B. Robison, "Stripped of Their Altars: Film, Faith, and Tudor Royal Women from the Silent Era to the Twenty-First Century, 1895–2014," in Julie A. Chappell and Kaley A. Kramer, eds., *Women During the English Reformations: Renegotiating Gender and Religious Identity* (New York: Palgrave Macmillan, 2014); see also Peter Marshall, "Saints and Cinemas: A Man for All Seasons," in Susan Doran and Thomas Freeman, eds., *Tudors and Stuarts on Film: Historical Perspectives* (New York: Palgrave Macmillan, 2008), 46–59; Parrill and Robison, *The Tudors on Film and Television*, 136–140.
6. *Henry VIII and His Six Wives* (1972, DVD: BSF Entertainment, 2002), www.imdb.com/title/tt0070170/; *Henry VIII* (1979, DVD: BBC Shakespeare Collection*, 2005), www.imdb.com/title/tt0080860/; *Henry VIII* (2003, DVD: Granada/HBO, 2004), www.imdb.com/title/tt0382737; *The Other Boleyn Girl* (2003, DVD: BBC Warner, 2008), www.imdb.com/title/tt0357392/; (2008, DVD: Columbia/Sony, 2008), www.imdb.com/title/tt0467200/; *Wolf Hall*; other on-screen Catherines include, from the silent era, in *Henry VIII* (1911) Violet Vanbrugh, *Anne Boleyn* (1911) unknown, *Anne Boleyn* (1912) unknown, *Cardinal Wolsey* (1912) Julia Swayne Gordon, *Anne de Boleyn* (1913) unknown, *A Tudor Princess* (1913) Margery Bonney Erskine, *Anna Boleyn* (1920) Hedwig Pauly-Winterstein, *When Knighthood Was in Flower* (1922) Theresa Maxwell Conover; in sound films and television shows, *The Tudor Touch* (1937) Antonia Brough, *Catalina de Inglaterra* (1951) Maruchi Fresno, *The Sword and the Rose* (1953) Rosalie Crutchley and *The White Falcon* (*BBC Sunday Night Theatre*, 1956) Margaretta Scott, *Heinrich VIII und seine Frauen* (1968) Eva Katharina Schulz, *Whatever Next?* (Episode 1:5, 1969) Antonia Fraser, *The Shadow of the Tower* (1972) Adrienne Byrne, *Mujeres insólitas: La segunda señora Tudor* (1977) Encarna Paso, *Monarch* (2000) Jean Marsh, *The Six Wives of Henry VIII* (2001

documentary) Karis Copp and Annabelle Dowler, *Juana la Loca* (2001) Nerea Garcia, *The Madness of Henry VIII* (2006 documentary) Georgeta Marin, *Tudor Rose* (2008) Tracey Allyn, *The Twisted Tale of Bloody Mary* (2008) Victoria Peiró, *Henry VIII: Mind of a Tyrant* (2009 documentary) Siobhan Hewlett, *Love Across Time* (2010) Stephanie Cervantes, *Fires of Faith* (2012 documentary) Valentina Cartago, *The Six Wives of Henry VIII* (2013) Michelle Coda, *Isabel* (Episodes 3:9–3:13, 2014) Natalia Rodríguez, *H VIII the Male Heir* (2015) Monique Rood Bos, *Carlos, Rey Emperador* (2015, Episodes 1:1, 1:3–1:5, 1:7–1:8, 1:10) Mélida Molina, *I Am Henry* (2015) Maria de Lima, *A Royal Love* (2016) Tamara van Sprundel; for discussion and filmographic details of all of the aforementioned films up through 2012, see Parrill and Robison, *The Tudors on Film and Television*, and for those after 2012, see the updates at www.tudorsonfilm.com.

7. On Catherine's education and life prior to Henry's decision to divorce her, see Davies and Edwards, "Katherine (1485–1536)," *ODNB*; Fox, *Sister Queens*, Chapters 1–25; Fraser, *Wives of Henry VIII*, Chapters 1–5; Mattingly, *Catherine*, part I; Starkey, *Six Wives*, Chapters 1–31; Tremlett, *Catherine*, Chapters 1–29; Williams, *Katherine*, Chapters 1–12.

8. Maxwell Anderson, *Anne of the Thousand Days* (New York: William Sloane, 1948); film: (1969, DVD: Universal, 2007), www.imdb.com/title/tt0064030/; Bordo, *The Creation of Anne Boleyn*, Chapter 10; Glenn Richardson, "Anne of the Thousand Days," in Doran and Freeman, ed., *Tudors and Stuarts on Film*, 60–75; Parrill and Robison, *The Tudors on Film and Television*, 17–20; on Anne, see G.W. Bernard, *Anne Boleyn: Fatal Attractions* (New Haven: Yale University Press, 2010); E.W. Ives, *The Life and Death of Anne Boleyn* (Oxford: Blackwell Publishing, 2004), and "Anne (c. 1500–1536)," *ODNB* [http://www.oxforddnb.com/view/article/557, accessed 10 November 2015]; Retha Warnicke, *The Rise and Fall of Anne Boleyn* (Cambridge: Cambridge University Press, 1989).

9. *The Six Wives of Henry VIII* (1970, DVD: BBC Warner, 2006, and *The BBC Tudors Collection*, 2011), www.imdb.com/title/tt0066714/; Parrill and Robison, *The Tudors on Film and Television*, 232–234; Robison, "Stripped of Their Altars."

10. Dormer, www.imdb.com/name/nm1754059/; Meyers, www.imdb.com/name/nm0001667/.

11. The scholarship on Henry VIII is voluminous, but for examples of scholarship recognizing his charismatic and appealing nature, particularly as a young man, see Robert Hutchinson, *Young Henry: The Rise of Henry VIII* (New York: Thomas Dunne Books, 2012); Suzannah Lipscomb, *1536: The Year that Changed Henry VIII* (Oxford: Lion Hudson, 2009);

J.J. Scarisbrick, *Henry VIII*, rprt. (New Haven: Yale University Press, 1997); David Starkey, *Henry: Virtuous Prince* (New York: Harper Press, 2009); see also Lauren Mackay, *Inside the Tudor Court: Henry VIII and His Six Wives Through the Writings of the Spanish Ambassador Eustace Chapuys* (Stroud, Gloucestershire: Amberley, 2014).
12. On Bessie Blount, see Beverley A. Murphy, 'Blount, Elizabeth (c. 1500–1539x41)', *ODNB*; online edn, January 2008 [http://www.oxforddnb.com/view/article/73234, accessed 15 November 2015]; Kelly Hart, *The Mistresses of Henry VIII* (Stroud, Gloucestershire: The History Press, 2009).
13. On the diplomatic summit, see Glenn Richardson, *The Field of the Cloth of Gold* (New Haven: Yale University Press, 2014); on Mary Boleyn, Jonathan Hughes, "Stafford, Mary (c. 1499–1543)," *ODNB*; online edn, January 2009 [http://www.oxforddnb.com/view/article/70719, accessed 15 November 2015]; Josephine Wilkinson, *Mary Boleyn: The True Story of Henry VIII's Favorite Mistress* (Stroud, Gloucestershire: Amberley, 2010).
14. On Fitzroy, see Beverley A. Murphy, "Fitzroy, Henry, duke of Richmond and Somerset (1519–1536)," *ODNB*, online edn, January 2008 [http://www.oxforddnb.com/view/article/9635, accessed 15 November 2015] and *Bastard Prince: Henry VIII's Lost Son* (Stroud, Gloucestershire: Sutton Publishing, 2001); see also Patricia Francis Cholakian and Rouben C. Cholakian, *Marguerite de Navarre (1492–1549): Mother of the Renaissance* (Columbia: Columbia University Press, 2005); William S. Maltby, *The Reign of Charles V* (New York: Palgrave Macmillan, 2002).
15. Bordo, *The Creation of Anne Boleyn*, Chapter 11.
16. For other depictions of Catherine since *The Tudors*, see above, note 6.

CHAPTER 4

The Tudors, Natalie Dormer, and Our "Default" Anne Boleyn

Susan Bordo

Portions of this piece are taken from Susan Bordo's *The Creation of Anne Boleyn: A New Look at England's Most Notorious Queen* (New York: Houghton Mifflin Harcourt, 2013).

HISTORICAL FICTION AS CULTURAL CONVERSATION

When I interviewed Hilary Mantel in 2011 while she was still writing *Bring Up the Bodies*, she described her characters as belonging to "a chain of literary representation." Her Cromwell, she told me, "shakes hands" with previous depictions, as does her Thomas More, a bold departure from earlier depictions such as the sanctified icon of conscience in Robert Bolt's *A Man for All Seasons*:

> What I was really up against [in *Wolf Hall*] was *A Man for All Seasons*: the older fiction having accreted authority just by being around for two generations. When I say to people, "Do you really think More was a 1960s liberal?" they laugh. "Of course not."[1]

Mantel's astute comments might be applied to all fictional representations of historical figures, in television and film as well as novels.

S. Bordo (✉)
Department of Women's and Gender Studies, University of Kentucky, Lexington, KY, USA

© The Editor(s) (if applicable) and The Author(s) 2016
W.B. Robison (ed.), *History, Fiction, and The Tudors, Queenship and Power*, DOI 10.1057/978-1-137-43883-6_4

"All historical fiction is really contemporary fiction," she told me. "We always write from our own time."[2] It is an insight to remember, whether we are assessing her fictions or those of *The Tudors*. As new generations of creative minds respond and add their voices to the "chain of representations" of the past, they both reflect the values and preoccupations of their own time and, almost invariably, stake their own territory through a reinvention of well-worn narratives and characters. Bolt's Thomas More—a witty, iconoclastic drop-out with proto-feminist leanings—was not a man "for all seasons" as much as a hero for the 1960s, and Mantel set out to smash that mythology, which had held popular consciousness in its grip for decades.[3]

Mantel's unkempt, "pinched, pedantic" More, "ready to torture heretics at the drop of a hat," enraged the Catholic establishment (as well as David Starkey and Simon Schama) when he made a mass-media appearance in the BBC miniseries based on *Wolf Hall* and *Bring Up the Bodies*.[4] In turn, Mantel defenders and Mantel herself insisted on the greater historical accuracy of her More: "Sadly for the bishops," she wrote in *History Today*, "history isn't just what you would like it to be."[5] In numerous remarks for the press, she stopped sounding like the artist that I interviewed and more like a keeper of the "the facts," as she touted the rigor of her research and emphasized how she had kept careful watch over the BBC's adaptation so as to avoid what she has called the "cascade of errors" and the "nonsense" of historical dramas such as *The Tudors*.[6] "History is never a convenient shape, it's true, but if you have the craft and the will to do it, you can find a way to tell a good story."[7]

The Mantel that I interviewed in 2011, however, did not promise "accuracy" from her books and was reluctant to criticize other authors for what she rightly described as their "choices." "I never knowingly distort facts," she told me. "But history is full of factual chasms and moral ambiguities," and "I might this very day be generating some vast error." "I make sure I never believe my own story," she declared.[8] I applaud that Mantel and wish she would make an appearance again.

The fact is that if you are looking for "facts" or "accuracy," you should not consult either *Wolf Hall* or *The Tudors*. They are both revisionist fictions that make selective use of historical material, fill in certain gaps while creating others, and service their own representational agendas. While *Wolf Hall* sets out to challenge the sedimented duality of heroic More/wicked Cromwell perpetuated by *A Man For All Seasons*, Hirst was intent on revising the "cartoon vision of Henry VIII" bequeathed to us by fat, chicken-munching Charles Laughton in Alexander Korda's 1933 *The Private Life of Henry VIII*. Each arguably went too far, ignoring and/or inventing various facts in the service of their visions (a Henry who never gets fat, a tender-hearted Cromwell who has not a truly mean bone in his body.) And each neglects events and/or caricatures key historical figures.[9]

While the BBC series is more "arty" and has far less sexual sleaze than *The Tudors*, it also takes more liberties with dialogue. *The Tudors* merges Henry's two sisters into one (a transgression that had historians frothing at the mouth), while *Wolf Hall* has Cromwell administering cardiopulmonary resuscitation on Henry after he's unconscious from a fall during a joust, and kills off his wife and two daughters in one 24-hour period, although the records indicate his girls survived his wife into the following year. In *The Tudors*, Francis I's sister, Marguerite de Navarre—author, intellectual light of the French court, and a deep believer in platonic love between men and women—appears as a visitor to the English court, bosom spilling out of her dress, casting hot glances across the dining hall at Henry as both bite into their roasted thighs and wings, Tom Jones fashion. Later that night, two guards stoically keep watch while Henry and Marguerite grunt and moan behind his bedroom door.[10] I seethed at *The Tudors* for that, but was far more angered by Mantel's representation of the Anne/Cromwell story, which imported ill-founded stereotypes of Anne "into the mind of Cromwell" rather than attempt to portray what history tells us was a much more complex relationship.

No fictional representations of the Tudors have been free from inventive elements. But we have very shifting standards when it comes to the "calling out" of those elements. Some depictions—Korda's *The Private Life of Henry VIII* (1933) is an example—get away with nonsense simply because they were created long enough ago that they are viewed as cultural artifacts. Others give offense because they are considered "pop" rather than "literary," and vice versa. Television and movies, because they carry the illusion of verisimilitude, are more likely to be criticized for historical inaccuracy than novels, no matter how often their creators insist that they are not meant to be entirely factual. If, however, they comport themselves with enough dignity—like the 1970 BBC production of *The Six Wives of Henry VIII* and the 2015 production of *Wolf Hall*—they are off the hook.

Perhaps, we ought to assess historical fiction, in whatever medium, less on factual "accuracy" and more on the insights and perspective that they bring to limited but generally accepted views and perhaps as well on the emotional satisfaction that new narratives and images provide. For example, the Tower scene in *Anne of the Thousand Days*, in which Anne gets to tell Henry off and leaves him with doubts about her fidelity that will haunt him to the end of his days, never happened, but it is immensely gratifying to see this alternative history acted.[11] Does a fictional representation expand our view of key characters and events? Or does it reproduce stale stereotypes and narratives? Does it provide new perspectives on who is a hero, who is a villain, or more significantly, put us in a muddle about those categories themselves? Do we leave the theater or turn off the television feeling we have gotten to know a character and/or understand his or her fate better? Those are the questions that matter to me far more than historical howlers. And with those questions in mind, *The Tudors* fares far better in its depiction of Anne Boleyn than its predecessors or *Wolf Hall* in challenging what I call our "default Anne"—the manipulative schemer whose motives are entirely those of ambition and whose religious commitments are, as Mantel describes them in her "notes on characters" for the play based on her books, purely "self-serving."[12]

Our Default Anne

"Incredibly vain, ambitious, unscrupulous, coarse, fierce, and relentless." The description comes from Paul Friedman's 1884 biography. But fans of Philippa Gregory will find her reincarnated as the sister from hell in *The Other Boleyn Girl*. In David Starkey's 2004 *Six Wives*, she is a vicious, vengeful harpy who "hardened" Henry's heart and judgment and who "rejoiced" when her enemies were "hunted down." And most recently, she has slithered her way into the higher literary reaches of Hilary Mantel's *Wolf Hall* and *Bring Up the Bodies*, where she appears as a predatory, anxious schemer with "a cold slick brain behind her hungry eyes." Manipulative. Calculating. Ambitious. Cold-hearted. A social climber who lured Henry into abandoning his faithful, devout wife of 15 years and would stop at nothing to become queen.[13]

Crafted *not* by Thomas Cromwell but by Eustache Chapuys, ambassador of Emperor Charles V at the court of Henry VIII from 1529 through the 16 tumultuous years that followed, our "default" Anne is the creation of a many-centuries-long telephone game that turned politically motivated lies into inflammatory gossip and alchemized that gossip into "history." Ironically, that "history" then became the inspiration for fictions—novels, movies, television shows—which in turn have assumed the authority of fact for many readers.

Chapuys was not a historian, a profession that did not exist at the time. His official job was to report court goings-on to Spain and to skillfully adjudicate between Henry and Charles. But his personal mission was to protect Catherine of Aragon and the Catholic cause from the turmoil brought about by the King's Great Matter and—as Chapuys saw it—the suspiciously "Frenchified" witch who had inspired the divorce proceedings and everything awful that Henry did thereafter: Anne Boleyn. Chapuys hated her with venom that he did not even try to disguise, disgustedly referring to her in his official communications as "the concubine" and "that whore"—or, with polite disdain, "the Lady." And everything dishonorable in Henry's behavior, including his shabby treatment of Mary (which actually persisted after Anne's execution), was the fault of the concubine's "perverse and malicious nature." He was convinced—and convinced many others at court—that Anne was continually plotting to murder both Catherine and Mary (no evidence of either). And he even charged Anne with chief responsibility for spreading the heretical "scourge" of Lutheranism throughout England. Anne probably was not a Lutheran, but she *was* an evangelical who promoted the English-language bible and disputed the authority of priests and pope to interpret scripture for us. For Chapuys, this was equivalent to being pro-devil, as from "anti-papal" to "heretic" to "witch" was a short step.[14]

Chapuys was hardly a credible witness to events. But Catherine's supporters did not ask for proof or logic, and Chapuys—spreading his tales around court and encouraging Catherine and Mary's suspicions of Anne—was able to generate an atmosphere of hostility toward Anne. Centuries later, his lengthy, gossipy letters became the prime source of all the early biographies of Henry and Anne. For narrative abhors a vacuum, and Chapuys was there to dress the slender skeleton of fact with juicy but unsubstantiated adornment. And while the earliest historians and biographers were justifiably suspicious of the veracity of his reports, they also leaned on them to stitch together a coherent story. Passed from one generation to another, that narrative ultimately overshadowed the suspicions, as Chapuys' venomous portrait of Anne's character and her manipulation of Henry crept into later histories, biographies, novels, films, television, and what we might call "the popular imagination."

Chapuys, of course, was not the sole architect of anti-Anne mythology. Wolsey's man Cavendish contributed his bit, and exiled Catholic polemicist Nicholas Sander later supplied some particularly salacious details, even going so far as to claim that Anne—besides having slept with most of the French court—was the daughter of Henry VIII and Anne's own mother Elizabeth Howard.[15] Nor has Anne lacked defenders. When Elizabeth came to the throne, Anne became for many Protestants the idealized, martyred heroine of the Reformation; for the Romantics, particularly in painting, she was depicted as the sorrowful, hapless victim of a king's tyranny. Victorian writers fought over whether her character was soiled by Henry's lust or her own wickedness. And when historical fiction became popular, authors won our sympathy by giving Anne an innocent adolescence, ruined by her scheming relatives. In *The Creation of Anne Boleyn*, I chart the cultural twists and turns of these and other versions of mutating Anne. But cold, ambitious Anne runs like a recurring pattern through the variations. Like Freddy Krueger in the "Nightmare on Elm Street" movies, our default Anne just will not die.

Natalie Dormer's Anne

If *The Tudors* is responsible for altering more than just Henry VIII's traditionally bloated body and highlighting the athletic, dynamic, but capricious young king of his earlier years, it is in challenging the hegemony of this "default" Anne. It did not happen in one season, however. For Anne did not begin her part in the series as much more than the captivating face and body that launched Henry VIII's battle with the church. In fact, Michael Hirst, who created and was chief writer for the show, freely admitted to me in an extended phone interview that when he wrote the first season, he was not even all that interested in Anne Boleyn. "I didn't even know if we'd be picked up for a second season at that point, and Anne was one of many people swimming in the ether. Wolsey and More—and, of course, Henry—were the more dominant figures." He also knew that the traditionally dignified BBC style of doing history was neither what the producers wanted nor, he suspected, what viewers jaded by the sex-and-sensation drenched world of cable television would warm to. He chose Natalie Dormer for the role of Anne largely because of the sparks between her and Jonathan Rhys Meyers, and he felt that to win audiences over to a historical drama they "had to push the boundary" when it came to sexuality. It was not entirely cynical however, as Hirst was intent on providing his young, athletic Henry and the guy-club that surrounded him with appropriately youthful hormones.[16]

Today, Hirst concedes, "We probably had a little too much sex in the beginning." You think? The sexual overkill was not only ludicrous, but turned all the women, save hair-shirted Catherine, into flirtatious tarts, including Anne. Through that first season, Anne entices, provokes, and sexually manipulates her way into the queenship, allowing Henry to get to every base except home, driving him mad with pent-up lust. "Seduce me!" she orders Henry, and a moment later we see her stark naked. (Surprise! It's a dream—a convenient way to get Dormer's clothes off without disputing the almost certain historical fact that it did not actually happen until marriage was assured.) A few episodes later, she taunts him to find a piece of ribbon that she has apparently hidden inside her vagina. In the last episode of the season, they ride into an appropriately moist and verdant forest, tear at each other's clothing, and just about do it before Anne pulls herself away from the embrace, leaving him to howl in frustration—and reminding me, unpleasantly, of high school. (We're told, early in the second season, that Anne had become acquainted, while a teenage resident at the French court, with the hand-job. Why did she not make use of it? It would have spared Henry and viewers alike some agony.) [17]

At the beginning of Season Two, it is also suggested that while at the French court, Anne slept with half the courtiers and possibly the French king. When Henry presents her, newly anointed as Marquess of Pembroke, to Francis and his court, she performs a Salome-style dance that makes one wonder just which historical series one is watching. At home, her bold flirting, confiding, and cuddling with Mark Smeaton makes the later charges of adultery with him quite plausible—and completely out of character with Anne, who was obsessed with being accepted as Queen and would never have condescended to treat a court musician in such an openly familiar fashion.[18]

This hypersexualization of Anne inevitably reduced Anne to her familiar role as the seductive, scheming Other Woman. Hirst says he never intended this and attributes it less to the script than to "deep cultural projections." He had initially seen Anne, he told me, as a victim of her father's ambitions and believed he was writing the script to emphasize that. He was surprised when "critics started to trot this line out: 'here she is, just a manipulative bitch.' Well, actually I hadn't written it like that. But they couldn't get out of the stereotypes that had been handed down to them, and that's what they thought they were seeing on the screen. It didn't matter what they were actually seeing. They had already decided that Anne Boleyn was this Other Woman, this manipulative bitch."[19]

I agree with Hirst about the power of cultural stereotypes; it is odd, however, that he would be so naive about the way that the show's own images reinforced them. Dormer, the then 26-year-old actress who had been chosen to play the role of Anne, believes it was indeed unconscious on Hirst's part, that in capitalizing on Anne's provocative sexuality while portraying Catherine as oh-so-pious and long-suffering, he slipped into a very common male mind-set. "Men still have trouble recognizing," she told me when I interviewed her in England in 2010—happily for me, at that point she no longer had any obligations to *Showtime*—"that a woman can be complex, can have ambition, good looks, sexuality, erudition, and common sense. A woman can have all those facets, and yet men, in literature and in drama, seem to need to simplify women, to polarize us as either the whore or the angel."[20]

Actually, the Anne/Catherine duality is not just a "male" mind-set; the Protestant/Catholic culture wars cast Anne as a witch and Catherine as a saint, and nineteenth-century female biographers such as the Stricklands kept the contrast going in their own Victorian way (Anne as "fallen woman" replacing Anne as witch). But Dormer is right that the "sensibility is prevalent, even to this day" and that it was initially present in *The Tudors*. She does not demonize Hirst: "I have a lot of respect for Michael as a writer and a human being, but I think that he has that tendency. I don't think he does it consciously. I think it's something innate that just happens and he doesn't realize it." But she did feel "compromised" by the script's portrayal of Anne, and felt she needed to do something about it:

> I lost so many hours of sleep, and actually shed tears during my portrayal of her, trying to inject historical truth into the script, trying to do right by this woman that I had read so much about. It was a constant struggle, because the original script had that tendency to polarize women into saint and whore. It wasn't deliberate, but it was there. I tried to fight that wherever I could.[21]

Dormer, a long-time British history buff who had hoped to study history at Cambridge (she misunderstood a question on her A-level exams and failed to get the necessary grade for acceptance), "didn't want to play [Anne] as a femme fatale—she was a genuine evangelical with a real religious belief in the Reformation."[22] Evangelical? Reformation? Fans of *The Other Boleyn Girl* (or even *Anne of the Thousand Days*), unless they were up on their Tudor history, would have known nothing of this Anne, for she had yet to make an appearance in popular culture.

The earliest well-known film versions—Ernst Lubitsch's silent *Anna Boleyn* and Alexander Korda's *The Private Life of Henry VIII*—portray Anne sympathetically, but as little more than a pretty face. In Lubitsch's version, Anne is a sacrificial lamb very much in the tradition of the wide-eyed, demure heroines that Mary Pickford made famous. Barely post-Victorian, she goes to her death unadorned, in a plain white smock. Merle Oberon, Korda's Anne, was the first of many elegant, hypnotic beauties who helped create the more glamorous version of femininity that reigned in the 30s—and that seems to be her main function in the film. She only has a few scenes to play, and each one seems designed to highlight the actress's regal (and, in those days, "exotic") beauty. As she prepares for her execution, she gazes into the mirror, fusses with her hair, ponders which headdress to wear. She preens, she suffers a bit, she looks beautiful, and then she is gone.[23]

Anne of the Thousand Days and the "Anne Boleyn" segments of the 1970 BBC *The Six Wives of Henry VIII*—the first to place Anne's character front and center—endowed Anne with brains and spirit but no spiritual commitments beyond some conventional praying to Jesus. *Thousand Days*, based on Maxwell's Anderson's stage play, followed the lead of Hackett's 1939 novel, *Queen Anne Boleyn*, in delivering an Anne who was "not a coquette nor a wanton" but "a high-spirited, high-minded girl who made this marriage a term of her being and who, in spite of this, delivered herself to ruin." Bujold's performance in the 1969 movie brought that "high-spirited girl" to memorable life. Her "Elizabeth Shall Be Queen" speech to Henry in the Tower—her hair disheveled, her dark eyes glittering with pride, desperation, hurt, and vengeance—transformed a potentially hokey (and, of course, completely invented) incident into an indelible, iconic moment. But she is pretty much oblivious to the religious crisis that has split England (as Anderson's Henry puts it) into "two bloody halves."[24]

Dorothy Tutin, in the six-part, multiauthored BBC miniseries, *The Six Wives of Henry VIII* (1970) first appears at the end of Rosemary Sisson's episode as a coldhearted, gossipy, and cackling harbinger of what is to come for Catherine. But in Nick McCarty's episode, devoted almost entirely (except for a brief montage of happier days) to Anne's fall, she suddenly becomes dignified, principled, and much more sympathetic. But although the role was not coherent and some viewers, possibly under the spell of Genevieve Bujold, said she was too old, Dorothy Tutin brought solidity to her Anne that those who followed her lacked.[25]

Charlotte Rampling was a credible vixen in a truly horrible 1972 condensation of the six-part BBC miniseries, which, as in the original, stars Keith Michell. He does an excellent job, but the events of Henry's reign are so compressed that we do not even get to see Anne's execution (one review said the made-for-television movie should have been titled, "Henry VIII and, By the Way, His Six Wives"). Helena Bonham Carter, playing Anne to Ray Winstone's Henry in the 2003 *Henry VIII* (a pretty decent TV movie that no one remembers anymore) was fine but indistinguishable from Helena Bonham Carter in any other role. The 2003 BBC version of *The Other Boleyn Girl* was almost entirely improvised, allowing the actors to interpret their roles as the mood struck them. Jodhi May, who was selected for the part of Anne on the basis of the fact that she was sensual but not conventionally pretty, was most notable for the excited deep heaving of her bosom, which never let up no matter what was happening in the plot. Excited: heave, heave. Anxious: heave, heave. Plotting: heave, heave. Awaiting her beheading: heave, heave, heave.[26]

Anne's promotion of Tyndale's bible? Her introduction to Henry of *Obedience of a Christian Man*? Her quarrel with Cromwell over the use of monastery money? The heavily coded sermon by Anne's almoner that compared Cromwell to Hamen, villain of the story of Esther? Nowhere in any of these productions.

Not that there is historical consensus about Anne's reformist leanings or activities. Eric Ives' scrupulous *Life and Death of Anne Boleyn*, several other historians of the Tudor era, and William Tyndale biographers David Teems and David Daniell credit Anne with significant intellectual and spiritual influence over the development of Henry's ideas about church and state. "She was the experimenter," writes Teems, "untangled and unbound from the old religion." Others are more skeptical, and some are downright enraged at the "fashionable" characterization—as George Bernard calls it—of Anne as an evangelical and patron of reformers. While such debate is legitimate, especially given the polemical nature of both pro- and anti-Anne writing of her own time, it astounded me to discover that Bernard's 700-page book, *The King's Reformation: Henry VIII and the Remaking of the English Church*, published in 2005, makes no mention whatsoever even of the issue of Anne's reformist leanings. Not a sentence.[27]

Mantel says in her notes on Anne Boleyn that "no one will ever know" if she was a convinced reformer. But this is to ignore a substantial stock of evidence. We know, from her books, that she was an avid reader of the radical religious works of the day (many of them banned from England and smuggled in for her), both in French and in English. Her surviving library includes a large selection of early French evangelical works, including Marguerite de Navarre's first published poem (*Miroir de l'ame pechersse*, 1531), which was later to be translated into English (as "Mirror of the Soul") in 1544 by Anne's 11-year-old daughter Elizabeth. Anne's library also included Jacques Lefevre d'Etaples' French translation of the Bible, published by the same man (Martin Lempereur) responsible for publishing Tyndale's New Testament, and numerous other French evangelical tracts. Significantly, James Carley, the curator of the books of Henry and his wives, notes that all the antipapal literature that Henry collected supporting his break with Rome dates from *after* he began to pursue Anne. So it is highly likely that it was indeed she who introduced them to him. In his introduction to Carley's book, David Starkey goes even farther and writes that Anne's books "demonstrate, beyond argument, that she was a convinced Evangelical. ... This implies in turn that she was not simply the occasion of religious change, but its acting, shaping agent."[28]

Far from being "self-serving," as Mantel suggests in her notes, the promotion and protection of the cause of reform was a dangerous business for Anne to engage in, because it was such a divisive issue (to put it mildly) and men's careers (and sometimes heads) would hang or fall depending on which side was winning. Anne took a risk in showing Tyndale and Simon Fish to Henry. It was a gamble, true, that initially paid off, as he immediately saw that they were on the side of kings rather than Rome when it came to earthly authority. But even if Henry had no objection to Anne's tutelage, others did, and their objections—a potent mix of misogyny and anti-Protestant fervor—created a political/religious "wing" of anti-Anne sentiment that could be exploited by Cromwell when he turned against Anne.

All of this is absent from the fictional representations that have dominated in the twentieth century, and the first season of *The Tudors*—except for a scene showing Anne introducing Tyndale's *Obedience* to Henry—seemed to be heading in much the same direction, to Natalie Dormer's dismay. So during a dinner with Hirst, who was still writing the second season, she shared her frustration and begged him "to do it right in the second half. He listened to me because we are friends and because he knew I knew my history. ... And I remember saying to him: 'Throw everything you've got at me. Promise me you'll do that. I can do it. The politics, the religion, the personal stuff, throw everything you've got at me. I can take it.'"[29]

Hirst took her at her word, and the result was a significant change in the Anne Boleyn of the second season, who was still sexy but brainy, politically engaged, a loving mother, and a committed reformist. Scenes were written showing Anne instructing her ladies-in-waiting about the English-language Bible, distributing alms to the poor, and quarreling with Cromwell over the misuse of monastery money. And Hirst's attention to Anne had changed. No longer was she simply a secondary character "in the ether." Rehabilitating her image became part of his motivation in writing the script:

> I wanted to show that she was a human being, a young woman placed in a really difficult and awful situation, manipulated by her father, the king, and circumstances, but that she was also feisty and interesting and had a point of view and tried to use her powers to advance what she believed in. And I wanted people to live with her, to live through her. To see her.[30]

To professional historians, it may seem as though Dormer's hard-won revisions amounted to little more than tweaking. But for young viewers of the show, the changes Dormer made, taken in combination with the sex appeal and flirtatiousness that Hirst had emphasized, went a long way toward creating what for them was a "multidimensional" Anne. "She portrayed so many sides of Anne," writes one 17-year-old, "strong, flirtatious, jealous, angry, intelligent, caring, loving ... and she did so without ever losing the matchless allure that makes Anne so fascinating." An 18-year-old: "Natalie captured the signature 'I am no fool' aspect of Anne's personality. Her Anne demanded attention; she brought feistiness to the English court, and embodied curiosity, intellect and charm in a manner I have never seen." A 19-year-old: "She gave the good, the bad, the vulnerable, the mother, and a sense that Anne was a very strong woman." A 25 year-old: "She captured the different sides of Anne very well—the innocent, the proud, the unsure, the angry, the strong. Anne is an extremely multidimensional character, and Natalie showed her as such."[31]

Winning Sympathy for the (She) Devil

The depiction of Anne's last days was especially important to both Hirst and Dormer. But Natalie knew that the Anne of the first season would not be able to win the audience's sympathies as deeply as she wanted:

It [the imprisonment] happened very shortly after she miscarried, remember. To miscarry is traumatic for any woman, even in this day and age. And to be in that physical and mental state, having just miscarried, and be incarcerated in the Tower! If only she'd had that child! It's horrific to confront how much transpired because of terrible timing, and how different it could have been. It's one of the most dramatic "ifs" of history. And it's why it's such a compelling, sympathetic story. But I knew by the time we'd finished the first season that we hadn't achieved it. That audiences would have no sympathy for her, because the way she'd been written [in the first season], she would be regarded as the other woman, that femme fatale, that bitch. Who had it coming to her.

She told Hirst: "By the end of the season, when I'm standing on that scaffold, I want the audience to be standing with her ... I want those who have judged her harshly to change their allegiance so they actually love her and empathize with her."[32]

This would require a lot of Natalie herself, especially since the show was not filmed in chronological sequence, and the execution scene was shot first, before the episodes that led up to it. At dawn, standing in the courtyard of Dublin's Kilmainham Jail, the site of many actual executions, she had "a good cry" with Jonathan Rhys Meyers. "It was incredibly haunting and harrowing—I felt the weight of history on my shoulders." But because she had "lived and breathed Anne for months on end," and had "tremendous sympathy for the historical figure," it did not require a radical shift of mood to prepare herself for the scene. "I was a real crucible of emotions for those few days. By the time I walked on to the scaffold, I hope I did have that phenomenal air of dignity that Anne had." Anne's resigned, contained anguish did not have to be forced, because by then Natalie was herself in mourning for the character: "As I was saying the lines, I got the feeling I was saying good-bye to a character. And when it was over, I grieved for her."[33]

Hirst, too, recalls the heightened emotions of shooting that scene: "That was an amazing day. Extraordinary day. After, I went in to congratulate her. She was weeping and saying, 'She's with me Michael. She's with me.'" And with thousands of fans who still write Dormer letters, describing the impact that the scene had on them. The episode averaged 852,000 viewers, according to Nielsen, an 83 % increase over the first season finale and an 11 % increase over the season premiere, and for many viewers—particularly younger women—the execution scene became as iconic as Genevieve Bujold's "Elizabeth Shall be Queen" speech. When I showed the episode to a classroom of historically sophisticated honors students, none of whom had watched the series, there were many teary eyes. Among devoted *Tudors* fans, for whom it was the culmination of a building attachment to the character, the effect of the scene—whose last moments were both graphic and poetic, lingering on Anne post-execution, her now-lifeless face still bearing her final sad, unbelieving expression, caught mid-air, suspended in space—was emotionally wrenching.[34]

Many viewers, in fact, watched the show listlessly after Anne/Dormer left; the rest of the story seemed anticlimactic to them. The following season's finale had the show's second smallest audience (366,000 viewers), and among those who stuck with it and continued to enjoy it (as I did), there remained a void where Natalie's Anne Boleyn had been. The ads for the remaining two seasons were successively more sensationalizing—the third season depicting Henry sitting on a throne of naked, writhing bodies, the last season described (on the DVD) as a "delicious, daring ... eight hours of decadence." But "those of us who were glued to this sudsy mix of sex and 16th century politics know the spark went out of the series when Dormer's Anne Boleyn was sent to the scaffold," wrote Gerard Gilbert in UK's *The Independent*.[35]

Today, hundreds of fan-sites are devoted to Natalie Dormer, who managed, despite being cast on the basis of "sexual chemistry," to create an Anne Boleyn that is seen by thousands of young women as complex and impossible to pigeon-hole in the previously available categories of "saint" or "sinner." Natalie still gets letters from them, every day, and finds them gratifying but depressing:

> The fact that it was so unusual for them to have an inspiring portrait of a spirited, strong young woman—that's devastating to me. But young women picked up on my efforts, and that is a massive compliment and says a lot about the intelligence of that audience. Young girls struggling to find their identity, their place, in this supposedly post-feminist era understood what I was doing.[36]

Dormer's perspective and knowledge, as a feminist who had done her homework with an eye to both the limitations placed on women during the Tudor era *and* the gender biases that affect most historical accounts of Anne's life, clearly informed her interpretation of Anne:

Anne really influenced the world, behind closed doors. But she's given no explicit credit because she wasn't protected. The machinations of court were an absolute minefield for women. And she was so good at that wonderful little thing that women do: making a man think that it's his idea. Let's not forget, too, that history was written by men. And even now, in our post-feminist era, we still have women struggle in public positions of power. When you read a history book, both the commentary and the first hand primary evidence, all the natural gender prejudices during the period will certainly be there. Anne was that rare phenomenon, a self-made woman. But then, this became her demise, because she was a challenging personality and wouldn't be quiet and shut up. So all the reasons that attracted [Henry] to her and made her queen and a mother were all the things that then undermined her position because she wouldn't change her personality. What she had that was so unique for a woman at that time was also her undoing. But she had her vindication, in her daughter, one of the greatest queens in British history. That really moves me.[37]

Is Dormer's Anne a feminist fantasy? Her comments above, except for the "self-made" part, are pretty spot-on, I think. While we have precious little on which to base our understanding of the "real" Anne—virtually all of her own letters are missing or destroyed, and the most detailed contemporary accounts of her personality and behavior were penned by her enemies—Dormer's "gendered" perspective on Anne's "challenging personality" as both the source of her appeal and a major cause of her downfall is shared by Eric Ives and David Loades, neither of whom identify as feminists. That the court was a "minefield" for women who refused to stay in their proper place is undeniable. And that Anne's reformist leanings had a significant intellectual influence on Henry "behind closed doors" is far better supported by the evidence than G.W. Bernard's denial that she played any role other than that of the prize to be won through the successful resolution of Henry's Great Matter.[38]

But the "facts" alone are not the only arbiter here. Just as Hilary Mantel's Cromwell and More are part of a cultural conversation that had become mired in stale stereotypes, so the Hirst/Dormer Anne should be seen as a response to the equally stuck recycling of our "default" Anne. This is not to turn Anne into a feminist "before her time" and before the term was invented (a description that can more justly be applied to Marguerite de Navarre or Christine de Pizan, who actually *did* argue for the equality, if not superiority, of women) but to recognize that the cold manipulative schemer is—like *A Man For All Season's* More—an ideologically motivated fantasy that requires revision. Bolt's More and the various fictional renderings of Chapuys' Anne may still provide archetypal gratification in the enjoyment of a black and white world of heroic martyrs and plotting *femme fatales*. But as representatives of "history"—or even of human beings—they are far too simplistic to let pass in our season.

Notes

1. Hilary Mantel, interview with author, e-mail, Lexington, Kentucky, October 5, 2011; *Wolf Hall* (London: Fourth Estate, 2009); *Bring up the Bodies* (London: Fourth Estate, 2012).
2. Ibid.
3. The play: Robert Bolt, *A Man for All Seasons* (London: Heinemann, 1960); the film: *A Man for All Seasons*, UK, 1966, http://www.imdb.com/title/tt0060665, Blu-Ray: Twilight Time, 2015; see also Peter Marshall, "Saints and Cinemas: *A Man for All Seasons*," in Doran and Freeman, eds., *Tudors and Stuarts on Film*, 46–59.
4. *Wolf Hall* (BBC, 2015), http://www.imdb.com/title/tt3556920/; DVD/Blu-Ray: PBS, 2015; Gregory Wolfe, "How 'Wolf Hall' Will Entertain Millions—and Threaten to Distort History in the Process," *The Washington Post*, April 5, 2015, accessed July 9, 2015, http://www.washingtonpost.com/news/acts-of-faith/wp/2015/04/05/how-wolf-hall-will-entertain-millions-and-threaten-to-distort-history-in-the-process/.
5. Hilary Mantel, "Hilary Mantel on Thomas More," *History Today*, July 1, 2015, accessed July 9, 2015, http://www.historytoday.com/hilary-mantel/hilary-mantel-thomas-more.
6. Hilary Mantel in Anita Singh, "Hilary Mantel: No 'Nonsense' in Wolf Hall Series," *The Telegraph*, October 12, 2014, accessed July 9, 2015, http://www.telegraph.co.uk/culture/culturenews/11157786/Hilary-Mantel-no-nonsense-in-Wolf-Hall-series.html.
7. Hilary Mantel in Jeananne Craig, "BBC's Wolf Hall is Good Drama but not Bad History," *Irish Examiner*, January 13, 2015, accessed July 9, 2015, http://www.irishexaminer.com/lifestyle/artsfilmtv/bbcs-wolf-hall-is-good-drama-but-not-bad-history-306560.html.
8. Hilary Mantel, interview with author, e-mail, Lexington, Kentucky, October 5, 2011.
9. *The Private Life of Henry VIII*, UK, 1933, http://www.imdb.com/title/tt0024473, DVD: Movies Unlimited, 2003; see also Greg Walker, *The Private Life of Henry VIII* (London: I.B. Tauris, 2003) and Thomas S. Freeman, "Henry VIII: A Tyrant for All Seasons," in Doran and Freeman, eds., *Tudors and Stuarts on Film*, 30–45.

10. *The Tudors*, Episode 1:4.
11. *Anne of the Thousand Days*, UK, 1969, http://www.imdb.com/title/tt0064030, DVD: Universal Studios, 2007; see also Glenn Richardson, "*Anne of the Thousand Days*," in Doran and Freeman, eds., *Tudors and Stuarts on Film*, 60–75.
12. Hilary Mantel, *Wolf Hall & Bring up the Bodies: The Stage Adaptation*, adapt. Mike Poulton (New York: Picador, 2015), 19.
13. Paul Friedmann, *Anne Boleyn: A Chapter of English History 1527–1536*, Vol. II (London: Macmillan and Co., 1884), 297; Philippa Gregory, *The Other Boleyn Girl* (New York: Touchstone, 2003); David Starkey, *Six Wives: The Queens of Henry VIII* (New York: Harper Collins Publishers, 2004), 443, 524, 527; Mantel, *Wolf Hall*.
14. For more of Chapuys's words, see *Calendar of State Papers, Spain* and *Letters and Papers, Foreign and Domestic, Henry VIII* at British History Online, http://www.british-history.ac.uk/; a recent study of Chapuys is Lauren Mackay, *Inside the Tudor Court: Henry VIII and His Six Wives Through the Writings of the Spanish Ambassador Eustace Chapuys* (Stroud, Gloucestershire: Amberley, 2014).
15. George Cavendish, *The Life and Death of Cardinal Wolsey*, ed. Richard Sylvester (London: Oxford University Press, 2003); Nicholas Sanders, *The Rise and Growth of the Anglican Schism* (London: Burns and Oates, 1877).
16. Michael Hirst, interview with author, telephone, Lexington, Kentucky, April 28, 2011. Hirst told me: "You know, Henry was eighteen when he became King, and I thought it was ridiculous that people were telling me he was really rather prudish and there was no sex because there was no heating in the palaces. But it's quite true that it was also a way of gaining an audience for something that wouldn't otherwise have been watched. Once I had my audience I could develop more complicated issues…" Some members of the cast, however, did not apparently care much about those "complicated issues." Sam Neill, who played Cardinal Wolsey, described the series as "Above all, about sex. Sex drives everything, including Wolsey, who had a mistress. The vow of celibacy didn't mean a lot to the good cardinal. Yes, sex drives everything. That's what makes the series such fun." Amazingly, this view of the period did not hamper Neill from doing a pretty fair job as Wolsey. Kristin Hohenadel, "The King Goes A-Courting," *Sun Sentinel*, 1 April 2007, accessed 15 January 2012, http://articles.sun-sentinel.com/2007-04-01/news/0703280572_1_tudors-rhys-meyers-henry-s-father/2.
17. Michael Hirst, interview with author, telephone, Lexington, Kentucky, April 28, 2011; *The Tudors*, Episodes 1:1, 1:8, 1:10.
18. *The Tudors*, Episodes 2:1, 2:2, 2:5, 2:7, 2:8.
19. Michael Hirst, interview with author, telephone, Lexington, Kentucky, April 28, 2011.

20. Natalie Dormer, interview with author, Richmond upon Thames, England, July 31, 2010.
21. Agnes Strickland and Elizabeth Strickland, *Lives of the Queens of England from the Norman Conquest* (Cambridge: Cambridge University Press, 2010); Natalie Dormer, interview with author, Richmond upon Thames, England, July 31, 2010.
22. Natalie Dormer, interview with author, Richmond upon Thames, England, July 31, 2010.
23. *Anna Boleyn*, Germany, 1920, http://www.imdb.com/title/tt0010962, DVD: Kino Lorber Films, 2006.
24. Maxwell Anderson, *Anne of the Thousand Days* (New York: William Sloane Associates, 1948); Francis Hackett, *Henry the Eighth: The Personal History of a Dynasty and His Six Wives* (New York: Liveright Publishing Corporation, 1945), 167.
25. *The Six Wives of Henry VIII* (BBC, 1970); http://www.imdb.com/title/tt0066714/; DVD: BBC Home Entertainment, 2006.
26. *Henry VIII and His Six Wives* (BBC, 1972); http://www.imdb.com/title/tt0070170/; DVD: Film Rise, 2014; Perry Fulkerson, "Henry VIII: Who Needs Wives?" *St. Petersburg Independent*, 5 November 1973, 10-B; *Henry VIII* (Granada Television, 2003); http://www.imdb.com/title/tt0382737/; DVD: 2003; *The Other Boleyn Girl* (BBC, 2003); http://www.imdb.com/title/tt0357392/; DVD: BBC Home Entertainment, 2008.
27. Eric Ives, *The Life and Death of Anne Boleyn* (Malden, MA: Blackwell Publishing, 2005); David Teems, *Tyndale: The Man Who Gave God an English Voice* (Nashville: Thomas Nelson, 2012), 121; David Daniell, *William Tyndale: A Biography* (New Haven: Yale University, 1994); G.W. Bernard, "Anne Boleyn's Religion," *The Historical Journal* 36 (1) (1993): 1–20, and *The King's Reformation: Henry VIII and the Remaking of the English Church*, (New Haven: Yale University Press, 2007).
28. Mantel, *Wolf Hall & Bring up the Bodies: The Stage Adaptation*, 18; David Starkey, introduction to *The Books of King Henry VIII and His Wives*, by James P. Carley (London: The British Library, 2004), 8.
29. *The Tudors*, Episode 1:10; Natalie Dormer, interview with author, Richmond upon Thames, England, July 31, 2010.
30. *The Tudors*, Episodes 2:3, 2:8, 2:9; Michael Hirst, interview with author, telephone, Lexington, Kentucky, April 28, 2011.
31. Marlessa Stivala (17), Michelle Kistler (18), Makenzie Case (19), Ilana Redler (25), interviews with author and Natalie Sweet, e-mail, Lexington, Kentucky, April 2011.
32. Natalie Dormer, interview with author, Richmond upon Thames, England, July 31, 2010.

33. Ibid; *The Tudors*, Episode 2:10.
34. Michael Hirst, interview with author, telephone, Lexington, Kentucky, April 28, 2011; Kimberly Nordyke, "'Tudor' Finale Doubles Its First-Season Ratings," *Hollywood Reporter*, June 4, 2008, accessed January 15, 2012, http://www.hollywoodreporter.com/news/tudor-finale-doubles-first-season-113105.
35. Ad language taken from promotional material found on *The Tudors*, Season 3–4, DVD cases; Gerard Gilbert, "Golden Girl: How Natalie Dormer Became the New Queen of the Screen," *Independent*, September 17, 2011, accessed January 15, 2012, http://www.independent.co.uk/news/people/profiles/golden-girl-how-natalie-dormer-became-the-new-queen-of-the-screen-2354626.htm.
36. Natalie Dormer, interview with author, Richmond upon Thames, England, July 31, 2010.
37. Ibid.
38. Ives, *The Life and Death of Anne Boleyn*; David Loades, *The Six Wives of Henry VIII*, 2nd ed. (Stroud, Gloucestershire: Amberley, 2010); Bernard, *Anne Boleyn: Fatal Attraction*.

CHAPTER 5

The Last Four Queens of Henry VIII in *The Tudors*

Retha M. Warnicke

Media observers understand how impossible it is for even a four-season television series like Showtime's *The Tudors* to mirror historical realities, as a monarch's reign must be squeezed into a few hours. However, Showtime's distortions arise from reasons other than this need for reduction. Michael Hirst includes gratuitous sexual scenes and seriously alters historical characters, including Henry VIII's last four wives. A complacent Jane Seymour (Anita Briem in the second season) seems willing to become Henry's mistress until she discovers the possibility of marriage, but in the third season Jane (Annabelle Wallis) appears as a devout Catholic. The next consort, Anne of Cleves (Joss Stone), finds his ulcerous leg repugnant but agrees to bed down with him after their annulment. Catherine Howard (Tamzin Merchant) represents an early-modern Lolita. Finally, the portrayal of Catherine Parr (Joely Richardson) closely reflects the queen's life after her royal marriage, but the courtship scenes are Hirst's creation. This chapter will analyze the consorts' characters and the actresses' interpretation of them. It will then provide a brief historical account evaluating these representations.

In the series, Henry initially sees Jane Seymour in September 1535 while he and Charles, Duke of Suffolk (Henry Cavill), dine with her father

R.M. Warnicke (✉)
School of Historical, Philosophical, and Religious Studies, Arizona State University, Tempe, AZ, USA

Sir John (Stephen Brennan) at Wolf Hall. They look up to see her entering the room clad in a white dress with a long train, her blonde hair falling around her shoulders. Henry immediately appears attracted to her, as she looks both regal and angelic, and decides to obtain her appointment to Anne Boleyn's household. While swearing to behave modestly as the queen's maiden of honor, Jane appears intimidated under Anne's watchful eye. Henceforth, when not clothed as a maiden, Jane wears pale outfits, signaling that her character differs from that of her extroverted mistress, who often wears bright and bold clothing.[1]

Soon Jane's modesty disappears. When Anne leaves her chambers accompanied by her ladies, they pass by an interested Henry at whom Jane smilingly looks back. Soon a messenger leads her to the king, who asks to "worship and serve" her as Lancelot did Guenevere. Although he refers to an adulterous affair, the obviously charmed Jane agrees. He kisses her hand, which she holds out toward him, smiling as he leaves. Later, her father and brother, Edward, future Earl of Hertford (Max Brown), warn her to protect her virtue since rumors claim that Anne might be replaced as queen. Jane's surprised response, "I thought," gives way to recognition of a possible royal match. Meanwhile, Henry continues playing Lancelot. At a tournament after he asks Jane for a favor, she offers a white ribbon, but soon the possibility of marriage gives her confidence to become less cooperative. When Suffolk brings her a letter and a purse of sovereigns from Henry, she appears pleased and kisses the unopened letter, placing it over her heart. But Suffolk later has to inform the king that she returned his letter and gift to protect her reputation, though she volunteered that Henry might give her money when she had an honorable marriage, obviously hinting for a royal match.[2]

The next scene with Jane incredibly shows her visiting the private chamber of the solitary Henry, who suffers from an ulcerous leg. Despite protesting his respect for her, he insists that she sit on his knee while he kisses her. Although he did not initiate this rendezvous, he promises never to meet with her again except in her relatives' presence. The pregnant Anne angrily interrupts them, but Henry continues wooing Jane, sending her a locket with his portrait that she eagerly accepts. However, following Anne's miscarriage, Henry sends Jane home. Trusting his promise that they will have their heart's desire, she smilingly prepares for his expected arrival. After he announces that they will be betrothed the following day at Hampton Court, she laughs. As they walk together in the garden, she asks him to return Mary to the succession but gladly kisses him after he refuses.[3]

The third season begins with their wedding at the queen's chapel at York Place before numerous witnesses with Stephen Gardiner, Bishop of Winchester (Simon Ward), presiding. Hereafter, Jane's character appears more consistent. Later, at a court reception, when Henry introduces her to Eustace Chapuys (Anthony Brophy), the Imperial ambassador, and leaves them alone, he asks her to restore peace between Mary (Sarah Bolger) and her father. Interrupting their conversation, Henry advises Jane to warn the ambassador to avoid foreign war. She next becomes involved in religious controversy by accepting Catherine of Aragon's crucifix and by requesting Henry to restore the monasteries. His response is to warn her against meddling in crown business and to remind her of Anne Boleyn's fate. Jane subsequently favors his daughters, whom she sends presents, and whose presence she requests at court. Henry snubs her plea and then distracts her with the gift of a dog. He finally permits Mary to return to court after she swears to accept the Reformation statutes. A final issue is Jane's pregnancy. She gives birth naturally after a lengthy labor amid a discussion about whether she should have a Caesarian section but dies of childbirth fever.[4]

Because of inconsistencies in Hirst's script neither Briem nor Wallis makes sense of Jane's personality. It also does not help the character's continuity that two different actresses played the role in the two seasons. The re-creation of Jane from a flirtatious maiden into a devout Catholic and dedicated stepmother is not convincing. That she kisses Henry, for example, after he refuses her request for Mary's return to the succession lacks credibility.

Surviving records indicate that Henry met Jane before 1535, as she served in Catherine of Aragon and Anne Boleyn's households. Unfortunately, most of the other evidence about her courtship comes from diplomatic rumors, especially those of Chapuys, who described her as pale of "middle stature and no great beauty." Like her relatives, she probably had brown hair.[5] Historians have mostly validated Chapuys's uncorroborated rumors.[6] In 1536, as he did not visit court until April 18, he relied solely on informants for his news. In February, for example, he referred to rumors that Anne blamed her miscarriage either on Henry's fall or his love for Jane. Nicholas Sander, a Catholic propagandist, later created the story about Anne's discovering Jane on Henry's knee. Actually, as his privy chamber staff guarded Henry's privacy, Jane could have only gained entrance at his invitation. The news about her rejection of the king's gifts was perhaps a staged event to distract Chapuys from the earlier rumors about her being Henry's love.[7]

The chivalric events in *The Tudors* are inventions. For example, although Henry did fall from his horse, according to Chapuys he was uninjured. After Anne's imprisonment, Jane stayed at Beddington, Surrey, not at Wolf Hall, and then at Hampton to be near Henry. Their betrothal occurred on May 20 and their wedding took place in the Queen's chapel at York Palace, not Hampton Court, on May 30 by an unidentified minister. Chapuys is the source for Jane's desire for Mary to be restored to the succession and for her hostility to the dissolution. In her interview with Chapuys, she agreed to favor Mary's interests but never promised to request the recovery of her succession rights. Jane did send Mary gifts and welcomed her to court after she capitulated to her father's demands.[8]

The dissolution controversy involved more complexity than Hirst's representation. The evidence for Henry angrily telling Jane, who allegedly wanted to save the monasteries, that she should not meddle in governmental matters is a rumor repeated by an unidentified writer to a French official. Actually, Henry refounded two dissolved monasteries, requiring them to provide prayers for Jane and himself. It is also unclear that she opposed obtaining monastic wealth. Some of her jointure income derived from former monastic possessions, and even Thomas, Duke of Norfolk, suggested that some of their confiscated valuables be granted to Jane.[9]

Finally, Jane died after delivering Edward, naturally following a lengthy labor. In Mary's reign, rumors claimed that Jane gave birth by Caesarian section but the medical personnel surely never discussed this still lethal procedure. Possibly part of her placenta remained in her womb, causing her to hemorrhage and die.[10]

Now returning to Showtime's series, shortly after Jane's death, Henry requires his councilors, including Sir Thomas Cromwell (James Frain), to seek a foreign bride for him. A reference to Anne of Cleves leads Henry to deny having heard any great praise of her beauty. Cromwell defends her candidacy, claiming the need for an alliance with Cleves because of the duchy's links to the Protestant League. Anne's brother William, Duke of Cleves (Paul Ronan), delays permitting the ambassadors, John Hutton (Roger Ashton-Griffiths) and Beard (Wesley Murphy), to see Anne, while denying his court is a "meat market." Hutton finally views the heavily veiled and identically dressed Anne and her sister, Amelia (Roxana Klein).[11]

When Cromwell orders Holbein (Peter Gaynor) to paint Anne as attractive, he inquires whether he should lie. Cromwell responds, "All art is a lie." After viewing the portrait, Cromwell reveals to Henry that Hutton describes her as more beautiful than Christina of Denmark, another possible bride, and that England needs a defensive Protestant alliance because of their enemies. Meanwhile, William surprises the ambassadors with news about Anne's betrothal to Francis, the Duke of Lorraine's heir, but after learning Henry will forfeit her dowry, he denies that the Lorraine contract is binding. Anne, still heavily veiled, leaves Cleves and reaches Calais where Suffolk greets her. She inquires in English about Henry's activities, and Suffolk teaches her to play cards as Henry does. Suffolk admits that the king does not like to lose when she asks if he always wins.[12]

When Henry learns that Anne has reached Rochester Castle, he says, "I want to possess this woman, this stranger." He impatiently travels incognito, enters the castle with a New Year's gift, and identifies himself to her. Disappointed by her appearance, he departs, upsetting her. Later, at a council meeting at Greenwich, Henry calls her a Flanders' Mare, but Cromwell still presses for the wedding since Charles V and Francis I have formed an alliance. When Anne arrives at Greenwich and Henry kisses her, she appears delighted and greets his daughters. Deciding to wed her, Henry protests to Cromwell about his poor treatment.[13]

Wearing a pale blue outfit and a German coronel, Anne walks hand-in-hand to the altar with the reluctant Henry. Later, he dismisses their attendants and points to the bed into which an anxious Anne climbs. Under her gown, he feels her loose breasts and full stomach, which cause him to believe she has already lost her maidenhead. When he proves impotent, she turns away. To his doctors he admits having night emissions and an ability to have sexual relations with others, just not with her.[14]

Later, Cromwell advises her to treat Henry more pleasantly so that she can become pregnant. She protests that despite his smelly leg, she will try to please him. When Lady Bryan (Jane Brennan) inquires about Anne's marital experiences, she admits that he kisses her, takes her hand, and says good night. Realizing she remains a virgin, Bryan advises her to "put his member inside" her "and stir it." Anne asks Bryan whether Henry will kill her if she cannot gratify him. That night Henry fails again to have relations with her.[15]

Henry informs the council that he believes her contract with Lorraine's son means he has wed another man's wife and that while they remain married, he will not be able to sire more children. Cromwell defends the Cleves alliance, but Henry responds that as Francis and Charles were enemies again, who needs Cleves? Henry then informs Anne that she will be removed to Richmond for her health and pleasure. There, Hertford reveals to her that parliament and the church convocations have invalidated her marriage. She is now Henry's sister with an annuity of £4000 and three estates: Richmond, Bletchingley, and Hever. Although she must remain in England, she may remarry. She replies that she hopes occasionally to see Henry and wishes him a long life. After Hertford departs, Anne weeps. Meanwhile, the imprisoned Cromwell writes a letter describing Henry's impotence. Later, he is executed.[16]

In 1541, Henry invites Anne to court. After sending New Year's presents to her successor, Catherine Howard, Anne arrives, and Henry introduces her to his reluctant consort. Anne appears delighted to meet her. Henry wearily departs, leaving them to talk pleasantly and to drink wine. Anne will not remarry, she confesses, and joins Catherine in dancing. The next morning Henry presents Catherine with a ring and a pair of spaniels, one of which she transfers to Anne, who is grateful for her kindness.[17]

Henry unexpectedly goes to Hever Castle, where Anne, accompanied by Elizabeth (Claire Macaulay), is in residence. She is pleased when he requests to stay for supper. Afterward Anne returns her wedding ring to the astonished king, calling it valueless and asking him to destroy it. When he thanks her for agreeing to their annulment, she expresses pleasure about her good treatment and for permission to remain in England. Anne also commends Catherine Howard's beauty and liveliness. Henry visits Hever once more and loses at cards to Anne, who admits she never drank wine or played cards at Cleves. He smilingly invites her to bed where they are seen together. She then disappears from the series.[18]

Joss Stone gives a credible performance as Henry's wife. Because she is attractive, however, it is difficult to believe Henry's reactions to her. It is easier to accept her negative attitudes about his ulcerous leg and impotence. Afterward, she becomes less credible. As she wept when learning of the annulment, her cheerfulness upon meeting her successor seems unrealistic. Furthermore, it is impossible to believe, given her marital experiences, that she would later willingly bed down with him. The problem lies less with her acting than with the screenplay.

As the historical record indicates that her father John, Duke of Cleves, entered antipapal alliances but forbade Lutheranism in Cleves, Cromwell did not press for this marriage to achieve Protestant goals. Worried about the Franco-Imperial friendship, Henry proved as interested in the Cleves alliance as Cromwell. It was Hutton, an English agent at Brussels, not Henry, who reported he had not heard any great praise of her. The ambassadors who negotiated with John's son William, were Nicholas Wotton and Richard Beard. Wotton saw an unveiled Anne whom he identified as a beauty and claimed Holbein's portrait of her was a true image. In the portrait she looks attractive if not gorgeous. He also admitted that she spoke only German and lacked musical accomplishments. William had probably delayed deliberations because of a dispute over Guelders. In 1527, his father had arranged Anne's betrothal to Francis of Lorraine and later signed an agreement, permitting William to gain Guelders if Anne married Francis.[19]

At Calais, Anne, who was unveiled, met William, Earl of Southampton, who described her as regal. She asked him to teach her to play cards and invited him and others to dinner to observe English customs. Later, Henry, like other contemporary monarchs who married foreigners they had not seen, greeted her in disguise. Although unfavorably impressed, he gave her a New Year's gift and stayed that night. He never called her a Flanders' Mare, as Bishop Gilbert Burnet first described her in 1682. Because Charles was visiting Francis in Paris, Henry married Anne. He concluded that she was a married woman, as she lacked the small breasts and flat stomach expected of maidens. His contemporaries viewed what modern scholars might define as psychological impotence as relative impotence, meaning when a man was unable to have relations only with a specific woman, he suffered from bewitchment.

Although Henry gave Cromwell permission to speak with Anne, he resisted, instead asking her lord chamberlain to advise her to act more pleasantly toward the king. Historians have argued that Henry had Cromwell executed because of his evangelical beliefs, although he swore he was a true Catholic.[20] Perhaps, Henry believed Cromwell had not done enough to free him from a marriage that would remain childless.

The investigation into the marriage's validity occurred after the council, not Henry, ordered Anne removed to Richmond. When several councilors informed her through an interpreter about the investigation, she fainted. The reason given for the annulment was that the Lorraine contract was binding. Three of her attendants, not Lady Bryan, supposedly asked her about her nights with Henry to confirm the lack of consummation. Their conversation almost certainly never occurred, for she still required an English interpreter. After tearfully accepting the annulment, she sent her ring to Henry to be destroyed. He granted his "sister" a pension of £4000 and Richmond Palace and Bletchingley for life, but after his death the crown substituted Hever and two Kentish estates for them. Following the annulment in 1540, Henry dined with her, invited her to court to meet Catherine in 1541, and dined with her again in 1543. With Catherine's disgrace, Anne hoped to resume the marriage, but they never bedded down again.

In Showtime's series, while the council investigates the validity of Henry's union with Anne, Sir Francis Bryan (Alan Van Sprang) visits Agnes, dowager Duchess of Norfolk (Barbara Brennan). Among her girls, Bryan discovers 17-year-old Catherine Howard. After he escorts her to court, Henry meets with her privately. She takes a ring, which he obtained from Becket's Shrine, and places it high between her legs, exciting him. After Henry in disguise gives her a ring, they have sexual relations. In bed another time, she laughs while reading Cromwell's letter detailing Henry's interaction with Anne. Later, Henry watches the nude Catherine swinging. Soon, amid rumors of their marriage, they appear at court, wearing crowns. Showing her ladies her jewels, she orders them to dress in the French fashion like herself.[21]

Catherine receives Mary, who appears unimpressed. Their meeting proceeds awkwardly, as Mary obviously disapproves of her new stepmother. Later, complaining about Mary's disrespectfulness, Catherine dismisses two of her attendants. Meanwhile, Jane, Lady Rochford (Joanne King), brings her a letter from Joan Bulmer (Catherine Steadman), an old acquaintance seeking to visit court. When Bulmer arrives, she refers to "you know who," meaning Francis Dereham (Allen Leech), who used to visit Catherine, hinting that she might reveal their affair. To silence her, Catherine gives a household office to Bulmer, who unsuccessfully attempts to seduce her, implying an earlier relationship.[22]

Catherine often plays juvenile games, tossing rose petals and taking a mud bath. When Henry introduces her to Elizabeth (Laoise Murray) and Edward (Eoin Murtagh), with a fan she hits Henry's face lightly and plays peek-a-boo with Edward. She also gives a necklace to Elizabeth. One evening, Catherine runs out to dance in the rain. Henry continues giving her presents, including a jointure containing Queen Jane's manors. On another night, Lady Rochford and Bulmer laughingly listen to the royal couple's lovemaking. Bulmer reveals Catherine's affair with Dereham to Lady Rochford and cautions her to keep it a secret, but later, intoxicated, her ladyship informs Sir Thomas Culpeper (Torrance Coombs). He decides to show Catherine a midwifery book that Richard Jonas dedicated to her. She giggles while examining the illustrations. When she complains about not recently seeing Henry, whose ulcerous leg has flared up, Culpeper hints about a royal mistress. At his behest Lady Rochford arranges his visit to Catherine's room. Later, the two rendezvous in Lady Rochford's chamber.[23]

As Henry discusses with his council a meeting at York with James V, Catherine interrupts him. Dressed in scarlet, she giggles while revealing her pregnancy. Afterward, Henry tells her about the journey, and she invites him into her bed. When he claims that it is too dangerous while she is with child, she denies her pregnancy, and he leaves angrily. Subsequently, Lady Rochford observes Catherine watching Culpeper from a window. Later, Catherine writes a letter to him, which Rochford in bed with Culpeper reads: "My heart will die if I can't be with you always." The court travels northward to meet James V. At Lincoln, Rochford escorts Culpeper to Catherine. At Pontefract, Henry orders Culpeper to bring Catherine to him. Preferring Culpeper, she suggests to Henry that he has more important matters on his mind than seeing her. After he takes her to bed, she returns to Culpeper. Meanwhile, Dereham appears at court, demanding a position. To silence him, she appoints him as her secretary. The jealous Culpeper argues with Catherine about Dereham, who brags about having been very close to her, but Culpeper and Catherine later reconcile, swearing their mutual love.[24]

When James fails to appear at York, the court returns south. While Henry worships with Gardiner, thanking God for Catherine, his perfect companion, someone leaves a letter on a seat that reveals her sexual encounters with Dereham and Henry Manox. The king orders an investigation, and Dereham confesses after torture that they were earlier contracted to marry but did not commit adultery. Manox admits fondling her. Thereafter, Thomas Risley (Wriothesley) (Frank McCusker) tells Catherine that her household is discharged and her title as queen is forfeited. She races from the room, trying to speak with Henry, who turns away. Gardiner then offers mercy to an anguished Catherine, if she will confess her faults. Crying that mercy is more than she can bear, she admits that Manox abused her and that she had sexual relations with Dereham, who used violence. She did not realize what a fault it was to hide the past. Gardiner discounts rape but believes that she entered into a contract that invalidates her royal marriage.[25]

After Dereham implicates Culpeper, Sir Richard Rich (Rob Hallett) questions Catherine about him. She admits only to flirting. Likewise, Culpeper denies adulterous relations. Thomas Seymour (Andrew McNair) also interrogates Lady Rochford, who admits witnessing their rendezvous. To the enraged Henry, Hertford reveals their confessions and shows to him Catherine's letter to Culpeper.[26]

Both Culpeper, who changed his plea to guilty, and Dereham are convicted and later executed. In prison, Catherine is seen dancing. Suffolk arrives to read the indictment and reveals that she must go to the Tower. She cries, almost falls, and the guards take her away. When informed that she is to die the next day, Catherine refuses a confessor but asks for a block on which to practice placing her head. She does this in the nude. Lady Rochford is executed first, and Catherine urinates while watching. She proclaims, "I die a queen but I would rather die the wife of Culpeper." Finally, she puts her head on the block, dripping with Rochford's blood, and the scene ends.[27]

As Hirst's Catherine is a more consistent character than Jane's and usually seen as an attractive woman, Tamzin Merchant has in some sense an easier role to play than the previous actresses. What fails to convince is the script itself, which calls for her often to appear nude and to play juvenile games. Merchant is less successful in portraying Catherine in the scenes after Henry discovers her sexual encounters. That she would admit at her death that she would rather die as Culpeper's wife than as queen seems unbelievable.

Most writers have argued that Catherine enjoyed Manox's fondling and Dereham's sexual advances. Some deny[28] while others believe[29] that she had intercourse with Culpeper, even speculating that she hoped he would impregnate her.[30] She was more likely the victim of sexual predators.[31] At her step-grandmother's, Manox, her music teacher, abused her when she was about 13. After Dereham entered the household, he seems to have protected her from the abuse, causing Manox to write an anonymous letter to the duchess about the goings-on in the maidens' chamber. When she was about 15, Dereham seduced her there. The affair ended about a year before her appointment in late 1539 as Anne of Cleves's maiden.

By April 1540, Henry had presented Catherine with gifts, and in late June he returned her to Norfolk House, where he visited her, preparatory to their July wedding after his divorce from Anne of Cleves. Lady Norfolk recalled that he took a fancy to Catherine the first time he saw her/ Catherine began appointing acquaintances, such as Bulmer and Dereham, to her household to silence them. According to Chapuys, she may have threatened to withdraw two maidens from the household of Mary, who was not at court, but he later noted that Catherine welcomed to court Mary, who encouraged Henry and her to visit Edward.

Her most dangerous opponent was Culpeper, who probably bribed Rochford to persuade Catherine to see him privately. He undoubtedly had learned about her relationship with Dereham and threatened to tell Henry. Catherine would have been aware that as a privy councilor, he had easy access to Henry. No evidence survives of her knowing about the book on midwifery. On the northern progress, she met Culpeper three more times. One of her maidens recalled seeing her staring out the window at him, surely worried about his plans. The message Catherine sent him was not a typical love letter. She would die if she could not always be in his presence because she needed assurances he would keep his promise to her, and she could conveniently see him only in Lady Rochford's presence. She changed the usual subscription, "yours during life" to "yours as long as life endures." Later, Culpeper described her as skittish and fearful during their rendezvous.

Catherine naively thought that Culpeper would reveal her past to Henry, but he would never have done so; even Cranmer had only enough courage to write the letter informing Henry about Dereham that he left in the chapel. She confessed about Manox and Dereham not to Gardiner but to Cranmer, who found her in a frenzy. She claimed Dereham used violence. Feeling ashamed, she cried when Cranmer offered mercy. Later, inquisitors disbelieved hers and Culpeper's denial about having sexual relations. In prison, Catherine cried like a madwoman and was convicted of treason by parliamentary attainder. Furthermore, parliament maintained that any future queen who did not reveal her illicit past would be guilty of treason. At her execution, Catherine admitted deserving death. According to social hierarchy, the queen was beheaded first. Eyewitnesses said she died a good death.

In the Showtime series, Sir Thomas Seymour visits the ailing John, Lord Latimer (Michael Elwyn) and his wife Catherine. Latimer requests Seymour to seek Henry's forgiveness for his disloyalty during the Pilgrimage of Grace. After leaving him, Catherine and Seymour question whether he "suspects" and discuss their future marriage. At Christmas, Catherine visits court alone. Sympathizing about Latimer's illness, Mary notes Henry's recovery from melancholy. At Catherine's approach, he confirms that he does not suspect Latimer or her of treason. Indeed, the rebels mistreated her. He questions whether her deceased first husband was insane. It was not a happy marriage, she explains. To his query about whether one exists, she replies, yes, and he praises her optimism.[32]

At home, when Catherine receives dress materials from Henry, Latimer wonders why he sent them. Later, Catherine thanks Henry for her lovely dress, and they play cards. To reward her for winning, he offers her a ring that she reluctantly accepts. He then sends Seymour to a permanent embassy abroad because he suspects him of trying to court Catherine.

After Latimer receives the last rites, Hertford and Risley tell Catherine about Henry's wish to wed her after her mourning ends. Gardiner ultimately marries them before a sizeable congregation, including Henry's daughters. Catherine plans to be a loving stepmother—she admits knowing Mary but wants to become better acquainted with Elizabeth and Edward. Henry will permit her to invite them to court but will not let them live there. Later, Catherine learns about the bursting of Henry's ulcer and moves her bed to his chamber to nurse him.[33]

Recovered and ready for war, Henry appoints Catherine to serve as regent during his absence in France. Later, Hugh Latimer (Jack Sandle) informs Regent Catherine about Gardiner's depriving him of his bishopric. She asks him to become her chaplain, but he hesitates until she explains the importance of Bible reading. Defending his appointment, Catherine informs her sister, Lady Herbert (Suzy Lawlor), that since she had to marry Henry, she will use her position to advance reform. As regent, Catherine writes to Henry, avowing her love and longing for his return. When Gardiner requests that she sign an indictment against heretics in the privy chamber, she responds that they must seek Henry's opinion about individuals so close to him. Catherine also decides to assist her stepchildren's scholarship. Mary shows the queen her translation of Erasmus's work on St. John, which is dedicated to her. Catherine next informs Edward that he should study with tutors and insists that Elizabeth learn the reformed faith of the Boleyns and appoints Roger Ascham as her tutor.[34]

At Dover, Catherine greets the victorious king. She later discusses her book, *Lamentation of a Sinner*, which she dedicated to him, calling him Moses who delivered his people from pharaoh (pope). Gardiner seeks Henry's permission to arrest Anne Askew (Emma Stansfield), a heretic who may have friends at court. Askew does not identity the queen as a friend, but Gardiner has already communicated with Mary about the queen's heresy that has caused an estrangement between the two ladies. With Gardiner, Risley, and others listening, Henry discusses Catherine's books with her. She admits having translated works by Erasmus and Savonarola and owning a psalter. When Henry warns that not all are able to read the gospel, Catherine responds that she is not afraid of the gospel, praises him for rejecting the monstrous Roman idol, and hopes he will purge the church of its "dregs." The unhappy king dismisses her.[35]

Henry agrees to permit Gardiner to arrest Catherine but insists on sparing her life. Gardiner immediately sends a messenger with a warrant for Catherine's arrest to Risley. Before delivering it to Risley, he shows it to Catherine's servant, who informs her. Henry hears someone weeping, discovers Catherine, and asks what is wrong. She fears, she responds, that she has displeased him. Twice he questions whether he has reason to be displeased. When she answers no, he departs, and Catherine orders her ladies to dispose of her religious books. Later, she approaches Henry, who inquires about what she learns from her books. She replies that, as he is head of the church, she can learn only from him. He accuses her of attempting to instruct him in theology, but she claims to have wanted only to distract him from his ailments. As a mere woman, she must defer to him as her lord and head. They are "perfect friends again," he exclaims. The next day when Risley arrives to arrest her, Henry angrily sends him away.[36]

Finally, Henry informs Catherine and his daughters that they will never again spend Christmas together and must say farewell. He orders his men to treat Catherine as though he were still alive and leaves her £7000 a year if she should remarry, plus her jewels and ornaments. As Henry leaves, the ladies weep and hold hands.

Richardson gives a moving performance as the queen who strives to be a good stepmother and to further gospel reading. But there are disconnections. Her character would have seemed more consistent if the scenes with her dying husband were omitted. That this pious lady exchanged vows of love with Seymour in their home seems incongruous. Knowing about her feelings for Seymour and reluctance to become queen makes it difficult to believe her moving letter as regent about how much she missed Henry. However, her abject submission when she believes Henry would punish her is convincing.

Biographical facts partially agree with Showtime's version. Before becoming queen, Catherine had wed twice: Edward Borough, whose grandfather was insane, and Latimer, who reluctantly participated in the Pilgrimage of Grace, after which rebels took Catherine and his children hostage. Before March 2, 1543, when he was buried, no record of her friendship with Mary or her interaction with Henry has survived. After his death, she wrote Seymour that when she was last free to wed, God prevented her from marrying him. Some biographers, probably inaccurately, have interpreted her statement to mean that Seymour courted her before she was widowed when she was not yet free to wed.[37]

Winchester married Catherine and Henry in July 1543, before the customary mourning year ended, in the queen's closet at Hampton Court in front of several witnesses. She never nursed Henry but did try to be a loving stepmother, although Elizabeth and Edward stayed with her mostly during her regency. From mid-July until mid-September 1544, she presided over the council, signing five royal proclamations while Henry seized Boulogne. She took an interest in her stepchildren's education but never chose Edward's tutors. She did appoint Roger Ascham as Elizabeth's tutor but only at her stepdaughter's insistence. When the children were not at court, she corresponded with them.[38] Despite their religious differences, she and Mary, who did not complete the translation of St. John because of illness, remained friends.

Knowledgeable about French and Italian, Catherine knew some Latin, since a few correspondents wrote Latin letters to her. But no holograph Latin manuscript of hers survives.[39] Relying on circumstantial evidence, Susan James, perhaps incorrectly, identified her as the translator of a work of Bishop John Fisher's, which was published anonymously. Catherine did read English translations of the books mentioned in the series. She utilized an English translation of the third book of Thomas à Kempis's *The Imitation of Christ* to write *Prayers and Meditations*, which was published in 1545. She did compose *Lamentation of a Sinner* during Henry's lifetime but published it after his death. Although she supervised the translation of Erasmus's Latin *Paraphrases on the New Testament*, she probably did not render any of them into English.[40]

The series repeats John Foxe's narrative about the conspiracy against her but with different details. For example, Henry found her in bed, claiming that her fear of having displeased him made her ill. Her submissiveness led him to cancel the warrant. Gardiner was probably not one of the plotters.[41] They did arrest her sister, but Hugh Latimer was never Catherine's chaplain. Henry was with her in early December 1546 but went to London at Christmas while she went to Greenwich. In early January, Catherine and Mary were at Westminster but Henry would not see them.[42] He provided legacies for Catherine in earlier documents not in his will.

An investigation of Showtime's series demonstrates how media have distorted historical events. Hirst could not decide whether Jane Seymour was careful or careless of her honor and wrote her both ways, first refusing gifts from Henry and then visiting him in private. Besides Henry's impotence, his interaction with Anne of Cleves is almost a total fabrication, as the German-speaking queen could not possibly have acted at court as was represented. As to Catherine Howard, she met with Culpeper secretly but not at first on her own initiative. Even so, the sensual scenes and juvenile games were largely inventions. The claim that both Henry and Seymour courted Catherine Parr while her husband lay dying is inconsistent with the view of her as a deeply religious woman. Except for some of the segments concerning Catherine Parr's religion and scholarship, Hirst did not attempt to present a vision of the queens that approached reality. The real story of their lives, although historians often disagree about how to interpret the surviving facts, is far more interesting and compelling than these fabrications that were created for entertainment.

NOTES

1. *The Tudors*, Episode 2:7.
2. *The Tudors*, Episode 2:8.
3. *The Tudors*, Episodes 2:8, 2:9. 2:10.
4. *The Tudors*, Episodes 3:1, 3:2, 3:3, 3:4.
5. Charles Wriothesley, *A Chronicle of England During the Reigns of the Tudors, from A.D. 1485 to 1559* (New York: Johnson Reprint, Corp., 1965), I, 43; *Letters and Papers, Foreign and Domestic of the Reign of Henry VIII*, ed. J.S. Brewer, J. Gairdner, and R.H. Brodie, 21 vols. in 35 (London: HMSO, 1862–1932) [hereafter *LP*], VII, no. 9 (ii); X, no. 90.
6. David Starkey, *Six Wives: The Queens of Henry VIII* (London: HarperCollins, 2003), 553–554, 561, 575, 584–610; Eric Ives, *The Life and Death of Anne Boleyn: 'The Most Happy'* (Oxford: Blackwell, 2004), 194, 291–293, 300–306, 350–356, 360, 365; Barrett Beer, "Jane [née Jane Seymour] (1508/9–1537), Queen of England, Third Consort of Henry VIII," *Oxford Dictionary of National Biography*, accessed 26 June 2012, http://www.oxforddnb.com; Pamela Gross, *Jane the Queen, Third Consort of King Henry VIII* (Lewiston, New York: Edwin Mellen Press, 1999); Elizabeth Norton, *Jane Seymour: Henry VIII's True Love* (Stroud, Gloucestershire: Amberley, 2009).
7. *LP*, X, nos. 282, 60; Nicholas Sander, *Rise and Growth of the Anglican Schism*, trans. David Lewis (London: Burns and Oates, 1877), 132.
8. *LP*, X, nos. 200, 908, 1069, 1204; XI, nos. 40, 1291.
9. *Great Britain, Statutes of the Realm*, 9 vols. (London: Dawsons of Pall Mall, 1963), III, 28 Henry VIII, c. 38 l; *LP*, XI, no. 860; XI, no. 422, XII (I), no. 1520, XII (II), nos. 34, 131.
10. Beer, "Jane Seymour," *ODNB*.
11. *The Tudors*, Episode 3:6.
12. *The Tudors*, Episode 3:7.
13. Ibid.
14. Ibid.
15. Ibid.

16. *The Tudors*, Episode 3:8.
17. *The Tudors*, Episode 4:2.
18. *The Tudors*, Episode 4:3.
19. Retha Warnicke, *The Marrying of Anne of Cleves: Royal Protocol in Tudor England* (Cambridge: Cambridge University Press, 2000).
20. Susan Brigden, "Thomas Cromwell and the 'Brethren,'" in Clair Cross, David Loades, and J. J. Scarisbrick, eds., *Law and Government under the Tudors: Essays Presented to Sir Geoffrey Elton, Regius Professor of Modern History on the Occasion of his Retirement* (Cambridge: Cambridge University Press, 1988), 57, where, for example, she almost calls him a Lutheran.
21. *The Tudors*, Episode 3:8.
22. *The Tudors*, Episode 4:1.
23. *The Tudors*, Episodes 4:1, 4:2.
24. *The Tudors*, Episodes 4:3, 4:4.
25. *The Tudors*, Episodes 4:4, 4:5.
26. *The Tudors*, Episode 4:5.
27. Ibid.
28. David Starkey, *Six Wives: The Queens of Henry VIII* (New York: Harper Collins, 2003), 645–649, 674–675, 680; Martin A. S. Hume, *The Wives of Henry VIII and the Part They Played in History* (London: E. Nash, 1905), 372–374, 393.
29. Lacey Baldwin Smith, *A Tudor Tragedy: The Life and Times of Catherine Howard* (New York: Pantheon Books, 1961), 9–10, 56, 67, 141, 171 (reprinted as *Catherine Howard*, Stroud, Gloucestershire: Amberley, 2009).
30. Joanna Denny, *Katherine Howard* (London: Portrait, 2005), 85, 88, 92, 108.
31. Retha Warnicke, *Wicked Women of Tudor England: Queens, Aristocrats, Commoners* (New York: Palgrave Macmillan, 2012), 45–76.
32. *The Tudors*, Episode 4:6.
33. *The Tudors*, Episodes 4:6, 47.
34. *The Tudors*, Episodes 4:7, 4:8.
35. *The Tudors*, Episodes 4:8. 4:9.
36. *The Tudors*, Episodes 4:9, 4:10.
37. Susan James, *Kateryn Parr: The Making of a Queen* (Aldershot: Ashgate, 1999), 90, stands corrected by Starkey, *Six Wives*, 814–815, n. 51, who noted that Catherine belatedly paid a clothing bill for her stepdaughter Margaret Neville, not Princess Mary, after she became queen. Sir Thomas Arundell, her royal chancellor, authorized the payment.
38. For her letters, see Janel Mueller, *Katherine Parr: Complete Works and Correspondence* (Chicago: University of Chicago Press, 2011), 75–128.

39. James Carley, *The Books of Henry VIII and His Wives* (London: The British Library, 2004), 140, doubts that she knew Latin and says she was a student of modern languages.
40. Erasmus, *The First Tome or Volume of the Paraphrase of Erasmus Upon the Newe Testamente,* trans. Nicholas Udall (London: Edward Whitechurch, 1548).
41. Thomas Freeman, "One Survived: The Account of Katherine in 'Foxe's Book of Martyrs," in Thomas Betteridge and Suzannah Lipscomb, eds., *Henry VIII and the Court: Art, Politics, Performance* (Burlington, Vermont: Ashgate, 2013).
42. James, *Kateryn Parr*, 285–286.

CHAPTER 6

The Significance of the King's Children in *The Tudors*

Carole Levin and Estelle Paranque

People's fascination with sixteenth-century England appears unending. From *The Private Life of Henry VIII* in 1933 to *The Other Boleyn Girl* in 2008, the public has shown a growing enthusiasm for historical movies and television shows on this time period. Showtime's *The Tudors*—actually only about Henry VIII, not the later Tudors—is mostly known for its sexualized view of history and sometime grotesque violence. As Jake Martin puts it, the show is "part stilted historical drama, part soft-core pornography."[1] But there are aspects of the series that go beyond that, with some interesting characterizations and shifting points of view, so that characters who are sympathetic at one point become far less so, and unpleasant characters gain our understanding. One theme is the occasional deep tenderness that Jonathan Rhys-Myer's Henry shows toward his young children. Along with all the adult drama, *The Tudors* shows that the royal children and the king's deep concern for a legitimate heir to the throne are central to understanding the political events that occurred in sixteenth century England.

C. Levin (✉)
Department of History, Medieval and Renaissance Studies Program, University of Nebraska, Lincoln, NE, USA

E. Paranque
Department of History, University College London, London, UK

© The Editor(s) (if applicable) and The Author(s) 2016
W.B. Robison (ed.), *History, Fiction, and* The Tudors,
Queenship and Power, DOI 10.1057/978-1-137-43883-6_6

This chapter examines how Michael Hirst—creator, writer of every episode, and executive producer—depicts the royal children and the king's relationship with them and what this suggests about popular cultural views of the importance of children in the life of the Tudor monarch. It analyzes the depictions not only of Mary, Elizabeth, and Edward, but also of the illegitimate son he recognized, Henry Fitzroy. The aim of this chapter is to explore the modern representation of Henry's progeny. While it notes historical inaccuracies, the emphasis is upon those instances when what happened historically might have been better drama, more effective at delivering Hirst's intended message.

The love and affection that Henry is capable of sharing with his children is evident from Episode 1:1, when Henry tells Catherine of Aragon that their daughter Mary "is the pearl of my world." In a number of episodes when she is about six years old, Henry lifts Mary up to cuddle her, telling her she is "the most beautiful girl in the world." It is obvious that Henry greatly loves his young daughter. Even when she is a young woman and accepted again at court in Season Three, he kisses her and asks her to call him "father" instead of "your majesty." Though the signs of affection are less explicit and appear less often with his younger daughter Elizabeth, they still exist. In Episode 2:7 Elizabeth hugs the king, calling him "my papa," to which he replies gently, "my Elizabeth." Years after the execution of Elizabeth's mother, Anne Boleyn, the series depicts Henry as still willing to show affection to his younger daughter. She is reestablished at court in Episode 3:3, though—as is discussed below—the series finale, Episode 4:10, shows how complex and difficult that affection was.

With his sons, Henry shows even more interest and affection. Episode 1:5 introduces his bastard son with Elizabeth Blount as "Henry Fitzroy." The king kisses the boy, who is dressed like a royal child, and puts him on a chair next to him. Though Henry Fitzroy is not his heir, the king seems to be willing to favor him and creates him Earl of Nottingham and Duke of Richmond and Somerset. As for his true and legitimate heir, the king refers to Prince Edward as a "special son" in Season Four. He seems deeply fond of him, showering him with affection and showing great concern about Edward's health.

Mary: Henry's First Heir: Brave, Pious, and Charismatic

Mary Tudor was born on February 18, 1516. She became queen in 1553 after the reign of her brother Edward VI (1547–1553) and did so without a battle despite the attempted coup in which John Dudley, Duke of

Northumberland, installed Jane Grey—his daughter-in-law and Mary's cousin—on the throne. However, the widespread support of the country wavered after her announcement that she intended to marry her Spanish cousin Prince Philip, and in early 1554 Wyatt's rebellion attempted to overthrow her in favor of Elizabeth. Between 1555 and 1558 she had almost 300 subjects burned as heretics, which led to her becoming known after her death as "Bloody Mary." Although *The Tudors* focuses on a younger and generally more pleasant Mary, it features numerous political and personal events that hint at how she became the queen she was.

Season One depicts Mary as child, played by Bláthnaid McKeown. In the remaining three seasons, Mary is a teenager or a young adult portrayed by Sarah Bolger. From the beginning, Mary appears as a bright, well-educated child who is shown speaking French and Spanish and is an accomplished dancer. Episode 1:2 depicts her as bold—when she kisses the young French dauphin and he is displeased, she knocks him down in front of everyone. Francis I, the prince's father, is clearly upset; however, though Henry reprovingly says "Mary," the look on his face shows that he is proud of his young daughter. Later, in courtship negotiations with the visiting Charles V, Mary is the only child who dances with the adults. Season One depicts not only Catherine's great love for her daughter but also her perception of Mary's future. In one scene the two speak in Spanish, and Catherine tells her daughter: "Be strong, my daughter. Remember who you are," adding, "One day you will be queen." The audience already knows this, but Catherine's statement puts it front and center from the beginning of the series.

One of the most significant aspects of Mary's portrayal is her religiosity, not only as a child but also—and more importantly—as a young woman. In Season Two, with her parents' marriage declared null and void, her official title is no longer "Princess Mary" but rather "Lady Mary." Her status and household change, and she no longer benefits from royal privileges. But Mary shows great devotion to her faith and to her mother. In Episode 2:3 she is brave enough to tell Anne Boleyn, who is attempting to win her over, "I recognize no queen but my mother, but if the king's mistress will intercede on my behalf, I will be grateful." Throughout Season Two—which describes the break with Rome, the marriage to Anne Boleyn, and the birth of Princess Elizabeth—Mary remains a zealous Catholic. In her most difficult times, Sarah Bolger portrays a calm, composed, strong hearted, and brave young Mary who faces adversities with dignity. In Episode 2.4, Mary meets Elizabeth and is told that she must serve her. Later, in her room, which is gloomy, dark, and far from royal expectations, the despair on her face is clear as she cries. Prayer becomes her main solace. However, in a subsequent scene, "the harlot" Anne Boleyn's fall and coming death please her, as does the knowledge that Elizabeth too will be called a bastard.

Mary's relationship with her father receives less attention as she grows up and is no longer the heir. Though he remains affectionate with her, once Anne Boleyn has been executed and Jane Seymour has asked for Mary to be reinstated at court, there are no scenes with just the two of them, which demonstrates a certain distance between father and daughter.[2] Moreover, before Mary can return to court, she has to recognize Henry as "head of the Church of England," as well as the nonvalidity of her parents' marriage, which is hard. In Episode 3:1 Hirst includes a scene, based on a real event, in which Sir Francis Bryan tells Mary when she refuses to take the Oath of Supremacy, "If you were my daughter, I would smash your head against the wall until it was as soft as a baked apple," a disturbing threat of violence highlighting the difficulties Mary faced (though actually it was Thomas Howard, 3rd Duke of Norfolk, who made this threat).[3] In the following seasons, Mary is more and more concerned about her status, her prospective marriage, and keeping her true faith. She appears more autonomous and the scenes with her father appear less often. She therefore becomes a crucial and independent character.

Another interesting aspect of Mary's representation in *The Tudors* is her relationship to her stepmothers and her siblings. The series accurately portrays her relationship with Anne Boleyn—who was the reason for her parents' divorce, the break with Rome, and her status as a bastard—as one of mutual dislike. Another queen whom Mary despises is the young, foolish Catherine Howard; however, when in Episode 4:1 Mary is rude to her, her manner demonstrates her royal breeding. Historically, Mary did show a lack of respect for Catherine Howard, who retaliated by having the king dismiss two of Mary's ladies. This scene is neatly contrasted to Elizabeth's politeness and poise when she meets Catherine Howard: "I am honored to be presented to you, and wish you every joy and happiness." When the pleased Catherine gives Elizabeth the necklace she is wearing, the girl promises to keep it forever.[4]

Mary's relationships with her other stepmothers are also somewhat complicated. She is closest to Jane Seymour, who shows her much affection, reconciles her with Henry, and thus facilitates her return to court. The strongest indication of the close bond between them is that Jane asks Mary to stay with her once she realizes her child is coming. Mary holds her hand, they speak of Catherine of Aragon, and she tells Jane: "I believe with all my heart she is with us." When Henry comes to see Jane after Edward is born, it is Mary who brings in the baby, though she looks a bit wistful as he is absorbed in his infant boy.

Mary also appears to admire and respect Anne of Cleves, though at first, in Episode 3:3, she scorns her for being a heretic. However, in Episode 4:4 Mary compares Catherine Howard harshly to Anne, telling Catherine that Anne deserves respect because of her dignity and modesty. Anne introduces Mary to Philip, Duke of Bavaria, whom Mary comes to care about even though he is a Lutheran. But when Henry decides to get rid of Anne, he also sends Philip home without regard to Mary's feelings. She walks away in tears but with her head held high, clearly a strong woman of royal blood—and one who would like to have an appropriate marriage arranged for her during her father's reign. Her last stepmother, Catherine Parr, is kind and loving, and at first they have a close relationship. Mary does a translation of Erasmus that she dedicates to Catherine. But when she realizes that Catherine is Lutheran in her beliefs, her feelings toward Catherine change and she keeps her distance.

The Tudors also depicts Mary's relationships with her siblings. Though Mary initially is pleased that Elizabeth too will be a "bastard," in subsequent scenes she clearly cares for both Elizabeth and Edward. Her affection for Elizabeth is consistent throughout the series. In Episode 3:4 Mary and Elizabeth share the same bed and talk about their new baby brother Edward. This scene intends to shed light on how intimate their sisterly relationship was. It also reveals their concerns regarding their gender, as Mary states, "The King has waited a long time for a son," adding, "A boy is more important." Elizabeth replies, "I don't think so." Then both smile looking at each other, joined as the less important sisters who do support each other.

While for much of the series Mary engages the audience's sympathy and respect, her actions and statements in Season Four mitigate that, exhibiting a hardness that foreshadows her reign as queen. Talking with Chapuys about Thomas Cromwell, she proclaims, "If I could, I would strip him from the king's side and burn him." In Episode 4:8, when Henry orders Chapuys out of the country, Mary is devastated by the loss of the only one she can truly trust, saying she is now all alone. Not only does she assert her distrust and growing distance from Catherine Parr, but also—with a clear sense of the relative important of sons and daughters—asks Chapuys, "Is it my fault? If I had been a boy England would be Catholic." When the ambassador attempts to comfort her, she replies that she does not know if she will ever be married or a queen, but that that if she does become queen, "I will heal this unfortunate realm. I would do whatever it takes. I would burn as many heretics as I have to."

Later, Mary learns that Chapuys is dead and agrees to support any action against Catherine Parr, whom she blames for raising her brother Edward as a heretic. Several times she consults with Bishop Gardiner over how the investigation of Catherine's ladies and the queen herself is progressing. In a scene between Mary and Catherine, she deliberately tells the queen about rumors that Henry is looking for a new wife. Catherine is stung and tells Mary that she loves her as she did before: "But you no longer love me as you did before. Why?" Mary refuses to answer. This strongly hints at the future Mary, who would do anything in pursuit of returning England to Catholicism, "the true faith."

Henry Fitzroy: A Bastard Who Plays the Role of Prince

Born in June 1519, Henry Fitzroy was the son of Henry VIII and his mistress, Lady Elizabeth Blount. Though there were rumors of others, he was the only illegitimate child that Henry publicly acknowledged. When he turned six, he was created Earl of Nottingham and Duke of Richmond and of Somerset. In *The Tudors*, Henry VIII is shown holding the baby boy with great joy as his mother watches. In Episode 1:5, we see the little boy again—played by Zak Jenrirargic—as he, wearing an ermine cloak, is formally brought to the king and given his titles. Henry kisses his son, places a hat on his head decorated with gold to make it look like a crown, and presents him with a miniature sword before he picks him up, caresses him, and then seats the boy next to him, obviously proud and deeply attached to his son. In the next scene with Fitzroy, his mother is bidding farewell to him as he is being sent to his own household. She promises to see him as often as she can, adding, "I love you, my darling boy, I love you."

But at the end of the episode the boy is dead of the sweating sickness, and we not only see his mother weeping over her son's body, but Henry alone weeping as well, with the boy's little cap trimmed in gold in front of him. This is a moving scene that presents a very human grief-stricken Henry, but it happens at the wrong time and it is a major shift from the historical record. We might wonder why Michael Hirst would change this important event and decide to only portray a young child. In the show,

Fitzroy's death is a trigger—this turn of events seems to have pushed further Henry's decision to break with Rome and to get a divorce with Catherine of Aragon. And the death of a child is an easy way to tug at the audience's heartstrings. Yet, we might also consider that Hirst missed an opportunity here; he could have continued the character until his historical counterpart's actual death in July 1536 at the age of 17. There could have been a powerful scene on the evening of Anne Boleyn's arrest where Henry, with tears in his eyes, tells his son how fortunate he is not to have been poisoned by the witch-like Anne.[5] And, at his father's command, Fitzroy was actually a witness to that queen's execution. His death in July 1536 left Henry with two daughters declared illegitimate, a wife who was not yet pregnant, and no son he could declare his heir, despite his illegitimacy. Suzannah Lipscomb contends that Fitzroy's death had a profound impact on Henry and that he reacted to it with "a mixture of denial, confusion and deep grief."[6] We are not arguing that a fictionalized portrayal needs to always be historically accurate, but Hirst could have used these historical facts to create effective drama and strengthen the point of the perils of the succession.[7]

Elizabeth: Disappointment, Bastard, Discreet Young Princess, and Future Queen

Henry VIII's second daughter is probably the one who has received most interest and fascination from scholars and the general public, and she is the subject not only of historical studies but also of many novels and films. Born on September 7, 1533 in Greenwich, Elizabeth was supposed to be the son who justified Henry's break with the Catholic Church and his turning his whole world upside down to marry Anne Boleyn, the woman he so passionately desired. In *The Tudors*, however, Hirst makes the decision to focus more on Mary, who is obviously older during her father's reign and therefore can play a more important role in the show. Some interesting representations of the younger princess are drawn, however. *The Tudors*' Henry was convinced, as was the historical king, that Anne's child would be a boy, and we see his stunned face in Episode 2:3, when he is informed that the baby is a girl. He walks in to see Anne, with the infant in her arms. In response to Anne's "I am so sorry," Henry regards her with some contempt but tells her—as the historical Henry actually did after the birth of Mary—"You and I are still young, and by God's grace boys will follow." He then walks out, and the next scene shows him in bed with the naked fictional Lady Eleanor, before it flashes back to Anne alone with a tragic face as she cuddles her infant daughter.

There are numerous scenes showing the close relationship of the very young Elizabeth with her mother. In Episode 2:4, Anne Boleyn wants to breastfeed her baby daughter, but Henry tells her dismissively, "Queens don't do that, especially for a daughter." Anne's demonstrations of love are numerous: "I love you Elizabeth, I love you with all my heart," "my own heart," "my dear girl," "my sweetheart." In 1536, when Anne realizes that her position is fraught, she says to one of her ladies, Nan Saville, a created character: "If anything should happen to me, will you promise to care for Elizabeth." In Episode 9:2, the last time Anne sees Henry and begs him for another chance, she is carrying Elizabeth, exclaiming to an unyielding Henry, "For the love you bear our child, for the love of Elizabeth." But it does no good, and the scene ends with Anne on the ground weeping and hugging her small child. These scenes suggest the deep loss that the young princess might have felt when her mother was executed and disappeared from her life without any warning.

In Episode 3:3, at Christmas court, Jane sits on one side of Henry and Mary on the other. They have the child Elizabeth brought in. She and Henry have not seen each other for quite some time, but he knows this is his younger daughter. She demonstrates her education by greeting him in French, and he puts her on his lap and responds in French to the court that she is family. Then he passes her to Mary, who lovingly takes her. Later in Episode 3:7, Elizabeth is introduced to Anne of Cleves and welcomes her to the court with a bunch of flowers. In *The Tudors*, Elizabeth never appears as particularly pious or religious. Rather she is portrayed as discreet, smart, fluent in several languages, affectionate with her younger brother Edward, playful, and modest.

The scenes with her father are quite sparse. Elizabeth does not receive much attention from the director and the scriptwriter. However, as mentioned earlier, Henry VIII is depicted as affectionate with his children. In our opinion, two important scenes reveal the affection and expectation that the king might have had toward his younger progeny. The first one is in Episode 2:4, when Henry visits the infant Elizabeth and says: "Who knows, Mistress Bryan, maybe one day this little girl will preside over empires." He kisses the baby several times, whispering—though of course an infant would not understand—"Please forgive me. I don't have much time."

Regarding the representation of Elizabeth's relationships with her siblings and her stepmothers, the audience can see a young girl who is easy to please and gets along well with her entourage. There is not one scene where Elizabeth is cold, spiteful, or mean to one of her siblings or stepmothers. Anne of Cleves describes Elizabeth as clever and affectionate in her conversation with Catherine Howard. Later in the episode, we see this cleverness and affection as Anne proudly watches Elizabeth learning to dance and the king surprises them. Significantly, at this moment Henry gives Elizabeth a book of Tacitus, telling her that without knowledge, life is not worth living.

Elizabeth loves her younger brother, whom in Episode 4:4 she calls "sweet Edward." In another episode, Elizabeth tries to teach Edward, who only wants to play, and says to him that he will be a good king. When Edward is ill, Elizabeth is the one who notices his fragile health and rushes to get help for him. Elizabeth is depicted as caring and loving—qualities that the historical character actually used as a ruler.

Hirst depicts a loving relationship between Elizabeth and Mary in the latter part of Henry's reign. In another critical scene for Elizabeth, Episode 4:6 begins with Mary rushing to share the news with Elizabeth that they have both been restored to the succession after Edward. She tells her younger sister, "It means that the king loves both of us." Elizabeth responds that it means, "You might be queen some day." Mary responds that so might Elizabeth, calling her jestingly "Queen Elizabeth," which is odd when one considers that the only way for Elizabeth to be queen would be for Mary to be dead. But Elizabeth is far more solemn than Mary and tells her older sister that because of Catherine Howard, she has made up her mind. "As God is my witness, I shall never marry." Apparently, Elizabeth did say this at the age of eight, but to Robert Dudley.[8] Nevertheless, the way it is represented in the series is one of the most compelling moments for Elizabeth.

Elizabeth's relationship with her final stepmother, Catherine Parr, is portrayed as caring and affectionate. In Episode 4:8, they hug, and Catherine tells Elizabeth, "I expect great things of you and I should not be disappointed." Elizabeth replies with a smile: "I hope not." While there are hints of the future waiting for Elizabeth, she remains a secondary character of the show.

Edward: The Promised and Special Son, the Hope for the Future

Edward, son of Henry VIII and Jane Seymour, was born on October 12, 1537. In the show he is played by Eoin Murtagh and for the last episode of the show by Jake Hathaway. We know in the series how important having a son is to Henry. In Episode 3:4, Henry has his head on Jane's stomach feeling the baby kick, and says, "My son, be strong."

The young prince appears as cheerful, playful, and sweet, and when Henry sees him he is very affectionate. The curly haired blond Edward is adorable when Henry introduces him to Catherine Howard. Always wanting to play, he is a contrast to the more serious Elizabeth, who is eager to learn. Henry is also concerned with his son's health, greatly fearing he will lose his only son. After Henry recovers from nearly dying in Episode 3:6, he shows himself to his people with his small boy Edward in his arms, reassuring the English populace the king is recovered and has an heir. Also, Henry is particularly affectionate with Edward, kissing his hands and in Episode 4:3 tells the boy how much he reminds him of his mother, Jane. The most touching and moving scene with the two of them comes in Episode 4:4, when Edward is ill and Henry spends the night with him crying and praying for his recovery.

The young prince is rarely seen with his older sister Mary unless Elizabeth is there as well. As we discussed earlier, Elizabeth and Edward spend some time together and play or learn together. There is no demonstration of affection from Mary to Edward, though she says she loves both of her siblings and worries about his religious faith. Edward seems to have barely any relationship with his stepmothers apart from Catherine Parr—in Episode 4:7, he tells her that he likes her. In this scene, he seems to doubt his father's love and tells Catherine, "He must love me; otherwise, he wouldn't give me these fine gifts." Catherine reassures the young prince and tells him that his father loves him and that he is very special to him. Later, she brings Edward to court so he can be with her and his sisters. Again, though Edward has the important role as the hope for the future of the Tudor dynasty, he appears as a secondary character in the show, as does Elizabeth. In the final episode, he greets the Lord Admiral in Latin, impressing the audience and making his father proud and then sits with his father on the throne, showing the continuity of the Tudor dynasty.

Henry and His Children

Of all Henry's children in *The Tudors*, the only one with a really significant role is Mary, probably since as a young adult she can truly be part of the political/sexual interactions. Fitzroy, Elizabeth, and Edward have far less screen time. Yet, despite that, for Henry, the boy is always the most important, and the daughters' significance comes as it relates the son. In Episode 4:10, as he is dying, Henry asks Mary "to be a kind and loving mother to your brother" and turns to Elizabeth adding, "You are so very young but you too can look after your brother." Edward definitely appears as the most important and most loved child, but he does not get much airtime. In the final episode, the children's importance is highlighted as the ghosts of Henry's three first wives, the mothers of his children, come back to haunt him, taunting him with what he did wrong. Catherine of Aragon tells Henry how he has neglected Mary, who should be married by now. Anne is also concerned with how he has neglected and does not really love his clever daughter Elizabeth. "I wish I could love her more," Henry tells Anne with Elizabeth now beside her. "But from time to time she reminds me of you and what you did to me." But Anne tells him she did nothing to him. The cruelest ghost is Jane Seymour, who tells Henry that Edward will die young and blames Henry for keeping Edward away from him to keep him safe: "You have killed him." Edward, as the longed-for heir, is of critical importance, but his symbolism is of more significance than the development of his character. For all the importance of Henry's children and his need for a son, the characters who matter the most in *The Tudors* are the ones who can engage in the sex, violence, and political intrigue that propel the four seasons of the series.

Notes

1. Jake Martin, "Regarding Henry," *American Magazine*, accessed November 10, 2014, http://americamagazine.org/issue/734/television/regarding-henry.
2. In *The Tudors*, Episode 3:1 Henry asks Mary to call him "father" again and kisses her forehead and in Episode 3:2 he swears to protect her.
3. The Duke of Norfolk and Lord Sussex, who were sent to administer the oath to her, told her that if she was their daughter 'they would knock her head against the wall till it was as soft as a baked apple.' *Dictionary of National Biography* Archive. Mary I (1516–1558), queen of England and Ireland, by Sidney Lee, Published 1893. Accessed November 12, 2014, http://0-www.oxforddnb.com.library.unl.edu/view/olddnb/18245.
4. Antonia Fraser, *The Wives of Henry VIII* (New York: Alfred A. Knopf, Inc., 1992), 334.
5. This is according to Eustache Chapuys. *Calendar of Letters, Dispatches and States Papers Relating to Negotiations between England and Spain 1485–1558*, ed. G.A. Bergenroth, et al. (1862–1954), V, 55.

6. Suzannah Lipscomb, *1536: The Year that Changed Henry VIII* (Oxford: Lion, 2009), 94.
7. For more on Fitzroy, see Beverley A. Murphy, *Bastard Prince: Henry VIII's Lost Son* (Stroud, Gloucestershire: Sutton, 2001).
8. BNF, MS FF 15970, fl. 14r-v in John Guy, *The Children of Henry VIII* (Oxford: Oxford University Press, 2013), 188, n. 31.

CHAPTER 7

The King's Sister(s), Mistresses, Bastard(s), and "Uncle" in *The Tudors*

Kristen P. Walton

Sex and tragedy shine throughout *The Tudors*. The series portrays Henry VIII as a rock star, constantly sleeping with different women and controlling the lives of those around him. It also regularly disrupts the space–time continuum to create what at first appears to be fictionalized history. Yet, it goes beyond that, for "*The Tudors* is best viewed not as a historical fiction but as a steamy period drama." Though writer Michael Hirst prides himself on the amount of research he conducted, he also admits, "The show is supposed to be an entertaining soap opera and not history." That statement accurately describes the entire series but is especially true of the way *The Tudors* portrays Henry's family and mistresses. From his fictitious uncle's assassination in the first scene of Episode 1:1 to the amalgamation of his two sisters into one person to the fabricated mistress Ursula Misseldon in Season Three, the series transforms history in a highly creative manner. This is important, for the stories Hirst invents about Henry, his extended family, and his mistresses produce much of the show's drama and help to increase both its sex appeal and its tragic moments outside of the well-known accounts of Henry and his wives.[1]

Most characters in *The Tudors* have some basis in reality, though in some cases it is just a similar name or the scant representation of rumor.

K.P. Walton (✉)
History Department, Salisbury University, Salisbury, MD, USA

© The Editor(s) (if applicable) and The Author(s) 2016
W.B. Robison (ed.), *History, Fiction, and* The Tudors,
Queenship and Power, DOI 10.1057/978-1-137-43883-6_7

Family and mistresses largely follow this convention, even when the show dramatically distorts their personas or relationships with Henry. In turn, Henry's interaction with these characters helps establish him as a man who is, in many ways, the opposite of popular stereotype ideas about him. Rhys Meyers' portrayal of a youthful king with a highly sexualized lifestyle (particularly in the first two seasons) shows a less familiar side of the king in a manner that is almost refreshing. Henry was, after all, the "It Man" of his day. Of course, in real life, he was not a "consummate philanderer," as most people imagine him, but instead was generally a one-woman man who had a good number of lovers but was fairly faithful to each while romantically involved. If the show does not depict his fidelity—in Episode 1:1 he sleeps with both Bessie Blount and another lady-in-waiting while attempting to fulfill his marital duties with Catherine of Aragon—it does show a Henry very different from the cantankerous tyrant he became in 1536 as his life imploded.[2]

Marcus Bull, Tatiana String, and others recently have developed the concept of Tudorism to describe the often presentist way subsequent generations have represented and interpreted the Tudor era. Tudorism is very much evident in *The Tudors*, which advances a distinctly twenty-first-century interpretation of Henry's reign. Yet one of the show's strengths is that it helps viewers recognize that Henry was more than just the fat king who caused the English Reformation and killed or disposed of all of his wives. The sexy Rhys Meyers' Henry is more like the young king Pasquagliano famously described in 1515 as "the handsomest potentate I ever set eyes on; above the usual height, with an extremely fine calf to his leg, his complexion very fair and bright ... and a round face so very beautiful that it would become a pretty woman."[3]

Henry was a complex person who won praise as a Renaissance man and criticism as a ruler more interested in increasing the pomp and stature of his court than in governing during his early years. If Hirst's focus on the king's mistresses and sex-filled court helps create a Henry who in his youth did not often resemble the ruthless tyrant of his later years, his treatment of the king's relationships with his family—including the bastard Henry Fitzroy—shows a side of Henry not usually seen in modern interpretations. Though their interactions and stories fall even farther outside the realm of true history, they help reshape the modern popular view of Henry.

The opening of *The Tudors* is a fascinating representation of how Hirst worked to add to the tragic story of Henry VIII and his court.

The first scene takes the viewer to the ducal palace of Urbino in 1518, where agents of Francis I of France assassinate the English Ambassador, Henry's uncle (played by Sean Pertwee). Historically, this moment never occurred. Neither did the uncle exist. On his father's side, Henry had one great-uncle, Jasper Tudor, who died before 1500. On his mother's side, there were no surviving males or else one would have been king instead of Henry VII. Though Elizabeth of York did have sisters who married, only Thomas Howard—married briefly to Anne of York—was still alive in 1518, and he plays a significant role in *The Tudors* as the 3rd Duke of Norfolk, so obviously he was not the assassinated ambassador. The only other option on whom Hirst might have drawn for this scene was Henry's great uncle by marriage, Sir Richard Wingfield, the husband of Elizabeth Woodville's sister Catherine. He was the English deputy of Calais in 1518, operated as ambassador to the court of Francis I in 1520, assisted in the arrangement of the Field of the Cloth of Gold, may have had a role in the "removal of Henry's minions" in 1519, and became ambassador to Charles V in 1521. He died of natural causes while ambassador in Toledo four years later.[4]

Whether or not Hirst based this ambassadorial uncle on Wingfield, the scene creates a dramatic setting for introducing Henry as a king who demands war with France in response to his uncle's murder. Henry is "mad with grief" and "inconsolable" about his uncle's assassination and immediately calls for war—before romping off to bed with Bessie Blount. In actuality, this story is off base in a number of ways. Not only did Henry have no uncle assassinated by the French in 1518, England and France were on good enough terms that the French had to create a new alliance with the Treaty of Rouen with Scotland in order to respect the friendship with England during the fall of 1517. However, the assassination also can be seen as setting a stage that in reality the Anglo-French War of 1513 created, without having to dredge up the history of Henry's first decade. This allows Hirst to move toward the Treaty of London of 1518, which arranged Princess Mary's engagement to the Dauphin and reenforced peace among England, France, and other European powers. It also establishes from the beginning a sympathetic vision of Henry, devastated by his uncle's death and consolable only by a beautiful young woman.[5]

Henry's interactions with other family members show another side of Henry, but this adds to the series' depth by developing side characters with whom the audience can develop connections. In Episode 1:3, during a masque to impress the imperial envoys Chapuys and Mendoza, the camera zooms in on a masked woman in white who is ascending the stairs of a castle where a group of wanton women guard other pure women in white. The first woman turns out to Anne Boleyn, and the scene opens the door for Henry and Anne's romantic tragedy. Meanwhile, though, standing next to her is another tragic—if less well known—figure, Henry's sister Margaret, played by Gabrielle Anwar. Earlier, Henry has asked Charles Brandon to escort her to wed the King of Portugal, and during the masque she challenges her brother about the proposed marriage. This scene continues Hirst's creation of "history." Similarly, his combination of Henry's two sisters into one who follows the historical path of neither demonstrates how he manipulates history for his own ends but in ways not always necessary for plot development.

In real life, Margaret was Henry's older sister and in 1503 went to Scotland to marry James IV. Her story is worthy of its own miniseries or movie, as it has enough soap-operatic tragedy to enthrall an audience. Margaret was only 13 when she married the 30-year-old James IV, and by the time of his death in 1513 she was mother to James V and pregnant with another son. Like her brother, Margaret had a passion for romance and was swept off her feet in late 1514 by the Scottish Archibald Douglas, 6th Earl of Angus, whom she divorced in 1527 so she could marry Henry Stuart, 1st Lord Methven, whom she also divorced. Margaret fled to England in 1515, but after only a year-and-a-half at Henry's court, she returned in June 1517 to Scotland, where she remained. In other words, Margaret was far from Henry's court by 1518, the approximate time when *The Tudors* begins.

Hirst's rewriting of history condemns *The Tudors* to end with Henry's reign by removing the connection between the English and Scottish thrones, a historical fact essential for understanding the later Tudor age. Margaret's granddaughter, Mary, Queen of Scots—from her marriage to James IV—was the target of the "rough wooing" by which England sought to marry her to Edward VI between 1543 and 1551, and she later was the bitter rival of Elizabeth I. In 1565, she married her first cousin, Henry Stuart, Lord Darnley—Margaret's grandson from her marriage to Angus—and the two became the parents of James VI and I. None of this could occur in Hirst's "history," where Margaret marries the king of Portugal and then Charles Brandon.

While Hirst uses Margaret's name for the one sister—probably because there are too many important Mary's in the show—the story he tells is much closer to that of Henry's younger sister Mary. Anwar—a stunning, tall, extremely thin, model-like figure who looks very Continental European—does not at all fit surviving images of either Margaret or Mary, who both had more rounded faces, denoting Renaissance figures nowhere near anorexic thinness, and reserved wardrobes that did not exude the sexuality that Anwar infuses into the character.[6] In any case, in Margaret's first interaction with Henry, she challenges his decision to marry her to the Portuguese king but eventually agrees to cooperate on the condition that Henry will allow her to choose her own husband for any future marriage. Henry actually forced his sister Mary to wed the 52-year-old Louis XII of France, and she made the same deal. In 1518, the Portuguese king was Manoel I "the Fortunate," who died of plague at the age of 52 in 1521, to be succeeded by his son João III "the Pious" at the age of 19. Thus, Manoel was about the age of Louis XII when Mary married him, which could be why Hirst chose him.

In the show, Henry elevates Charles Brandon to the position of Duke of Suffolk to make him a suitable guardian when accompanying his sister to Portugal, but in history Brandon became Duke of Suffolk in 1514 during a period when there was a question of marriage (or at least a prime flirtation) with Margaret of Savoy, the Regent of the Netherlands, not either of Henry's sisters.[7] Episode 1:4 opens with Henry giving his sister and Brandon a stiff farewell as they sail off to Portugal. Margaret and Brandon verbally spar on the ship, building sexual tension as they sail across the seas. Margaret longingly watches Brandon undress in the cramped quarters, leading her to invite him for a card game that quickly turns into a steamy sexual encounter. Upon their arrival in Lisbon, Margaret faints and then timidly follows through with her marriage to the old Portuguese king, who is unattractive, crippled, and has dirty feet. He also is amorous, and after the curtain is drawn across their marriage bed, sounds of lovemaking reverberate through the room, after which the king holds his chest in pain.

Rumors from early 1515 suggested that Louis XII died on January 1, less than three months into his marriage with Mary, of heart problems due to too much sexual activity. Thus, replacing Louis with Manoel was not a far-fetched decision, given the chronological changes on the show and Margaret's assimilation of Mary's history. However, the show then takes a dramatic turn. Margaret, distressed about Brandon's imminent departure from Lisbon, decides to smother the king with a pillow, killing him and turning herself into a murderess. Although the real Margaret once tried to kill her husband Angus by aiming cannon at him as he entered into

Edinburgh, neither sister was a murderess. Therefore, this development completely changes the character of Henry's sister(s).[8]

The remainder of Margaret/Mary's story in *The Tudors* diverges significantly from historical fact, and there is no obvious reason why Hirst decided to change that history. Although Margaret does marry Brandon, it is after he proposes on the ship on the way back to England. In actuality, following the death of Louis XII, Mary was in isolation and worried that Henry would not live up to his promise for her to marry where she pleased, so she turned to Francis I, who helped to secure the secret marriage with Brandon at Cluny in February 1515. Henry forgave them after a short while and allowed a second marriage in May 1515 at Greenwich Palace. In the historical record, the marriage appeared to be relatively strong and loving, with Mary bearing four children before she died in 1533, including two daughters who survived to adulthood, the Lady Frances—mother of the Grey contenders to the throne, Jane, Catherine, and Mary—and the Lady Eleanor.[9] In the show, Henry learns of the marriage upon the ship and banishes both Margaret and Brandon from court, leading to their fighting, throwing things, and making up with passionate sex. In Episode 1:6, Brandon speaks with Thomas Boleyn—who tries to win him over to support the Anne marriage—and Norfolk in order to oust Wolsey from power. Margaret overhears the conversation, reminds Brandon of Wolsey's past kindness, and encourages him not to support Anne, but he rejects her, widening the gap between the spouses.

Mary never supported Anne Boleyn but remained close to Catherine of Aragon, with whom she had maintained a good relationship from childhood, and Hirst has Margaret portray this side of her well. Brandon joins forces with the Anne conspiracy and goes to Henry, where he begs forgiveness for his boldness in marrying Margaret and is welcomed back to court. During Episode 1:7–1:9, the tension between Margaret and Brandon increases significantly as Brandon sleeps around. Margaret remains largely isolated until finally she declines Brandon's invitation to return to his bed and goes to the bathroom, where she begins coughing up blood. Margaret dies shortly after, covered in blood and alone while her husband has sex with another woman.

The truth was far different. From the beginning, Mary was always Henry's favored sister, and he forgave her for her marriage to Suffolk fairly early on. The marriage between the two was considered one of the better ones in the Tudor age, and their relationship was apparently strong and relatively happy. On the show Margaret becomes isolated, has no children or heirs to carry on her line to the throne, and is a murderess with a cold relationship both with her brother and husband. Neither of Henry's sisters corresponds with Hirst's depiction of Margaret. The manner in which she appears rarely and essentially fades into the background until her death in Episode 1:9 does not advance the plot significantly, nor does it show much relation to historical reality. Possibly it can be seen as a vehicle to demonstrate the changing nature of Henry, who was devastated by his imaginary uncle's death but, after an immediate challenge to Brandon for not reporting his sister's illness, seems quickly to forget he ever had a sibling. Just as Margaret's lack of children erases from history the Stuart line leading to Mary, Queen of Scots, and James VI and I, the complete absence of her sister Mary eliminated Jane Grey and her sisters.

Henry's coldness toward his sister is contrary to the heat in his bedroom throughout the series. His first romantic encounter—with Bessie Blount—occurs five-and-a-half minutes into the first episode, right after he declares war on France and the opening credits stop running. The graphic scene shows Henry kissing Bessie's inner thighs and feet, and the two throw themselves into passionate throes of love while the guards stand still outside the door. Henry follows their lovemaking by asking about Bessie's husband, though she did not actually marry until 1522 after their affair ended. The show significantly condenses the length of this relationship, though as Henry is already having a romantic tryst with Blount at the beginning, it is likely meant to be a continuation of an earlier affair. Blount caught Henry's eye as early as October 1514, when in a letter to Henry from France, Brandon refers to her and Elizabeth Carew (another possible mistress who does not appear in *The Tudors*).[10] The affair, though, likely did not begin in until 1517 or 1518, so the chronology concerning Bessie is relatively accurate, as she gave birth to Henry's only recognized bastard in 1519.

Henry never advertised his affairs, so the historical proof is scant, but from rumor and records of favors, it is likely he had been unfaithful to Catherine since as early as 1510, possibly with Lady Anne Stafford, whom Hirst makes into a lover of Brandon and not Henry. Blount is portrayed relatively accurately. She was supposedly beautiful, a good dancer, and one of the more accomplished ladies at Henry's court.[11] Ruta Gedmintas plays her in a very appealing manner during her run on the show, which lasts until episode five of the first season. By the end of Episode 1:1, though, the king returns to Catherine but finds her at prayer and turns to another Lady in Waiting, Jane Howard, a Hirst-created mistress who appears only in Episode 1:1 and may represent an affair that Henry may have had with Jane Popincourt around 1515 or 1516.[12]

By the end of Episode 1:1, the plot thickens as Bessie reveals to Wolsey that she is pregnant with Henry's child. The following episode has Bessie's imaginary husband promoted to an earldom and given additional estates. In actuality, Bessie and Henry likely continued their affair until 1522, when he married her to Gilbert Tailboys, and the following year parliament granted her land in her own name for life. On the show, the pregnancy apparently concludes the affair between Bessie and Henry. Furthermore, though Henry recognizes their child, Henry Fitzroy (Zak Jenciragic), as his own and bestows honors and titles upon him, the boy dies as a young child of about five or six. In reality, Fitzroy lived until 1536, and Pope Clement VII contemplated legitimizing him and sanctioning his marriage to his half-sister Mary in order to prevent the English Reformation. Bessie also had a daughter born likely in 1520, who was possibly a daughter of the king, but Henry did not acknowledge young Elizabeth Tailboys, and there is no hint of her or of Henry's other probable illegitimate children in the series.[13]

Henry's role as a sexual potentate continues until he becomes enthralled with Anne Boleyn and reemerges as he becomes disillusioned with her. Episode 1:2 includes not only Henry Fitzroy's birth but also the king's relationship with Mary Boleyn, Anne's sister. Perdita Weeks actually looks a fair amount like paintings of Mary Boleyn, and she interests Henry with her "French graces," but this affair is condensed as much as Bessie's was in the first episode. The entire relationship with Mary seems to last no more than a few weeks in 1520, whereas the real Mary married William Carey in 1520 and only entered Henry's bed in 1521–1522. She continued to have a relationship with Henry for three to four years and likely bore him at least one and possibly two children, Catherine and Henry Carey. Though Henry never recognized either child, both are widely assumed to have been royal offspring, particularly Catherine, who was born at the height of their affair. In the show, Henry gets bored by Mary very quickly and tells her to leave his bed almost immediately upon their return from France to Whitehall in 1520.

Henry then moves onto his next conquest. In Episode 1:3, as he begins to develop an interest in Anne Boleyn, he has a quick affair with an unknown woman played by Rachel Montague. She enters Henry's chamber in a luxurious gown that immediately falls to the floor in a scene that follows a touching moment between Catherine of Aragon and Princess

Mary. Hirst uses her primarily to build sympathy for Queen Catherine, the good mother waiting for her husband while he indulges himself with the thin, busty young woman. In Episode 1:4, Hirst exercises even greater historical license by bringing Marguerite of Navarre, one of the greatest female minds and scholars of the sixteenth century, before Henry shortly after Anne Boleyn first rejects his presents. The two gaze longingly into each other's eyes as Henry suggests that she must be compensated for leaving behind her husband. Marguerite was Francis I's sister and married both Charles of Alençon and Henri II of Navarre, but was unmarried at the time when this fictional tryst occurs. Wolsey brings Marguerite to Henry's attention to distract him from Anne, and Henry happily shares his bed with her as an insult to Francis. This is the most fictionalized of the relationships Henry has with an actual historical figure and is really just a gratuitous affair that occurs without any real advancement of the plot.

Henry's external relationships heat up again in the second season when he begins to tire of Anne Boleyn. In Episode 2:3, as a pregnant Anne further embraces the Protestant faith, Henry notices the invented Eleanor Luke dancing. When the child turns out to be the girl Elizabeth, Henry—who looked forward to having a legitimate son—invites Eleanor into his chamber for a game of naked chess and sleeps with her, ending his faithfulness to Anne. During Episode 2:4 Anne dismisses Eleanor, accusing her of stealing jewelry, and then follows her father's suggestion that she choose a mistress for Henry so his eyes will not wander too far from her. She chooses her cousin Madge Shelton (played by Laura Jane Laughlin), encourages Madge to go to Henry, tells her that the king admires her, and pretends that she is fine with Madge sleeping with the king. However, as the king and Madge ride off into the country, Anne is left in tears. In real life, the affair was with Mary Shelton, although historians for some time were confused between the two due to difficulty reading Chapuys' handwriting. It is unlikely that Anne pushed Mary on Henry, as this easily could have backfired, but Mary did not keep Henry's attention for long, as Chapuys states that the affair lasted only about six months. Chapuys was a strong supporter of Catherine and wanted the king's marriage to Anne to end, so his writings cannot be fully accepted; however, he suggests that Henry had several more affairs between 1534 and 1536, when he settled on Jane Seymour as his next bride.[14]

Henry's primary affair in this part of the series is with William Webbe's wife, Bess. The story behind this is that a rumor surfaced in 1537 that the king had met William Webbe and his wife and committed adultery with Bess. Cromwell and others investigated and found the story false, which supposedly cost Webbe his position in Westminster Sanctuary. Hirst brings this tale back to 1535 in Episode 2:5, when Henry stops Webbe and his beautiful wife, kisses Bess, and leads her to his bed. She is never seen again in the series. Analyzing this scene, Shannon McSheffrey determines that Hirst probably found material in the work of popular historian Alison Weir, who originally created a similar version of the story. She also emphasizes the need for sex in visual entertainment as an excuse for Hirst's representation of the mistresses.[15]

The final major mistress in the show is Ursula Missledon, played by Charlotte Salt in five episodes of Season Three. She is another creation of Hirst's imagination and allows him to bring Hans Holbein into the story by having him paint her in the nude as part of the seduction scene. Henry's extramarital sex life adds the juice to *The Tudors* to keep the audience enthralled and to maintain his image as a sex-hungry monarch.

As Jerome de Groot argues, *The Tudors* deconstructs history to revise twenty-first-century opinion of Henry VIII.[16] Henry's interactions with his extended family and his mistresses paint the picture of an on-screen king at least as complex as the historical Henry, even though his true historical persona is not accurately represented. Hirst moves far from history, at times with some artistic or plot advancing purpose and at times for no observable reason. The images he produces, though, of Henry's uncle, sister(s), bastards, and mistresses increase the sex appeal and the tragedy of the series and influence our own interpretations of Henry's life.

Notes

1. Allan Hazlett and Christy Mag Uidhir, "Unrealistic Fictions," *American Philosophical Quarterly* 48 (1) (2011): 43; Chris Curtis, "Michael Hirst, The Tudors," accessed May 21, 2009, http://www.broadcastnow.co.uk/michael-hirst-the-tudors/5001701.article.
2. Kelly Hart, *The Mistresses of Henry VIII* (Stroud, Gloucestershire: The History Press, 2009), 11–12; for the argument on the changes made by 1536, see Suzannah Lipscomb, *The Year that Changes Henry VIII: 1536* (Oxford: Lion Hudson, 2009), *passim*.
3. Tatiana C. String and Marcus Bull, eds., *Tudorism: Historical Imagination and the Appropriation of the Sixteenth Century* (Oxford: Oxford University Press, 2011), passim; Pasquagliano, "Description of Henry VIII, 1515," in C.H. Williams, ed., *English Historical Documents, 1485–1558*, V (London: Eyre & Spottiswoode, 1967), 388.

4. Richard Glen Eaves, *Henry VIII's Scottish Diplomacy, 1513–24* (Jericho, NY: Exposition Press, 1971), 70; Greg Walker, "The 'Expulsion of the Minions' of 1519 Reconsidered," *The Historical Journal* 32 (1) (1989): 8, 13; "Instructions to Sir Richard Wingfield, Ambassador to the Emperor, 7 May 1521," in J.S. Brewer, ed., *Letters and Papers, Foreign and Domestic, Henry VIII*, vol. 3 (London: Her Majesty's Stationery Office, 1867), 481–484, accessed March 3, 2015, http://www.british-history.ac.uk/letters-papers-hen8/vol3/pp481-484.
5. Eaves, *Henry VIII's Scottish Diplomacy*, 67–68.
6. For more on the two sisters, see Nancy Lenz Harvey, *The Rose and The Thorn: The Lives of Mary and Margaret Tudor* (New York: Macmillan, 1975); Hester W. Chapman, *The Sisters of Henry VIII* (London: Jonathan Cape, 1969).
7. For more on Brandon, see: S.J. Gunn, *Charles Brandon, Duke of Suffolk, c. 1484–1545* (Oxford: Basil Blackwell, 1988).
8. Patricia Hill Buchanan, *Margaret Tudor, Queen of Scots* (Edinburgh and London: Scottish Academic Press, 1985), 207.
9. Erin Sadlack, *The French Queen's Letters: Mary Tudor Brandon and the Politics of Marriage in Sixteenth-Century Europe* (New York: Palgrave Macmillan, 2011), *passim*.
10. "Charles Brandon to Henry VIII, October 25, 1514," BL Cotton Caligula DVI, f. 155, cited in Elizabeth Norton, *Bessie Blount, Mistress to Henry VIII* (Stroud, Gloucestershire: Amberley, 2013), 122–123.
11. Norton, *Bessie Blount*, 95.
12. Hart, *The Mistresses of Henry VIII*, 35–38.
13. Norton, *Bessie Blount*, Chapter 11.
14. Hart, *The Mistresses of Henry VIII*, 122–124.
15. Shannon McSheffrey, "William Webbe's Wench: Henry VIII, History, and Popular Culture," in Mariem Pagès and Karolyn Kinane, eds., *The Middle Ages on Television: Critical Essays* (Jefferson, NC: McFarland, 2015), 53–77.
16. Jerome de Groot, "Slashing History: *The Tudors*," in String and Bull, eds., *Tudorism*, 243–260.

CHAPTER 8

The King's In-Laws in *The Tudors*

Anne Throckmorton

In *On the Family*, Leon Battista Alberti identified acquiring awful in-laws as one of the most calamitous things that could happen to a man in search of a wife: "I think that no one is so great a fool that he would not rather remain unmarried than burden himself with terrible relatives."[1] Henry VIII was unusual in that he had six opportunities to get it right—or wrong—when it came to assessing the tolerability of the in-laws he acquired along with his spouses. Indeed, the monarch was fortunate in the talent and industry he was able to extract from the male relatives of his English brides while those queens were in favor. Unlike the families to which Alberti alluded, the king did not have to suffer horrible relatives for very long because they were discarded as easily as his wives. Ironically, while *The Tudors* depicts a highly proactive family politics wherein relatives strategically engineer liaisons and marriages to the king, Michael Hirst—executive producer and writer of the series—is just as reactive as the historical Howard, Boleyn, and Seymour men. Whereas they had to react to the vagaries of their king's lust, Hirst has to respond to the vagaries of actor availability, the tight time constraints of commercial television, the viewing audience's ability to follow tangled family relationships among people

A. Throckmorton (✉)
Department of History, Randolph-Macon College, Ashland, VA, USA

© The Editor(s) (if applicable) and The Author(s) 2016
W.B. Robison (ed.), *History, Fiction, and* The Tudors,
Queenship and Power, DOI 10.1057/978-1-137-43883-6_8

who often shared the same names, and the need to showcase Jonathan Rhys Meyers as Henry VIII along with his complicated marital history.

Though Henry's first set of in-laws provided plenty of drama in real life that television might exploit to good effect, *The Tudors* begins around 1518, by which time Catherine's parents were dead, as were all her siblings except Joanna "the Mad," who was imprisoned. Otherwise, Season One establishes the series' distressing propensity for conflating historical personages as well as introducing pivotal characters only to have them disappear. It is never entirely clear in the first season whether Henry Czerny is playing the 2nd or 3rd Duke of Norfolk, both of whom were named Thomas Howard; in fact, he seems to be an amalgamation of both men. The 2nd Duke was Anne Boleyn and Catherine Howard's grandfather, while the 3rd Duke was the uncle of both queens. As Thomas Howard, Czerny presides over the trial of the traitorous Duke of Buckingham and is also the father of Henry Howard, the ill-fated Earl of Surrey. In reality, it was the 2nd duke of Norfolk, a man in his 70s, who pronounced Buckingham guilty in 1521 and his son, the future 3rd duke of Norfolk, who sired Henry Howard. Czerny, a youthful and handsome 40-something when he filmed *The Tudors*, in no way resembles the septuagenarian 2nd Duke of Norfolk who reportedly wept as he sentenced Buckingham to death.

In the series, Charles Brandon, Duke of Suffolk—played by Henry Cavill—suborns Norfolk into delivering a guilty verdict against Buckingham. Brandon—who takes his orders directly from Henry VIII— accosts Norfolk in a palace hallway along with his son Henry, who appears to be about ten years old, although the historical Henry Howard could not have been more than three or four at the time. Brandon reminds Norfolk of his responsibilities and gives him a ring. Again, confusion reigns. Upon receiving the ring, Norfolk says, "This is my father's ring. He was executed by his Majesty's father. Did you know that?"[2] But any English courtier worthy of the designation knew the genealogy of Tudor executions, and John Howard, 1st Duke of Norfolk—father of the 2nd Duke and grandfather of the 3rd—was not executed but died in battle in 1485 when Henry VII defeated Richard III at Bosworth.[3] The 2nd Duke fought alongside his father and then spent the next two decades rehabilitating the family's reputation. In 1513, he won a great victory against the Scots at Flodden, a year later Henry restored his dukedom, and the family continued its conservative strategy of supporting the crowned king.[4] Yet, when Brandon confronts Norfolk, it is as if it is 1485 all over again, and the Howards still have substantial toadying to do. Brandon warns Norfolk to see to his son's future: "It would be terrible, for example, if some action of yours were to deprive him of a father, a title, and a ring."[5]

As it turned out, the real son's shenanigans almost deprived the historical 3rd Duke of his life, but the viewers never see this because Czerny did not return after the first season of *The Tudors*, compounding the errors of conflating the two Dukes. There may have been practical reasons for this decision to amalgamate Norfolk. Certainly, it is cheaper to pay one actor rather than two. Also it is undeniable that if one were to shout for Thomas in a Tudor palace, a crowd of important people might respond. Perhaps, Hirst feared that viewers would have difficulty distinguishing between so many characters named Thomas and so many sets of fathers and sons.

Still, the decision to combine the two Norfolks had major plot implications for the series after Czerny's departure. Rather than replace him, Hirst allows the character to melt into an off-air background, after which only Anne Boleyn refers to him—once in Season Two. This is unfortunate, for in real life, the 3rd duke of Norfolk continued the family tradition of playing the king's reliable angel of death when he presided over the trials, convictions, and executions of Anne and George Boleyn. Much later in Henry's reign, Norfolk leveraged the king's lust for another of his nieces into more power and position, only to desert that niece—Catherine Howard—in her time of trouble in order to save his own life. He was also instrumental in the destruction of another of the king's great ministers, Thomas Cromwell. In *The Tudors*, Cromwell and Howard never meet on screen. In the waning days of the king's rule, the real Norfolk sought to position himself to dominate the next reign, but his machinations earned him a long stay in the Tower of London and contributed to the death of his son, Henry Howard, Earl of Surrey. It is a shame that due to the apparent lack of actor availability, Hirst opted to eliminate from his series one of the most important political actors in the reign of Henry VIII.

With no Norfolk, Hirst creates incongruous alliances among other characters to move the narrative forward. For example, he has the Seymour brothers colluding with Brandon to put Catherine Howard in the path of the king. While the Seymours could be friendly with the Howards if it benefited them, they never would have promoted a woman from a rival family, especially when it could be expected that the lands settled on the dead Jane Seymour would be transferred from Seymour to Howard control—which is exactly what happened.[6] Norfolk is not the only essential character to disappear because an actor left the show. Thomas Cranmer, the theological architect of England's Reformation, apparently goes on indefinite embassy to the continent after actor Hans Matheson leaves for more prestigious roles on the big screen. The only character in the series to be recast is Jane Seymour, Henry's third wife, with Annabelle Wallis replacing Anita Briem for Season Three. Apparently, a wife of Henry VIII is indispensable.

One strength of Season One, with its very present and active Duke of Norfolk, is the establishment of a hierarchy of deference within the Howard and Boleyn clans with Norfolk properly assuming the mantle of head of the family and Thomas Boleyn serving as junior partner to his father-in-law. The interaction between Norfolk and Boleyn reveals the latter to be a wily politician who keeps his own counsel and is beholden to his father-in-law, but at the same time resents his subordinate position. For example, when they update each other on their plan to use Boleyn's daughter Anne to ensnare the king, Norfolk observes, "When she opens her legs for him, she can open her mouth and denounce Wolsey. They do say the sharpest blades are sheathed in the softest pouches."[7] As Norfolk walks away, Boleyn glowers impotently at his father-in-law's receding back.

Not only did Thomas Boleyn owe deference to Norfolk, so too did his children. There was a pecking order not only among courtiers but also within families, who were bound by blood and marriage but not necessarily by affection. In Episode 1:2, Anne Boleyn—played by Natalie Dormer—greets her uncle, Norfolk, by kneeling and kissing his hand. By the season finale, Anne openly chafes at her family's cadet status at a dinner party with her uncle. At this juncture, Wolsey is out of favor but appears to be working his way back into the king's affections. Norfolk informs his niece that the king is pondering a pardon for his erstwhile minister. Anne asks Norfolk how he responded to the king. He replies, "I agreed with His Majesty that the cardinal has many talents."[8] As the acknowledged favorite of the king, Anne proceeds to do what few women of the Tudor age could afford by challenging a male authority figure and questioning Norfolk's actions: "I cannot believe you did this! Have you not spoken yourself of the terrible vengeance he [Wolsey] would exact on all of us if he ever again had the power?"[9] Anne Boleyn then scowls and throws her napkin on the table in disgust, at which point the scene abruptly ends. There was much promise in this interchange. The historical Anne's notorious arrogance grew with her power. By the time she became queen, she had begun to alienate even her supporters, including Norfolk, who behind her back called her "the great whore."[10] The promise of this interaction is unfulfilled because Czerny and the character of Norfolk disappear.

The introduction of Thomas Boleyn in Season One establishes a series device whereby a character talks about the traits of another character in order to condition viewer perception of the person being discussed. For example, the audience is introduced to Boleyn when he is summoned into the presence of the Duke of Buckingham, who upon meeting Boleyn says, "They tell me you are an excellent ambassador."[11] Later, Boleyn visits a rusticated Charles Brandon to enlist him in the plot to orchestrate Wolsey's downfall. In the course of the meeting, Brandon observes: "You're a clever man Boleyn. That is what people say. They say you are charming and clever."[12] This series was ambitious in scope and expensive to produce. Under pressure to generate episodes of roughly 55 minutes each, Hirst perhaps did not have the luxury of allowing each of the show's characters to develop organically. He quickly had to establish identities for actors appearing in a limited number of episodes before they were, in most cases, killed off or left the series for other projects.

Hirst's determination to showcase Jonathan Rhys Meyers as Henry VIII and to focus on marital politics at the Tudor court explains why viewers might well believe that sex was the only way to cultivate royal favor. The emphasis on Henry's marital misadventures means that the series ignores the very real accomplishments of Norfolk and Boleyn prior to Anne's rise. In fact, both had achieved much long before Henry's eyes lit upon Mary or Anne Boleyn.[13] As mentioned before, the 2nd Duke of Norfolk won a great victory at Flodden with aid from his son. The 3rd Duke played a major role in suppressing the Pilgrimage of Grace—a role Brandon assumes in Season Two following Czerny's departure—and won another major victory against the Scots in 1542. He also served Henry in a variety of other roles such as Lord Treasurer and Lord High Admiral.

Boleyn had compiled a distinguished record as a diplomat even when Anne was in the schoolroom. Indeed, his achievements were instrumental in providing his daughter with an exceptional education. Boleyn served so capably as Henry's ambassador to the Netherlands that he secured Anne a position as maid of honor to Archduchess Margaret at the most sophisticated court in Europe.[14] In real life, as in the series, Boleyn also played a major role in organizing the Field of Cloth of Gold meeting between Henry VIII and Francis I in 1520, by which time Anne was serving as lady-in-waiting to Queen Claude of France.

In spite of their significant historical roles, the primary function of Norfolk and Boleyn in *The Tudors* is to engineer Anne's marriage to the king. In the series, they summon her home from France when Henry's interest in her sister Mary starts to wane. Nick Dunning's Thomas Boleyn bribes the Master of Revels at the Tudor court to include Anne in a pageant being staged for the imperial ambassador. In the course of besieging the fictional *Chateau Vert*, Henry falls in love with Anne Boleyn. Both Anne and Mary appeared in the historical pageant of 1522, as did Henry, but apparently he did not notice either Boleyn sister. Mary became his mistress first, and the royal eye did not fix its gaze upon Anne Boleyn until 1526 at the earliest, and as William Robison has noted, when Anne caught the king's attention, she did so without her father or uncle's assistance or insistence.[15] The series makes another incongruous historical leap when Norfolk and Boleyn betray the traitorous Buckingham. In reality, Buckingham had no trouble betraying himself, and Norfolk and Boleyn's collective sense of self-preservation would never have allowed them to be near the duke when he self-destructed.

The character and historical personage of Thomas Boleyn benefits from *The Tudors* in that he receives more face time than in any other on-screen Tudor treatment to date. Nick Dunning brings a forceful presence to the role and effectively depicts the wily, urbane diplomat who leverages every opportunity to advance himself and his family. Unfortunately, Dunning's Boleyn has to bear too much of the weight of Season Two because in addition to his own duties, he also takes on the tasks reserved for the absent Norfolk. Dunning's Boleyn lobbies parliament and convocation to approve the break with the Roman Church and hires Richard Rouse to poison John Fisher, the Bishop of Rochester and a major stumbling block to the annulment of the marriage between Henry and Catherine of Aragon.[16] Dunning's Boleyn also appears to be one of the primary compilers of the *Valor Ecclesiasticus*, a damning inventory of monastic houses that triggered their dissolution. In his spare time, Dunning's Boleyn travels all the way to Ludlow Castle on the Welsh marches to inform Mary Tudor of her bastardization by parliament and periodically goes to France to spar with Francis I about his refusal to recognize Anne as queen.

In the midst of all this activity, Dunning's Boleyn prods his children to stay on task. He never allows Anne, Mary, and George to forget that they must pursue power, even at the expense of personal happiness. Thomas Boleyn reminds Anne in Season One that it is her duty to use the king's love to do Cardinal Wolsey "a great hurt."[17] In Season Two, when Mary turns up pregnant and married to a man of low degree, Boleyn abruptly disowns her. When George balks at marrying Jane Parker, father strides up to his son at the altar, physically forces him to bow his head, and whispers to him, "Get on with it!"[18] While it is doubtful that the historical Anne ever felt hesitant about doing Wolsey a bad turn or that George protested his arranged marriage, Boleyn's treatment of Mary and the expectation that noble children put family fortunes first is certainly accurate. Boleyn's callous casting aside of Mary also reflects patriarchal attitudes of the time. Dunning expresses this sentiment beautifully in Season Two when he confronts Anne for challenging her husband's chief minister, Thomas Cromwell, about how funds from the Dissolution of the Monasteries are being spent. He castigates his daughter for having the temerity to challenge male authority: "Anne, I did not bring you up to have opinions or to express them or to quarrel with those closest to the Crown."[19]

Boleyn's dressing down of his daughter and his regular servings of reality to her—"The danger to you and us, is not that the king takes a mistress, but that he takes the wrong one"—alternate with an almost lover-like reverence for his offspring.[20] For example, when he enlists Anne to replace Mary in the king's affection, he observes that she has the skill not only to capture but also to keep Henry's interest. "There's something deep and dangerous in you, Anne," he says as he strokes her face. "Those eyes of yours are like dark hooks for the soul."[21] In the second season, Boleyn displays a tender regard for Anne's pregnant condition, warning her to not allow the king's attentions to Jane Seymour to upset her or her unborn child. Once Anne gives Henry a son, father reminds daughter, her rival will disappear. At this juncture, Dunning says, "Think that I am the angel come down to tell you that you carry the Christ child in your belly."[22] He then kneels down, places his hands tenderly on Anne's stomach and reverently kisses it. The historical Boleyn probably never did this, but he and his family certainly regarded the delivery of a healthy boy as the family's salvation. When Anne miscarried, many jealous courtiers started circling the Boleyn clan, looking for opportunities to destroy the family.[23]

When Anne and George Boleyn are arrested, Dunning's Boleyn heartlessly abandons his children. During an interrogation, he condemns his daughter and her alleged paramours: "All those men, whatever their rank or station who deceived the king and slipped between the sheets with his lawful wife ... for such awful adultery, there should be only one punishment."[24] He refuses to watch his son's execution and smiles when he learns he will keep his earldom, although he is being deprived of the offices that bring him in contact with the king. When he is released from the Tower, he looks up at his daughter and then turns his back on her. Some care was actually taken to spare the historical Thomas Boleyn during the trials of his children. As a peer, he would have been expected to serve on the jury and pass judgment, but he was excused from this duty. The real Boleyn also was relieved of his offices but retained his earldom even as he retired to his estates, presumably to ponder all he and his family had lost. The historical Boleyn continued to fulfill his duties as a peer by playing a major role in the christening of Prince Edward, the son of his former son-in-law and his daughter's replacement, Jane Seymour.[25] Dunning does not reappear in the series after Anne is executed, although in Season Four Brandon refers to his recent death in conversation with the imperial ambassador, who observes that the only ones who mourned the passing of the Boleyn patriarch were "the ghosts of his children."[26]

The ghost of George Boleyn surely came back to haunt Michael Hirst for the way he is maligned in *The Tudors*. During the first season, George, portrayed by Padraic Delaney, is the annoying brother, snatching the king's love letters from Anne and reading the more treacly parts aloud. As he grows to understand the possibilities of his sister's royal popularity, he acts like a randy, entitled fraternity boy, approaching two of Catherine of Aragon's maids of honor and promising them great riches and fame if they agree to be guided by him in their sexual exploits. In Season Two, Hirst has George engage in a number of actions that are mostly unsupported by the historical record. For example, he engineers the ouster of the king's new (imaginary) mistress Elizabeth Luke by framing her for theft, embarks on a homosexual love affair with Mark Smeaton, turns up drunk at his wedding, and brutally rapes his new wife.[27] George's immature, brutal on-screen behavior is hard to square with the perceptive and learned persona that Hirst simultaneously tries to create for him, mainly through the observations of other characters. While George is shown procuring sexual favors and romping with the hired help, the audience is supposed to believe he is persuading English bishops to accept the Royal Supremacy and that he favors religious reform. The historical George certainly was a gifted politician and diplomat, as well as a student of theology and the so-called New Learning.[28] However, it is difficult for the audience to glean these aspects of Boleyn's character when, in one of the more ridiculous scenes of the series, Boleyn fails to recognize a technological innovation that had been around for at least 70 years: "Oh my Lord! What is God's name is that," Boleyn exclaims to Thomas Cromwell. "It's a printing press, my lord. And it will change the world," responds the minister.[29]

Whether George Boleyn and Mark Smeaton had a sexual relationship is the subject of historiographical debate. What is indisputable is that *The Tudors* inaccurately depicts their nonsexual interaction. As a musician, Smeaton never would have initiated conversations with his betters, let alone made emotional demands upon them as he does in the series. For example, at the celebration of Catherine of Aragon's death, Smeaton—played by David Alpay—asks George if he has told his wife about their relationship. But such a relationship would have been shrouded in secrecy because sodomy was a capital offense, and while wives might have been aware of their husbands' extramarital exploits, sexual double standards of the day meant that most would have hesitated to castigate their husbands about such dalliances. Nonetheless, this unlikely interchange between Boleyn and Smeaton provides Delaney with his best line in the series: "If you could read Greek, Master Smeaton, you'd know that even the gods had problems with their wives."[30] Aside from depicting George as a rapist, a procurer of sex and murder, and a feckless playboy, Hirst denies this character what should have been his finest hour. During his trial for treason and incest, the historical George acquitted himself so well that many spectators were sure he would be exonerated. But the series does not show his trial. Instead, viewers are treated to a craven, blubbering man who deserts the sister to whom he hitherto has been so loyal.

When the Boleyn family fell from favor, it was the Seymour family's turn to enjoy the royal largesse inevitably showered upon the king's in-laws. *The Tudors* does not pay much attention to Sir John Seymour, the patriarch of the queen's family, who is portrayed by Stephen Brennan. John Seymour only appears in Season Two, and his main function is to remind viewers of the physical and spiritual purity of his daughter, Jane. Brennan's Seymour is a kindly man who recognizes that the king is charmed by his daughter and quickly enlists his son Edward to cultivate the royal interest. Like their historical counterparts, John and Edward Seymour of *The Tudors* employ the Boleyn strategy of dangling Jane's innocence before the king with Edward warning his sister not to succumb to sexual temptation.

When the real Jane Seymour first caught Henry's eye, the historical John Seymour had retired to his estates after a long and distinguished career as a soldier and a courtier. He died not long after his daughter wed the king. As a result, his son Edward benefited most from being related to the queen. In *The Tudors*, as in real life, Sir John retires early from the drama, and Edward Seymour, played by Max Brown, becomes a major political player at court. Despite Brown's somewhat accurate depiction of

Edward as aloof, ambitious, and gifted with the talent of forging alliances with people close to the king, there is one important thing that Brown's Seymour does in the series that his historical counterpart never would have done, that is, tolerating the adulterous adventures of his wife. In one of the series' most egregious character assassinations, Anne Stanhope—played by Emma Hamilton—has affairs with Sir Francis Bryan and her brother-in-law, Thomas Seymour, and engages in heavy petting with the Earl of Surrey. In the series, Edward Seymour is aware of his wife's infidelities but, though annoyed by them, does not cast his wife aside. In contrast, when the historical Edward Seymour suspected his first wife of adultery, he repudiated her and apparently refused to recognize the legitimacy of the children born during their marriage. His second wife was Anne Stanhope, a strong-minded woman and staunch evangelical who was said to rule her husband.[31]

In the series, Anne Stanhope has a child, but it is not her husband's. The baby is the result of her liaison with her brother-in-law, Thomas Seymour, played by Andrew McNair. The historical Thomas Seymour was something of a philanderer and rake, pursuing marriages with rich, politically well-connected women, including Catherine Parr, the sixth queen of Henry VIII.[32] However, there is no evidence that he had an affair with his morally upright sister-in-law. McNair's Thomas conveys the simmering resentment that his historical counterpart had toward his more talented older brother but with none of the dashing charm the real Thomas possessed. In the series, Thomas is written as a bland punching bag for the king who not only insults his courtier and brother-in-law but also steals his woman. Additionally, the Thomas of *The Tudors* is not nearly as reprehensible as the historical Thomas. As David Starkey has argued, Seymour tried to marry Mary and Elizabeth Tudor before settling for Catherine Parr. Once married to Parr, he became Elizabeth's guardian and may have sexually abused her when she was a teenager.[33] His vaunting ambition led to his execution during the reign of his nephew, Edward VI.

The end of Henry's reign witnessed a power struggle among conservative and evangelical factions at court to control the future King Edward VI during his minority. Edward Seymour triumphed in this struggle, which pitted him against Thomas Howard, 3rd Duke of Norfolk, and his son, Henry Howard, the Earl of Surrey.[34] In Season Four of *The Tudors*, Surrey reappears to duel with the Seymour brothers and is the beneficiary of soap-opera style aging. The young boy seen in Season One manages to age at least 30 more years in the 15-year time span covered by the series.

David O'Hara was in his early 40s when he took on the role of Surrey, and he looks more mature and has more presence than Jonathan Rhys Meyer's Henry, whose historical counterpart was old enough to father Surrey. The historical Surrey was brought up in a royal household with Henry Fitzroy, Henry's illegitimate son. When Fitzroy died in 1536 at the age of 17, there was no one of comparable rank with whom Surrey could associate, and he was vocal in his assessment of the relative inferiority of other English peers.[35] Unfortunately, in *The Tudors*, the relationship between Fitzroy and Surrey is not explored because Hirst kills off Fitzroy at the age of three or four in the first season. By not showing the Fitzroy-Surrey connection, a rich source of motivation for the arrogance and anger that O'Hara so effectively displays is ignored. Not showing the relationship also makes it difficult for viewers to believe Jonathan Rhys Meyers when he claims that he has long loved Surrey but that the earl has destroyed that love and so must be destroyed.

The decision by Hirst to not recast the Duke of Norfolk after the first season meant that in Season Three, an unlikely band of confederates—including the Seymour brothers, Charles Brandon, and Francis Bryan—orchestrate the marriage between Henry and his fifth wife, Catherine Howard. This unfortunate queen was Norfolk's niece and Surrey's cousin. Because O'Hara was only hired for the final season and Norfolk had disappeared, the family exploitation of the rise of Catherine Howard is not shown. Only once in passing in Season Four does O'Hara remind Catherine of their connection. During the queen's execution scene, O'Hara's Surrey pointedly snubs the queen when he passes her on the scaffold.

The historical Surrey's illustrious pedigree was the defining feature of his character, and O'Hara's Surrey stays true to this in *The Tudors*. He constantly bemoans the advancement of inferior persons and is quick to assault any man who cast aspersions on his family name. Surrey is depicted quite rightly as a man whose ancestry weighs heavily upon him and for whom being denied the opportunity to serve his king is akin to exile. Such a denial of service did in fact take place when the historical Surrey suffered a major loss at the skirmish of St. Etienne in 1546 and Henry recalled him. This defeat served to underscore Edward Seymour's position as the leading general of the 1540s when he replaced Surrey in France.[36] *The Tudors* does not show the defeat at St. Etienne, but news of it does mark a turning point in the king's trust of one of his higher-ranking nobles, an accurate echo of what happened between the historical Henry and Surrey.

The military defeat and Surrey's recall from France set in motion his downfall in reality and on *The Tudors*. However, the series does not address a major reason for Surrey's trial for treason. In the last months of Henry's reign, a power struggle developed between the old nobility and the new men at court. Most courtiers knew the king was dying, but Surrey was foolhardy enough to proclaim loudly and often that his father, Norfolk, should act as regent for Edward VI until he came of age. To speak of the king's death was treason, and such rash words landed Surrey and his father in the Tower of London. Father and son were convicted, and Surrey executed on January 19, 1547. In *The Tudors*, Norfolk is not around for Surrey to promote as the future powerbroker of the monarchy. However, he is convicted of quartering the arms of St. Edward the Confessor with the arms of the Howards, an indication to the king and other powerful people that Surrey has designs on the throne of England. The historical Surrey was also condemned for quartering the arms of Edward the Confessor with his own, but as Lucy Wooding had pointed out, his conviction was more a function of the old king's fears of impending death and worries about safely passing his crown to his young son.[37]

The Tudors is diverting to watch. It features beautiful actors with perfect teeth wearing beautiful clothes and jewelry and having beautiful sex. The series scores high in entertainment value, particularly in the first and second seasons, and is especially effective at showcasing the young, charismatic Henry VIII, who is frequently represented in other television and film versions by the old, fat, bitter Henry VIII of the late 1530s and 1540s. There is serendipity in casting Jonathan Rhys Meyers, who won a Golden Globe award and earned an Emmy nomination for his portrayal of the young Elvis Presley, who is frequently lost in the polyester, sequined, and jump-suited memories of his later years. Like the young—and old—Elvis, Henry owned every stage he walked on at every age in his life. In an effort to capture Henry's charisma, his instinctive showmanship, and surprisingly modern insistence on being in love with his wives, Hirst keeps the supporting players of Henry's life in their places. In the process, factual integrity is often lost and some historical personages are unfairly maligned or just disappear. While *The Tudors* imparts a strong sense of the allure and danger of family politics at the Tudor court, it reduces many people with many accomplishments to two-dimensional beings. Ironically, to make it at the real court of Henry VIII, most courtiers had to mask their true feelings and motives, so perhaps Tudor politics got what it deserved in *The Tudors*.

Notes

1. Leon Battista Alberti, *On the Family* in *Sources of the West*, 2nd ed., vol. 1, ed. Mark A. Kishlansky (New York: HarperCollins College Publishers, 1995), 213.
2. *The Tudors*, Episode 1:2.
3. Paul Murray Kendall, *Richard the Third* (New York and London: W.W. Norton & Company, 2002), 439–440.
4. Edwin Casady, "A Reinterpretation of Surrey's Character and Actions," *PMLA* 51 (3) (September 1936): 627.
5. *The Tudors*, Episode 1:2.
6. Antonia Fraser, *The Wives of Henry VIII* (New York: Vintage Books, 1994), 332–333.
7. *The Tudors*, Episode 1:3.
8. *The Tudors*, Episode 1:19.
9. Ibid.
10. Fraser, *Wives*, 218.
11. *The Tudors*, Episode 1:6.
12. Ibid.
13. Lucy Wooding, *Henry VIII* (London and New York: Routledge, 2009), 123.
14. Ibid., 113.
15. Retha M. Warnicke, *The Rise and Fall of Anne Boleyn* (Cambridge University Press, 1989), 38.
16. Boleyn involvement in this infamous incident has never been established beyond reasonable doubt, although as Lucy Wooding points out in her biography of Henry VIII, "Popular rumour blamed the Boleyns," Lucy Wooding, *Henry VIII*, 164.
17. *The Tudors*, Episode 1:6.
18. Ibid.
19. *The Tudors*, Episode 2:7.
20. *The Tudors*, Episode 2:4.
21. *The Tudors*, Episode 1:2.
22. *The Tudors*, Episode 2:8.
23. Wooding, *Henry VIII*, 198.
24. *The Tudors*, Episode 2:9.
25. Julia Fox, *Jane Boleyn, The True Story of the Infamous Lady Rochford* (New York: Ballantine Books, 2007), 226.
26. *The Tudors*, Episode 4:1.
27. Retha Warnicke argues that a homosexual relationship did exist between George Boleyn and Mark Smeaton and that the reputation of sexual licentiousness in the queen's court contributed to the downfall of Anne Boleyn, Warnicke, *The Rise and Fall of Anne Boleyn*, 191–233.

28. Fox, *Jane Boleyn*, 30.
29. *The Tudors*, Episode 2:6.
30. *The Tudors*, Episode 2:7.
31. Fraser, Wives, 235.
32. David Starkey, *Rivals in Power, Lives and Letters of the Great Tudor Dynasties* (New York: Grove Weidenfeld, 1990), 115.
33. David Starkey, *Elizabeth: The Struggle for the Throne* (New York: HarperCollins Publishers, 2001), 67.
34. Christopher Haigh, *English Reformations: Religion, Politics and Society under the Tudors* (Oxford University Press, 1993), 164–167.
35. Susan Brigden, "Henry Howard, Earl of Surrey, and the 'Conjured League,'" *The Historical Journal* 37 (3) (September 1994): 509–510.
36. David Grummitt, "The Court, War and Noble Power in England, c. 1475–1558," in Steven Gunn and Antheun Janse, eds., *The Court as a Stage, England and the Low Countries in the Later Middle Ages* (Woodbridge: The Boydell Press, 2006), 152–153.
37. Wooding, *Henry VIII*, 271.

CHAPTER 9

The King's Friends in *The Tudors*

Victor L. Stater

The Tudor monarchy was a personal one in a very real sense. The sovereign's personal choices, his priorities, his desires, even his whims had a dramatic effect upon the course of English history in the sixteenth century. While reality always constrained Henry VIII—even though he often raged against it—he was perhaps the only person in his realm capable of setting or altering the course of English history through his personal choices. Policy was made at Court, where Henry and the royal family lived, worked, and played. The bureaucratic and institutional structures that later dominated government and politics—parliament, the Exchequer, and the courts of law—paled in significance when compared to the intimate spaces of the royal court. Here power and reward, as well as danger and even physical survival, depended first of all upon personal relationships. Courtly life revolved around alliances and rivalries forged through family ties, local and regional connections, and a constantly changing calculus of personal interests. Apparently rock-solid relationships—such as that between Anne Boleyn and Thomas Cromwell—might vanish virtually overnight in the struggle for power and survival. *The Tudors* skillfully reflects this atmosphere—while there are important scenes set outside the palace, most of the action takes place at court, and rightly so.[1]

V.L. Stater (✉)
Department of History, Louisiana State University, Baton Rouge, LA, USA

"Let nothing draw thee from court" was the advice given to Elizabeth I's ill-fated favorite, the Earl of Essex, and the advice was sound. Proximity to the court was vital—and in Essex's case prolonged absence spelled doom—but no less important for the ambitious was staying close to the monarch. Among courtiers, the hope was to be chosen for positions affording easy access to the king, especially as a member of the king's Privy Chamber. The most envied position at court was that of the Groom of the Stool, the officer whose formal duty was to attend Henry when he was at his close stool. We cannot assume that the Groom of the Stool actually emptied Henry's chamber pot—though we should not rule the possibility out—but we know that he had privileged access to the king, access that could easily be parlayed into powerful influence. Henry had four Grooms of the Stool during the course of his reign, two of whom are depicted in *The Tudors*: Sir William Compton, played by Kris Holden-Ried, and Sir Henry Norris, played by Stephan Hogan. Compton and Norris are among the few courtiers who we know were Henry's friends before his accession in 1509. But only Compton shows up in Season One.[2]

The historical Compton served as a page to Henry when he was Duke of York, so their friendship must have begun before Henry was 11 years old. Although Compton maintained a low profile politically, he missed no opportunity to profit by his relationship to the king. Henry appointed him to a wide range of offices and sinecures, the profits of which allowed him to expand his family's estate dramatically. By the time he died in 1528, he had built an impressive estate centered upon the great Warwickshire mansion, Compton Wynyates, still today the home of his descendant, the seventh Marquis of Northampton. In *The Tudors*, Compton appears in the first seven episodes of Season One, where he is one of Henry VIII's closest companions, along with Charles Brandon, played by Henry Cavill, and the semifictional Anthony Knivert (based on Sir Thomas Knyvett), played by Callum Blue. For example, the three accompany the king to the Field of the Cloth of Gold in 1520 and place bets on the infamous wrestling match between Henry and Francis I. Compton also takes the lead in the rather inaccurately depicted arrest of Edward Stafford, 3rd Duke of Buckingham in 1521. In one of writer Michael Hirst's more peculiar deviations from history, Compton becomes the lover of composer Thomas Tallis, who appears at the Tudor court more than two decades earlier than he did in reality and becomes a bisexual philanderer in the process. Episode 1:7 correctly portrays Compton dying as a victim of a nationwide outbreak of the mysterious disease called the "sweating sickness," but invents a pathos-laden scene in which Tallis mourns his death.[3]

If the real Compton represents the rewards of close friendship with the king, the fate of Henry's second Groom of the Stool, Sir Henry Norris, shows that royal friendship could be deadly. Norris had been close to the King from the mid-1510s. His family, like Compton's, were landed gentry with a history of court connections—his father, grandfather, and great grandfather all had held minor posts at court. His father was an early supporter of Henry VII, probably fighting for him at Bosworth in 1485. So Norris would have been quite familiar with the court and its ways when he came to the young king's attention, most likely at the regular jousts and courtly entertainments staged for Henry's amusement. By 1518, the year in which *The Tudors* opens, he was a gentleman of the privy chamber and in constant attendance upon Henry. The king relied upon him for personal services of all kinds—paying his debts, and even serving as a witness to Henry and Anne Boleyn's private marriage in early 1533. By this time Norris was Groom of the Stool and the Chief Gentleman of the Privy Chamber, and he exercised considerable influence on royal patronage—he became for many the gateway to office, and he profited accordingly. But *The Tudors* shows none of this, for it often has characters appear late, for example, Norris, Sir Francis Bryan, and the Earl of Surrey; or disappear at the end of a season, for example, the Duke of Norfolk, Thomas Cranmer, and again Bryan.[4]

Norris, like his predecessor Compton, accumulated offices and lands that raised him high; indeed, by 1536, his income was greater than that of many nobles. However, this prosperity came with risks—Norris was a close friend to Henry, generally popular at court, and as such he excited Thomas Cromwell's jealousy. Cromwell's ambitions allowed for no rivals in the distribution of Henry's favors, and the destruction of Anne Boleyn offered him the opportunity to remove a troublesome competitor. It is at this point that Hirst inserts Norris into *The Tudors*. Recently widowed, he gets the king's permission to marry Madge Shelton, a marriage he did consider but never carried out. Norris also appears as the king's adversary during the joust when he was knocked unconscious. The series depicts Anne seeking his help in urging Francis I to agree to a French marriage of her daughter Elizabeth, Norris visiting her chamber, the queen teasing him about preferring her to his intended bride, and Madge—jealous of their relationship—naming him to Cromwell as one of the men the queen entertained inappropriately.[5]

In the midst of a lavish May Day joust organized at Greenwich, the real Norris, preparing to lead a team into the lists, was suddenly called away to return to London with the king. A bewildered Norris found himself personally accused by Henry of adultery with Anne. The scene is admirably played in *The Tudors*. Henry offered Norris a pardon in return for a full confession, but Norris refused to admit guilt—indeed he was certainly innocent. Cromwell manipulated gossipy accounts of a sharp exchange of words between the Queen and Norris into evidence of an affair. The result was a foregone conclusion—charges of high treason, a swift conviction and execution on May 17, 1536. Cromwell's desperate plot to eliminate the queen and his most dangerous rivals was a success, and Norris' 20-year long friendship with the king earned him no more than the favor of beheading rather than drawing and quartering.[6]

Another of Henry's friends caught up in the catastrophe that befell Anne and Norris was Sir Thomas Wyatt. Played by Jamie Thomas in *The Tudors*, Wyatt appears in 14 episodes, making him one of the more prominent characters in the series, though its depiction of his life is often inaccurate. The historic Wyatt was no less interesting than the television version. Younger than the king by a dozen years, Sir Thomas was born in 1503. As with many of Henry's chosen companions, Wyatt came from a family with close connections to the court—his father, Sir Henry, had been a reliable supporter of the Tudors even before Henry VII seized the throne. Master of the King's Jewels and a member of Henry VII's council, Sir Henry was close enough to the monarch to be named an executor of his will in 1509. He was well placed to introduce his talented eldest son into the court of the new king, Henry VIII. Thomas' first known role at court came in 1516, when, aged 13, he participated in the infant Princess Mary's christening. He attended St. John's College, Cambridge, a well-known center of humanist learning. Although he did not earn a degree, Thomas' time at Cambridge provided him with the tools he used to build a reputation as the leading poet at Henry VIII's court.[7]

He followed his father into the Jewel House in 1524, where he was appointed clerk of the king's jewels. A year later he became an esquire of the king's body, granting him privileged access to Henry, who was clearly impressed by him. He was prominent in courtly entertainment, participating in, for example, the Christmas revels of 1524, a scene enacted in Season One of *The Tudors*. Henry sent Sir Thomas on the first of many diplomatic missions in 1526. Charged with congratulating the French king Francis I on his release from imperial captivity, Wyatt made a favorable impression. He became a trusted and active diplomat, representing Henry on embassies to Spain, Rome, and on numerous occasions France. Wyatt married

Elizabeth Brooke, daughter of Thomas Lord Cobham, at 17. His parents arranged the marriage, seeking to expand their local political influence, and the couple were unhappy. By the late 1520s, they were separated, and Elizabeth complained that her husband refused to support her. At the same time, Sir Thomas began an affair with another Elizabeth—Darrell, played in *The Tudors* by Krysten Pellerin—who bore him at least one son. She was one of the ladies of Catherine of Aragon, with whom Wyatt had very good relations—she may have recommended him to Henry as an ambassador to Charles V. In addition, he was acquainted with and admired Princess Mary.[8]

Wyatt also knew Anne Boleyn, and this relationship drew Thomas into grave danger. Exactly when or how Thomas and Anne became acquainted is unknown, but the Boleyn and Wyatt families, who both had Kentish roots, had known each other for years. As Henry's infatuation for Anne grew, Wyatt benefitted from his family's ties to the Boleyns. From the fall of 1529, Sir Thomas received a variety of favors from the king: lucrative import licenses and profitable sinecures came his way, probably in some measure due to his friendship with the new Queen, at whose coronation in June 1533 he was sewer-extraordinary. Some scholars have argued that Wyatt and Anne were romantically involved; there are hints in his poetry, but in reality we do not know for certain. *The Tudors* offers a version of this romance and takes liberties with Wyatt's relationship with Elizabeth Darrell. In the series, Wyatt tries to woo Anne, telling her he is to be divorced, but when Henry VIII asks about their relationship, he claims that he has admired her only from a distance and emphasizes that he is married. Later, a flashback "reveals" that Wyatt and Anne have slept together. He meets Elizabeth Darrell only when she is attending Catherine of Aragon in exile at the More and forces himself upon her. After Catherine's death, she hangs herself, though in reality she outlived Wyatt and remarried.[9]

What is undoubtedly true is that in May 1536 some at court believed Wyatt was guilty of something. When Anne's alleged lovers were arrested, he found himself in the Tower along with them. In later years he blamed the Duke of Suffolk for his arrest, saying that the duke bore him a grudge. He was still in a cell when the other prisoners were executed on May 17. Ultimately, though, Wyatt escaped the fate of Anne's other alleged lovers. For this he could probably thank Cromwell, who was his father's executor and had succeeded the elder Wyatt as master of the jewels upon his retirement in 1532. Thomas himself had been closely associated with Cromwell for some time, and since the coup directed against the queen was largely of the secretary's making, he could rescue the poet. Wyatt was duly released in June after Anne's death. At this point he disappears from the story in *The Tudors*. In reality, however, this brush with disaster seems to have had little impact upon Wyatt's friendship with Henry or his career at court.[10]

Henry appointed Wyatt sheriff of Kent, granted him the stewardship of Conisbrough Castle, and in March 1537 named him ambassador to Charles V. The honor of being ambassador to the Holy Roman Emperor was considerable, but the burden was a serious one, and once again Wyatt found himself in deep waters. He left for the continent in April 1537 and spent over two years abroad in a frustrating mission to restore Anglo-Imperial relations, badly damaged by Henry's divorce from Charles' aunt. Wyatt's instructions directed him to arrange a match between the now-bastard Lady Mary and the heir to the Portuguese throne—a proposal with very small hope of success, given Mary's status. Following Jane Seymour's death, Wyatt was further instructed to woo the newly widowed Duchess of Milan on behalf of his master. Duchess Christina, a 16-year-old Danish princess, wanted nothing to do with Henry, who she considered a very poor risk as a husband, "for her Council suspected that her great aunt [Catherine of Aragon] was poisoned, that the second [wife] was put to death and the third lost for lack of keeping her child-bed." And no less difficult was the requirement that he prevent reconciliation between Charles and Francis.[11]

The embassy was a failure; there was no royal marriage and a treaty between the emperor and Francis was in fact signed, to Henry's fury. Wyatt's experience demonstrates an important point about friendship with the king. Henry imposed heavy responsibilities upon his friends, and though the rewards could be great, the consequences of failure were also high. Recalled by the king and in bad odor, he returned to England in May 1540. Sir Thomas was delighted to be home. He had neglected his personal affairs while in Europe, and his distance from the court enabled rivals to gain headway in the king's affections. But his homecoming soured very quickly, for in June came Thomas Cromwell's fall. The disastrous marriage between Henry and Anne of Cleves emboldened the secretary's legion of jealous enemies, and by July Wyatt's greatest protector—barring the king himself—was dead. Sir Thomas was present at Cromwell's execution, and Cromwell's last words were directed at Wyatt from the scaffold.[12]

Shorn of his powerful patron's protection, Wyatt stood exposed before his enemies, who did not wait long to act. Edmund Bonner, a clerical diplomat in Henry's service, had traveled with Wyatt on the continent in 1538, and their partnership evidently had been unhappy. Bonner charged that Sir Thomas had conspired with Henry's bête noir, the fugitive traitor Reginald Pole, while serving as ambassador. Bonner was probably motivated by his hatred of religious reformers, with whom Wyatt was identified, his questionable sexual morality notwithstanding. While Cromwell was alive, the charges went nowhere, but they reemerged in late 1540. Carted once again to the Tower in January 1541, this time in chains, Wyatt's prospects were grim indeed. Royal officials descended upon his country house, Allington Castle, where they confiscated his horses and plate, and dismissed his servants, leaving his pregnant mistress Elizabeth Darrell to fend for herself. A prosecution for treason appeared imminent. But Wyatt's enemies had not reckoned on the poet's value to the king, for Henry ordered his release in March, and soon courtiers were remarking upon how close they seemed. Within a month Henry was granting him former monastic lands and still more valuable offices. More diplomatic service awaited Wyatt, but by October 1542, ground down by stress and overwork, his health collapsed and he died, aged only 39. Again, none of this appears in *The Tudors*.[13]

Among the mourners Wyatt left behind was Sir Francis Bryan, one of the more fascinating members of the group often called Henry's minions, as was Wyatt. Bryan appears in eight episodes of *The Tudors*, played by Alan van Sprang, and the television version shares much with the historical character, who was notorious. Having lost an eye in a joust, Bryan earned a reputation for hard living: drinking, gambling for high stakes, and womanizing. By the 1530s, he had been nicknamed "the Vicar of Hell," and the cautious gave him a wide berth. Like many of Henry's friends, Bryan's family had a long history of courtly connections. His father—Sir Thomas—was a knight of the body to both Henry VII and Henry VIII as well as vice-chamberlain to Catherine of Aragon, but his mother—Lady Margaret (né Bourchier)—was better known because from 1516 on she served as governess to the king's children, serving all three of Henry's legitimate offspring. She later claimed that Henry made her a baroness in gratitude—which if true was an exceptionally rare honor for a woman. He also was the brother-in-law of Sir Nicholas Carew, who married his sister Elizabeth but who does not appear in *The Tudors* despite being another of the minions.[14]

Like most of Henry's close friends, Bryan initially garnered Henry's attention through his daring performances in the lists. In 1515, the king was loaning Bryan horses and armor for competition, and he became a frequent companion in the king's indefatigable bouts of hunting. By 1518, Bryan had become a gentleman of the privy chamber and was very often to be found in Henry's company. He caused offense and alarm shortly afterward, when, along with the other minions, he engaged in a variety of raucous japes when in Paris visiting the court of Francis I. They left a trail of broken heads and windows behind them and considerable embarrassment for Henry's more sedate diplomats. His outrageous behavior—and Thomas Wolsey's jealousy—resulted in a temporary banishment from court for much of 1519. But Henry missed the boisterous Francis and recalled him within five months. Bryan's brush with exile from court seems to have spurred him to make himself more useful to the king. Henry frequently called upon his close friends, as in the case of Sir Thomas Wyatt, to undertake significant responsibilities. For Bryan, these tended to be military and diplomatic. He had already served at sea, commanding one of the king's ships in 1513. By the mid-1520s he had also gained experience on land, commanding troops against the French and Scots in separate campaigns.[15]

Henry called upon Sir Francis—knighted in 1522 when in service against the French—to undertake a variety of sensitive diplomatic duties, especially during the years dominated by the king's "Great Matter." Bryan was Anne Boleyn's cousin, and he became a valuable envoy. He accompanied Cardinal Campeggio on his trip from Rome to England in 1528 and returned to Rome in November to forward Henry's case before Pope Clement. He also visited Francis I, with whom he had a good relationship, on several occasions in pursuit of his master's goals. But Bryan was not a textbook diplomat. He was willing to employ unorthodox methods—in Rome, for example, he allegedly bedded a cardinal's professional mistress in order to obtain inside information. Strangely, none of this appears in *The Tudors*, where Bryan appears only in Season Three, which begins after Anne's death.[16]

For the most part, Bryan's actions on-screen are nonhistorical, though in keeping with the real man's character. He seduces the fictitious Ursula Misseldon (who also sleeps with the king), threatens Princess Mary (he actually supported her restoration to the succession) and later makes an ill-considered joke to her about cunnilingus (one of the show's most gratuitously tasteless scenes), conducts an imaginary affair with Anne Stanhope and has an invented feud with her husband Edward Seymour, digs up incriminating evidence on Margaret Pole (Countess of Salisbury), in a pimp-like moment procures Catherine Howard for the king's diversion, and joins Thomas Seymour in an all-night drinking bout with Cromwell's executioner that leads to his botched beheading the next day (the executioner did a poor job but not as the result of drinking). However, while serving as Henry's ambassador in Paris in 1537, Sir Francis did mastermind (unsuccessful) plans for kidnapping or assassinating Reginald Pole, which is somewhat overdramatized in *The Tudors* but grounded in historical truth.[17]

Unfortunately for Bryan, however, his undiplomatic tendencies outweighed his dramatic unorthodoxy. He drank and gambled heavily, contracting large debts that left him embarrassed and unable to pay his bills. His friend and fellow ambassador Sir Thomas Wyatt was forced on one occasion to lend him £200 to cover gambling losses. On an important mission to France in 1538, charged with forestalling the same Franco-Imperial rapprochement Wyatt attempted to undo at Charles V's court, Bryan's diplomacy failed utterly. Frequently drunk, indiscreet in his language even when sober, and deeply in debt, he alienated King Francis, who refused to see him. A furious King Henry recalled his erstwhile ambassador. Sir Francis returned to court to find his influence much diminished. He had managed to avoid the wreck of the Boleyns in 1536 by a quick adherence to Cromwell—an about-face that drew criticism. But after his failed embassy to Francis in 1538, Henry no longer had confidence in him as a diplomat—there were even rumors that his plot against Cardinal Pole failed because he had secretly warned him. He undertook one more very brief mission to Charles V's court, but the remainder of his service to Henry was military. He held various commands against the French and Scots, and his friendship with the king continued, bringing him a variety of valuable grants and places. And his political instincts remained sharp—in 1546 he swiftly abandoned his Howard cousins as they careened to destruction, and he emerged as a firm ally of the winning Seymours, in possession of a number of offices once in the hands of the condemned Earl of Surrey. Following Henry's death, Bryan, no longer connected to the court by ties of close friendship, moved to Ireland where he married a wealthy widow, Joan Butler, dowager countess of Ormond. He died in Ireland in 1550, a reprobate to the end. His last words were "I pray you, let me be buried among the good fellows of Waterford, which were good drinkers." Again, this is missing from *The Tudors*.[18]

Of all Henry's close friends depicted in *The Tudors*, Henry Cavill's portrayal of Charles Brandon, Duke of Suffolk, figures most prominently. Cavill appears in every episode of the series, and his performance is often crucial to the story. *The Tudors*' Brandon is shaped and manipulated by the demands of drama, though his real history is hardly less fascinating than the fictional one in the series. Like nearly all of Henry's closest friends, Brandon came from a gentry family with close connections to the court.[19] His father died at Bosworth in August 1485, serving as Henry Tudor's standard-bearer—killed in the final moments by Richard III himself. Fatherless as an infant and losing his mother by his tenth birthday, Brandon was probably raised by his uncle, Sir Thomas Brandon, a prominent figure at the first Tudor's court. He began modestly, serving Henry VII at table, but by 1507 was an esquire of the body. More importantly for his relationship with Prince Henry, Brandon was an acknowledged master of the joust. His first known appearance in the lists was in the tournament held to celebrate Prince Arthur's wedding to Catherine of Aragon in 1501. Prince Henry would have witnessed Brandon's performance, and we must assume that he was impressed. Martial skill was important to Henry, and Brandon was possibly the best jouster at court—though he was shrewd enough to know that when engaged against the king, winning was not necessarily everything.[20]

By the time the action of *The Tudors* begins in 1518, Brandon was well established as the king's most intimate friend. He and Henry participated in many tournaments as a team, dressed in identical suits of armor, challenging all comers. At the same time, Brandon began accumulating ever-increasing marks of Henry's favor: marshal of the royal household in 1511, a knighthood in 1512, master of the horse in October of the same year, and the Order of the Garter in 1513. Henry elevated Charles to the peerage as Viscount Lisle in 1514, an exceptional honor—very few of the king's friends ever received a noble title. His good fortune continued when in February 1514 he became Duke of Suffolk—one of only three dukes in the kingdom. Proof of the strength of Henry's regard for Brandon came in the aftermath of his impetuous marriage to the king's sister Mary in February 1515. In depicting these scenes, *The Tudors* sacrifices accuracy for drama. Perhaps in an effort to simplify the complex family relationships, the series combines the king's two sisters, Margaret and Mary, into one. The real Princess Margaret married to James IV of Scotland in 1503. Her younger sister Mary was betrothed to Louis XII of France rather than the Portuguese monarch, as Showtime would have it. Louis died after only a few weeks of marriage, and Henry sent Suffolk to Paris to bring the widow home. But before they returned—and less than a month after her first husband's death—Suffolk and Mary wed without

Henry's permission. Many were shocked, although Henry had promised Mary free choice of a second husband, and she and Brandon had been acquainted for years. The king was certainly angry about the marriage, but his forgiveness was ensured by the newlywed's promise to surrender a substantial amount of money in plate, jewels, and cash. From this point forward Suffolk was assured a lasting place in Henry's circle—as both friend and in-law.[21]

Suffolk's position as brother-in-law to a king brought both substantial rewards and risks. His landed property was relatively modest at his marriage, and his rank required much more. Henry endowed him with substantial estates, many of which had been salvaged from the wreck of another part of the Tudor family—Henry's cousins, the de la Poles. Brandon also benefited from a considerable stream of income from his wife's French property, though this money came irregularly, often subject to the ups and downs of Anglo-French relations. The duke also had to endure living uncomfortably in the shadow of his wife, who as a royal-born queen dowager outranked him socially. Mary's seal was twice the size of his, and when the couple traveled, it was the duchess who tended to attract public attention. He also had to manage his wife's prejudices, for example, her dislike of Anne Boleyn. He was active in Henry's service in the 1520s, leading English troops on campaign in France in 1523, 1524, and 1528, and heading an embassy to Francis I in 1529, but his relations with the Boleyns were ambivalent at best. Brandon dutifully carried out Henry's orders to bully Princess Mary into accepting the end of her parent's marriage, but without relish. For these reasons, he and his wife preferred to avoid the court in these years, although Suffolk remained a significant figure. Obviously, with no Mary in the series, none of this appears in *The Tudors*.[22]

The difficulties of being a royal in-law ended unexpectedly in June 1533, when Mary Tudor died, aged 37. Suffolk was no stranger to the benefits of marriage—he had married twice before Mary—and lost no time finding a new bride. His choice was his son's 14-year-old fiancé, Catherine Willoughby, whose great advantage was her status as an heiress who stood to inherit very large estates in Lincolnshire—with the end of his French income, Suffolk badly needed new sources of revenue. His marriage into a family at the top of Lincolnshire society was a boon to Henry, who badly needed loyal supporters there. The great rebellion known as the Pilgrimage of Grace broke out there in October 1536, and Henry relied upon Suffolk to put it down. In the end, the rebellion largely collapsed before

Suffolk arrived with troops, but the threat of fire and sword at his hands certainly dampened the pilgrims' enthusiasm. However, historical reality and the drama of *The Tudors* are here again at odds. Though the series has Suffolk suppress the entire Pilgrimage, it was the Duke of Norfolk (missing after Season One) who took the lead against the main rebellion in Yorkshire and farther north. Although the show portrays Suffolk as reluctant and conscience-stricken, there is no evidence that Suffolk had much sympathy for the rebels or their cause.[23]

Through the years of factional struggle that followed the king's marriage to Jane Seymour, Suffolk trod a fine line, never wholly committing himself to any group. It was clear that in religious terms he was more traditional in his outlook, but he avoided any serious entanglement with the likes of Stephen Gardiner, champion of the conservative cause. Suffolk maintained good relations with Cromwell and the other reformers at court, and his young wife was linked to them. In the final analysis, it was the king to whom Suffolk owed his allegiance, loyally supporting him in every situation, vindicating Henry's confidence in him.[24]

In his later years, Suffolk continued to labor in Henry's behalf, as Lord President of the Privy Council and as a commander at the siege of Boulogne in 1544. But as early as 1538, observers commented on his ill health and lack of energy. By the time he arrived in France on his last campaign, he was hardly less obese than his master and suffering from a variety of ailments. He certainly was in no condition to begin a passionate affair with the daughter of a French officer, a development chronicled in the final season of *The Tudors*. Henry granted him a place of honor in the occupation of Boulogne, and granted him significant estates in Lincolnshire as a reward. But the acquisition of Tattershall College was not the last honor Henry bestowed upon his oldest friend. Suffolk died on August 22, 1545 and, at the king's command, was buried in St. George's Chapel, Windsor, where Henry himself would be interred less than two years later. Tragically, Suffolk's surviving sons, Henry and Charles, both died within half an hour of each other in an epidemic of the sweating sickness in 1551. The Dukes of Suffolk, monuments to the power of royal friendship, endowed with thousands of acres, numerous offices and titles, and a vast income, vanished from history like a morning dew.[25]

The king's friends played a crucial role in the history of Henry VIII's England. These men were the kingdom's elite, a handful personally chosen by Henry, nearly all of whom came from a narrow segment of the landed gentry. Interestingly, very few were peers or the sons of peers, perhaps reflecting the well-known Tudor wariness of the titled aristocracy. Most of them—like Charles Brandon, Francis Bryan, William Compton, and Thomas Wyatt—were from families with long-standing connections to the court, but whose estates were relatively modest. And they were uniformly successful practitioners of the martial arts—nothing recommended a man to Henry more than ability to wield a lance on horseback or to triumph in a melee on foot. The benefits of Henry's friendship were manifest, as the careers of Brandon, Bryan, Compton, and Wyatt show. But the risks were great too, for the court was a dangerous place, and success there attracted jealousy and enmity. Norris demonstrates that point, for though Henry VIII was generous, he was also mercurial and dangerous. The picture provided in *The Tudors*, while not always historically accurate, nevertheless reveals a great deal about life in the company of England's most famous king.

Notes

1. See David Loades, *The Tudor Court* (Totowa, NJ: Barnes and Noble, 1987).
2. For the advice to Essex, *Calendar of State Papers, Domestic Series, of the Reigns of Edward VI, Mary, Elizabeth, James I, 1547–1625: Preserved in the State Paper Department of Her Majesty's Public Record Office*, ed. Robert Lemon, 12 vols. (Nendeln, Liechtenstein: Kraus Reprint Ltd., 1967), vol. 4, 533; David Starkey, "Intimacy and Innovation: The Rise of the Privy Chamber 1485–1547," in Starkey, ed., *The English Court from the Wars of the Roses to the Civil War* (London, 1987), 71–118.
3. G.W. Bernard, "Compton, Sir William (1482?–1528)," *Oxford Dictionary of National Biography* (Oxford University Press, 2004); online edn, January 2008 [http://www.oxforddnb.com/view/article/6039, accessed October 24, 2015], hereafter *ODNB*; *The Tudors*, Episodes 1:1–1:7.
4. E.W. Ives, "Norris, Henry (*b*. before 1500, *d*. 1536)," *ODNB*; online edn, May 2009 [http://www.oxforddnb.com/view/article/20271, accessed October 24, 2015].
5. Ibid.; *The Tudors*, Episodes 2:6–2:9.
6. Ibid.; *The Tudors*, Episode 2:9; the best account of Anne Boleyn's fall may be found in Eric Ives, *The Life and Death of Anne Boleyn*, 2nd ed. (Oxford: Blackwell Publishing, 2004).
7. Colin Burrow, "Wyatt, Sir Thomas (*c*. 1503–1542)," *ODNB*; online edn, May 2015 [http://www.oxforddnb.com/view/article/30111, accessed October 24, 2015]; see also Susan Brigden, *Thomas Wyatt: The Heart's Forest* (London: Faber & Faber, 2012).
8. Ibid.

9. Ibid.; *The Tudors*, Episodes 1:3–1:4, 1:6, 1:10, 2:1–2:4, 2:6–2:10.
10. Ibid.
11. Ibid.; the quote is in J.J. Scarisbrick, *Henry VIII* (Berkeley: University of California Press, 1968), 358.
12. Ibid.
13. Ibid.
14. Susan Brigden, "Bryan, Sir Francis (*d.* 1550)," *ODNB*; online edn, January 2008 [http://www.oxforddnb.com/view/article/3788, accessed October 24, 2015]; the evidence for Lady Margaret's elevation depends upon her own assertion, G.E. Cokayne, Vicary Gibbs, et. al., eds., *The Complete Peerage*, 2nd ed., vol. 2 (London: St. Catherine Press Limited, 1910–1959), 363; Stanford Lehmberg, "Carew, Sir Nicholas (*b.* in or before 1496, *d.* 1539)," *ODNB*; online edn, October 2007 [http://www.oxforddnb.com/view/article/4633, accessed October 24, 2015].
15. "Sir Francis Bryan," *ODNB*.
16. Ibid.
17. *The Tudors*, Episodes 3:1–3:8.
18. "Sir Francis Bryan," *ODNB*.
19. S.J. Gunn, "Brandon, Charles, First Duke of Suffolk (*c.* 1484–1545)," *ODNB*; online edn, May 2015 [http://www.oxforddnb.com/view/article/3260, accessed October 24, 2015], and *Charles Brandon, Duke of Suffolk, c. 1484–1545* (Oxford: Blackwell Publishing, 1988).
20. Ibid.
21. Ibid.; *The Tudors*, Episodes 1:1–1:10, 2:1–2:10.
22. Ibid.
23. Ibid.; *The Tudors*, Episodes 3:1–3:8.
24. Ibid.
25. Ibid.; *The Tudors*, Episodes 4:1–4:10.

CHAPTER 10

Postmodern and Conservative: The King's Ministers in *The Tudors*

Robin Hermann

It is perhaps too much of a truism among historians that popular culture, specifically Hollywood, almost always gets history wrong. Every few years, it seems, another Oscar-chasing film or prestige premium cable drama will claim, as *The Tudors* did in its opening credits, to tell the "real story," undergraduate students will entertain some very dubious ideas about subjects near and dear to their history professors' hearts, and the rot will spread, as illustrated by the belief that HBO's *Game of Thrones* is somehow "medieval."[1] As readers of this volume undoubtedly know, this problem is particularly acute when it comes to Henry VIII and his reign, not the least because as Mark Rankin, Christopher Highley, and John N. King recently have argued, Henry's image was remarkably unstable in his own lifetime, as polemicists and playwrights sought to manipulate the figure of the king for their own political and aesthetic purposes.[2] As a result, construction of the myth of Henry VIII had already begun before the real Henry's death, and in the intervening five centuries that myth has only grown, relentless in its omnivorous hunger for new expressions, emphases, and idioms. Such iterations inevitably present their narrative of Henrician England as the "right" one, hoping the audience will forget that stories are products

R. Hermann (✉)
Department of History and Geography, University of Louisiana at Lafayette, Lafayette, LA, USA

of their time and tell us more about the moment in which they were produced than the historical figure, period, or process they purport to depict with accuracy.

Shakespeare's *Henry VIII* was an attempt to legitimate the reigns of his daughter, Elizabeth I, and her successor, James I. The antiauthoritarian themes of *A Man for All Seasons*, in which all institutions are always corrupt and the common man is always wise, were as familiar to Britain after World War II as they would have been horrifying and alien to the actual Thomas More. Similarly, the historical Thomas Cromwell would have been profoundly surprised to know that he sought to reform the English church and state for the good of the subject. Such is our cynicism concerning government and corporations that when the Cromwell of *Wolf Hall* works to increase financial transparency and legal clarity against the forces of reaction and mystification, it is all too easy for twenty-first century readers to imagine that, as Hillary Mantel has Cromwell crossing swords with a reactionary nobility and a regressive Catholic Church, she has another, implicit target in mind: the unholy, assuredly corrupt institutions deemed "Too Big To Fail." Would it not be nice to think that there was someone in government like Cromwell, who worked for the good of the common man, against the priesthood, the cabals, the privileged orders that seem to run the world?

To say *The Tudors* is guilty of such presentism as well is therefore hardly controversial; creator and executive producer Michael Hirst proclaimed himself drawn to tell Henry's story because of its epic sweep—according to Hirst, "[Henry] presided over the change from the medieval to the modern world"—and the "totally familiar, almost commonplace" reality of the love triangle between Henry, Catherine, and Anne.[3] In a way, Hirst's admission at the outset of the series (albeit in a paratextual document) that *The Tudors* would function primarily as entertainment and have little, if any, value as an historical inquiry is refreshing. For, as any half-decent historiography seminar will demonstrate, Hirst has acknowledged the commission of two of the worst errors an historian could make, as Herbert Butterfield warned us against, over 80 years ago. By looking to Henrician England as the point of transition between the medieval and the modern world, Hirst is "riding after a whole flock of misapprehensions if he goes to hunt for the present in the past."[4]

Such a failure to treat the past on its own terms leads to further error, as Hirst throughout the series treats Henry as a modern figure whose drama audiences could see themselves in, since, as he argued, "Kings and queens act out, on a vast and public stage, the dramas that fill and define our lives."[5] As other chapters in this volume will illustrate, to make such an argument for Henry borders on the absurd, but such an attitude nicely highlights some of the historical and aesthetic problems of *The Tudors* that are the subject of this chapter. Hirst's desire to, in Butterfield's words, "seize ... upon those personages ... in the past who seem ... analogous to our own"[6] reduces the complexity of the past and casts the historical narrative in an almost exclusively modern, and therefore incorrect, context. Once the backlash to the historical infidelities of *The Tudors* began to set in,[7] defenders of the series argued that if Showtime and Hirst had attempted to maintain historical accuracy, there would have been no audience. Besides, this line of attack went, our knowledge of Henrician England will always be incomplete, so what does it matter if the show plays fast and loose with the facts?[8]

Indeed, from the outset, Hirst obligingly signaled his essential alignment with such a position:

> I was very happy to dramatize [the] extreme contradictions and events of [Henry VIII's reign]. After I had done so, there was a conference call with, among others, Robert Greenblatt, the head of programming for Showtime. Bob didn't mince his words. He told me: "Michael, we really only have one question to ask you—is *any* of this true?" It was a big moment ... but I replied, as casually as possible, "About 85 percent." *Of course the percentage was an invention* [emphasis added]—but I wanted to make the point that everything I wrote was based on historical research and historical "fact" (as reported, that is, by historians!).[9]

Hirst's admission that his widely quoted "about 85 percent" degree of accuracy[10] was itself fiction suggests, in miniature, the semantic thicket historians find themselves in when trying to correct the historical narrative of the series. As Professor Robison notes in the introduction, we would likely have been willing to accept a filmic narrative of Henrician England that was in fact 85 % accurate, but even that number, like the historical "facts" Hirst cavalierly dismisses, cannot be trusted. As Tom Betteridge astutely notes, *The Tudors*, in both content and form, approaches history essentially from the postmodern perspective: if facts are really "facts," and historical narrative is only "truth,"[11] then what historians think they know about Henry's reign is just another cinematic device to be utilized, or not, when necessary.

As Eric Josef Carlson argues, however, it is possible—or at least it could be possible—to enjoy Hirst's approach to Tudor history as entertainment largely separate from fact.[12] Arguably, this is true: Hirst's *Elizabeth* (1998), despite the film's casual relationship to history, largely succeeds because of the skills of its director and the strength of its cast. Unfortunately, the same cannot be said of *The Tudors* largely because Hirst's postmodern approach to history undercuts and weakens three of the strongest actors in the cast: Sam Neill as Cardinal Wolsey, Jeremy Northam as Thomas More, and James Frain as Thomas Cromwell. As we will see, Hirst handicapped *The Tudors* almost from the beginning because of his decision to focus almost exclusively on Henry VIII "as a human being,"[13] and treat the revolutionary events of the period as incidental accidents that might (or might not) delay Henry from yet another tryst. For a show with a cast of hundreds and over four decades of history, the focus remains frustratingly small: Henry' dynastic concerns.

Gina Bellafante appeared a bit bewildered at the decision of the series to "make … it seem as if the entire creation of the Anglican Church boiled down to Henry's wish to remarry and sire a male heir,"[14] but I will argue that it is because *The Tudors* views history from a postmodern perspective that the series "articulates a profoundly conservative model of history,"[15] in which only Henry's decisions and goals explain the many controversies and answer the questions of his reign. Without venturing too far down the rabbit hole of postmodernist theory and criticism, the proposition that *The Tudors* can be both conservative and postmodern depends in part on Michel Foucault's analysis of discourse and Fredric Jameson's Marxist approach to the culture of capitalism.[16] Foucault, of course, characterized all discourse and language as expressions of, and therefore constrained by, existing "power relations." Taken to its logical (and depressing) extreme, such an argument holds that language and speech cannot effect any change in those relationships of power, since discourse is always subject to the authority of the state. Language is subject and therefore subjective; it has no inherent, objective meaning and becomes just another commodity, in Jameson's analysis, in the ongoing movement of late capitalism to place a value on everything in the global marketplace.

The Tudors embodies this postmodern paradigm, which is why the series is so often dramatically inert. Betteridge accurately described how the series "treats history as simply a commodity," while at the same time so "desirous of authenticity" that it is a "fetish."[17] This is the postmodern condition: meaning can become so subjective that culture seeks the authentic, or real, even though such goals are unobtainable where diachronic history—the determinant of the truly authentic real—has vanished into the eternal moment of the synchronic present.[18] The aesthetic and historical confusion that resulted from Hirst's preoccupations confused and angered reviewers and scholars alike. Bellafante criticized the show's "struggle to calibrate a tone ... that might feel true to its period without feeling absurdly anachronistic," as a result of which "Henry shifts from regal formal locutions to outbursts that make him seem like the ornery head of a construction company, and the effect is disorientating, as if you're seeing someone at a memorial service in clothing exclamatory or garish."[19]

Such disorientation on the part of the viewer is what I am referring to as the inert drama of the series. In the first episode, for example, Henry VIII speaks formally—as we might expect—to Wolsey, More, and his privy council about war with the French, but Hirst has the king, as he exits the scene, inform the council that since Wolsey has matters in hand, "Now I can go play."[20] From a historical perspective, it is extraordinarily unlikely Henry would have said any such thing to Wolsey, More, and his council; from a dramatic perspective, the contradictory disorientation makes it similarly difficult to take Henry seriously as a king. Unfortunately, such confusion only worsens over four seasons, as Hirst increasingly has his characters speak lines of dialogue taken—it appears—verbatim from the archives, but in the postmodern context of *The Tudors* these attempts at authenticity only lessen the show's dramatic impact. Patrick Collinson, when reviewing *Elizabeth*, noted Hirst's tendency to rearrange chronology and character to no clear purpose: it was "as if the known facts of [Elizabeth's] reign, plus many hitherto unknown, were shaken up like pieces of a jigsaw and scattered on the table at random."[21] Early modern academics watching *The Tudors* know far too well how little had changed in Hirst's approach between *Elizabeth* and the series; I would add, however, that such an approach not only makes for (at best) flawed history, at least in the case of *The Tudors*, but made for flawed television. In the case of the king's ministers, such a failure is particularly disheartening, because accurate representations of Wolsey, More, and Cromwell would have made for a truly exciting and interesting series.

The first error *The Tudors* commits concerning the king's ministers, similar to the confusion about the character of the king described above, stems from the fact that Hirst's scripts provide the very gifted actors portraying these men with wildly inconsistent material. It often feels, to echo

Bellafante's criticism regarding the series' lack of calibration, as if Hirst vacillated between using the ministers either to articulate the transition from medieval to modern, to stray into deeply anachronistic territory for "dramatic" effect, or to behave or speak with some degree of historical accuracy. The portrayal and characterization of Thomas Wolsey—just in Episode 1:1—illustrates this disjunction, which plagued the series throughout its run. In the shooting script for the first episode, Hirst describes Wolsey as "a man with soft, almost effeminate features."[22] As with so much else in *The Tudors*, this is a change from the historical record—no contemporary image of Wolsey would ever fit that description—and it not only has no basis in reality, but appears to have no dramatic purpose either. If we consider, however, that one of Hirst's stated purposes in dramatizing Henry's reign was to chronicle England's "progress" from the (presumably backward) Middle Ages to the (ostensibly enlightened) modern period, and the break with Rome and the creation of the Anglican Church was a crucial point in such a shift, Wolsey—cardinal and papal *legate* that he was—must be represented as weak and suspect.

In the aggressively misogynistic narrative of *The Tudors*, where men may indulge in all sorts of sexual abandon, assaults, and crimes without consequence while even the hint of impropriety is enough to bring down Anne Boleyn,[23] there is a cynical logic in Hirst's decision to describe Wolsey as effeminate. As we will see, Wolsey's weakness is largely in keeping with the portrayal of the king's ministers throughout the series, an aesthetic decision that has much to do with Hirst's conception of history. And yet, what makes the show so difficult, simply at a narrative level, is that the Wolsey who becomes increasingly flummoxed and undone by Henry over the course of the first season is also given to throwing bishops against walls, demanding payment for saving Bishop Bonnivet's "master's arse,"[24] and calling Cardinal Campeggio a "stupid cunt" (Episode 1:9). While it is of course true that such a canny political operator as Wolsey would never have said or done any of these highly impolitic things,[25] it makes little narrative sense for a theoretically "weak" character to do them, or for either of these versions of Wolsey to propose a "Treaty of Universal and Perpetual Peace,"[26] as the real Wolsey did with the Treaty of London in 1518.

As if that were not confusing enough to the average viewer, let alone an historian, Hirst gives in to his presentist impulses as More tries to sell Henry on this treaty, describing it as "entirely new in the history of Europe, committing all of its signatories to the principle of collective security and universal peace ... [through] the creation of pan-European institutions."[27] As *A Man for All Seasons* demonstrates, the impulse to modernize More is not new, and at least *The Tudors* was honest enough to depict More's persecution and burning of heretics.[28] Again, it seems doubtful that the same character who advocated the establishment of an institution far more similar to the League of Nations or the United Nations than any early modern league or diplomatic process would also burn men for heresy. Hirst's desire to read the past in terms of the present while at the same time striving for historical accuracy results in inconsistent and confusing characterization—the root, I would argue, of the series' narrative incoherence.

The irony of such inconsistency in the script and incoherence in the narrative, of course, is that Hirst could have avoided many of the problems illustrated above—and made much more effective television—if he had presented Wolsey and More as the people they were in the historical record. If he had attempted, in other words, to represent More, as historians are trained to do at a very early stage in their career, in terms that More himself would have understood, he and Jeremy Northam could have created a More who would have been entirely comfortable with advocating a universal peace and burning heretics, because More would have seen both actions as serving the greater good of Christianity and the Catholic Church. In *The Tudors*, More refers to himself and to Henry as humanists, and although there is some vague hints that humanists prefer peace to war, the series never engages fully with what Christian humanism meant to More (or anyone else in the English Renaissance who described themselves as humanists). Christian humanists like More were urgently concerned with the improvement of life in this world[29] and would have believed something like the Treaty of London to be necessary, not only for social and political reform and improvement but to unite Europe against the Lutheran heresy.[30] More's deeply felt conviction of the need to safeguard the unity of Christendom against the Lutherans and the ravages of war was entirely in keeping with his great apprehension of the mystery of God and profound fear of the darkness of lost faith. This, then, was the More who could write both the *Utopia*, urging men to build a better and more just society here on earth, and *A Supplication of Souls*, hectoring men to prayer and charity for fear of eternal damnation.[31] This More would have reconciled all of the seeming contradictions of the series' version, explained with much greater clarity why a man of his religious convictions could never have acquiesced to the break with Rome,[32] and been a far more interesting character.[33]

Such a poor understanding of More illustrates one of the greatest failings of *The Tudors*: its inability, or unwillingness, to take the ideas of the king's ministers as important to—or as sufficient motivation for—the momentous events of the reign. Again, whether he was conscious of this or not, Hirst treats ideas, language, and belief as if it is all only discourse: subject to the true power and authority of the state, or in this case the head of state's desires, wants, and lusts.[34] That focus, however, ignores the complexity of his ministers' convictions—convictions that shaped the course and contour of what we used to call "the Tudor revolution in government."[35] Geoffrey Elton may have been wrong to assert that Henry and Thomas Cromwell, during the break with Rome, created the first modern nation-state with an efficient, rational bureaucracy at its core, but Henry, Cromwell, and like-minded ministers during the 1530s and 1540s *did* drastically alter the nature and purpose of Tudor government.[36] The full extent of such change is beyond my scope here, but in brief: Cromwell *did* seek to expand the power of the monarchy in order to secure the break with Rome, largely through statutes such as the Act in Restraint of Appeals, which invested the crown with *imperium* throughout the monarch's dominions.[37]

Cromwell recognized that in order to make such an audacious claim to sovereignty legitimate in the Tudor polity, the king's responsibility toward his subjects would have to expand concomitantly with his power over them. Hence Cromwell's repeated appeals throughout the Reformation statutes to the good of the commonwealth; such language signaled his belief that the government was charged with the maintenance of the economy, provision for the poor, support of Protestantism, and the care of its subjects generally.[38] Unsurprisingly, nearly of all this is absent from *The Tudors*. More briefly mentions the Act of Restraint of Appeals (Episode 2:3), and of course the series dramatizes the royal supremacy and the dissolution of the monasteries, since without them the series would have been less violent in Seasons Two and Three. On screen, Cromwell appears to have little positive motivation other than to strengthen the position of the king. That much was certainly true, up to a point, but by ignoring Cromwell's quite public conviction of the responsibility of the government toward the governed, Hirst not only fails to represent Cromwell as a fully realized character, he also evades the question of how the government portrayed in *The Tudors*, which seems to revel in war against foreigners and torture of its subjects, could have stayed in power for so long. Early in the series, Henry and More discuss Machiavelli's *The Prince* (Episode 1:2), and Henry wonders if it is better to be loved or feared. Part of the secret to Henry's success was his ability, with the careful management of his ministers, to be both—feared for his anger and his tendency toward judicial murder, loved for his government's stated commitment to the common good.

If, as I have argued, all that matters in *The Tudors* is power and the license that power allows, it is not enough for Hirst to badly misrepresent the king's ministers and their beliefs; these characters must also be *shown* to be weak relative to Henry's authority and character. As many scholars have argued, no minister other than Wolsey ever held power near to that of the king,[39] but in weakening all of his ministers the series articulates that very conservative and old-fashioned interpretation of history, mentioned above, in which only the great are agents of change. This crippling dynamic is at work throughout the series. Wolsey, for example, always seems to be at least one step behind Henry in diplomacy and politics, as when Buckingham's death sentence surprises Wolsey (Episode 1:2), when in reality the cardinal was the architect of Buckingham's fall. Similarly, in the same episode, Henry's comment that Hampton Court is a finer palace than any the king owns so terrifies Wolsey that he gives it to Henry on the spot. In reality, Henry was only able to claim Hampton Court after Wolsey's fall from grace began in 1529. Wolsey's treasonous correspondence with Charles V and Francis I in 1530 goes unmentioned. Each of these changes and many others like them in and of themselves would perhaps not amount to much, but taken together Wolsey's stature as a political player in Henry's court is reduced while Henry's stature grows. It is much the same for More and Cromwell. At More's trial, for example, he does not question—as he did in reality—Richard Rich's highly suspect testimony concerning More's alleged speech against the Act of Supremacy; as a result he appears far more passive and much more a victim of events beyond his control (Episode 2:5). In much the same way, Cromwell suffers a botched execution because the king's councilors Sir Francis Bryan and Sir Thomas Seymour, who have spent much of the third season sneering at his low birth, must play one last conspiratorial trick on him and get the executioner drunk (Episode 3:10).[40] All three men are playthings of the king's will to a much greater extent than the historical record will support. In the end, such a flawed representation of three of the most important men in Henry's life illustrates the show's postmodern, yet highly conservative approach to history as entertainment. If the king's ministers have no agency or beliefs of any consequence, because their actions and ideas are all subject to and constrained by the king and his desires, the only explanation *The Tudors* offers for historical change is the actions of great and powerful men.

Notes

1. For an excellent analysis of why *Game of Thrones* is really a representation of the early modern world, see Benjamin Breen, "Why 'Game of Thrones' Isn't Medieval—and Why that Matters," http://www.psmag.com/books-and-culture/game-thrones-isnt-medieval-matters-83288.
2. Mark Rankin, Christopher Highley, and John N. King, eds., *Henry VIII and His Afterlives: Literature, Politics, and Art* (Cambridge: Cambridge University Press, 2009), 5–6.
3. Michael Hirst, *The Tudors: It's Good to be King* (New York: Simon Spotlight Entertainment, 2007), xii.
4. Herbert Butterfield, *The Whig Interpretation of History* (New York: Norton, 1931), 10.
5. Hirst, *The Tudors*, xii.
6. Butterfield, *Whig Interpretation of History*, 29.
7. Alex Cohen, "*The Tudors* Battles with the Truth," http://www.npr.org/templates/story/story.php?storyId=89182466.
8. http://www.sfgate.com/news/article/Review-Tudors-Henry-sheds-frat-boy-crown-3221632.php.
9. Hirst, *The Tudors*, xiii.
10. See, for example, Tom Betteridge, "Henry VIII and Popular Culture," in Rankin, Highly, and King, eds., *Henry VIII and His Afterlives*, 208–222, 214.
11. Hirst, *The Tudors*, xv.
12. Eric Josef Carlson, "Teaching Elizabeth Tudor with Movies: Film, Historical Thinking, and the Classroom," *The Sixteenth Century Journal* 38 (2) (Summer, 2007): 419–428.
13. Hirst, *The Tudors*, xv.
14. Ginia Bellafante, "Nasty, but not Brutish and Short," http://www.nytimes.com/2008/03/28/arts/television/28tudo.html?_r=0.
15. Tom Betteridge, "Henry VIII and Popular Culture," 216.
16. Michel Foucault, *Discipline and Punish: The Birth of the Prison*, trans. Alan Sheridan (New York: Vintage Books, 1979); Fredric Jameson, *Postmodernism, or, the Cultural Logic of Late Capitalism* (Durham: Duke University Press, 1991).
17. Betteridge, "Henry VIII and Popular Culture," 214–215.
18. Jameson, *Postmodernism*, 16. For a positive interpretation of this mindset, see Frances Fukuyama, *The End of History and the Last Man* (New York: Free Press, 2006).
19. Bellafante, "Nasty, but not so Brutish and Short."
20. Hirst, *The Tudors*, 39.
21. Quoted in Carlson, "Teaching Elizabeth Tudor," 420.
22. Hirst, *The Tudors*, 36.

23. Betteridge, "Henry VIII and Popular Culture," 214–215.
24. Hirst, *The Tudors*, 70.
25. See Cavendish's account in George Cavendish and William Roper, *Two Early Tudor Lives: The Life and Death of Cardinal Wolsey by George Cavendish and The Life of Sir Thomas More by William Roper* (New Haven: Yale University Press, 1962), and Michael Everett, *The Rise of Thomas Cromwell: Power and Politics in the Reign of Henry VIII* (New Haven: Yale University Press, 2015), 202.
26. Hirst, *The Tudors*, 66.
27. Ibid, 67.
28. Unsurprisingly, however, the series depicts More burning in 1529 a heretic—Simon Fish—who died of the plague in 1531.
29. *The Tudors* nods to this imperative by showing him teaching his daughters to read, but not why this was radical, or, of course, why he did it in the first place.
30. William Rockett, "Wolsey, More, and the Unity of Christendom," *The Sixteenth Century Journal* 35 (1) (Spring, 2004): 133–153.
31. J Patrick Coby, *Henry VIII and the Reformation Parliament* (New York: Pearson Longman, 2006), 143–150.
32. William Rockett, "The Case Against Thomas More," *The Sixteenth Century Journal* 39 (4) (Winter, 2008): 1065–1093.
33. To be fair, it seems difficult for filmic adaptations to get Thomas More right. As noted, the More in *A Man for All Seasons* is too modern and liberal; in *The Tudors* he is an intellectual lightweight; and in *Wolf Hall* he is too concerned with punishing heretics and barely interested in humanist reform.
34. It is not for nothing that the last episode of the first season opens with Henry masturbating while a servant attends. It is difficult to think of a clearer symbol of the series' obsession with Henry's sex life.
35. G.R. Elton, *The Tudor Revolution in Government* (Cambridge: Cambridge University Press, 1953). For one rebuttal, see Conrad Russell, "Thomas Cromwell's Doctrine of Parliamentary Sovereignty," *Transactions of the Royal Historical Society* 7 (1997): 235–246.
36. John Guy, "Thomas Wolsey, Thomas Cromwell and the Reform of Henrician Government," in Diarmaid MacCulloch, ed., *The Reign of Henry VIII: Politics, Policy and Piety* (Basingstoke: Macmillan, 1995), 35–57.
37. Derek Hirst, *Dominion: England and Its Island Neighbours, 1500–1707* (Oxford: Oxford University Press, 2012), 32–37.
38. C.S.L. Davies, "The Cromwellian Decade: Authority and Consent," *TRHS* 7 (1997): 177–195.
39. Guy, "Wolsey, Cromwell, and the Reform of Government," 39.
40. Of course, there was no such conspiracy at Cromwell's death. His executioner bungled the execution without any outside influence.

CHAPTER 11

A Cardboard Crown: Kingship in *The Tudors*

Glenn Richardson

Henry VIII first appears in *The Tudors* wearing a crown. It is so that we know he is the king—for we might not otherwise. He arrives to chair a meeting of his council. Jonathan Rhys Meyers' Henry wears something like an über version of the gold cardboard crowns much favored by the three kings in school Nativity plays. As with the best of those, it is pointy and glittery. Wearing it, the king looks every bit as authentic as the child kings *imagine* themselves to be before their disbelief-suspending audience. It is thus an apt symbol of the simulacrum of kingship presented in this television extravaganza.[1]

In the century before the Tudors became the English royal dynasty, the concept of European kingship was comprehensively reinvented. Throughout most of Europe, monarchs encountered serious challenges from their own most powerful subjects. They faced rebellion and civil wars, not least of them the Wars of the Roses, which eventually brought the Tudors to power over the last Plantagenet king. Monarchy was forced to reassert and, to some extent at least, redefine itself in response to these challenges. New fiscal and legal mechanisms were developed whereby the power of rulers was more effectively brought to bear upon "over-mighty subjects." Though many were novel in operation, they were presented in

---

G. Richardson (✉)
School of Arts and Humanities, St. Mary's University College, Twickenham, UK

© The Editor(s) (if applicable) and The Author(s) 2016
W.B. Robison (ed.), *History, Fiction, and* The Tudors,
Queenship and Power, DOI 10.1057/978-1-137-43883-6_11

high-flown rhetoric as things of ancient authority and time-honored precedent. Kingship's rights, responsibilities, and limitations were fused into a complex model of sovereignty—now often referred to as "Renaissance Monarchy." This derived in some measure from forms of rule in the ancient world, from those of the Germanic tribes of the early Middle Ages, and from the medieval experience of monarchy. It was characterized by a belief among the principal European rulers that they must show themselves to be effective governors, great patrons, and—above all else—great warriors.[2]

Sixteenth-century European monarchs, Henry most of all, saw themselves as ultimately accountable only to God for the exercise of their divinely ordained power. All Renaissance commentators agreed on the importance of equipping those born to rule with the knowledge and skills needed to do so justly and effectively. Education was therefore crucial. Classical languages, literature, and philosophy and the study of history were the chief tenets of a curriculum sometimes called the *studia humanitatis*, from which we ultimately derive our sense of "the humanities." There was a world of difference, however, in Erasmus of Rotterdam's neo-Platonic "ideal" ruler, described in his treatise *The Education of a Christian Prince* (dedicated at one point to Henry VIII), and those espoused by Machiavelli in *The Prince*. There is a general sense in *The Tudors* of Henry having begun his reign more or less as the schoolboy to Wolsey and Sir Thomas More, which—albeit crudely done—does correspond with the historical record. We see the young king discussing humanist principles (and, anachronistically, even Machiavelli) with his two mentors, comprehending the potential advantages of Wolsey's plans for a "universal peace," and generally appreciating that ideas are important, even if these "conversations" are short and meanly scripted.[3]

The education of the prince in good government was crucial, but—like all European monarchs—Henry also operated within personal and constitutional frameworks designed to protect his subjects from purely arbitrary rule. Fifteenth- and sixteenth-century authors drew upon Plato, Aristotle, Cicero, and Seneca, among others, for models of ideal leadership. According to most such authorities, the capacity to maintain justice was the key attribute of kingship. This meant not only the making and upholding of fair laws but also equitable dealing with all subjects. Henry's government involved a significant degree of negotiation between the crown and the powerful vested interests. These included the church, the nobility and gentry, the wealthy merchants and town councils, as well as lawyers and even the crown's own administrative and judicial officers. The parliament and his own judges were the formal sources of law making, advice, and restraint upon Henry. The royal (eventually the privy) council was the primary executive body of the realm and the final court of appeal. The importance of good "counsel" occupied political commentators greatly. Most warned against overly large councils or ones too narrow in compass and membership. Kings were warned against the flattery of self-serving councilors, and there was a strong anticourtier tradition in the literature in England going back at least as far as Walter Mapp in the twelfth century.

In *The Tudors*, we see Henry meeting his council to discuss war when a young man and after the siege of Boulogne. We see him summoning parliament to discuss his marriages and changes to religious practice at several points in the series. There is some sense of advice being offered by the council, minimal though this is, but Henry usually just berates parliament to get his way—and the real Henry's agents and minister did indeed bully parliament into obeying the king's will. Yet, beyond these formal bodies, Henry—like all monarchs—ultimately relied upon his people at all social levels to accept his authority voluntarily and to cooperate with his regime. Otherwise, he could not properly maintain law and order. The series notes this in the episodes dealing with the Pilgrimage of Grace, which was the most serious rebellion ever faced by a Tudor monarch and one that nearly brought Henry down. It was less suppressed than temporized with until it ran out of impetus. Henry was finally saved by his subjects' loyalty to him.[4]

As Henry's reign went on, there was considerable overlap between the personnel of the council and the court, and *The Tudors* notes the close proximity of one to the other in the portrayal of the council members and in the rise of Thomas Cromwell—although the latter appears much earlier in time in the series than he did in historical reality.[5] As Baldassare Castiglione advised in his *Book of the Courtier*, ambitious men or women should make their way into service of the prince through the court, maintain favor through displaying the right combination of useful talents, and be called to advise him formally or informally.[6] The prime example of this in the historical record of Henry's reign and in *The Tudors* is, of course, Cardinal Wolsey. Sam Neill's portrayal in Season One captures well how close was Wolsey's relationship with the king and how hard he worked to make Henry a powerful ruler at home and a respected one abroad. It captures the friendship between the two men and how Wolsey was to some extent a mentor to the young king but also how completely the cardinal was dependent upon Henry's favor. It also shows how Wolsey's influence on Henry was never total and how dangerous "the court" could be for him. The cardinal's forlorn reverie in his final moments captures that sense of betrayal and final disappointment with himself that we are told the real Wolsey felt in the days before he died a miserable death from dysentery as he was being brought to London for trial. Having his life end in despairing suicide as he cuts his own throat, as happens in *The Tudors*, is just stupid.[7]

Monarchs like Henry were shown respect and interacted with through the complex ceremony and deferential etiquette, which daily surrounded them at court. Its details varied considerably across Europe, but royal ritual focused on the times when the person of the monarch was encountered most directly, was also at its most vulnerable, and therefore in greatest need of mystification. Key moments were the ruler's rising in the morning, retiring at night, and meal times. Some aspects of this ceremony are evoked reasonably often throughout *The Tudors*. Courtiers bow and scrape, doff caps, and curtsey predictably enough and as we expect them to do. They lower their heads and eyes in the royal presence—although the women's eyes usually rise longingly and flirtatiously to the king's immediately afterward. The servants are often shown overhearing, if not actually listening in to, the king's incessant sexual activity. Inadvertently or otherwise, the series does show how closely notionally "invisible" servants lived to the high and mighty. *Downton Abbey* does the same thing of course for a later age. Like the staff, we are outsiders in this world, but unlike them, we get to see the behind-closed-doors action.[8]

The Tudors also hints at some aspects of more formal daily ceremonial and the organization of the royal household. We see Henry being undressed and put into his night attire by gentleman attendants and being offered a crucifix to kiss before going to be a husband to Catherine of Aragon, in hopes of begetting the longed-for male heir. He is shown as having his own apartments separate to those of the queen, the male-only "king's side" as it was called. Why exactly the king's chamber should also be populated by two skimpily clad lovelies is not revealed by any surviving Tudor household account books. It is handy that they are there, however, because, finding his wife at prayer, the king returns to vent his sexual frustration on one of them—who has been forewarned by a courtier to stand by for boarding.[9]

High-ranking courtiers such as the Duke of Buckingham are shown attending the king and Cardinal Wolsey. Buckingham spills water from a hand-washing dish on Wolsey's feet, an intimation of the hostility between them and an episode derived from the real duke's having served the cardinal with water for ritual washing at the high Mass at the Field of Cloth of Gold in 1520. Buckingham is also shown serving Henry and Catherine of Aragon a platter of food during a meal in which Henry's doubts about their marriage are first sounded.[10] Aristocrats did personally attend and serve the monarch at times, but not usually in the daily round at court in the way this scene suggests. Most such service at meal times was undertaken by lower-ranking nobles and higher gentlemen who had salaried household offices such as "carver" or "sewer" and who lived at court in these capacities serving the king or queen for about three months a year—or a "quarter" as the wages rolls of the household have it.

The most important of such courtiers under the real Henry VIII were the Gentlemen of the King's Privy Chamber, who occupied the private space of the monarch and helped to dress and undress him, assisted by Grooms. They kept the king company, gambled with him, hunted, jousted, and danced with him, and escorted him informally wherever he went. The office had developed during the first decade of Henry's reign, finally modeled on an analogous one at the court of Francis I of France. The leading Gentleman was known as the Groom of the Stool because he attended the king when he used the close-stool or toilet, a position of great trust and esteem because this individual attended the monarch when he was at his most humanly vulnerable. In the early years of Henry's reign, the Groom was Sir William Compton. While *The Tudors* offers no indication of Compton's important court office, he appears in the series as a close friend of the king—and, bizarrely, sexually infatuated in the 1520s with a young Thomas Tallis, who did not in fact appear at court until about 20 years after Compton's death. In Season One, he and his fellow courtiers show us "the pastime with good company" that characterized the early years of Henry's reign, when he and Catherine were happy and presided over one of the most glamorous of European courts. The whole subject of the Privy Chamber, its staffing, and the implications for how its politics worked has been among the principal developments in the historiography of Henry's reign. It was a major impetus in the foundation of the field of academic "court studies" in Britain during the last two to three decades.

Understandably, perhaps, one observes little that is specific about court structures and office-holding in *The Tudors*, but the series does show "the court" to be wherever the king is. It is shown to have wide and narrow spaces and places, as well as public, private, and secret ones, and there is a general sense that life there is competitive. Personal and family advancement was at heart of Tudor politics, and the series shows well enough that it was a risky and at times downright dangerous business dealing with a king like Henry. One point the series hammers home is that getting and safeguarding one's access to the king is vital for status and political power. Several characters scream "majesty, majesty" at the moment of their downfall and usually toward the retreating king's back. More mundanely, who is in his favor and who is not obsesses the characters in *The Tudors* in believable ways and the power of the royal "favorite" is clear. We have noted Wolsey's closeness to Henry, but it is Henry Cavill's Charles Brandon, Duke of Suffolk, who is the first real star "favorite" of the series. He appears on-screen more than anyone but the king and always as the "boon companion" or best buddy in all his enterprises—just as the real Suffolk was described as being. His sexual charisma and technique match or exceed Henry's, made explicit in his winning their (fictional) 100 crowns bet about seducing Buckingham's daughter.

Suffolk is also the first favorite to be seen to lose royal favor but, unlike so many others, also to recover it. The invention in Season One of his marriage to the king's older sister Margaret after her fictional marriage to and murder of the king of Portugal is only one of the many fatuous attempts by the scriptwriter to "improve" on history. For reasons unfathomable, Suffolk's unauthorized marriage to Henry's youngest sister, Mary, which took place in France in early 1515 after the death of her first husband Louis XII, is confusingly and ludicrously elided with Margaret Tudor's second marriage, to Archibald Douglas, 6th Earl of Angus after the death of her first, James IV of Scotland, at Flodden in 1514 (though the series makes no references to the Scottish king). Henry is infuriated, banishes his friend from court, and threatens to have him executed. They are eventually reconciled through an arm-wrestling bout, which Suffolk wins. The real Wolsey made the most of the king's anger in securing the gratitude of the couple as he assisted their rehabilitation in royal favor. Suffolk submitted abjectly to Henry but in reality his life was never seriously in danger. In fact, Suffolk, Thomas Howard, 3rd Duke of Norfolk, and William Fitzwilliam, 1st Earl of Southampton, were the three great survivors of Henry's reign. All were deeply involved in its various machinations, yet none died at Henry's hands, albeit only by a hair's breadth in Norfolk's case. By contrast, the tragic consequences in Season Two for the Boleyn family of its vaunting ambition are conveyed movingly in the scenes around Anne's arrest and execution, especially in her father's abandonment of his two children.

Yet, as the king's personal relationships with Suffolk, Wolsey, his wives, and others show us, the individual ruler still had to bring to the majesty of the office of king and to education for its correct exercise a personality that could secure the obedience, the loyalty, and ideally the love of the ruled at all social levels. Therein lay the secret of effective kingship. The character traits or "virtues" that might best constitute this disposition, and which might be inculcated through the best education, had been discussed since Antiquity and reexamined in the course of the Renaissance. The preeminent virtue was wisdom or prudence, by which the right course could be determined according to correct understanding. Temperance was the next virtue, which meant maintaining a balance, proportion, and order, as much in the ruler's personal disposition as in the affairs of the realm, for the former was held to influence the latter. Fortitude encompassed bravery in action, stamina, and patient perseverance in adversity. Mercy, as Portia reminds the Doge and Shylock in the *Merchant of Venice*, was perhaps the most divine virtue of sovereignty. Sparingly and rightly exercised, it had a transformative quality upon all whom it embraced, ruler and subject alike. Like unto it was magnificence, an expansive and sustaining generosity that reassured the subjects—just as surely as its opposites, profligacy and wastefulness, unsettled them. Possessing or, more precisely, being regarded as possessing these supposedly masculine qualities was expressed in the Latin word *virtus* or manliness. *Virtus* compelled respect and obedience from the governed, at all social levels and gave a ruler personal honor and esteem.[11]

Before turning to what, if any aspects of *virtus* are portrayed in *The Tudors*, two aspects of it are conspicuous by their absence. Religious faith was not a prescribed aspect of *virtus* in the writing of most Renaissance political commentators, but it was assumed by all. The real Henry VIII did not become "religious" in the course of his life and through the trauma of his various marriages as the series suggests; rather, he was profoundly religious from the start. In the opening episodes, all the religiosity is done by Catherine, who is frequently seen in her private chapel chanting the rosary and praying before statues of the Virgin Mary. She has been here before on screen, most notably in the 1969 film *Anne of the Thousand Days*. As in that movie, so in *The Tudors*, her piety is contrasted sharply with the wantons of the court, not least Anne herself. In *Anne of the Thousand Days*, it ennobles her suffering as a good wife trying to meet her husband's need.[12] In *The Tudors*, it almost becomes the reason she cannot do so—as in the scene referred to earlier, when Henry goes to be with her and finds her at prayer. Henry is seen praying—a bit. He weeps in or near a confessional over his lack of a son, but there is no sense at all of the complex religious life of the court led by a king who routinely heard five masses and more a day and observed the seasonal festivals and rituals of the church with great sincerity.[13] As an amateur theologian from an early age, the king genuinely believed himself suited for taking the leadership of the church in England upon himself when this became the only apparent outcome of the struggle with an uncooperative papacy.

The patronage of architecture and art was an important aspect of the magnificence enjoined upon sixteenth-century monarchs. It often had practical implications such as designing new accommodation for ever-expanding courts.[14] Henry was very interested in a range of artistic endeavors. He took some hand in the designs of Beaulieu Palace in Essex, the temporary palace at the Field of Cloth of Gold, of Hampton Court after Wolsey made it over as a gift, and of Whitehall, the largest palace complex in Europe at Henry's death. He also oversaw military architecture in the chain of fortifications he ordered to be built around the south coasts of England and Wales. Henry owned a large number of paintings, maps and charts, and numerous musical and scientific instruments, and he patronized the Horenbout family of miniaturists and, of course, Hans Holbein. We get some sense in *The Tudors* of the opulence of the king's surroundings, of his clothes and jewels. And of gifts given to his favorites and received from them. Henry is shown composing "Greensleeves," something the real Henry never did, but his claims to musicianship are thereby noted. The vast range of Henry's artistic and architectural patronage was an important aspect of the projection of his power and status as monarch and of his posthumous legacy.[15]

The concept of *virtus* encompassed actively expressed masculinity. This had formal and informal, public and private aspects. A king had to look the part and express his will clearly and express his authority at all times. In *The Tudors*, this requirement upon kings is often rendered as petulant shouting. From the outset Henry seethes with anger and menace. His eyes narrow suspiciously or else stare in the same unblinking fury whether he believes himself betrayed by his heart's love or his shaving water is cold. At its worst, Rhys Meyers' Henry resembles a young and ambitious middle manager of an Internet sales company, who shouts, shakes his fists, and stamps as he drives his cowed team on to exceed their monthly targets so that he can get a bigger bonus. He is a nasty little bully. At its best, in moments of crisis such at the scene of the Blackfriars' trial or the immediate aftermath of Anne's execution, the performance shows us the fallible and delusional inner Henry well enough.[16] We have a sense of a man struggling to make himself and others believe that what he wants for himself is also best for his kingdom. But that is where it ends. This Henry has a brittle, crystalline, magnetism but no real warmth, or that charismatic ease of manner, "the common touch," that we are led to believe the real Henry had. Though he flashes his teeth at them regularly, this Henry's courtiers bow to him out of terror, not love or a genuine desire to serve.

As knights and as the chief military officers of their realms, kings were expected to express their authority and manliness, bravery, and aggression in defense of the realm or the prosecution of their territorial rights and claims. Leading men in battle (real or simulated) was *the* authenticating action of kingship. Going to war was seen as part of the magnificence of monarchy, especially as kings sought to focus the loyalty of their nobles upon themselves and to direct their aggressive energies outward. Whatever the complexities of international treaties and other constraints upon them, such as a lack of resources (financial and otherwise) the desire for personal renown drove young kings on, and no king of early sixteenth-century Europe was more bent on personal renown than Henry. He was proud of his own physicality and strength as a young man and never wasted an opportunity to show himself off.[17]

Here, *The Tudors* is typically puzzling. As the narrative begins in 1518 or thereabouts, it completely ignores Henry VIII's first and in one sense most significant war—that against France in 1513. For this actual "just war" in support of papacy against a schismatic Louis XII, it substitutes Henry roaring about "just causes" for war against Louis' successor, Francis I, who has "captured northern Italy" and connived at the murder of a fictional royal uncle. Henry talks a good deal about war, has a picture of his hero Henry V in his private quarters, and shows his ships to Charles V when he visits England. We do eventually see Henry at war in the 1544 siege of Boulogne, which is presented almost as a pitched battle at points and before which Henry, dressed in a surcoat of the royal arms and his snazzy crown, does a short pastiche of Shakespeare's Henry V's St. Crispin's Day speech before the battle of Agincourt—right down to crying for God, Harry, England, and St. George. Henry otherwise shouts and berates as usual over the length of the siege but returns a victorious hero. Of the French counterattack and the sinking of the *Mary Rose* in the Solent in July 1545 we hear nothing, save a dark warning from Suffolk of rumors of a French fleet assembling. It is not heroic having one of your capital ships sink before your eyes due to the incompetence of the crew, so that incident does not fit with *The Tudors*' narrative.[18]

Henry was also a master of "quasi-warfare," the aristocratic sports of the tournament and hunting, in which he self-consciously displayed his masculine prowess. In dozens of tournaments in the early years of his reign, his participation was carefully choreographed to focus attention on his physical strength and paramilitary prowess as a model of aristocratic and royal manliness. In *The Tudors*, the crowd greets his entry to the competition at one tournament with surprised delight and excitement. He unhorses several fictional noble opponents while tilting at the barrier, but we get no sense that here is an exceptional tournament competitor such as the real Henry was. We are told often that the king is out "hunting," but we actually see him only riding at pace with friends, unarmed, but apparently in pursuit of quarry invisible to us.[19] Of Henry's legendary skill in archery—which enabled him to demonstrate bodily proof, as it were, of his descent from the great princes whose armies had used archery to devastating affect against the French in the Hundred Years War—we see nothing.[20] We do see him at tennis dressed only in his shirt and hose, which the real Henry is reported to have been when he played. Henry also practiced at the sports of grappling, throwing, and over-balancing maneuvers now more commonly associated with the martial arts. There is a depiction of the famous wrestling bout with Francis I at the Field of Cloth of Gold, which Henry lost. In *The Tudors*, this provokes a complete temper tantrum in which Henry wrecks furniture in fury at being beaten by a better man—and here a taller one in the person of the actor Emmanuel Leconte. It becomes the reason for his repudiation of his alliance with Francis.[21]

It was not just in the sporting arena that Henry demonstrated his masculine strength and implied to watching audiences his fertility and to some extent at least even his virility. In the series, the camera dwells lovingly on young Henry's chiseled pecs and six-pack and those of his friend Suffolk, quite as much as on the heaving bare breasts and spread thighs of the women they seduce. This caters fully to modern sensibilities, which eroticize the chest and abdomen and upper arms of the young male body. It contrasts, however, with early-sixteenth-century European culture, where the primary sites of male desirability were the bearded face, the neck and shoulders, the thighs, and legs. Short, wide doublets, stockings and hose, and the legendary codpiece all emphasized these parts of the body to the fullest extent within the bounds of propriety. And they were best displayed while dancing. Henry VIII was an enthusiastic and accomplished dancer.

At a banquet in August 1514, he was reported as having spent "almost the whole night in dancing with the damsels." He had "done wonders" on the dance floor, leaping "like a stag." As with the tournaments, so in the banqueting hall, his entry and participation were causes of great excitement and wonder to all assembled. And, again, this rather crucial aspect of Henry's masculine physicality is entirely absent from *The Tudors*. The music and choreography in the frequent banqueting scenes are as aberrant as any other aspect of this production. It veers, often in the same scene, between imagined-to-be medieval fife and drum yomping and the sort of genteel country dancing familiar to the Bennet sisters in *Pride and Prejudice* but alien to the Tudor court. Henry does none of it. Instead, he walks around the guests smilingly, like the mayor of Netherfield (to pursue the Austen analogy), leering at his next potential conquest from a distance. The real Henry would have been at the center of the dancing and using it as the perfect way to get up close and personal.[22]

In the end, it all comes down to sex. And only sex. The whole complex driving force in Henry VIII's personality and thus his kingship, that monstrous but profoundly insecure ego, is reduced to his libido and his anxiety over the lack of a male heir. Albeit in a rather serious register, Henry is once more caricatured as an insatiable lothario, a very Casanova or Don Juan of sixteenth-century England and a paragon of priapic potency— even to the point of virtual rape in one scene. This is *The Tudors*' great disservice to England's most famous king, whose "real story" it purports to tell. Peddling the myth is presumably meant to make him heroic or at least compelling to modern audiences. It would certainly not have made him so in his own time. As Katherine Crawford and others have observed, contrary to modern expectations, the obsessive pursuit of sex might actually expose a ruler to accusations of effeminacy and tyranny.[23] In patriarchal theory, it was women, not men, who were held to be incapable of controlling their sexual urges. A prince who could not bridle his sexual instincts demonstrated that his own masculinity was insecure, precisely because it risked ceding to women a man's control over himself and his divinely ordained authority over them. It went further. If a prince was obsessed with his own private appetites, how could he devote his attention to the best interests of his people? How could he be trusted to respect the rights, property (including of course the women) of other men, chiefly those of his peers? These were exactly the accusations leveled at Alessandro de' Medici, Duke of Florence, in the early 1530s. His successor, Cosimo I, very carefully and very publicly honored his marital vows to Eleonora di

Toledo and thus secured the approbation of contemporary commentators for respecting and honoring women, and for his wise rule of the duchy.[24] Henry did have known mistresses in Elizabeth Blount and Mary Boleyn—and doubtless some other brief encounters besides—but these relationships were within the patriarchal norms as applied to kings. In contrast to his contemporary Francis I of France whose philandering was notorious, Henry was essentially a serial monogamist.[25]

Henry's own view of himself in these matters is presented in the most iconic image we have of him, the one that has virtually become his trademark and which is presented in *The Tudors* as essentially Henry's creation, rather than that of the artist. Hans Holbein's mural portrait of the king made for the Privy Chamber at Whitehall was painted to celebrate the birth of Prince Edward in October 1537. Much of Henry's modern and misplaced reputation as an inveterate womanizer (which originated only in the eighteenth century) derives from the pose and costume of the king in the painting. In Holbein's portrait, the king's shoulders and his arms held with hands on hips create an inverted triangle. This sits atop another triangle formed by his spread-legged stance. The apexes of the two triangles meet at the king's groin and there, of course, at the famous codpiece. This has been read as a reference to the king's supposed sexual appetite and capability. The codpiece was actually designed to protect and emphasize the "coddes," that is the testes (hence the name), and thus the wearer's reproductive capacity, his own security and maturity as a man, and that of his dynasty.[26] Seen within the painting, which also depicts Henry VII, Elizabeth of York, and Jane Seymour, Henry's position and stance proclaim his personal legitimacy as a king divinely charged with bringing true religion to England. Holbein presents him as a greater sovereign than his own father and as himself a father, not just to Prince Edward (referenced in Jane), but also to his whole people as God the Father's earthly representative in the realm.[27] In short, Henry's stance and costume celebrate not the endless sexual conquests for which *The Tudors* wants to make him primarily famous, but his own sense of his fame and reputation as the religious king of England.

For all the hype about the series and its sensationalist titillation, the portrayal of King Henry VIII in *The Tudors* is one of the most conventional and least convincing ever offered on screen. Its single distinguishing characteristic is that in the first two seasons it offers us the youngest Henry ever. Jonathan Rhys Meyers' Henry is famous for never really growing older until the last moments of the last episodes or obese or even credibly ill. The notoriety of the series derives from the portrayal of the dashing and sexually desirable hero that the real Henry certainly was—for a time. Rhys Meyers' Henry has plenty of exuberance, and he captures the unpredictability, paranoia, and the rather schizoid nature that most historians have detected in the king. The problem is that all of these things are there more or less from the outset. There is some dynamism in Henry as he begins to become his own man through his pursuit of Anne Boleyn, the fall of Wolsey, and the rise of Cromwell. That done, however, the work to establish Henry's character is essentially finished by Anne's fall. There is little believable development in the king's personality across the whole length of the series beyond Season Two. The rest is just repetitious variation on the theme (performed with slightly more facial hair) until the end, which is an exaggerated reiteration of what we saw at the start and the series fails in the face of the complexity of kingship as public office and role in the medieval and early-modern world.[28]

This is less a criticism of Rhys Meyers' performance (he won ten acting awards for his Henry, so it must be good) than of the series' writer and various directors. They were so antagonistic toward the historical record that the resultant plot bars the viewer from ever seeing Henry properly in any kind of plausible context, for all the attention lavished on apparent (though not actual) "authenticity" in costumes, scenery, and so on. As if the record of his life is not extraordinary enough, the sequence of events and even the people who form that record are thrown around so recklessly that virtually anything can, and does, happen. It makes understanding why Henry did exactly what he did *as a king* almost impossible.

The Tudors is entertainment, not a history documentary of course. All screen portrayals of historical characters amend and alter the record to fit the dramatic and technical demands of the medium. This is usually done, however, with some sense of respect for the historical record rather than determined indifference to it. Done well, as it has been, it can offer meaningful insight to wider audiences and become part what Robert Rosenstone has called "historical drama." Such a performance was given, for example, by Genevieve Bujold in *Anne of the Thousand Days*, where she played Anne Boleyn as an intelligent feisty proto-feminist and dynastic politician in her own right. Robert Shaw offered a memorably charming yet menacing Henry in *A Man For All Seasons*—and at least he looked a bit like Henry Tudor.[29] Knowingly or otherwise, both these characterizations worked with the grain of contemporary explorations of psychological motivation in historical characters and a revised view of how Tudor power worked. This is not true of *The Tudors*. Its publicity boasts that it has "redefined historical drama." It does nothing of the kind because it has no regard for, or integrity in dealing with, the history it ostensibly presents. It remains at best a bare-chested, heaving-bosomed, frenetic, "costume drama." It has more in common with *Carry on Henry* than any other film about the Tudor period. But while *Carry On* set out to be funny, the portentous *Tudors* ends up being merely laughable because its creators had no real understanding of, or interest in, the driving force of Henry VIII's life—namely, his kingship.

Notes

1. *The Tudors*, Episode 1:1.
2. Glenn Richardson, *Renaissance Monarchy: The Reigns of Henry VIII, Francis I and Charles V* (London: Hodder, 2002), 6–34.
3. Ibid., 24–27; David Starkey, *Henry, Virtuous Prince* (London: Harper Press, 2008), 118–135 and 172–183 on Henry's education and his relationship with More; *The Tudors*, Episodes 1:1–1:2.
4. *The Tudors*, Episodes 1:1, 1:10, 2:4, 2:9, 3:6–3:8, 4:1–4:3, 4:5–4:10 for the council; 1:10, 2:1–2:4, 3:8, 4:5, 4:9 for parliament; 3:1–3:4 for the Pilgrimage of Grace.
5. Christopher Coleman, and David Starkey, *Revolution Reassessed: Revisions in the History of Tudor Government and Administration* (Oxford: Oxford University Press, 1986).
6. Baldassare Castiglione, *The Book of the Courtier*, translated from the Italian by George Bull (London: Penguin, 1967).
7. Steven J. Gunn and Peter Lindley, eds., *Cardinal Wolsey: Church, State and Art* (Cambridge: Cambridge University Press, 1991).
8. Ronald Asch, and Birke, A.M., *Princes Patronage and the Nobility, The Court at the Beginning of the Modern Age c. 1450–1650* (Oxford: Oxford University Press, 1991); David Starkey, et al., *The English Court from the Wars of the Roses to the Civil War* (London: Longman, 1987).
9. *The Tudors*, Episode 1:1.
10. Ibid., Episodes 1:1–1:2.
11. Richardson, *Renaissance Monarchy*, 24–27.
12. *Anne of The Thousand Days* (1969), DVD: Universal Studios, 2007; http://www.imdb.com/title/tt0064030/; Glenn Richardson, "Anne of a Thousand Days," in Susan Doran and Thomas Freeman, eds., *Tudors and Stuarts on Film: Historical Perspectives* (New York: Palgrave Macmillan, 2008).

13. Fiona Kisby, "The Royal Household Chapel in Early-Tudor London, 1485–1547," unpublished University of London PhD dissertation, 1996.
14. Kent Rawlinson, "Architectural Culture and Royal Image at the Henrician Court," in Suzannah Lipscomb and Tom Betteridge, eds., *Henry VIII and the Court: Art, Politics and Performance* (Farnham: Ashgate, 2013), 93–114.
15. Maria Hayward, "'Dressed to Rule: Henry VIII's Wardrobe and His Equipment for Horse, Hawk and Hound,'" in Maria Hayward and Philip Ward, eds., *The Inventory of King Henry VIII, vol. II Textiles and Dress* (London: Harvey Miller Publishers, 2012), 67–108; *The Tudors*, Episode 1:9.
16. *The Tudors*, Episodes 1:8, 2:10.
17. Richardson, *Renaissance Monarchy*, 36–72.
18. *The Tudors*, Episodes 4:7–4:9.
19. Glenn Richardson "Hunting at the Courts of Francis I and Henry VIII," *The Court Historian* 18 (2) (December 2013): 127–142.
20. Starkey, *Virtuous Prince*, 221–233 on Henry's enthusiasm for jousting from a young age.
21. Glenn Richardson, *The Field of Cloth of Gold* (New Haven and London: Yale University Press, 2013), 138–140 for an explanation of the wrestling episode; *The Tudors*, Episode 1:2.
22. Margaret McGowan, *Dance in the Renaissance, European Fashion, French Obsession* (New Haven and London: Yale University Press, 2008), especially 94–98.
23. Katherine Crawford, *The Sexual Culture of the French Renaissance* (Cambridge: Cambridge University Press, 2010), 1–22; Ruth Karras, *From Boys to Men: Formations of Masculinity in Late Medieval Europe* (Philadelphia: University of Pennsylvania Press, 2003).
24. Nick Scott-Baker, "Power and Passion in Sixteenth-Century Florence: The Sexual and Political Reputations of Alessandro and Cosimo I de' Medici," *Journal of the History of Sexuality* 19 (3) (2010): 432–457.
25. Robert J. Knecht, "'Born Between Two Women … Jules Michelet and Francis I,'" *Renaissance Studies* 14 (3) (2000): 329–343, on Francis' posthumous sexual reputation. See also David Potter, "Politics and Faction at the Court of Francis I: The duchesse d'Etampes, Montmorency and the Dauphin Henri," *French History* 21 (2) (June 2007): 127–146.
26. Tania String, "Projecting Masculinity: Henry VIII's Codpiece," in Mark Rankin, Christopher Highley, and John King, eds., *Henry VIII and His Afterlives Literature, Politics and Art* (Cambridge: Cambridge University Press, 2009), 143–159, and Christopher Highley, "The Remains of Henry VIII," in the same volume, 160–189.

27. Tania String, "Henry VIII and Holbein: Patterns and Conventions in Early Modern Writing about Artists." in Lipscomb and Betteridge, eds., *Henry VIII and the Court*, 131–141.
28. Glenn Richardson, "Boys and the their Toys: Kingship, Masculinity and Material Culture in the Sixteenth Century," in Sean McGlynn and Ellie Woodacre, eds., *The Image and Perception of Monarchy in Medieval and Early-Modern England* (London: Cambridge Scholars Publishing, 2014), 183–206.
29. Ruth Ahnert, "Drama King: The Portrayal of Henry VIII in Robert Bolt's *A Man for All Seasons*," in Lipscomb and Betteridge, eds., *Henry VIII and the Court*, 207–221.

CHAPTER 12

The Tudors and the Tudor Court: Know Your Symptom

Thomas Betteridge

what the nostalgic image conceals is not the historical meditation but on the contrary the unhistorical traumatic kernel which returns as the Same through all historical epochs (in Marxist terms, the nostalgic image of idyllic pre-capitalist society as opposed to capitalist antagonism ultimately conceals the class struggle which is what *remains the same* in the passage from feudalism to capitalism).

Slavoj Žižek[1]

The Tudors is a historical drama that stages, compulsively, the production of the male body as that which stays the same, which escapes the demands of history. The Tudor court as constructed in *The Tudors* is a machine for the endless staging of the encounter, or perhaps more accurately the nonencounter, between history and masculinity. There is, therefore, a strange disturbing sense in which the Tudor court functions as a romance space—it is a place in which the viewer is constantly taught how to recognize real, as opposed to historical, manhood. Of course, this repetition is itself a sign of the instability of the romance of masculinity as staged through the court in *The Tudors*. Jonathan Rhys Meyers' body has to be lauded and staged over and over again in order to publicly

T. Betteridge (✉)
Department of Arts and Humanities, College of Business, Arts, and Social Sciences, Brunel University, London, UK

© The Editor(s) (if applicable) and The Author(s) 2016
W.B. Robison (ed.), *History, Fiction, and* The Tudors, Queenship and Power, DOI 10.1057/978-1-137-43883-6_12

defeat historicism and in the process sustain a notion of the male body as desirable across or even beyond history. This public production of the male body depends upon the court as a symbolic space capable of bearing the burden of history. The problem is, as with all good romances, the court/narrative takes on a life of its own and in the process creates a genuinely historical image of Henry's court.

This chapter is in three parts. The first section discusses the way in which the court functions in *The Tudors*, while the second section looks in detail at the series' depiction of the fall of Anne Boleyn. The final section broadens the argument to suggest relationships between the court as depicted in *The Tudors* and the ways in which the poet Thomas Wyatt presented the court to his readers. Henry's court was always an object to be consumed and the consumption of the Henrician court is invariably political. The gaze follows the king, or the queen, or the mistress, or the servant, or the poet, and in the process makes political choices concerning who matters and what needs to be excluded from view in order to protect the fantasy of the court.

Producing the Tudor Court

John Skelton's poem *The Bowge of Courte* (c. 1498) is a dream vision in which the narrator sees a ship of vices which, it becomes clear through the course of the poem, is a metaphor for the court. The narrator recounts his encounters with various courtly figures including Riot, Suspicion, and Dissimulation. It is, however, a final conversation with Dread that drives the narrator panicking from the boat/court. The poem ends on a profoundly ambiguous note with narrator simultaneously undermining the nature of his vision and suggesting it did indeed contain some truth.

> I wyll not saye it is matter in dede,
> But yet oftyme suche dremes be founde trewe.
> Now constrewe ye what is the resydewe.[2]

The narrator refuses to say whether his vision was indeed truthful but he then goes on to remind the reader that dreams are often found to be true. He leaves the reader to ponder what is left, what residues, once the competing claims of fictionality and truthfulness have been weighed up. *The Bowge of the Court* was written about the court of Henry VIII's father, but it invokes a world that is instantly recognizable to a viewer of *The Tudors*.

Skelton's court is one whose protagonists engage in an endless game of lying, seducing, and scheming. They are united only in a desire to keep out any newcomers who might disrupt their deadly game. Henry VIII's court as depicted in *The Tudors* appears at times to be a parodic version of Skelton's. The acting is so wooden and the characterization so simplistic that it is as though one is watching a film version of *The Bowge of the Court*. This would, however, be unfair. *The Tudors* is a study in a particular kind of postmodern historical tourism in which a residue of genuine historical insight constantly appears amid all of the inevitable anachronism.

The court in *The Tudors* is above all centered on the person and persona of Henry VIII. Peter Marshall has recently commented:

> [I]t seems unlikely that attempts to fathom and comprehend Henry VIII's psychological make-up and personality facets will cease any time soon. For the enduring fascination of Henry for both popular and academic biographers stems from the fact that his "tyranny" was not so much an expression of a system of governance as the toe of the governing web of personal relationships. He remains an unrivalled case-study in the effect of untrammelled power on the development of a personality, and of a personality of power.[3]

The Tudors uses images of the court and of courtliness to create a sense of Henry's power and the web through which it operated.

In Season One a key conflict is between Henry and the Duke of Buckingham, played by Steven Waddington. Indeed, before the advent of Anne Boleyn, the struggle between Buckingham and Henry is the central source of narrative motivation for the series. The court plays a central role in this struggle since it is through his role as cup bearer and royal servant that Buckingham's status as a subject to Henry is played out. In these terms the intricacies of the court come to stand for hierarchy and historical specificity. Viewers confront the reality of the contest between Buckingham and Henry as a form of history lesson. Court ceremony is the place in *The Tudors* where history appears or is noted. This is, however, partly because the program deploys a profoundly ahistorical model of masculinity to sustain its construction of the conflict between Henry and Buckingham. Waddington has played heroic masculine roles in a number of television shows and films. *The Tudors* depicts him as a conventional, even stereotypical, male hero. In particular, he is portrayed as noticeably more muscular and substantial than Jonathan Rhys Meyers' Henry. The tension that is articulated around and through court ceremony in *The*

Tudors is given a particular valance by the different models of masculinity that Waddington and Meyers represent. This is not complex. The Tudor court as it functions in Season One of *The Tudors* is a machine that forces real men, father figures, to be menial servants to much less manly figures—Buckingham is the man to Henry's boy.

This aspect of the court is further emphasized when Henry provokes his confidante Charles Brandon, played by Henry Cavill, to seduce Buckingham's daughter, although in fact the character name, Anne Stafford, was that of the duke's sister. *The Tudors* depicts Buckingham surprising Anne and Charles having sex in a side room at court and reacting violently to what he regards as a slur to his honor and the family name. The series sets up a clear division between Henry, Brandon, and Anne (by implication, although she is denied all agency) on one hand and Buckingham on the other in relation to sexual norms. While *The Tudors* depicts the latter as holding dated, old-fashioned ideas concerning family honor, it treats Brandon's seduction of Anne as modern and endorses it as a natural or at least presents it to the viewer in a way that suggests sexual pleasure. The *Tudors* therefore creates a symbolic tension between the court as a place of formality, which operates to undermine the masculinity of figures like Buckingham, and a place where under the formal surface, often literally, sex takes place. The spaces behind arrases, side rooms, and corridors are all marked in *The Tudors* as sites for various forms of illicit behavior, which in term are represented as modern or transhistorical. The formal surface of the court is where history is located while modernity lurks in the shadows.

In this context, there is an interesting and potentially homoerotic aspect to the Tudor court which centers on the relationship between Henry and his various close male companions. In particular, here is a clear homoerotic charge to Henry's friendship with Brandon as portrayed in *The Tudors*. Brandon's seduction of Anne is as a result of a bet he had made with Henry and there is a sense in which Brandon is Henry's sexual surrogate. At the same time, this sexual defeat reinforces Buckingham's status as a man out of place in the court. In the symbolic *ménage à trois* between Henry, Brandon, and Anne, there is no place for a real man like Buckingham. Thomas S. Freeman has recently commented that, "The most recent television portrayal of Henry ... *The Tudors* ... is strikingly different from the tyrannical alpha male of almost all post-war film depictions of the king."[4] This is particularly true in terms of the ways in which it shows Henry relating to the sexual norms of the court. *The Tudors* consistently depicts him as a man driven by an almost overwhelming sex drive that appears able to find its full expression only in the court. The courtly Henry VIII in *The Tudors* is certainly a flamboyant Renaissance monarch and a man of politics but he is also someone who cannot pass a beautiful woman without desiring her and often seducing her. Jonathan Rhys Meyers' Henry is aggressively masculine outside the court, but inside he becomes strangely feminine through his sexualized displayed body. This is not simply a matter of the display of Meyers' body, which is constant, but it is also because the court is itself shown to a dangerously feminine space.

Voyeurism is the logic of the court in *The Tudors*. It pervades all the court's aspects, and consistently the viewer is invited to view the court as a space in which behind every arras or door their fantasies will be taking place. Ann Snitow argues:

> Promiscuity by definition is a breakdown of barriers. Pornography is not only a reflector of social power imbalances and sexual pathologies; it is also these imbalances run riot, run to excess, sometimes explored *ad absurdum*, exploded. Misogyny is one content of pornography; another content is the universal infant desire for complete, immediate gratification, to rule the world out of the very core of passive helplessness.[5]

Of course, *The Tudors* is not pornographic. It does, however, validate and normalize promiscuity as a sexual norm and tactically implies that anyone who is not promiscuous is in some way restricted and flawed. Indeed, in the context of the Tudor court promiscuity is a signifier of modernity. The formal straitlaced historical surface of the court is compared consistently with the promiscuous modern depth. The fantasy that *The Tudors* offers the viewer is that it is the norms of modern sexuality, which in Žižek's terms remain the same across history. The sexual imagery in *The Tudors* offers the viewer the fantasy of immediate uncomplicated gratification without having to engage with the pressure, the burden, of history. You do not need to know who Brandon and Anne are in order to enjoy the pleasure of their toned eroticized bodies.

The Fall of Anne Boleyn

The fall of Anne Boleyn is the climax to the second series of *The Tudors*. Episode 2:8 opens with a highly conventional cinematic moment. Jane Seymour is shown being instructed in how to be a maid of honor. Anne is depicted as seeing Jane as a potential rival for no explicit reason other than Jane's attractiveness. Clearly, Anne has already watched Episodes 2:8 and 2:9 of *The Tudors*. The shot is framed so that Anne is positioned on the right, the established/old, and Jane on the left, emerging and new. It is as though the director was not confident that the viewers would understand the significance of Jane's appearance. At one level, this opening sequence is of a piece with *The Tudors* simplistic and plodding version of history by numbers, the sense that the series gives of a need to paint in very bold colors. There is, however, more to this moment than clunky television making. Episodes 2:8 and 2:9 of *The Tudors* have to perform the delicate task of changing the focus of the program's romance narrative from Anne to Jane. In this structure, the court is a key symbolic space. The program consistently depicts Jane as sitting above politics. In these terms she represents the idealized promise of romance as a genre.

Mary Poovey comments:

> [T]he fundamental assumption of romantic love—the reason it is so compatible with bourgeois society—is that the personal can be kept separate from the social, the one's "self" can be fulfilled in spite of—and in isolation from—the demands of the marketplace.[6]

The court in *The Tudors* is a place of romance, or perhaps more accurately, it is a place where romance happens. This is an important distinction since one way in which the program changes the focus from Anne to Jane is through its construction of their relationships to the court. Having set up the tension between Jane and Anne as a key issue, the next scenes in Episode 2:8 are a series of courtly moments in which various male characters are shown engaged in the process of Tudor government. The viewer sees the imperial ambassador Eustace Chapuys plotting, then discussing foreign affairs with Henry before the latter is depicted in conversation with Thomas Cromwell. The next scene in Episode 2:8 is set in an ecclesiastical setting and concludes with an exchange of charged gazes between Jane, Henry, and Anne. This scene is followed by one in which Anne is shown dispensing charity to the poor on Maundy Thursday.

The narrative of Anne's fall as *The Tudors* depicts it is a process of expulsion from the space of romance into that of the court. Despite all the politics that surrounded her fall, it is the moment when Henry's nonpolitical, implicitly nonhistorical, gaze falls on Jane that the viewer—and, in fact, Anne herself—knows that she is doomed. The court operates as a space in which Anne's fall is mediated, enacted, and enabled. Jane's innocence is constructed against the strictures of the court. Her affection for Henry, in the face of pretty compelling historical evidence, is represented as being chaste and based entirely on a genuinely romantic attachment between two adults—who happen to be a king and a lady. This process has two very useful effects for the program makers. It allows them to represent Anne's fall as a failure of femininity. It also reassures the viewer that romance can survive the pressures of history and can exist in or even beyond a world of power politics and factional scheming. *The Tudors* consistently distinguishes through Henry's behavior the difference between Anne's downfall and Jane's elevation. In the process, *The Tudors* interestingly resolves the historiographical issue of Anne's guilt—Anne is guilty, if not of multiple adulteries, then certainly of failing as a romance heroine.

At a crucial moment during the narrative of Anne's fall, the poet Thomas Wyatt is in a gallery overlooking the court. He comments to his companion, "Something is going on here but I don't know what it is." Wyatt's gaze is occupied by a swirling whirl of courtly activity. In one corner Anne is entertaining various foreign ambassadors with anti-French jokes, in another her father and brother are plotting, while Henry is everywhere and nowhere. Wyatt's perplexity reflects both a literal and a symbolic lack of knowledge. The surface of the court seems to be wrong from his viewpoint. This is partly because he is positioned, like a television viewer, watching and not participating in the court. It is also because it is obvious to everyone that there is a monumental political change happening, but it is not clear what it is. This is because the public surface of the court is being disrupted by the private investigation of Anne's behavior going on behind the scenes led by Cromwell. It is almost as if *The Tudors* has a Marxist subtext with the imp of history being played by Henry's desire to be rid of Anne. The court in this context functions as the site of formal, even acceptable, history while in the background the real issues are played out.

As always, at the center of this process is Henry. Ruth Ahnert has recently commented that in series one of *The Tudors*, "Jonathan Rhys Meyers's Henry is both anachronistically youthful, and a brooding, troubled soul, torn between the guidance of More on the one hand, and Wolsey on the other."[7] This binary division is given a different but equally powerful articulation in the fall of Anne when we have the romantic ahistorical Henry courting Jane and the powerful but torn historical king convinced the woman for whom he transformed the country is actually a witch and a whore. It is not clear in *The Tudors* to what extent Henry really believes in the various accusations against Anne. Or perhaps more accurately, it is not clear how hard he has to work to convince himself that she is an adulterer. Certainly by the end of Episode 2:9, when Henry is confronted by a pleading Anne with the Princess Elizabeth is her arms, he is fully committed to Jane. Indeed, this scene is a perfect illustration of Anne's fall since she commits the ultimate romance scene of having a child and therefore referring to precisely the kind of social realities that Poovey suggests romance allows its consumers to avoid. Anne and Jane are valuable on the marketplace because of their ability to produce children, preferably male. Anne has to be executed in the end because history demands it and because she can no longer play the role of the romance heroine.

This romantic failure is given an increasing symbolic charge in *The Tudors* in Episode 2:8 and 2:9 as there are a number of moments when Natalie Dormer's Anne speaks words derived from the evidence used to convict the historical Anne. In particular, *The Tudors* makes much of the allegation that Anne told Henry Norris that he looked "to step into dead men's shoes." There is something unnerving for someone who knows the facts of Anne Boleyn's trial and the testimony about hearing it reproduced in a fictional work like *The Tudors*. It is as though the romance narrative operates as the enabling frame for historical facts to emerge into the cold light of day. Narrative is the trans- even a-discourse that provides the shape for the shards of Tudor dialogue to break through. In these terms, the court in *The Tudors* creates an ethos of symbolic space that is strangely accurate as a representation of Henry's court, albeit not in terms of historical facts.

In his poem, "Circa Regna Tonat," Thomas Wyatt reflects on the cost of being a courtier. This poem contains a famous reference to Anne's fall and is quoted by the character Wyatt in *The Tudors*.

> The bell tower showed me such a sight
> That in my head sticks day and night.
> There did I learn out of a grate
> For all favour, glory, or might,
> That yet *circa Regna tonat*.[8]

Wyatt uses Latin within the discursive frame of his poem as a statement of fact. This is partly a question of Wyatt using the poem to display his talent for using classical tags, but it is also a way of separating the central argument of the poem from the more elliptical, topical, and potentially dangerous matter of the English lines. Of course, the use of original dialogue in *The Tudors* is not as sophisticated as Wyatt's, but in the context of the way the program constructs the court, there are some interesting overlaps.

Above all, when Anne the character quotes the testimony of Anne the real person, executed for crimes she almost certainly did not commit, the ethics of television history are brought into sharp relief. Indeed, this is particularly the case given that while the surface portrayal of Anne's fall in *The Tudor*'s is relatively sympathetic to her and makes it clear that much of the motivation for it came from Henry's desire for Jane, the narrative framing makes Anne guilty. She is tarred with the historical brush of courtliness, she is the one left in the historical court while Jane and Henry take central stage in the ahistorical world of romance. Anne's fall reflects the extent to which the court in *The Tudors* is a symbolically charged site whose status changes and mutates depending on the nature of the storyline being pursued. At times, it enables the promiscuity that the program makers clearly deploy to add to the series' popularity. At other times, it works to elide or smooth away the tensions of history or indeed the need to engage with history at all—the court will do this while Henry/the viewer can indulge in their desire for romance and sex.

THE COURT AS A SCREEN FOR MASCULINITY

Wyatt's poem, "They Flee from Me," is a perfect distillation of anxious courtly masculinity. It opens with the far-from-trustworthy narrator lamenting the fact that he is no longer sought out by the women who used to seek him out. The second verse conquerors up an image of a specifically courtly erotic tryst.

> Thanked be fortune it hath been otherwise
> Twenty times better, but once in special,
> In thin array after a pleasant guise,
> When her loose gown from her shoulders did fall
> And she me caught in her arms long and small,
> Therewithal sweetly did me kiss
> And softly said, 'Dear heart, how like you this?'[9]

The erotic charge in this verse is between the agency of the narrative voice and male passivity as depicted in the lines. The woman, with "arms long and small," catches the male narrator and kisses him in an image that suggests a sexual encounter in which the weak woman renders the strong man infantile—and this is what he wants and desires. Wyatt is clearly conscious of the extent to which the narrator of "They Flee from Me" is torn between desire and repulsion.

The Tudors uses the court to create a similar oscillation between the harsh truths of history and the world of romance. This is particularly true in Season Three, where the producers were confronted with the need to stage the Pilgrimage of Grace. In Episode 3:4, the viewer is faced with a constant movement backward and forward between the court where Jane is making friends with Henry's daughters, particularly Mary, and the grim events in the North. The scenes cut from the image of a field full of hanging bodies to Jane's entry into court. There are scenes with Henry plotting with Francis Bryan to kill Reginald Pole and then action returns to the court and a feast. There is even time for a typical court scene from *The Tudors* when Bryan is shown having sex with Edward Seymour's wife, Anne Stanhope, before the viewer is taken back to York to see Robert Aske's execution. What happens in this episode is that the viewer is shown historical reality, which in the case of the suppression of the Pilgrimage of Grace is brutal and violent, in relatively small pieces interspaced with far more palatable courtly images—both of the surface of the court, feasts, and ceremonial events, and of its underside, plotting, and sex. In Wyatt's poetry, there is a constant sense of a power or pressure that bears down on his narrators. In "They Flee from Me" a key element in the narrator's anger is that the erotic moment when he was rendered powerless by the women dressed in "thin array" was also a moment when he no longer had to live up to the impossible crushing demands of male courtliness by which he now finds himself oppressed again.

In *The Tudors*, it is above all Henry who has to carry the charge or sign of masculinity. Arguably, this is entirely historically accurate. Tatiana String has recently pointed out that the representation of Henry in the famous Whitehall mural is not at all conventional.

> In the Whitehall mural, unlike many other images of the period, nothing is occluded, or allusive, or buried underneath ritual. The concatenation of masculine signifiers is not an unusually compacted rehearsal of visual clichés. Holbein was breaking new ground, not ticking boxes, in this unusually intensive concentration on masculinity. Masculinity was typically nuanced and inflected, selectively or discreetly rendered. But Holbein's construction permitted no ambiguity in the viewer's response to Henry's evident and maximal self-fashioning in masculine terms that fully personalized the exercise of political power.[10]

Henry VIII consistently used his court as a stage for his particular masculinity exceptionality. In many ways this is a key and underappreciated facet of Henry's realm. There were numerous reasons why the Pilgrims of 1536 had to be treated harshly, some entirely legitimate. But at least one of them was Henry's sense of wounded, even offended, masculine pride. Not for him, in any situation, to be shown to be weak or to be caught in arms "long and small." One of the more disturbing and interesting aspects of Meyers' portrayal of Henry is the way he captures the king's mercurial personality. At one moment he treats Jane as the heroine in a classic romance tale and at another complains to her because she is not pregnant. The Henry of *The Tudors* and the Henry of history always construct themselves as a cynosure of the action—except when the action will tarnish the royal reputation or be difficult to achieve. At these moments Meyers' Henry, like at times the historical Henry, gets others to do his dirty work. In the process, however, what is thrown into stark relief is the extent to which Henry's masculinity is far less total and perfect than it is portrayed either in paint or on the screen. The court may be a site for romance and at times function as the historical foil to other transhistorical aspects of the show, but it always wins in the end.

As the program progresses there is a sense in which the burden of history becomes more and more pressing. This is reflected both in the surface of the program in some rather strange plot twists—Henry being visited by the ghost of his father being perhaps the most strange—and also by an increasing divergence from the facts of the past. The latter is of course entirely understandable. There is a real sense that from Jane's death the program loses its way. This is partly because the counterweight to Henry's masculinity provided by strong women like Catherine, Anne, and Jane disappears—or is replaced by new female characters like Brandon's French mistress, Brigitte Rousselot, who are not historical. What Seasons Three and Four of *The Tudors* reveal is the extent to which the entire series is predicated on a denial of history in order to accommodate some particularly transhistorical representations of gender, in particular masculinity. Slavoj Žižek comments:

> We do not have the public "repressive" rule of law and order undermined by undercover forms of rebellion—mocking public authority, and so on—but rather its opposite: the public authority maintains a civilized, gentle appearance, whereas beneath it there is a shadowy realm in which the brutal exercise of power is itself sexualised. And the crucial point, of course, is that

the obscene shadowy realm, far from undermining the civilized semblance of the public power, serves as its inherent support.[11]

In *The Tudors* the public authority is history, and in many ways it is expressed in and through the court. The shadowy realm is the need to entertain the audience and satisfy the demands of popular television. These two competing pressures meet in and around the twin poles of Henry and the court. The producers made a conscious decision to accept Meyers' refusal to get fat as Henry ages in order to protect his sex appeal. This has interesting and at times unfortunate effects on the program. For example, it makes the portrayal of Catherine Howard's adultery particularly problematic and critical of the queen. It also, however, reflects the extent to which, at a fundamental level, it is the romance narrative that is important to the program makers, and in this discourse bodies do not age or grow fat. Anne fell, and the viewers knew she had, when she appeared on screen carrying the baby Elizabeth and pleading with Henry to take her back. In a sense, Elizabeth at this point reflected both the public face of history but also its obscene shadowy realm.

Conclusion

Thomas S. Freeman has recently commented, "The more [*The Tudors*] subverts the traditional Henry, the more strongly it re-establishes it."[12] In many ways this is also true of the way in which the series depicts the Henrician court. Despite its emphasis on courtly promiscuity and its tendency to flatten court ceremony to such an extent as to render it almost meaningless, there is a historical kernel in representation of the Tudor court by the makers of *The Tudors*. And this is that it is the presence of the monarch—of Henry—that renders the court meaningful and important. The camera follows Henry around—he is always the center of the action, and he is the one person who can intervene and safely disrupt the court's smooth surface. Despite some of the critical comments that I have made in this chapter about the series, *The Tudors* has been genuinely innovative in the way it has used court space as a narrative tool and a frame for politics. I wonder if *Game of Thrones* would have been so confident in its portrayal of its various and varied courts without the example set by *The Tudors*.

NOTES

1. Slavoj Žižek, *Enjoy Your Symptom: Jacque Lacan in Hollywood and Out* (London: Routledge, 1992), 81.
2. John Skelton, *The Complete English Poems*, ed. John Scattergood (London: Penguin, 1983), 61.
3. Peter Marshall, "Henry VIII and the Modern Historians: The Making of a Twentieth-Century Reputation," in Mark Rankin, Christopher Highley, and John N. King, eds., *Henry VIII and His Afterlives* (Cambridge: Cambridge University Press, 2009), 263.
4. Thomas S. Freeman, "A Tyrant for All Seasons: Henry VIII on Film," in Susan Doran and Thomas S. Freeman, eds., *Tudors and Stuarts on Film: Historical Perspectives* (London: Palgrave, 2009), 44.
5. Ann Snitow, "Mass Market Romance: Pornography for Women is Different," in Susan Ostrov Weisser, ed., *Women and Romance: A Reader* (New York: New York University Press, 2001), 316.
6. Mary Poovey, "Persuasion and the Promises of Love," in Weisser, ed., *Women and Romance: A Reader*, 269.
7. Ruth Ahnert, "Drama King: The Portrayal of Henry VIII in Robert Bolt's A Man for All Seasons," in Thomas Betteridge and Thomas S. Freeman, eds., *Henry VIII and History* (Basingstoke: Ashgate, 2012), 207–221, 221.
8. Thomas Wyatt, *The Complete Poems*, ed. R.A. Rebholz (London: Penguin, 1978), 155.
9. Ibid, 117.
10. Tatiana C. String, "Projecting Masculinity: Henry VIII's Codpiece," in Rankin, Highly, and King, eds., *Henry VIII and His Afterlives*, 155.
11. Slavoj Žižek, "'I Hear Your with My Eyes': Or, The Invisible Master," in Renata Salecl and Slavoj Žižek, eds., *Gaze and Voice as Love Objects* (Durham: Duke University Press, 1996), 100.
12. Thomas S. Freeman, "A Tyrant for All Seasons: Henry VIII on Film," 45.

CHAPTER 13

"The Dyer's Hands Are Always Stained": Religion and the Clergy in *The Tudors*

Caroline Armbruster

A poignant scene in the first season of *The Tudors* begins in the bright sunshine of a stable yard in Paris, where Thomas Wolsey and Thomas More discuss the price of a career in royal service. Wolsey insists a man must be prepared to compromise his principles. He declares, "The dyer's hand is always stained by the elements he works with." More refuses to accept this assertion. Dipping his own hands into a nearby bucket of water, he retorts, "Here is my element. The spiritual element. The higher element. Now, you tell me—am I stained by it?"[1] So ends an excellent exchange, underscoring the contrasting dispositions of Sam Neill's Wolsey and Jeremy Northam's More. While the former is invariably concerned with the demands of this world, the latter refuses to compromise his principles regardless of the cost. Like the ambitious Wolsey, *The Tudors* is also stained by the elements with which it works. Comprising a total of 38 episodes, the series has more than enough opportunity to explore the complexity of the Tudor era. Concerned with both attracting and keeping a popular audience, however, the script chooses to focus on the more gratuitous aspects of Henry VIII's reign. The theme of religion—"the spiritual element"—is visible throughout, but it is undermined by a simplistic approach to difficult concepts and an obvious preference for entertainment.

C. Armbruster (✉)
Department of History, Louisiana State University, Baton Rouge, LA, USA

Unlike the world of *The Tudors*, religion was inescapable in sixteenth-century England. Church doctrine dictated both belief and practice, infusing every stage of life with Christian ritual. Books of hours—popular devotional works of the time—provided users with a regimented, daily schedule of prayer and introspection. The clergy, too, made their presence felt on a regular basis by administering the sacraments, providing charity and education, as well as occasionally investigating heresy. Men of the cloth often also served as government officials, merging thoroughly the spiritual and the secular. With the coming of the Reformation and the destruction of England's long-established ties with the Roman Catholic Church, questions of belief and practice became even more inescapable. Thus, the early sixteenth century was undeniably a time of religious piety, fervor, and revolution.

The four seasons of *The Tudors* cover the majority of Henry VIII's tumultuous reign, including the onset of the English Reformation and its consequences. Despite its scope, the series is often condemned for its historical inaccuracy and its preoccupation "with sins of the flesh."[2] Critics claim that writer and creator, Michael Hirst, simply reduces "the era's thematic conflicts to simplistic struggles over personal and erotic power."[3] Although *The Tudors* certainly never misses an opportunity for shameless spectacle, its script does occasionally force viewers to engage with sixteenth-century spiritual concerns. Religion and the clergy monopolize a respectable amount of screen time. Yet, instances of historical inaccuracy, anachronism, and oversimplification abound. When religion takes center stage, the resulting portrayal is usually superficial. Popes, cardinals, and bishops impress in their splendid robes, but this merely serves to underscore a theme of rampant corruption among the clergy. Characters clutch at bejeweled rosaries, read from ornate Bibles, kneel somberly in prayer, and attend mass in splendid cathedrals, but only rarely does the script engage with serious issues of faith and belief. Hirst reserves genuine religiosity for a select few characters, overlooking the simple fact that religion affected all aspects of life in Tudor England.

The series begins in approximately 1518, well before the beginning of Henry VIII's "Great Matter." From the first episode, however, Henry is troubled by his unproductive marriage to Catherine of Aragon. The story of the king's prolonged efforts to abandon his first wife, marry again, and produce a male heir is a familiar one. Film, television, and the stage have all depicted Henry VIII's marital drama and ensuing impasse with the Roman Catholic Church. What sets *The Tudors* apart, however, is that it has the luxury of nearly 35 hours to devote to the narrative. Yet, the series refuses to take full advantage of this time, delivering a distinctly unimaginative interpretation while operating under the belief that the "whole show is about love."[4] With Henry's private life as the central theme, the complicated origins of the English Reformation are oversimplified, leading the audience to believe that the establishment of the Church of England was almost entirely the outcome of the king's marital dilemma. Aside from Henry VIII's "Great Matter," there were other forces at work contributing to England's abandonment of Catholicism.[5] For example, the script generally disregards the king's genuine belief in his role as Christian monarch.[6] Jonathan Rhys Meyers' Henry is instead motivated by personal vanity and egotistical ideas about his authority, treating religion as a mere instrument for political gain.

Most historians agree that Henry VIII was, in fact, devoutly religious and well versed in theology. He heard mass on a daily basis, participated in holy pilgrimages, and read scripture habitually.[7] But *The Tudors* only occasionally reminds the audience of this religiosity. The young king is presented, for example, as the sole author of the theological treatise, *Assertio Septem Sacramentorum*—though the historical Henry likely had help with its composition.[8] In a much later episode, the aging king manages to briefly fulfill the role of Christian monarch by performing the royal touch—placing his hands on the heads of the sick, offering his blessing, and then distributing alms.[9] Aside from such perfunctory demonstrations of faith, *The Tudors*' Henry concerns himself with satisfying his ambitions. The script presents him as a Catholic who "would have neither pope, nor Luther, nor any other man set above him." For example, as proof of his megalomania, Henry ludicrously—and inaccurately—decides to rewrite the Ten Commandments and the Lord's Prayer for his new church.[10] Rhys Meyers himself sums up the series' approach to the king by stating bluntly that the character is "wracked with ego, vanity and thoughts of his own divinity."[11]

The clergymen of *The Tudors* are likewise not exempted from excessive worldliness, and among their ranks, Cardinal Thomas Wolsey certainly looms largest. As a progressive and levelheaded politician, Sam Neill's Wolsey is both appealing to a modern audience and fairly consistent with those historical assessments more sympathetic to the cardinal's memory.[12] Yet, the clergymen of *The Tudors* usually exemplify clerical abuses rather than virtues, and Wolsey is no exception. Among other indiscretions, he keeps a mistress and illegitimate children from the public eye, siphons funds from the royal coffers, negotiates secretly with foreign ambassadors, and even threatens a fellow papal legate with force.[13] In exchange for a life of political ambition, Neill's Wolsey sacrifices his religious principles. The cardinal of George Cavendish's biography, who allegedly heard mass twice a day and wore a piece of the true cross around his neck, is not to be found in *The Tudors*.[14] Yet, the series' Wolsey, like his historical counterpart, uses his position to display ecclesiastical power and prestige. He dresses in clerical finery, travels through crowds with pompous ceremony, conducts magnificent services for European dignitaries, and convenes ecclesiastical councils in the king's name. Hirst's script also dramatizes his bid for the papal tiara in 1521, though historically, the cardinal was probably less than enthusiastic to stand for election.[15] Above all, Neill's Wolsey, like his king, sees religion as a way to amass political influence and further his own agenda.

The historical Wolsey died of illness on the road to London in 1530. Forced from office and eventually charged with treason, the cardinal's natural death saved him the disgrace of trial and probable execution. *The Tudors*' Wolsey meets a violently dramatic end by taking his own life. Before drawing the dagger to his throat, however, he spends his last moments in prayer. Stripped of political position and ostentatious finery, Wolsey bares his soul to God and recognizes that his offenses do not deserve forgiveness. Meanwhile, his enemies at court stage a farcical play that mocks the cardinal and foreshadows the destruction of papal supremacy in England. This clever bit of symbolism suggests the advancement of anticlericalism at the royal court after the cardinal's downfall.[16]

Mirroring the historical record, Hirst's script has Rhys Meyers' Henry slowly turn his back on Rome as he becomes amenable to more radical opinions. The first and second seasons of *The Tudors* thus draw adequate attention to the spread of evangelical ideas at court after Wolsey's fall. Although the script never fully explains reformist belief, often reducing evangelical arguments to mere anticlerical jargon and restricting its portrayal to elite social groups, it is clear to the audience that reformers constitute an influential network at court. Thomas Cromwell, Thomas Cranmer, as well as Anne Boleyn and her family are all shown to be vigorous proponents of religious reform.

The series effectively demonstrates that the advancements of both Cromwell, played by James Frain, and the Boleyn family were based on a mutually beneficial alliance, centered on religious reform. Historians continue to dispute the nature of Cromwell's religious beliefs, some contending that his reformist leanings were not as radical as once presumed.[17] *The Tudors* nevertheless places the king's ill-fated chief minister firmly within the militantly Protestant camp. Hirst's script also gives Cromwell a variety of anachronistically modern ideas. For example, early in the first season, he attends a pro-Lutheran meeting, led by an unnamed German reformer who spouts vague messages of anticlericalism and spiritual "liberty." Yet, only in the third season does the audience catch a glimpse of Cromwell's theological beliefs, when he states simply that, to pray and speak to God, "there is no need for bells and books and candles—all you need is your soul." Although this scene drastically simplifies the Protestant doctrine of salvation by faith alone, it provides Frain's Cromwell with a rare moment of tangible piety.[18]

Aside from brief insights into his beliefs, Hirst's script usually portrays Cromwell as a one-dimensional character who is radically anticlerical. In conversation with Thomas Boleyn, for example, Cromwell reveals dramatically that his ultimate goal is to destroy, rather than reform, the Roman Catholic Church. This attitude is erroneous, however, for early English reformers did not see themselves as a destructive force—they believed their efforts were bringing the church back to its authentic roots.[19] *The Tudors* instead presents Henry VIII's chief minister as a corrosive force and ignores his contributions to the English Reformation.

Although many historians consider the developments of the 1530s to be essentially a political reformation, the changes instituted by Cromwell undoubtedly helped lay the foundations of English Protestantism.[20] Hirst's script overlooks many of these achievements, such as the Great Bible—arguably the most significant religious contribution of Henry's reign next to the concept of royal supremacy.[21] Attention is focused instead on the various pieces of legislation issued by the Reformation Parliament, such as the praemunire charges against the clergy, the Act in Restraint of Appeals, the Acts of Succession, and the Act of Supremacy. The series does a fair job of communicating the significance of these measures.[22] Yet, in its haste to depict Henry VIII's Reformation as a legislative process designed to expand royal authority, *The Tudors* neglects most religious developments.

The series' preoccupation with the secular facets of the Henrician Reformation stems chiefly from its lack of interest in certain ecclesiastical figures, particularly Archbishop Thomas Cranmer. The script's retelling of the Reformation becomes weaker with the exit of Hans Matheson's Cranmer after Season Two, for this places the push for religious reform largely in the hands of laymen, such as Cromwell. This decision ignores much English Reformation scholarship, which usually credits both Cromwell and Cranmer with laying the legal and theological foundations of the Church of England.[23] Hirst's failure to replace Cranmer after Matheson's early exit further underscores the decision to concentrate on Henry VIII's personal life. For, when Anita Briem, the actress portraying Jane Seymour, also left the series after the second season, she was replaced immediately. *The Tudors* therefore clearly prioritizes Henry and his six wives over Cranmer and other significant figures of the period.

Despite his brief presence in the series, Matheson's Cranmer comes across as a man of fierce personal religious convictions. The script accurately depicts his crucial suggestion to Henry VIII that he approach his annulment matter from a theological perspective by canvassing university opinion.[24] Additionally, while Cranmer is present in the series, Cromwell appears to be genuinely interested in religious reform. The two men together champion a few important causes, including the suppression of the monasteries and the assault against the cult of images.[25] Yet, their apparent devotion to reform is undermined by Cromwell's inconsistent attitude toward religion, as well as by the Archbishop of Canterbury's unexplained departure.

Thomas Cranmer's wife—mistakenly identified as Katharina Prue—also makes a short, but memorable appearance.[26] In conversation with her husband and Cromwell, she asserts that, as a woman, she deserves "equal respect" for her ideas and the right to debate religious reform. Although *The Tudors* is often critical of the Protestant Reformation and its effects, it allows reformist characters to promote remarkably progressive, albeit anachronistic, ideas about intellectual and spiritual freedom. Cranmer's wife, played by Julia Wakeham, represents a faulty view of Protestantism, which argues that the Reformation freed women from the constraints of medieval Catholicism. While some women did find a modicum of independence as leaders, preachers, and authors in the early stages of the movement, once Protestantism became institutionalized, they were usually excluded from such roles.[27] Hirst's script also perpetuates the fallacious story of Cranmer traveling throughout England with his illegal wife in a box—an eccentrically humorous tale based on rumor that emerged only after the archbishop's death.[28]

In addition to Cromwell and Cranmer, Natalie Dormer's Anne Boleyn is also shown to be an advocate of religious reform. As with Frain's Cromwell, however, her evangelical leanings are inconsistent. Earlier episodes depict her as merely a hypersexualized political schemer, but by the second season she becomes a major proponent of the Reformation. Like her historical counterpart, Dormer's Boleyn gives Henry VIII a copy of William Tyndale's *The Obedience of a Christian Man*, makes the English Bible available to her household, patronizes reformers, and supports both charity and education.[29] Furthermore, Hirst's script incorporates her feud with Cromwell regarding the uses of monastic wealth.[30] This addition gives Anne Boleyn's downfall a religious dimension that is usually lacking in portrayals of Henry VIII's ill-fated second wife.

The audience is provided with an accurate depiction of sixteenth-century Catholic religiosity through Maria Doyle Kennedy's performance as Catherine of Aragon, the king's first wife. Hirst's script furnishes continual evidence of Catherine's piety, particularly after the annulment of her marriage and her exile from court. She is shown praying regularly, attending confession, supporting the cult of the Virgin Mary, and standing firm in her defense of the papacy.[31] Catherine also passes on her Catholic beliefs to her only child, Mary. Henry VIII's eldest daughter, played by Sarah Bolger, remains as demonstrably pious as her mother. Throughout later seasons, the series also alludes to Mary's hatred of heresy. She persists in being steadfastly Catholic despite her father's animosity toward the papacy and the growth of Protestantism in England. Against the growth of "heresy," she vows to do all within her power to "make England faithful again."[32]

Supporting Catherine of Aragon, Mary Tudor, and the Catholic faith are various international clergymen and dignitaries, including Ambassador Eustace Chapuys, Emperor Charles V, Pope Paul III, Cardinal Lorenzo Campeggio, and Cardinal Reginald Pole. Aside from strong performances by Anthony Brophy as Chapuys and Peter O'Toole as Paul III, *The Tudors*' depiction of Henry VIII's Catholic adversaries is inconsistent. This flawed portrayal stems mostly from Hirst's repeated emphasis on the violence of religious fanatics and the venality of clergymen. For example, O'Toole's Paul III sanctimoniously bemoans his inability to die as a martyr for the church, yet he is guilty of both nepotism and political conspiracy. Additionally, William Brereton, whom the series insists on making a Jesuit missionary, embarks on a fanatical (and purely fictional) mission to assassinate Anne Boleyn. He inadvertently succeeds by being caught up in her trial for adultery, but he also manages to kill an innocent bystander during one of his earlier attempts.[33] More compelling than any of these depictions are the performances given by Bosco Hogan as Bishop John Fisher and Jeremy Northam as Sir Thomas More, two Catholics who sacrificed everything in defense of their faith.

Against the venality of Cardinal Thomas Wolsey, the egotism of Henry VIII, and the secular radicalism of Thomas Cromwell, *The Tudors* presents a fervently pious Thomas More. Throughout his journey to martyrdom, More remains steadfastly, even fanatically, devout. He is also exceptionally unconcerned with personal or political gain—a striking contrast to most of the series' characters. Whether he is chastising Wolsey's corruption, burning heretics and their writings, lecturing his family on the importance of faith, or praying furiously in Latin, viewers are given continual proof of More's piety and self-righteousness. Aside from his hatred for heresy and his loyalty to the papacy, however, the script never fully reveals his views on the theological debates that divided much of Europe in this period. In fact, More's documented talent for religious polemic is sadly missing from this portrayal. Unlike the calm and mild-mannered character of the series, the historical More was capable of violent (even crude) language. He wrote a number of derisive harangues against reformers such as Simon Fish, William Tyndale, and Martin Luther.[34]

Simon Fish, author of *Supplication for the Beggars*, even makes a brief appearance in *The Tudors*. More interrogates the reformist author regarding his antipapal views, and Fish's retorts manage to hint at the Protestant doctrine of justification by faith alone. He declares, "I am a Christian man, a child of everlasting joy, through the merits of the bitter passion of Christ. This is the joyful answer." Although his words actually belong to a sermon delivered by Hugh Latimer in 1529, they provide viewers with a brief, albeit unexplained, glimpse into sixteenth-century theology.[35] The historical Simon Fish died of the plague, but the reformer of *The Tudors* meets his end at the stake, with a resignedly regretful Thomas More standing witness.[36] Unlike most fictional portrayals of More, which focus on his heroic martyrdom, the series does not hesitate to engage with the more unappealing aspects of his character, such as his reactionary stance on heresy and reform.[37] Northam's More does go to his inevitable death with dignity. But before the battle over his religious principles begins, he is more concerned with suppressing the growth of heresy in England.[38]

Another devotedly Catholic and ill-fated character in *The Tudors* is Robert Aske, played by Gerard McSorley. Aske makes an appearance in the series' third season as the leader of the Pilgrimage of Grace, the largest rebellion of the Tudor period. Overall, the series provides an accurate and engrossing depiction of the rebels (or "pilgrims") as champions of traditional religion. In writing the scripts for later seasons, Hirst was determined to provide the audience with a fresh perspective on the early English

Reformation and its effects. He was particularly concerned with depicting the dissolution of the monasteries, for though "we tend to think of [the Reformation] as a good thing ... the fate of generations was destroyed."[39] As a result of this viewpoint, *The Tudors* concentrates heavily on what was lost after the dissolutions and the brutal suppression of the Pilgrimage of Grace. The series' Robert Aske encapsulates the sorrow felt by many with the destruction of monasticism in England, stating that the abbeys provided charity, education, and spiritual guidance to their communities. Quoting the historical Aske, McSorley's character refers to the abbeys as "one of the beauties of this realm."[40] Although the series undoubtedly glosses over the fact that the majority of religious houses in England stood in dire need of reform at the time of the dissolutions, Hirst's script poignantly conveys the most visibly striking development of the Henrician Reformation.[41]

The dissolution of the monasteries was arguably the most radical of Henry's religious changes, yet in the early 1540s the king's innate conservatism halted any further reform. *The Tudors* devotes a surprising amount of time to its depiction of religious uncertainty in England during Henry VIII's later reign, focusing on the clash between the conservative and reformist factions at court. Beginning with the formation of the Six Articles at the end of the third season, the script indicates that, despite the break with the papacy, the king's traditional beliefs have not changed. The series correctly emphasizes the Catholic nature of the Six Articles, which upheld such traditional beliefs as transubstantiation, private masses, confession, and clerical celibacy and chastity.[42] Although Henry VIII is inaccurately named as the author of the articles, it is clear that they constitute a victory for conservatives at court. The leader of these conservatives is Bishop Stephen Gardiner, played by Simon Ward, who appears in the third and fourth seasons of the series. Regrettably, the absence of Thomas Cranmer weakens the dramatic portrayal of Gardiner's campaign to eliminate heresy, as does that of the 3rd Duke of Norfolk. Without the Archbishop of Canterbury, the well-known struggle between Cranmer and Gardiner over church doctrine is eliminated. Yet, with the Six Articles as their weapon, Ward's Gardiner and his supporters set out to attack heresy at the royal court.[43]

After Cranmer's departure from the series and Cromwell's execution at the end of the third season, Edward Seymour and Catherine Parr become the leaders of the evangelical cause. Notwithstanding his confusing role in Cromwell's downfall, Seymour, played by Max Brown, is portrayed as a devoted (if somewhat ruthless) proponent of religious reform. For example, Robert Testwood, a musician whom Gardiner later arrests for heresy, flees to the Earl of Hertford's household in the hope of sanctuary. Seymour's wife, Anne Stanhope, mirrors her husband's ruthlessness by turning Testwood away and commanding his discretion by way of threats to his family.[44] Yet, the script also endeavors to highlight the evangelical leanings of Stanhope, played by Emma Hamilton. Despite her brutal dismissal of Testwood, she risks exposure by aiding her friend and Protestant martyr, Anne Askew, whom Gardiner also arrests for heresy.

By closely replicating the historical record, *The Tudors* does an excellent job of presenting the story of Anne Askew, played by Emma Stansfield, who was arrested for preaching against transubstantiation, tortured for information on Catherine Parr and her household, and finally burnt at the stake. Her interrogation gives the audience its first explanation of the debate over the Eucharist, which was a fundamental distinction between Catholics and Protestants in the sixteenth century. Additionally, by drawing a connection between Askew and Catherine Parr, the script effectively underscores the intense reformist beliefs of Henry VIII's sixth and final wife.[45]

Catherine Parr, played by Joely Richardson, is perhaps the character who most accurately exemplifies sixteenth-century evangelical religiosity. Like her historical counterpart, Richardson's Parr patronizes reformist clergymen, encourages theological discussion in her household, influences the education of Elizabeth and Edward Tudor, and writes her own theological works.[46] Above all, she uses her position as queen to further "the cause of the reformation" so that she can address God "with a clear conscience and an honest soul." This depiction conforms to the historical Catherine Parr, who was the first woman to publish under her own name in English and who, of Henry's six wives, deserves the title "Protestant Queen."[47]

Catherine Parr's Protestantism nearly caused her downfall, for, according to John Foxe's *Book of Martyrs*, Gardiner and the conservatives almost succeeded in arresting the queen for heresy. Hirst's script pulls this story straight from Foxe's work, and Richardson adroitly recites Parr's speech to Henry VIII, in which she defends herself against charges of heresy.[48] By failing to bring down Catherine Parr, Ward's Gardiner is undone and neatly banished from court.[49] Without the conservative faction, Seymour and the reformers stand poised to influence the king's heir, the future Edward VI. Until the old king's death, however, it is clear that the state of religion will remain unchanged. During his final speech to parliament, Rhys Meyer's Henry, like his historical counterpart, concerns himself with halting religious conflict in England. This speech consists of paraphrased excerpts from Hall's *Chronicle*.[50] He states that, as "God's appointed vicar," he "will see these divisions extinct." Thus, *The Tudors*' Henry VIII belatedly manages to present himself as a monarch who is genuinely concerned with the state of religion in England. Despite this overdue demonstration of piety, Rhys' Meyers Henry, along with the majority of the series' characters, remains inadequately devout and overly concerned with worldly pursuits.

Despite plenty of screen time throughout its four seasons, *The Tudors* only halfheartedly and sporadically engages with the topic of religion and the clergy in Henry VIII's reign. Yet, one exceptional instance stands out in the form of an early episode depicting the 1528 outbreak of sweating sickness. In this episode, the series manages to provide an authentic, yet frustratingly brief glimpse of sixteenth-century piety. The onset of the sweating sickness interrupts the usual political drama and gives the audience a rare glimpse into the characters' more spiritual concerns.[51]

When confronted with illness and death in this episode, the king and his court turn to religion by attending mass, confessing their sins, and searching their souls. Henry VIII, worrying that his own sins are to blame for England's suffering, attends confession and asks a priest for forgiveness "not as a king, but as a man." At her family home in Hever, Anne Boleyn drifts between life and death after contracting the sweat. The king's physician suggests to her father and brother that they should summon a priest to perform extreme unction. Even the worldly Cardinal Wolsey experiences both the physical and spiritual effects of the sickness. After recovering from the disease, he exhibits a rare moment of piety by arranging for a pilgrimage of thanksgiving to the shrine of Our Lady of Walsingham. The more devout Thomas More mirrors the actions of his king by searching his soul for the cause of God's punishment, coming to a more ominous conclusion. He explains to his daughter that the growth of heresy—"the disease of Lutheranism"—poses a more significant threat than any bodily illness. Much like his historical counterpart, More sees England's spiritual sickness and the fragmenting of Catholic Christendom as the reasons for God's displeasure.[52]

In this unique episode, each character fleetingly displays a variety of authentic sixteenth-century reactions to illness and death. Thus, Hirst presents an alluring illustration of what might have been, had his series given religion and the clergy appropriate consideration. Yet other episodes fall short of this high standard. The script continually prioritizes the personal life of Henry VIII and its other main characters and does not allow the audience to truly engage with sixteenth-century spiritual concerns. Entertainment triumphs over accuracy, allowing *The Tudors* to provide a frustratingly superficial depiction of religious life in Tudor England.

Notes

1. *The Tudors*, Episode 1:6.
2. Brian Lowry, "*The Tudors*: Review," *Variety*, March 28, 2007, accessed February 2, 2015, https://variety.com/2007/film/reviews/the-tudors-3-1200509343/.
3. Ginia Bellafante, "Nasty, but not so Brutish and Short," *The New York Times*, March 28, 2008, accessed February 2, 2015, http://www.nytimes.com/2008/03/28/arts/television/28tudo.html?_r=0.
4. Jim Halterman, "Interview: '*The Tudors*' Creator Michael Hirst," *The Futon Critic*, April 3, 2009, accessed March 25, 2015, http://www.thefutoncritic.com/interviews/2009/04/03/interview-the-tudors-creator-michael-hirst-30921/20090403_tudors/.
5. A.G. Dickens, *The English Reformation*, 2nd ed. (University Park, PA: Pennsylvania State Press, 1989), 106.
6. Richard Rex, *Henry VIII and the English Reformation*, 2nd ed. (New York: Palgrave Macmillan, 2006), 82–84; J.J. Scarisbrick, *Henry VIII* (Berkeley, CA: University of California Press, 1968), 248.
7. Scarisbrick, *Henry VIII*, 43; Michael A. R. Graves, *Henry VIII: Profiles in Power* (London: Pearson Longman, 2003), 56.
8. Scarisbrick, *Henry VIII*, 112–113; *The Tudors*, Episode 1:3.
9. On the royal touch, see Carole Levin, *The Heart and Stomach of a King: Elizabeth I and the Politics of Sex and Power* (Philadelphia: University of Pennsylvania Press, 1994), 21–22; *The Tudors*, Episode 4:3.
10. *The Tudors*, Episode 3:5.
11. Jeanne Wolf, "Jonathan Rhys Meyers: 'I'm Glad to Say Goodbye' to Tudors," *Parade*, April 6, 2010, accessed February 28, 2015, http://parade.com/133670/jeannewolf/0406-jonathan-rhys-meyers-tudors/.
12. See, for example, Scarisbrick, *Henry VIII*, 240, and Peter Gwyn, *The King's Cardinal: The Rise and Fall of Thomas Wolsey* (London: Pimlico, Random House, 1990), xv–xviii.
13. Wolsey did have a mistress and two children, Thomas and Dorothy. See A.F. Pollard, *Wolsey* (London: Longmans, Green and Co., 1929), 306. Wolsey slams the fictitious Bishop Bonnivet against the wall in *The Tudors*, Episode 1:1.

14. Ibid., 346.
15. Ibid., 387; Scarisbrick, *Henry VIII*, 107–110; Wolsey actively seeks the papacy in *The Tudors*, Episodes 1:1–1:2.
16. *The Tudors*, Episode 1:10.
17. A.G. Dickens, *Thomas Cromwell and the English Reformation* (New York: The Macmillan Company, 1959), 178–179; Robert Hutchinson, *Thomas Cromwell: The Rise and Fall of Henry VIII's Most Notorious Minister* (New York: St. Martin's Press, 2007), 266.
18. *The Tudors*, Episodes 1:4, 3:7.
19. Dickens, *Thomas Cromwell and the English Reformation*, 179.
20. See Christopher Haigh, *English Reformations: Religion, Politics, and Society under the Tudors* (Oxford: Clarendon Press, 1993), 103–167, and Rex, *Henry VIII and the English Reformation*, 56–106.
21. Rex, *Henry VIII and the English Reformation*, 151.
22. *The Tudors*, Episodes 2:3–2:5.
23. See, for example, Diarmaid MacCulloch, *Thomas Cranmer: A Life* (New Haven, CT: Yale University Press, 1996), 1, and Dickens, *Thomas Cromwell and the English Reformation*, 43.
24. MacCulloch, *Thomas Cranmer*, 45–46; *The Tudors*, Episode 1:10.
25. *The Tudors*, Episodes 1:10, 2:3–2:7.
26. Cranmer actually married a woman named Margarete—the niece of Katharina Prue and her husband, Andreas Osiander, a German reformer and theologian. See MacCulloch, *Thomas Cranmer*, 72; for the misidentification of Margarete as Katharina in credits for *The Tudors*, see http://www.thetudorswiki.com/photo/6412595/Julia+Wakeham+as+Katharina+Prue(Cranmer's+wife).
27. Lyndal Roper, *The Holy Household: Women and Morals in Reformation Augsburg* (Oxford: Clarendon Press, 1989), 1–3; Kirsi Stjerna, *Women and the Reformation* (Malden, MA: Blackwell Publishing, 2009), 72; Katharina M. Wilson, *Women Writers of the Renaissance and Reformation* (Athens, GA: The University of Georgia Press, 1987), xxvii.
28. MacCulloch, *Thomas Cranmer*, 250; *The Tudors*, Episode 2:2.
29. Eric Ives, *The Life and Death of Anne Boleyn: "The Most Happy"* (Malden, MA: Blackwell Publishing, 2004), 133, 260–263, 269, 283–287; *The Tudors*, Episodes 1:10, 2:3.
30. Ives, *The Life and Death of Anne Boleyn*, 307–312; *The Tudors*, Episode 2:9.
31. Antonia Fraser, *The Wives of Henry VIII* (New York: Alfred A. Knopf, Inc., 1992), 79–80; *The Tudors*, 1:1–1:2, 1:5, 1:7, 1:9, 2:1.
32. Linda Porter, *The Myth of "Bloody Mary": A Biography of Queen Mary I of England* (New York: St. Martin's Griffin, 2007), 41–42, 158; *The Tudors*, Episodes 2:4, 2:6, 2:10, 3:1, 3:3, 4:2, 4:4, 4:8–4:10.

33. In reality, William Brereton was not a fanatical Jesuit missionary, but merely a groom in Henry VIII's privy chamber who had the misfortune of being caught up in Anne Boleyn's downfall. Ives, *The Life and Death of Anne Boleyn*, 319; *The Tudors*, Episodes 2:3–2:4.
34. *The Tudors*, Episodes 1:1–2:5.
35. Hugh Latimer, *Select Sermons and Letters*, ed. William M. Engles (Philadelphia: Presbyterian Board of Publication, 1842), 17; *The Tudors*, Episode 1:10.
36. Alistair Fox, *Thomas More: History and Providence* (New Haven, CT: Yale University Press, 1982), 115–120.
37. Fox, *Thomas More*, 118.
38. *The Tudors*, Episode 2:5.
39. Chris Curtis, "Michael Hirst, The Tudors," *Broadcast*, May 21, 2009, accessed March 25, 2015, http://www.broadcastnow.co.uk/michael-hirst-the-tudors/5001701.article. This interpretation disagrees with traditional Whig history and is in congruent with that of revisionist historian Christopher Haigh. See Haigh, *English Reformations*, 15–16.
40. Susan Brigden, *New Worlds, Lost Worlds: The Rule of the Tudors, 1485–1603* (New York: Penguin Books, 2000), 127.
41. For a more critical discussion of the state of sixteenth-century English monasticism, see Dickens, *The English Reformation*, 76–77; *The Tudors*, Episodes 3:1–3:4.
42. Rex, *Henry VIII and the English Reformation*, 124.
43. *The Tudors*, Episodes 3:5–3:6.
44. Historically, Robert Testwood was executed for heresy in 1543. See Dickens, *The English Reformation*, 206–207; *The Tudors*, Episode 4:6.
45. Susan James, *Catherine Parr: Henry VIII's Last Love* (Stroud, UK: The History Press, 2008), 233–234; *The Tudors*, Episode 4:9.
46. James, *Catherine Parr*, 115–119, 121–134, 157–199.
47. Ibid., 189–194; *The Tudors*, Episodes 4:6–4:10.
48. Ibid., 247–248; *The Tudors*, Episodes 4:9–4:10.
49. In reality, Gardiner was banished from court over a property dispute with the king. See Scarisbrick, *Henry VIII*, 490.
50. Edward Hall, *Hall's Chronicle; Containing the History of England, During the Reign of Henry the Fourth and the Succeeding Monarchs to the end of the Reign of Henry the Eighth* (London: Printed for J. Johnson, etc., 1809), 865–866; *The Tudors*, Episode 4:9.
51. Brigden, *New Worlds, Lost Worlds*, 26; *The Tudors*, Episode 1:7.
52. Brigden, *New Worlds, Lost Worlds*, 84; Richard Marius, *Thomas More: A Biography* (New York: Alfred A. Knopf, 1984), 386–406.

CHAPTER 14

Fact, Fiction, and Fantasy: Conspiracy and Rebellion in *The Tudors*

Keith Altazin

Michael Hirst, creator and writer of *The Tudors*, weaves conspiracy and rebellion into the plotline from beginning to end. Among the many story lines are the 3rd Duke of Buckingham's alleged conspiracy to overthrow Henry VIII, a fictitious papal plot to kill Anne Boleyn, Thomas Cromwell's very real conspiracy to remove her from power, the most dangerous rebellion that any Tudor monarch faced—the Pilgrimage of Grace of 1536–1537—and the Exeter Conspiracy. In assessing the series' depiction of these and other events, it is important to keep in mind that Hirst's primary objective was to produce an entertaining series, which he certainly did. However, if portions of his story have some historical basis, he often abandons proven fact, fictionalizing history or indulging in outright fantasy and leaving his viewers to decide which is which.

Season One of *The Tudors* introduces the first of many conspiracies, that of Edward Stafford, the 3rd Duke of Buckingham. The plotting and treachery that are so central to the entire series begin in Episodes 1:1–1:2, in which Buckingham's desire for the throne—which he claims is his birthright—forms an important subplot. Hirst's depiction of the alleged Buckingham plot is representative of his mixture of fact and fiction. Steven Waddington portrays Buckingham as an overly proud, angry, and arrogant

K. Altazin (✉)
Social Studies, University High School, Baton Rouge, LA, USA

malcontent. His anger, as portrayed in the series, has two general sources. First, Buckingham is particularly resentful over the king raising up base-born men to positions of rank and power. He aims much of his antipathy at Cardinal Thomas Wolsey—portrayed brilliantly by Sam Neill—a man who represents all that is wrong with Henry VIII's court as Buckingham sees it. The second source of his rage is the "new men" who form Henry's inner circle of friends, for example, Charles Brandon, William Compton, Anthony Knivert (based on Thomas Knyvett), and Thomas Wyatt. Henry raised several such individuals to high office, granting some titles of nobility. *The Tudors* portrays Brandon, played by Henry Cavill, as Henry's most trusted friend and ally, and he is one of the mainstays of the entire series. As a reward for his friendship, Henry bestows upon Brandon the title of Duke of Suffolk. Buckingham regards such "new men," who come from the gentry, as unworthy of high office, particularly while he—scion of one of England's oldest families—has no power or influence.[1]

Episode 1:1 is typical of Hirst's convoluted manner of shaping the historical record to blend with his script. Buckingham is outraged when he discovers Suffolk in bed with his daughter. When Suffolk makes light of the situation, Buckingham barges in on the king and demands that Henry punish the insolent and lecherous courtier. Instead, the king rebukes Buckingham and angrily dismisses him. This incident, which transforms Buckingham's discontent into treason, is strikingly similar to one the Spanish Ambassador Luis Caroz reported involving the king, one of Buckingham's married daughters, and William Compton. In Caroz's report, it is unclear if the king or Compton was involved with Buckingham's daughter. However, Buckingham confronted Compton and "reproached him in very hard words." When Henry heard of this, he upbraided the duke angrily. Hirst alters the details of the original incident to accommodate other inaccuracies in his script, for example, given that he depicts Compton as homosexual, he makes Suffolk the guilty party. Caroz mentions no bedroom confrontation; rather Buckingham met his daughter to discuss how to handle court gossip surrounding her.[2]

In *The Tudors*, Buckingham plots to remove Henry from the throne and attempts to involve the Duke of Norfolk, played by Henry Czerny, and Thomas Boleyn, portrayed by Nick Dunning. He tells them in no uncertain terms that he is the rightful heir to the throne, that he has royal blood in his veins, specifically that of Edward II. In a scene that ultimately leads to his doom, he boasts that he will kill Henry. To his guests' shock and horror, he demonstrates how he will carry out the deed by kneeling before the king and, while Henry is standing over him, pulling a knife from the sleeve of his gown and driving it into the king's chest.[3]

The Tudors depicts Buckingham's character, his hatred of Wolsey, and his opposition to the French alliance fairly accurately. Buckingham never understood that by criticizing Wolsey's policies, he was also criticizing Henry. On the other hand, although Hirst portrays Buckingham as actively plotting to kill the king, there is no evidence of such a conspiracy or of the duke swearing his followers to support him therein, as he does on the show. The scene in which Buckingham acts out how to kill the king before Norfolk and Boleyn is fiction, based loosely on the testimony of his servants, Charles Knyvett and Robert Gilbert, which reveals that he had been incautious but not an overt conspirator. Following the Star Chamber trial of another servant, Sir William Bulmer, in 1519, Buckingham rather suggestively described how his father—Henry Stafford, 2nd Duke—planned to stab Richard III. However, Hirst ignores other serious charges against Buckingham, notably that he listened to the prophesies of the Carthusian monk Nicholas Hopkins that he would someday be king and speculated that he would be regent if Henry should die without an heir. This was, indeed, treason according to the law. The actual indictment against Buckingham accused him of compassing and imagining the death of the king.[4]

The scene depicting Buckingham's execution also ignores the historical record. For some reason Hirst decided to depict the duke as a weak, sniveling coward as he approaches the block. Out of fear, he fails to offer the customary forgiveness to the executioner and refuses to stretch out his arms to signal when he is ready. Sir Anthony Knivert, portrayed by Callum Blue, moves toward the gallows and forces Buckingham to stretch out his arms. This entire scene, with the exception of the duke's beheading, is completely fictional. Accounts indicate that Buckingham went to his death with the dignity befitting his high status. Anthony Knivert, a semi-fictional character based on Thomas Knyvett, certainly did not hold out the duke's arms. In fact, Buckingham, "after reciting the penitential psalms ... took off his gown, and his eyes blindfolded," placed his head on the block, meeting his fate with great courage.[5]

Season Two begins with two more conspiracies, one a highly fictionalized version of the attempt to poison Bishop John Fisher and the other a completely invented plot to assassinate Anne Boleyn. In Episode 2:1, Thomas Boleyn bribes Fisher's cook, Richard Roose, to poison him and even supplies the poison, which ends up in the soup. Boleyn wants to eliminate Fisher due to his support of Catherine of Aragon and outspoken criticism of Henry's religious reforms. The poisoning itself is based on historical fact. Several people supping with Fisher were poisoned, and two eventually died. Fisher's cook was arrested and confessed to the crime, for which he was boiled alive. However, there is no evidence that the Boleyns were involved.[6]

In the same episode, Pope Paul III, played by Peter O'Toole, meets with Cardinal Campeggio to discuss Henry VIII's Great Matter and suggests that in order to solve the problem, someone should "get rid of" Anne Boleyn. The result is a murder plot that runs through the whole of Season Two until the queen's arrest in Episode 2:9. The key figure in this plot is William Brereton, played by James Gilbert. Brereton, as depicted in *The Tudors*, becomes an almost completely fictionalized character. In actuality, he was a Groom in the Privy Chamber and did not serve in Anne's household, as he does in the series. However, Hirst depicts Brereton as a devout Catholic, deeply troubled by Henry VIII's break with Rome. Eustace Chapuys, the Imperial Ambassador to England, played by Anthony Brophy, recruits Brereton to assassinate Anne. After failing twice, Brereton journeys to Rome and somehow gets an audience with Paul III, becomes a Jesuit, and receives papal instructions to rid England and Christendom of "the great whore." Though he fails to assassinate Anne, Brereton completes his mission in a sense when he confesses to having sexual relations with the queen and helps to bring her down. On-screen, he goes to the gallows—as he did in reality—for this alleged offense.[7]

Obviously, such cloak-and-dagger conspiracy adds to the drama of Season Two; however, it has no historical basis. To begin with, there are problems with the time line. The poisoning of Bishop Fisher took place in 1531 and Roose's execution took place on April 5 of that year. Pope Paul III did not become pope until 1534 and so could not have suggested that someone murder Anne in 1531. William Brereton never became a Jesuit and never traveled to Rome, much less had an audience with the pope. Brereton did not confess to fornication with Anne Boleyn and, like others accused in the scandal, protested his innocence. Although both Pope Clement VII and Paul III might have desired to see Anne Boleyn "go away," there is absolutely no evidence of any plot involving either of them. Chapuys, while no friend of Anne Boleyn or the Henrician Reformation, certainly was too savvy a minister to involve himself in such a plot.[8]

Another interesting subplot in this story line is the alliance between Cromwell and Chapuys to bring down Anne Boleyn. In Episode 2:7, a rift occurs between Anne and Cromwell over their differing views of the best use of the monastic lands and buildings obtained through the dissolution of the lesser monasteries. Anne wants the money to go to poor relief and education. When Cromwell attempts to defend the sale of the monastic lands, she threatens to destroy him. Thus begins the battle between queen and chief minister. Although there is evidence that a falling out between Anne and Cromwell occurred, no absolute proof exists that he masterminded the queen's arrest and subsequent execution. Eric Ives, Diarmaid MacCulloch, and Alison Weir contend that he did. Others, such as J.J. Scarisbrick, Suzannah Lipscomb, David Starkey, and Greg Walker, argue that the driving force behind Anne's fall was Henry.[9]

However, evidence does exist that suggests Cromwell engineered Anne's fall. Chapuys reported a conversation on March 7, 1536 in which Cromwell intimated that Anne's fall was at hand. The two men were talking about Catherine of Aragon's physician entering into employment in Henry's court. The doctor was afraid that Anne would retaliate against him. But Cromwell assured Chapuys that there was no "obstacle at all for before three months there would be most perfect friendship" between Charles V and Henry.[10] The obstacle was Anne. On April 1, Chapuys reported that Anne "would like to see his [Cromwell] head off his shoulders."[11] Furthermore, he informed Charles V that this information came directly from Cromwell. In the conversation, Chapuys warned Cromwell not to antagonize the queen further and "to guard against her attacks more effectually than the cardinal [Wolsey]."[12] Cromwell responded "that the day might come when fate would strike him as it had struck his predecessors in office: then he would arm himself with patience and place himself for the rest in the hands of God."[13] This implies that Cromwell, ever the practical politician, recognized that he had to destroy his former ally. On June 6, Chapuys reported that Cromwell claimed that he "planned and brought about the whole affair" of Anne's downfall. All of this suggests that a plot to bring down the queen, masterminded by Cromwell, was afoot.

A number of prominent historians disagree with this interpretation of events; most discount the argument that Cromwell, fearing his power threatened by Anne, sought and engineered her destruction. It is clear that that by 1536, Henry had gotten tired of Anne and turned his affections toward Jane Seymour. As early as March 6, 1536, reports suggested that Anne feared that Henry planned to leave her and marry another woman. Chapuys heard the same rumor and reported it to Charles V on April 1.

Shortly thereafter, Anne miscarried and thus sealed her fate. Henry ordered Cromwell and Norfolk to investigate. In a letter dated June 6, Chapuys reported that Cromwell said the king "authorized and commissioned" him to investigate the queen's behavior. This is the same document in which Cromwell claims to have authored Anne's downfall. Obviously, therefore, the plotline in *The Tudors* concerning Anne's fall has some historical merit even though historians disagree as to what role Cromwell played.

Hirst's capable portrayal of Cromwell's role in Anne's fall marks the zenith of historical accuracy in *The Tudors*. However, Season Three and the portrayal of the Pilgrimage of Grace revert to gross inaccuracies, lapsing into pure fiction and even fantasy at several points. Episode 3:1 interjects the Lincolnshire Rebellion and the Pilgrimage of Grace into the storyline. Historical inaccuracies abound in the depiction of the rebellion and its leaders. While Hirst does a credible job of summarizing the grievances of the northern rebels, often using direct quotes from primary sources, there are numerous instances where he fictionalizes the rebellion for no apparent reason. Because the Duke of Norfolk disappears after Season One, Suffolk replaces him as leader of the royal forces sent to quell the Pilgrimage of Grace. Suffolk did play a role in Lincolnshire, but not in Yorkshire, and he never met or dealt directly with Robert Aske.[14]

Several of the characters are highly fictionalized, confused, or terribly miscast. The character of John Constable, played by Robert Doyle, is a good example of a character that is highly fictionalized and most likely confused with another participant in the Pilgrimage of Grace, in this case Robert Constable, who did become one of the chief captains of the Pilgrims. Constable did argue in favor engaging the royal forces in battle upon returning from London. However, he did not participate in the attack on Carlisle. The attack on Carlisle Castle grew out of a combination of the simmering suspicions about the royal pardon and the Doncaster Agreement and local disputes that had little to do with the Pilgrimage of Grace. Constable accepted the king's pardon, but ignored the king's command to appear in London. He did not accompany Aske and Lord Darcy to London, nor did he go to the block as depicted in Episode 3:3. Only those of noble blood met their deaths by beheading; thus, Constable as a commoner was hanged at Hull in June 1537.[15]

The character of Robert Aske, portrayed by Gerard McSorley, is highly fictionalized. McSorley, when cast for the role, was 20 years older than the historical Robert Aske was. At the time of his execution, Robert Aske was 37 years old. As depicted in *The Tudors*, Aske has a wife and two children;

in reality, he never married. McSorely portrays Aske as a tortured soul, only reluctantly joining the Pilgrimage of Grace. The historical record does not support that portrayal. Aske, although he did not seek to become the "great captain" of the Pilgrimage of Grace, did not hesitate to accept the role once given it. The relationship between Aske and Constable is pure fiction. Constable did not recruit Aske to join the rebellion. There is no evidence that these men knew each other before the Pilgrimage of Grace. The Lincolnshire rebels captured Aske, swore him to their oath, and made him one of their captains. Lord Thomas Darcy, the other leader of the Pilgrimage, lacks any sort of character development in *The Tudors*. He is one of several characters who appear with no introduction or reference. Although an important figure in Yorkshire, Darcy becomes nothing more than window dressing in the episodes that concern the Pilgrimage of Grace.[16]

Hirst does have a working knowledge of the historical record but often deviates from it. Aske did march on York and did lay siege to Pontefract Castle, which Lord Darcy surrendered after only three days. Norfolk (replaced on-screen by Suffolk) did parlay with the rebels at Doncaster Bridge and agree to a truce, and he did escort to London two representatives of the Pilgrims, who brought with them a list of grievances for Henry to review. However, John (Robert) Constable did not travel to London. The Pilgrims chose Sir Ralph Ellerker and Robert Bowes to carry their grievances to the king. Norfolk did attempt—again Suffolk is a stand-in—to have Darcy betray Aske and, as depicted, Darcy refused. Ellerker and Bowes did not return from London with news of a royal pardon. Claiming the articles too vague for a reply, Henry proposed that 300 representatives of the rebels meet Norfolk at Doncaster in December. The king insisted on a pardon with exceptions and a submission of the Pilgrims before he would answer their articles.

A heated discussion among the Pilgrim leadership did occur, with a group lobbying of war, while Aske and Darcy successfully argued that the best course of action was to negotiate first. Constable did lobby for a military confrontation with Norfolk and, as depicted, failed to gain Darcy and Aske's support. Robert Constable accepted the pardon and worked hard to maintain the truce established at the first meeting with Norfolk. But there is nothing in the historical record to indicate that John (Robert) Constable participated in the attack on Carlisle. Yet, in Episode 3:3, Constable rejects the truce, questions whether the king will honor the pardon, and leaves for Carlisle. In fact, none of the leaders of the Pilgrimage of Grace participated in the attack on Carlisle Castle. This episode would have the audience believe that Constable went off to Carlisle immediately after Aske returned from London.

Actually, Aske arrived back in Yorkshire in early January, and the attack on Carlisle began on February 12, 1537. Another problem is the rebels in Cumbria actually attacked Carlisle Castle and failed. *The Tudors* would have us believe that Lord Dacre attacked while the rebels prepared to attack the castle. Lord Dacre did, in fact, attack the rebels but only after they had failed to capture Carlisle Castle. However, neither Suffolk nor Norfolk took part in the defense of Carlisle Castle. Norfolk did not participate in the attack on the Carlisle rebels; he was in Ripon, too far away to aid Sir Christopher Dacre. Norfolk did write to Dacre to encourage him to defend Carlisle against the rebels or lose the love of his king. He wrote, "Make true mine old sayings, that Sir Christopher Dacre is a true knight to his sovereign lord … and a man of war. Finally, now, Sir Christopher, or never. Your loving cousin if ye do well, or else enemy forever."[17]

The depiction of the interrogation of Aske, Darcy, and Constable has a number of historical flaws. First, the record of Darcy's interrogation no longer exists; only the questions put to him by Cromwell remain. Obviously, the scene that has Cromwell questioning Darcy is total fiction. The scene depicting John Constable's torture is also questionable, since there is no direct evidence that any of the Pilgrimage leaders were subjected to torture. As mentioned earlier, John Constable (Robert) was not beheaded at Tyburn, but rather he was hanged at Hull.

The depiction of the punishment meted out by Suffolk is not merely fiction but lapses into fantasy. Initially, Norfolk did have 74 rebel leaders hanged. However, he had to resort to martial law because he could not find enough loyal men to sit on juries. Hirst has Cromwell inform Suffolk that his execution of 74 rebels is far too lenient and tell him that some question his desire to carry out the king's orders in the North. He advises Suffolk that many, including the king, believe that he is loyal to the old faith. Next, Cromwell notifies Suffolk that he must return to the North and inflict extreme retribution on a much greater number than 74. Suffolk confides to his wife that he "must kill hundreds, thousands of men, women, and children or lose the love of my king." Henry did actually command Suffolk (the real one) that if the rebels continued their traitorous behavior, he was to "run upon them and with all extremity destroy, burn, and kill man, woman, and child to the terrible example of all others."[18] However, the target of the order was the town of Louth, where the Lincolnshire rebellion began. Although Hirst has Suffolk carry out the king's order in complete compliance, in reality no such action was taken. The total number of executions for both the Lincolnshire rebellion and the Pilgrimage of Grace totaled 199, a far cry from "thousands."[19]

Season Three also addresses the Exeter Conspiracy, for which, historically, Henry Courtney, Marquess of Exeter, his wife, and young son found themselves arrested, along with Sir Nicholas Carew, Margaret Pole, Countess of Salisbury, and her two sons, Sir Geoffrey Pole and Henry, Lord Montague. However, in *The Tudors* there is no mention of Exeter, his family, Carew, or. Sir Geoffrey Pole, whose testimony played a pivotal role in bringing about the executions of his mother, brother, and cousin, Henry Courtenay. Rather, the plotline of Episodes 3:5–3:7 focuses on Henry's destruction of the Poles—the so-called White Rose faction—which it attributes entirely to the actions of Cardinal Reginald Pole, the youngest son of the countess. A one-time favorite of Henry, he became one of the chief critics of the break with Rome, and his publication *Pro Ecclesiasticae Unitatis Defensione* in 1536 and his call for the princes of Europe to immediately overthrow Henry led the king to declare him a traitor.[20]

In Episode 3:5, Henry confides to Sir Francis Bryan that although he cannot touch Pole, "he will see him eat his heart." The implication is that in order to get at Pole, Henry will destroy his family. Thus, in Episode 3:6, Bryan arrests the Countess of Salisbury, Lord Montague, and his young son Henry on charges of treason. Bryan finds a White Rose flag and a Five Wounds of Christ flag among the countess' belongings. The latter indicates that the Poles supported the Pilgrimage of Grace, as it was the symbol of the rebellion. Both the countess and Lord Montague are executed, though not on-screen. Episode 3:6 ends ominously with Edward Seymour taking young Henry Pole by the hand and leading the lad out of his cell in the Tower.

As with much of series, there are a number of problems with the timeline and a number of historical inaccuracies in the depiction of the Poles' destruction besides the absence of Exeter and Sir Geoffrey Pole. The countess neither went to the Tower with her son nor did she go to the block with him. She went to the Tower in May 1539 and went to her death in 1540. Henry's agents found no flags of any kind among her belongings, although they did discover a suit of armor with the king's arms surrounded by the pansies of the Pole family. This implied that Pole intended to marry Lady Mary and claim the throne. The discovery of the

Five Wounds flag is pure fiction; Montague actually raised men and traveled north to confront the rebels.

As usual, there is some semblance of an historical framework. Henry did have the Pole family arrested and executed. Lord Montague's warning to Seymour that "the king never made man but he destroyed him" reflects a statement attributed to him; however, his words were from a private conversation—not with Seymour—and reported by one of his servants. Montague and Exeter went to the block on Tower Hill on January 9, 1539. However, the countess was not beheaded until 1541. While the show leads the audience to believe that young master Henry Pole went to his death shortly after his father, there is no evidence that the boy was ever executed. Young Henry was alive as late as 1542, after which there is no mention of him.

Historically, there is no evidence of any conspiracy involving the Poles and/or Exeter. It seems that all the Poles were guilty of was loose talk about the king's policies and ministers. Perhaps, Hirst portrays the Poles' destruction because he believes Henry destroyed them because of his hatred for Reginald Pole and as a result chose to depict the events as such. However, why fictionalize so much of the story? Why have a "Plantagenet royal flag" and the Five Wounds flag discovered among countess Salisbury's belongings?

In assessing the depiction of conspiracy and rebellion throughout the four seasons of *The Tudors*, one cannot escape the feeling of being shortchanged. Many of the historical figures have little depth or character development; they become something akin to stick figure drawings. As a representation of history, the series falls well short of the mark. There is clear evidence that the writers researched Henry's reign but consistently and for no apparent reason chose to fictionalize much of the story. One might argue that Hirst, in his depiction of the conspiracies mentioned above, expresses a particular historical interpretation. That line of thought certainly has some merit with regard to his portrayal of Cromwell's involvement in Anne Boleyn's destruction and Henry's destruction of the Pole family. However, the outrageous departure from the historical record depicted in the retribution carried out by Suffolk following the Pilgrimage of Grace undermines any historical interpretation argument. Then there is the obviously fictitious depiction of Buckingham's desire to remove Henry from the throne and the completely fictional plot to assassinate Queen Anne. If we remove the rather weak representation of history and look at the entertainment value, then the series comes off a bit better.

However, Seasons One and Two were far superior to Seasons Three and Four. With a subject of such substance as the reign of Henry VIII, there could have been a better balance of historical accuracy and entertainment.

Notes

1. On Buckingham, see C.S.L. Davies, "Stafford, Edward, Third Duke of Buckingham (1478–1521)," *Oxford Dictionary of National Biography* (Oxford University Press, 2004); online edn, January 2008 [http://www.oxforddnb.com/view/article/26202, accessed October 26, 2015], and Barbara Harris, *Edward Stafford, Third Duke of Buckingham, 1478–1521* (Stanford, CA: Stanford University Press, 1986).
2. Alison Weir, *Henry VIII—The King and His Court* (New York: Ballantine Books, 2001), 121–122.
3. *The Tudors*, Episodes 1:1–1:2.
4. Harris, *Edward Stafford, Third Duke of Buckingham*, 182.
5. Ibid., 187.
6. Richard Rex, "Fisher, John [St John Fisher] (*c.* 1469–1535)," *ODNB*, [http://www.oxforddnb.com/view/article/9498, accessed October 26, 2015].
7. For Brereton's actual life, see E.W. Ives, "Brereton, William (*c.* 1487x90–1536)," *ODNB*; online edn, January 2008 [http://www.oxforddnb.com/view/article/70865, accessed October 26, 2015].
8. For a recent account of Chapuys, see Lauren Mackay, *Inside the Tudor Court: Henry VIII and His Six Wives Through the Writings of the Spanish Ambassador Eustace Chapuys* (Stroud, Gloucestershire: Amberley, 2014).
9. For a useful summary of the debate, see Suzannah Lipscomb, "Why Did Anne Boleyn Have to Die?" http://www.historyextra.com/feature/tudors/why-did-anne-boleyn-have-die.
10. *Letters and Papers, Foreign and Domestic of the Reign of Henry VIII* (Vaduz: Kaduz Reprints, 1965), X, no. 429. Hereafter noted as *LP*.
11. Spain: April 1536, 1–20, *Calendar of State Papers, Spain, Volume 5 Part 2: 1536–1538* (1888) [http://www.british-history.ac.uk/report.aspx?compid=87958, accessed November 18, 2014].
12. Ibid.
13. Ibid.
14. Scholarship on the Pilgrimage of Grace is substantial, see, for example, Claire Cross, "Participants in the Pilgrimage of Grace (*act.* 1536–1537)," *ODNB* [http://www.oxforddnb.com/view/theme/95587, accessed October 26, 2015]; Madeleine Hope Dodds and Ruth Dodds, *The Pilgrimage of Grace and the Exeter Conspiracy*, reprint, (Cambridge:

Cambridge University Press, 1971); R.W. Hoyle, *The Pilgrimage of Grace and the Politics of the 1530s* (Oxford: Oxford University Press, 2001); Geoffrey Moorhouse, *The Pilgrimage of Grace: The Rebellion That Shook Henry VIII's Throne* (Phoenix, 2003). The Pilgrimage of Grace is one of the main storylines in *The Tudors*, Episodes 3:1–3:4.

15. Cross, "Participants in the Pilgrimage of Grace"; Christine M. Newman, "Constable, Sir Robert (1478?–1537)," *ODNB* [http://www.oxforddnb.com/view/article/6110, accessed October 26, 2015].
16. R.W. Hoyle, "Aske, Robert (*c.* 1500–1537)," *ODBN*, online edn, October 2008 [http://www.oxforddnb.com/view/article/797, accessed October 26, 2015], and "Darcy, Thomas, Baron Darcy of Darcy (*b.* in or before 1467, *d.* 1537)," *ODNB*, online edn, January 2008 [http://www.oxforddnb.com/view/article/7148, accessed October 26, 2015].
17. *LP* XII (1), no. 426.
18. *LP* XI, no. 780.
19. S.J. Gunn, "Brandon, Charles, First Duke of Suffolk (*c.* 1484–1545)," *ODBN*; online edn, May 2015 [http://www.oxforddnb.com/view/article/3260, accessed October 26, 2015].
20. J.P.D. Cooper, "Courtenay, Henry, Marquess of Exeter (1498/9–1538)," *ODNB*; online edn, January 2008 [http://www.oxforddnb.com/view/article/6451, accessed October 26, 2015]; Dodds, *The Pilgrimage of Grace and the Exeter Conspiracy*; Thomas F. Mayer, *Reginald Pole: Prince and Prophet* (Cambridge: Cambridge University Press, 2007), and "Pole, Sir Geoffrey (*d.* 1558)," *ODNB* online edn, January 2008 [http://www.oxforddnb.com/view/article/22447, accessed October 26, 2015]; Hazel Pierce, *Margaret Pole, Countess of Salisbury, 1473–1541* (University of Wales Press, 2003).

CHAPTER 15

Crime, Punishment, and Violence in *The Tudors*

Krista J. Kesselring

That *The Tudors* opens with an entirely fictional killing of a person who never existed—the assassination of Henry VIII's supposed uncle—tempts one to focus a discussion of crime, punishment, and violence in the series on the inaccuracies.[1] But one might also see the opening sequence as an early alert from the show's creators that they are presenting not a work of history but a fiction based only loosely on historical facts, something to be watched for what it is rather than derided for what it is not. Indeed, one should not expect to learn one's history from a series such as this any more than one expects to pick up useful surgical techniques from a hospital drama. Yet, of course, some people do accept what they see on screen as true; cinema and television have sometimes created or perpetuated myths about the past that have had power in the present.[2] More generally, others find themselves drawn by shows like this to learn more about history as it happened. As such, I found it both surprising and encouraging how many aspects of *The Tudors* have some ring of truth. In her review of the series for *The Guardian*, historian Anne Whitelock suggested that beneath its many and manifest misrepresentations lay a "not inaccurate" presentation of Henry's court politics.[3] The cautious caveat

K.J. Kesselring (✉)
Faculty of Arts and Sciences, Department of History, Dalhousie University, Halifax, NS, Canada

of the negative construction seems suitable here, too: despite (and sometimes precisely because of) its many divergences from the facts, *The Tudors* offers its viewers a "not inaccurate" portrayal of crime, punishment, and violence in early modern England. The ethics of presenting and viewing such violence as entertainment is another matter, though, arguably made all the more problematic by the series' creative crossings of the lines between fact and fantasy.

I came late to *The Tudors*: I have more patience for historically themed dramas than some of my colleagues, I think, but have exhausted my store of it for programs that use degrading violence against women simply as plot devices. The show's promotional materials suggested it might be historical fiction of the shoddier sort, selling itself not only with sex, but also with sexualized violence (interest in the personal life of Henry VIII sometimes seems to stem not just from his having married six women, but also from his killing two of them). The busty but headless women of Season One's ads suggested that the show might be appealing to something more than simple prurience, a sense strengthened by the key image advertising the Season Two, which eroticized the physical aggression of a man we know would kill the woman he married. The picture's power came in part from its—and the show's—blurring of the lines between fact and fiction: while it was an actress being groped and throttled in the image, she played a real woman who really was killed by her husband. It was this blurring that eventually drew me in, as more and more students asked whether some part or another of an episode bore any resemblance to reality. As I caught myself saying, "Well, actually, yes" to some of their more incredulous reports, I became curious about just what mix of fact, fiction, and fantasy they were picking up from the show. In respect to crime, violence, and punishment, I found, its "not inaccurate" presentation offers a salutary dose of blood and anguish to what can easily become an unduly sanitized version of early modern English history, even while prompting potentially useful questions about the ways in which we view such "not inaccurate" violence as entertainment.

The Tudors depicts its protagonist presiding over a brutally bloody age; he did, and it was. Yes, one easily finds fabrications, but they are often balanced by elements that are based in fact, despite seeming to some too brutal to be true. Simon Fish died of the plague rather than being burned as a heretic, for example; but yes, Thomas More did have others very like Fish reduced to ashes. We have no reason to think that Bishop Fisher's cook Richard Roose was an assassin hired by the Boleyn family; but yes, the authorities did actually boil him to death.[4] The narrative of the Pilgrimage of Grace and the suppression of its subsequent revolts take many liberties—not least in that the Duke of Norfolk, not Suffolk, took charge of the task in reality; but yes, at one point, he really did select precisely 74 people to be executed en masse.[5]

Alongside the glaring distortions sometimes appear small, strange details drawn from life. Yes, for example, one of Henry's first gifts to Catherine Howard really was the rather unromantic (and perhaps foreboding) grant of property forfeited to the crown upon a murder, stripped from the killer's family and taken by the king to dole out as he pleased—in this case, to a woman he wanted to woo.[6] As Thomas More's wife noted earlier in the series, when men were found guilty of felony or treason, their families lost not just a loved one and provider, but also all their goods.[7] The forfeiture of criminals' property was thought to act as a disincentive to disobedience, and hope of its mitigation presumably helped explain the tone of some of those strikingly submissive scaffold speeches—another element that seems implausible to some but turns out to be based in truth.[8]

Cumulatively, the series ably conveys something of the violence of Henry's reign. Mid-twentieth-century historians, thinking perhaps of the violent regimes of their own day, sought to refute earlier characterizations of a "Tudor despotism" by showing that executions (usually) proceeded according to known laws.[9] They came to emphasize consent rather than coercion. More recently, perhaps cognizant of our own acquiescence and collaboration in systems of governance and commerce that rely on violence of another sort, historians have explored the ways in which power was negotiated, diffused, and based on broad participation.[10] Henry VIII did indeed recognize the constraining force of law and had to put many decisions before groups of his more powerful subjects gathered in courts, convocations, and parliaments. Any sentence of death required the concurrence of jurors or members of parliament. The king had no professional police force or salaried bureaucracy, as such, and thus relied upon the cooperation of active "agents"—people who did not simply do as they were told but operated according to their own ideas and interests, as they were able. And yet none of this should blind us to the fear and force that lay behind it all. Just because many people agreed that the violence was just or useful does not make it any less violent.

Of course, if one's definition of "violence" includes a notion of illegitimacy, of force wrongly applied, then we must also recognize that a good many acts of physical harm and coercion were not deemed violent at the time—something the show also conveys. Men could legitimately physically correct and control their wives and other dependents to ensure disciplined households; courts could legitimately impose sentences of death and mutilation in pursuit of a well-disciplined realm. People certainly disputed the legitimacy of particular instances, but generally accepted the use of force to ensure order and obedience.[11]

Even more so than violence, "crime" is a relative concept—a notion to which the series nods, at least implicitly. James Sharpe's definition is useful: simply, "crime is behaviour which is regarded as illegal and which, if detected, would lead to prosecution in a court of law or summarily before an accredited agent of law enforcement."[12] Some behaviors that were considered the most heinous of crimes in the past are no longer crimes today; some things that are crimes today were nothing of the sort in days gone by. The list of actions deemed criminal in early modern England lengthened significantly in the reign of Henry VIII. The early modern English divided their crimes into three broad categories of increasing severity: misdemeanors, felonies, and treasons. The latter two categories of offenses had death as their sanction. Henry's parliaments passed 11 statutes that expanded the scope of treason and 15 that made new felonies, along with dozens more that created lesser offenses to be punished with imprisonment, corporal punishment, or fines.[13] Along with witchcraft, "buggery" also became an offense punishable with death. Priests who took wives upon the mistaken belief that the Reformation brought with it freedom to marry, as it did elsewhere in Europe, risked death in the wake of Henry's Act of Six Articles. And the list goes on. This growth in the scope and severity of the criminal law constituted part of the "increase in governance" that marked the sixteenth century in general, and Henry's reign in particular.

As the scope and severity of the law increased, so too did the need for flexibility and discretion. Justice and mercy existed in tandem, even if for the most pragmatic of reasons: having too many of the poor and pitiable hanging from gallows at the end of a court session might weaken the intended lessons of law. Sanctuary had long afforded some offenders safety: people might flee to any church and there, upon confession of their crimes, obtain permission to leave the country or, if they fled to one of a select group of permanent sanctuaries, spend their days within its borders, immune from arrest.[14] Sanctuary had a long history, but fell victim to Henry's attacks on the church and its privileges, not least to his closure of the monasteries. Royal mercy—pardons from the king himself—replaced it. Tudor monarchs issued pardons to individuals upon petitions for clemency and to groups, too, in spectacles carefully calibrated to advertise the king's godlike mercy.[15] As the Henry of *The Tudors* does in one episode, so did the real king on several occasions, offering forgiveness to those who humbled themselves by appearing with halters about their necks in dramatic acts of contrition and submission.[16] The series might exaggerate for effect the capriciousness and degree of the king's discretion, but discretion he had.

So, too, does the series somewhat caricature the significance of status and hierarchy in the era, but this might offer a salutary reminder to those—professional historians included—who sometimes assume that societies which recognize the rule of law also endorse the equality of all before that law. Early modern justice was emphatically not indifferent to status, nor was it intended to be. The law's privileging of status emerged not from a simple failure of justice, a disjunction between rhetoric and reality, but from a different notion of how and to whom justice applied than what prevails today. Only equals required equal treatment. Rights varied according to one's position in society.[17] Free and unfree constituted fundamental categorical distinctions, as did birth within or outside the king's dominions. Sex and marital status distinguished some from others. Differences depending on estate mattered, too. Clergy, nobility, and commons belonged to distinct orders. Whether by birth or by sacrament, nobles and clerics differed from commoners and received fundamentally different treatment at law.[18]

The privileges of clerics came under sustained attack in the reign of Henry VIII, however, a development that receives some mention in the series. Under Henry, the clergy became subject to the same courts and to the same laws that applied to others, losing many of the incidents of their status as a distinct order. "Benefit of clergy" had ensured that clerics not be tried in the king's courts; clerics lost that privilege, and the so-called benefit of clergy instead became a legal fiction supervised by the king's justices and open to any man who could satisfy a reading test, allowing him to exchange the death penalty for a lighter punishment of branding, forfeiture of property, and perhaps some time in gaol upon conviction for one of a shrinking list of offenses.[19]

The legal privileges of the second great estate continued, though, with the greater nobility—the peers—retaining legal immunities and privileges they received by right of birth. They were free from arrest for everything save treason, felony, and breaches of the peace. They could not be imprisoned for debt or outlawed or asked to depose on oath. Significantly, too, for offenses punishable with death, lords were free from the common law criminal courts, tried instead by their fellows in the court of the Lord High Steward or in the House of Lords, a privilege first given statutory backing in 1442 and entrenched over the following two centuries.[20] The series gives its viewers two notable instances of such special trials, those of the Duke of Buckingham at the beginning and the Earl of Surrey near the end.[21] Both depictions simplify and speculate, but convey something of the significance attached to trials of the nobly born and the political risks the king took in prosecuting such individuals.

The inaccuracies in such historical dramas are often not "errors," as such: they are choices made for some hoped-for effect. On occasion, that choice may itself harken more effectively to a truth than attempting a more factually accurate depiction might have done. The execution scenes sometimes seem wrong, for example, in being relatively empty and quiet, more akin to nineteenth-century gaol-yard hangings, when in fact authorities staged such executions as spectacles for public consumption. Often rowdy, raucous affairs, executions were meant as examples and often served as entertainment. Large crowds came to watch. The show's creators use such crowds to good effect in some such execution scenes, but in others opt for lonelier spaces not because they "got it wrong," but because they sought to evoke a particular sense in a different sort of audience, one comprising modern television viewers rather than sixteenth-century men and women gathered before a scaffold. As director Ciaran Donnelly noted in the production notes for Season Four, the sheer number of executions that needed to be shown in the series caused concern that simple repetition would dull the effect. Inventiveness seemed necessary.[22] And in the depictions of Simon Fish's (fictional) burning and that of John Lambert, for example, the relative emptiness of the scenes is perhaps more effective than a more accurate shot of crowds might have been in conveying a sense that burning a man to death for a matter of religious belief had become almost routine.[23]

Whatever the choices made in portraying individual deaths, cumulatively they convey something of the visual force and frequency of Henrician executions. Hanging was by far the most common form of capital punishment, used for the bulk of felonies and prized for its supposedly exemplary, deterrent effect. These hangings were not the relatively quick affairs of the late nineteenth and early twentieth centuries: the standard drop and long drop developed only in 1866 and 1872, respectively, meaning that earlier instances were typically slow strangulations that could take half an hour or more to kill a person. For high treason—defined as offenses that violated one's loyalty to the king—men faced being dragged through the streets, briefly hanged, then disemboweled and divided into quarters, though a beheading with block and axe was typically substituted for noble-born offenders. Heretics were indeed burnt at the stake. So, too, were women who killed their husbands, which the law defined not just as murder but more seriously as an act of "petty treason," a deed that violated the bonds of obedience and loyalty one owed one's immediate lord and master. (The judges at Queen Anne's trial sentenced her to *either* burning *or* beheading, already unusual in its imprecision, and made more unusual when the king decided to employ a continental executioner, trained in using a sword rather than an axe.[24]) Notably, though, women convicted of witchcraft in England were not burnt at the stake, as they were in legend and in Scotland; when witchcraft was first made a capital crime in England, in 1542, it was made a felony to be punished with hanging, like most any other crime of its class.

While the English prided themselves on not having some of the more imaginative and gruesome forms of execution used on the continent, they did make exceptions for what they saw as exceptional crimes. Briefly after 1531, those who used poison to kill risked death by boiling, as happened to Bishop Fisher's cook Richard Roose and at least one woman in these years.[25] Some punishments evoked parallels with the crimes committed: Alice Wolfe and her husband John, for example, were sentenced to be tied to a stake at the Thames' low tide, left there to drown as the waters rose, having killed foreign merchants while ferrying them cross the river.[26] The authorities killed yet other offenders by gibbeting or hanging in chains, as shown in the horrifying depiction of Robert Aske's execution in the series, or after first severing some offending body part.[27]

Death came for many offenses, in many varieties, and in many places. In and around London itself, the Tower offered the main site of execution for elite or exceptional offenders, either on full public view just outside the walls or somewhat more privately inside. The Smithfield market area, Wapping Docks, and Tyburn field served as favored sites, but almost any church yard or open space that accommodated a crowd hosted executions, too. Charing Cross, Cheapside, St. Paul's Churchyard, Westminster's Tothill, and Old Palace Yard all saw executions in these years. After a set of riots in 1517, people were hanged at each of London's city gates, with special gallows set up at such places as Aldgate, Bishopsgate, Gracechurch

Street, and Leadenhall Street.[28] As the series ably intimates, many people witnessed the power of the king's law to take life.

Exactly how many people died as traitors, felons, and heretics in Henry's reign we cannot know. Extrapolating from pockets of surviving court records, Philip Jenkins has estimated that anywhere from 600 to 1200 people a year suffered judicial executions in early modern England.[29] The archives that allow us even these imprecise estimates come mostly from the reigns of Elizabeth and her successors, though; relatively few court records survive from Henry's reign that provide the all-important indications of whether or not sentences were actually carried out. One frequently sees cited online and in older historical accounts claims that Henrician authorities executed some 72,000 (or 70,000) thieves and vagabonds. This number is at once shocking and also not completely out of line with our extrapolations from Elizabethan and early Stuart records. It is also, however, grounded on nothing more than the hearsay report of a visitor to England, which was then included (in slightly altered form) in an Elizabethan chronicle and thence passed on to posterity.[30]

Trying to find somewhat stronger sources of evidence, we might turn to the chronicle of Henry's reign left by the royal herald Charles Wriothesley. Though he noted only the executions of high profile or unusual offenders, he mentioned specifically the deaths of 234 individuals (along with "diverse others," unspecified), with some 29 of those people beheaded, 118 hanged and quartered, 43 simply hanged, 43 burnt, and one boiled.[31] The letters Christopher Jenney sent to Thomas Cromwell give us some sense of executions for regular crimes, in another urban center. Jenney was a traveling judge, sent out on the twice-yearly circuit courts that emptied the gaols throughout the country. In one letter reporting on a court day in York in March 1535, he noted that 76 prisoners had been tried, with 18 convicted, though one and possibly two of the condemned had escaped execution thanks to their clerical status and a pardon.[32] His report of the August 1535 court date mentioned 42 prisoners, of whom 6 went to their deaths. (In that letter, he noted too his stop at Hull, where he tried a 20-year-old "boy" for "meddling carnally with a cow": both the young man and the cow were killed, the latter burned in the place where the deed had been done.)[33] In a third letter, reporting a court session in April 1538, he noted that he had tried at York 80 prisoners, with 18 executed, but had not bothered to travel to Durham as he had word that the city had no prisoners in its gaol at the moment.[34] We might choose to be impressed by either or both facts that only about 20 % of those charged with capital offenses suffered death, or that the small city of York witnessed a minimum of 40 executions resulting from these three court days alone.

In at least a general sense, then, the series' depictions of crime, punishment, and violence accord with what we know or have good reason to think to be true of the era's realities. What of its frequent scenes of torture, though? "Torture," properly speaking, refers to torments used to gather information to investigate and prosecute crimes, not to the destructive or degrading punishments imposed thereafter. It was a routine part of criminal procedure in continental Europe, but had no place in English common law. Even so, English authorities did use it over the sixteenth century, at least on occasion. We know of 81 cases over the years from 1540 to 1640, with the bulk in Elizabeth's reign, thanks to warrants for its use in surviving privy council registers. Both Edward Seymour, Earl of Hertford, and Charles Brandon, Duke of Suffolk, received authorization from these warrants to torture suspected offenders, for example.[35] Those registers only began to be kept in 1540, though, so we do not know much about torture's use in earlier years, save through stray mentions in (or inferences from the steadily weakening signatures on) other documents left from the period. *The Tudors*' depictions of torture, then, seem broadly plausible, but also bring us up against the limits of our ability to know for sure what really happened—in more ways than one.[36]

The case of Anne Askew, depicted in the program's penultimate episode, brings many of these threads together.[37] Yes, she was racked; we know this from her own account. Yes, she had to be carried to the stake because her body was so badly broken and, yes, she was burned. In the series, Askew is shown being burnt alone, however, when in fact three others—John Lascelles, John Adams, and Nicholas Belenian—died alongside her. Can the series be faulted for not including these others, or for failing to mention one of the most interesting and unusual things about Askew, that she left written accounts of her interrogations that were later published? Perhaps. But if so, we first need to recognize the limits on our ability to know all the details of the real burning against which we want judge the show. Two Protestant reformers, John Bale and John Foxe, later published reports of Askew's death that we use as our main sources of evidence, but their accounts differ in detail from one telling to the next. Foxe's own version of the story differed from the 1563 edition of his book to the 1570 edition, with the latter adding bits about the Lieutenant of the Tower leaving the racking in some dismay (though not because the law supposedly forbade the torture of women specifically) and about the use of gunpowder at the execution (though not provided by Lady Hertford as a kindness, rather there in his account to suggest the timorousness of the councilors sent to watch the execution). The changes from one version to another reflect in part the altered preoccupations and concerns of the authors as they edited or composed, choices made for some hoped-for effect. Foxe's changes, for example, seem part of his critique of the slow pace of religious reform in Elizabeth's reign, intended to use Askew's story to stiffen resolve in his own day.[38]

Or, instead of faulting the series for its divergences from what we know (or think we know) to have been true, we can accept that the series did not set out to be historically accurate, but simply to entertain. If we view it as entertainment, though, the ethics of presenting or watching so much violence, some of it sexualized, might give one pause. Given the creative license already used throughout the program, and evidence for the influence of media depictions of violence against women on viewers' attitudes, one might wish that the creative license had been used a bit more liberally and responsibly.[39] The semifictional nature of much of the show's narrative perhaps makes it easier to watch its graphic scenes of violence, allowing viewers to forget that they are watching reenactments of pains inflicted on real bodies. That they are somewhat fictionalized accounts, however, elides the few good reasons to view violence, such as bearing witness and attempting to understand in order to amend. The ethical issues involved in using accounts of other people's suffering to one's own ends are shared by historians, though, so perhaps in raising such issues in so graphic a format *The Tudors* does us a service. At least, too, while the violence sometimes seems gratuitous, it is not glorified; the series presents torture as a flawed means of attempting to learn the truth that also diminishes those inflicting the pain, for example. We see signs here of present-minded concerns, perhaps. As many of the show's viewers live in societies that continue to condone capital punishment or torture in hidden chambers, if *The Tudors*' portrayals of crime, punishment, and violence prompt reflection on such issues today, then perhaps a bit of ahistoricism is not all a bad thing. The show's "not inaccurate" depictions of violence, crime, and punishment might well prompt us to rethink the histories we write and those which we create.

NOTES

1. *The Tudors*, Episode 1:1.
2. Thomas Freeman, "Introduction: It's Only a Movie," in Susan Doran and Thomas D. Freeman, eds., *Tudors and Stuarts on Film: Historical Perspectives* (Basingstoke, 2009), 1–29, makes a strong-enough case for engaging with inaccuracies in historical dramas to weaken my usual skepticism about the merits of doing so.
3. Anna Whitelock, "Was Henry VIII Really an Oaf in Leather Trousers?" accessed July 7, 2014, http://www.theguardian.com/theguardian/2007/oct/05/features11.g2.
4. *The Tudors*, Episodes 1:10, 2.01; K.J. Kesselring, "A Draft of the 1531 'Acte for Poysoning,'" *English Historical Review* 116 (2001): 894–899.
5. *The Tudors*, Episode 3:2; The National Archives, Public Record Office [hereafter TNA], SP 1/116, fol.108. [See J.S. Brewer, J. Gairdner, and R.H. Brodie, eds., *Letters and Papers...of the Reign of Henry VIII*, 21 vols. (London, 1862–1910, 1929–1932), XII, i, no. 498].
6. *The Tudors*, Episode 3:8; *Letters and papers ... of the reign of Henry VIII*, XV, no. 613 (12).
7. *The Tudors*, Episode 2:5; for the historical context, see K.J. Kesselring, "Felony Forfeiture and the Profits of Crime in Early Modern England," *The Historical Journal* 53 (2) (2010): 271–288 and "Coverture and Criminal Forfeitures," in *Women, Transgression and Discipline in Early Modern Britain*, ed. Richard Hillman and Pauline Ruberry-Blanc (Farnham, 2014), 191–212.
8. See L.B. Smith, "English Treason Trials and Confessions in the Sixteenth Century," *Journal of the History of Ideas* 15 (1954): 471–498 and J.A. Sharpe, "Last Dying Speeches: Religion, Ideology and Public Execution in Seventeenth-Century England," *Past & Present* 107 (1984): 144–167.
9. See in particular works by G.R. Elton, e.g., *The Tudor Revolution in Government* (Cambridge, 1953).
10. See, for example, key works on the early modern state: M.J. Braddick, *State Formation in Early Modern England, c. 1550–1700* (Cambridge, 2000) and Steve Hindle, *The State and Social Change in Early Modern England, c. 1550–1640* (Basingstoke, 2000). For a recent restoration of violence to the heart of our understanding of early modern governance, see Ethan Shagan, *The Rule of Moderation: Violence, Religion and the Politics of Restraint in Early Modern England* (Cambridge, 2011).
11. See Susan Amussen, "Punishment, Discipline, and Power: The Social Meanings of Violence in Early Modern England," *Journal of British Studies* 34 (1995): 1–34.

12. J.A. Sharpe, *Crime in Early Modern England, 1550–1750* (London, 1999), 6.
13. K.J. Kesselring, *Mercy and Authority in the Tudor State* (Cambridge, 2003), 37–38.
14. For sanctuary's history, see Karl Shoemaker, *Sanctuary and Crime in the Middle Ages, 400–1500* (New York, 2011).
15. Kesselring, *Mercy and Authority*, passim.
16. *The Tudors*, Episode 3:2.
17. See, for example, Edward Powell, "Law and Justice," in *Fifteenth Century Attitudes: Perceptions of Society in Late Medieval England*, ed. Rosemary Horrox (Cambridge, 1994), 31 and G.R. Evans, *Law and Theology in the Middle Ages* (London, 2002), 85–119.
18. See, for example, Georges Duby, *The Three Orders: Feudal Society Imagined* (Chicago, 1980); Jeffrey Dunton, ed., *Orders and Hierarchies in Late Medieval and Renaissance Europe* (Toronto, 1999); and Bernard Jussen, ed., *Ordering Medieval Society: Perspectives on Intellectual and Practical Modes of Shaping Social Relations* (Philadelphia, 2001), trans. Pamela Selwyn.
19. On benefit of clergy see, for example, J.G. Bellamy, *The Criminal Trial in Later Medieval England* (Toronto, 1998), 143–147 and Kesselring, *Mercy and Authority*, 46–55.
20. See M.L. Bush, *The English Aristocracy: A Comparative Synthesis* (Manchester, 1984), esp. 18, 20–28 and Colin Rhys Lovell, "The Trial of Peers in Great Britain," *American Historical Review* 55 (1949): 69–81.
21. *The Tudors*, Episodes 1:1, 4:10.
22. Interview with Ciaran Donnelly in Production Notes for Season 4 on *The Tudors* website, accessed July 14, 2014, http://www.thetudorswiki.com/page/CREATORS+of+The+Tudors.
23. *The Tudors*, Episodes 1:10, 3:6.
24. Nadia Bishai, "'Which Things Had Not Before Been Seen': The Rituals and Rhetoric of the Execution of Anne Boleyn," in *The Rituals and Rhetoric of Queenship*, ed. Liz Oakley-Brown and Louise Wilkinson (Dublin, 2009), 171–185.
25. See Kesselring, "A Draft of the 1531 'Acte for Poysoning,'" 894–899.
26. See Ibid., 895 n.6.
27. *The Tudors*, Episode 3:4.
28. See Kesselring, *Mercy and Authority*, 157–159 and contemporary Edward Hall's account, in H. Ellis, ed. *Hall's Chronicle* (London, 1809), 587–590. For the full range of corporal punishments, also visible and violent, see too J.A. Sharpe, *Judicial Punishment in England* (London, 1990).
29. Philip Jenkins, "From Gallows to Prison? The Execution Rate in Early Modern England," *Criminal Justice History* 7 (1986): 52.

30. William Harrison's "Description of England," included in Raphael Holinshed's *Chronicles of England, Scotland and Ireland* (London, 1587), vol. 1, p. 314 seems to be the most commonly cited source for this number, but as Harrison notes, he acquired it only "by report" passed on by one Gerolamo Cardano, a visiting Italian scholar, who in turn heard the number from the "Bishop of Lexovia" (possibly Lisieux, in France). See Thorsten Sellin's tracing of the story in "Two Myths in the History of Capital Punishment," *Journal of Criminal Law and Criminology* 50 (1959–1960): 114–117.
31. *A Chronicle of England ... by Charles Wriothesley*, ed. William Douglas Hamilton (Camden Society, 1875), *passim*.
32. TNA, SP 1/91, f. 144.
33. TNA, SP 1/95, f. 33.
34. TNA, SP 1/242, f. 10.
35. John Langbein, *Torture and the Law of Proof* (Chicago, 1976), esp. 73–82, 94–95.
36. *The Tudors*, Episodes 2:9, 4:5, 4:9.
37. *The Tudors*, Episode 4:9.
38. Thomas S. Freeman and Sarah Elizabeth Wall, "Racking the Body, Shaping the Text: The Account of Anne Askew in Foxe's 'Book of Martyrs,'" *Renaissance Quarterly* 54 (2001): 1165–1195. For Askew's own text and its publication history, see Elaine Beilin, ed., *The Examinations of Anne Askew* (Oxford, 1996). The variations between Foxe's first and second editions can easily be seen in the texts presented on www.johnfoxe.org: 1563 edition, book 3, pp. 725–734 and 1570 edition, book 8, pp. 1452–1460. For the broader utility of accounts of women martyrs, see Megan Hickerson, *Making Women Martyrs in Tudor England* (Basingstoke, 2005).
39. Notably, one study which argues that the strength or subordination of the female characters shapes the effects of portrayals of violence used an episode of *The Tudors* as an example of a show with sexual violence and passive female characters, to contrast not just with nonsexual/nonviolent shows but also with programs with sexual violence but stronger female characters. See Christopher J. Ferguson, "Positive Female Role-Models Eliminate Negative Effects of Sexually Violent Media," *Journal of Communication* 62 (2012): 888–899. The study indicated that shows in *The Tudors*' category did more than those in either of the other two to increase the anxiety of female viewers and the negative attitudes of male viewers toward women.

CHAPTER 16

Humanism and Humanitarianism in *The Tudors*

Samantha Perez

A central component to the Renaissance revival of antiquity, humanism was an educational model centered on the study of Greek and Roman texts that glorified the classical ideal and promoted a curriculum rooted in rhetoric, grammar, and philosophy. With champions like Leonardo Bruni, Rodolphus Agricola, and Erasmus, the intellectual movement quickly spread out of the Italian peninsula and across Europe. Henry VIII and his court were instrumental in fostering humanism in England. Scholars such as Richard Pace, Richard Morison, and Thomas Starkey advanced classical studies, and the library at the Syon Monastery in Isleworth, just west of London, amassed Latin texts.[1] Henry and Catherine of Aragon supported the introduction of Greek studies at Oxford.[2] In 1519, Erasmus wrote that humanism would flourish in the Low Countries, if only they had a king like Henry.[3] As a result of these academic endeavors, the exploration of humanism becomes an interesting, if complicated, pursuit within *The Tudors*. Although the show presents an anachronistic definition of humanism as humanitarianism, *The Tudors* incorporates historically accurate aspects of the Renaissance movement by exploring Thomas More's *Utopia*, the education and treatment of educated women, and the methods of effective kingship based on Niccolò Machiavelli's *The Prince*.

S. Perez (✉)
Department of History, Tulane University, New Orleans, LA, USA

Despite the Henrician court's historical involvement in humanism, *The Tudors* depicts a postmodern understanding of the intellectual movement as a human-centric, peace-focused endeavor, devoid of any dependence on the classical ideal. In the series' opening episode, Henry and More define humanism as a promotion for the preservation of human life and the antithesis of war:

More: As a humanist, I have an abhorrence of war. It's an activity fit only for beasts, yet practiced by no kind of beast so constantly as by man.

Henry: As a humanist, I share your opinion. As a king, I'm forced to disagree.[4]

Humanism for *The Tudors* implies the protection and advancement of all society. Henry describes the European peace treaty as "the application of humanist principles to international affairs,"[5] and Wolsey bemoans that his humanist values are often at odds with a contemporary world that finds value in war and corruption.[6] The show's conceptualization of humanism is never more fully explored beyond these brief mentions, which often unsatisfactorily rely on circular definition to explain the concept. In this way, "humanism" serves more as a historical prop used by the writers to establish the cultural setting of Henry's fictionalized court rather than a commentary on the actual Renaissance curriculum. In fact, of the five times humanism is directly referenced in the series, two occur in the first episode and four in the first season. In the rare instances when humanism is mentioned by name, the characters maintain this anachronistic definition of the term, arguably more relatable to the show's audiences, rather than complicating its meaning with the incorporation of classical elements. It is not until the final season that classical writers are referenced to any meaningful degree, and when they are, the characters make no apparent association between ancient texts and humanism. Henry presents the teenage Elizabeth with a book by Tacitus, highlighting the importance of classical authors in her education, but makes no mention of humanist curriculum as a motive.[7] Likewise, the Earl of Surrey is shown translating Martial's X.47 epigram, "Ad Seipsum," clearly a humanist-influenced undertaking, but that does not correct or complicate Henry and More's earlier definition of humanism as a pro-humanity movement.[8] Instead, interest in classical texts and humanism remain two separate, unconnected themes within the series, and *The Tudors*' portrayal of humanism becomes synonymous with humanitarianism.

Even though *The Tudors* does not directly associate humanism with education or classicism, events within the show still relate to the endeavors of a more historically accurate Renaissance definition, beginning with More's *Utopia*. Published in 1516 in Latin, *Utopia* details the travels of Raphael Hythlodaeus, who describes to the self-fictionalized More an island in the New World where inhabitants share common goods, condemn wealth, and promote the merits of education. *The Tudors* never gives the specifics of More's text, nor does it detail the plot. In the brief, one-time mention of the book, Henry only describes *Utopia* as "utopian" when he compares it to *The Prince*.[9] Despite this lack of description, elements of More's work still manifest themselves in the series. In fact, the show's humanitarian value for humanism derives more from *Utopia* than from historical humanism. Hythlodaeus finds fault in princes, who "have more delight in warlike matters and feats of chivalry ... than in the good feats of peace,"[10] erecting a war/peace dichotomy that serves as one of the primary thematic undertones lasting the entire series:

More: I must urge you that instead of spending ruinous amounts of money going to war you should spend it rather on the welfare of your people.

Henry: Thomas, I swear to you I intend to be a just ruler. But tell me this: Why is Henry V remembered? Because he endowed universities? Built alms houses for the destitute? No. He is remembered because he won the battle of Agincourt. ... That victory made him famous, Thomas.[11]

More's utopian ideals provide a moral standard to which Henry can aspire, even if he ultimately fails as Hythlodaeus predicts. It is the responsibility of the philosopher, as More suggests in *Utopia*, to work within those corrupt systems to correct them as best possible: "[Y]ou must with a crafty wile and a subtle train study and endeavor yourself, as much as in you lieth, to handle the matter wittily and handsomely for the purpose; and that which you cannot turn to good, so order it that it be not very bad."[12] Compromise between ideals and reality was central to More's philosophy, and Jeremy Northam's character paraphrases such sentiments when he advises his children, "If you cannot be good, be the least bad you can be."[13] Toward such ends, he tries to actualize his utopia as much as possible in Henry's court. Like the people of Utopia, he ignores the allure of material possessions, avoiding the trappings of office when he takes over as chancellor, unlike predecessor Wolsey.[14] More must face the issue of compromise when petitioned by Henry to accept the position as chancellor. Henry recognizes More's disapproval of the King's Great Matter but assures More he will not have to act against his conscience; with such an agreement, so in line with his utilitarian view of philosophy, More accepts the appointment.[15] Although only name-dropped in passing, *Utopia*'s glorification of simplicity and peace and the juxtaposition of ideal and reality inform More's character and by extension influence Henry's reign.

The Tudors has a much stronger grasp on another cornerstone of Renaissance humanism: education, specifically the education of women. Before the nurturing of humanist interests in England in the sixteenth century, English women had little opportunity to expand their education. In a sermon for Margaret Beaufort, the grandmother of Henry VIII, Bishop John Fisher mentioned that "she complained that in her youth she had not given her to the understanding of Latin," an interesting commentary on the changing times regarding both her lack of education and her apparent thirst for one.[16] However, prominent humanist scholars such as Leonardo Bruni on the continent and Richard Hyrde in England advocated their schooling based on the classical curriculum. Hyrde even dedicated his treatise on the education of Christian women to Catherine of Aragon, asking, "For what is more fruitful than the good education and order of women, the one half of all mankind?"[17] Henry VIII's fostering of humanism introduced new opportunities for the education of women, especially those closest to the royal family. Catherine was a celebrated patron of artists and employed William Blount, Lord Mountjoy, a student of Erasmus, as her chamberlain.[18] Fluent in Latin and Greek herself, she subsidized the study of poor students at English universities and made a tour of Wolsey's Oxford in 1518.[19] Anne Boleyn's experiences in the French court likely exposed her to the intellectual circle of Marguerite de Navarre, Francis' sister and a proponent of humanism.[20] The seventeenth-century historian John Strype labeled Anne as a "great favourer of learning."[21] Even with these vocal supporters, the education of women was still largely a novel concept during Henry's reign, and the problematic undertaking was not intended to dismantle the established gender hierarchy. Bruni believed that daughters should be educated with the same care as sons but warned against their applied use of rhetoric because "contests of the forum, like those of warfare and battle, are the sphere of men."[22] Hyrde remarked that women were susceptible to "many peevish fantasies in their minds, which must needs be occupied either with good or bad, so long as they be waking."[23] As King Francis remarks and Henry translates with a smile in Episode 2:2, "Women are often variable. Only madmen believe them."

The Tudors reflects this historical change in access to education for elite women in Henrician society, so much so that when the show discusses education, it is mainly associated with women. As in history, the fictionalized More, identified by Henry as "the greatest humanist in all England,"[24] spearheads this social change by requiring equal education of both his son and his daughters:

Henry: How are your children?
More: They are well, thank you, your Majesty. I encourage them all to their studies, even the girls.
Henry: Always the idealist.
More: At some point, I imagine, it will be considered ordinary enough and nothing strange for a girl to be educated.[25]

Henry's gift of Tacitus to Elizabeth stresses the importance of Latin within quality instruction for girls.[26] Likewise, Mary, who studied Latin and Greek in reality, also receives a rigorous classical education, at which she excels. Catherine of Aragon praises her intelligence, telling Henry, "She writes to me in perfect Latin, and tells me she dances the galliards every day, and can play the lute, much to everyone's satisfaction and joy. You should be proud of her."[27] Catherine herself is depicted as articulate and educated with many learned colleagues, including real-life humanists More and Fisher. When she realizes her lawyers are not supporting her case against divorce, she employs legal and religious arguments to condemn them for having more loyalty to Wolsey than God.[28] Anne Boleyn mentions her tutor Dr. Knight in a conversation with Cromwell,[29] is proficient in French and Spanish,[30] and is frequently shown reading. When she swears in her ladies-in-waiting, she shows them the copy of Tyndale's Bible kept on display for her women to "read … and draw spiritual nourishment from it. For the old days are gone. Everything is changed now."[31] She recognizes the value in education and combats Cromwell over the use of funds gained from dissolved monasteries, demanding that some money go to a "better use" such as "endowments to charitable and educational causes, which even Wolsey did."[32] Interestingly, even though the show links its understanding of humanism with male characters—Henry, More, Wolsey—it is the women in *The Tudors* who most exemplify the historical movement's actual basis in education. The portrayal of these important female characters as highly educated, receptive to learning, and eager to employ their intelligence reflects the rapid changes in the education of women in Henrician England.

Although promoting their education, humanism did not necessarily authorize women to utilize the resulting knowledge to the same extent as their male peers, creating tension between the allowance for female education and society's treatment of educated women, both within an accurate historical context and within the show. In a conversation with Wolsey in Episode 1:9, Catherine of Aragon recognizes this disparity with a tongue-in-cheek belittling of her capabilities, claiming, "I am surprised to receive such a request from such a wise and noble man as you. I am but a poor woman, lacking both in wit and understanding." Similarly, Wolsey disparages Anne, snidely asking, "What would a silly girl like you have to say to a King?"[33] When Catherine Parr is caught advancing her Protestant beliefs against Henry's more moderate reform, she quickly relies on gender to excuse her actions: "Majesty, I think my meaning has been mistaken, for I have always held it preposterous for a woman to instruct her lord."[34] A conversation with Cromwell, Cranmer, and his wife, Margarete, best captures the new license of educated women with their remaining social constraints. Margarete questions the two men concerning their implementation of Reformation practices in England but finds their progress unsatisfactory:

Margarete: That's very good, gentlemen. But allow me to chide you. I don't think you are going far enough or fast enough.
Cromwell: Your wife is, uh, quite radical, Thomas.
Cranmer: She is. And illegal. *Laughter between Thomas and Cromwell.* Two reasons to hide her.
Margarete: Being carried around in a box does not make you laugh.
Cranmer: My dear, I am sorry about that.
Margarete: I am not "your dear." I am nobody's dear. I am a woman, and I demand equal respect for my ideas. For me, the practices of the Catholic church are evil. The way people are kept in total ignorance and made to feel guilty about their own bodies and their own thoughts. And even worse, the idea that the rich can buy a plot in heaven for their souls!
Cromwell: I agree with you. The Catholic church is corrupted. It's irredeemable.

Margarete: Then you should smash and destroy it utterly and totally and without pity. That is my advice to you, Mr. Cromwell. *Stands up.* Now you can put me back in my box![35]

The Tudors reflects the careful balance women in Henrician England were expected to maintain: humanism's emphasis on education afforded them new access to classical philosophy, literature, and rhetoric, but they were still largely restrained, whether socially or politically, from exercising the acquired knowledge.

Even while limited by traditional gender boundaries, it is most often educated women within the show who are able to exercise agency and promote a socio-political agenda beyond their own self-interest. Catherine of Aragon does not hesitate to voice her opinion about Henry's political policies, especially concerning France and the Holy Roman Empire, even though Henry sternly reminds her, "You are not my minister, you are not my chancellor, but my wife."[36] She shows political awareness and subtlety when she meets with the imperial ambassador Mendoza and asks for Charles V's help disputing Henry's desired divorce.[37] Later, the educated Mary Tudor champions her Catholic cause, capitalizing on the humanist education her mother insisted she receive as she orchestrates a return to papal obedience in Henry's court. Perhaps the best example is Anne Boleyn, who employs every resource available—from scholarly interests to sensuality—to further her ambitions and Protestant cause to great success before her ultimate fall from power. She introduces Henry to Protestant texts[38] and holds her own against male authorities like Wolsey and Cromwell. After Wolsey returns from his failed conclave in Paris, Henry invites him to speak freely about religious–political matters in front of Anne, commenting that "she knows everything" and is deeply involved in his affairs of state.[39] Thomas Boleyn tries to argue that their family's fortune was due to male organization, in which she was only a pawn, but Anne recognizes that it was in part her own effort—and her own intellect—that achieved the family's success:

Thomas: Anne, I did not bring you up to have opinions or to express them or to quarrel with those closest to the crown.
Anne: But I am closest to the crown. I am the king's wife!
Thomas: And you should remember how you got there!
Anne: I know how I got there. And it was not all you. It was not all you or Norfolk or George or any other *man* that you want to

name! It was also me. He fell in love with me, he respected me and my opinions.[40]

Her father's intent with her upbringing is moot; Anne has learned the means to assert her skills and recognize her own effort—precisely the inherent problem of equal education Bruni identified when he cautioned against women learning and actually employing rhetoric. In one of her final scenes, Anne cradles a book in her hand while she remembers her life in the court of Margaret of Austria and recounts how she once played "the Queen of the Amazons, with a naked sword in [her] hand and a crimson headdress with a great plume."[41] The comparison between Anne and the Amazons, one of the most famous symbols of female power from classical sources, is striking: the book in her hands as she retells the story mirrors the image of her holding the naked sword, both instruments for her that lead ultimately to power and death. The scene ends with her pointedly setting the book onto the table, relinquishing her means of power, and surrendering herself to her death which soon follows. In a show that makes a clear distinction between the efforts of educated women like Anne, Catherine, and Mary, and women whose education is lacking or unknown, like other ladies of the court and Henry's later wives, education, the cornerstone of Renaissance humanism, serves as the means by which women are able to participate actively in the social, political, and religious spheres typically dominated by men.

The most fully explored example of Renaissance humanism in *The Tudors* is an examination of Machiavelli's *The Prince* within Henry's political policies, focusing on the effects of fear and love for a stable kingship. Living in the troubled political climate of the heart of the Renaissance movement, Machiavelli became a leading humanist figure in Florence and applied classical political theory, especially an emphasis on republicanism, to contemporary government concerns. Key engineers within Henrician court were certainly familiar with *The Prince*, first published in Rome in 1532, as well as Machiavelli's other texts. In spring 1539, Henry Parker, Lord Morley, sent a copy of *The Prince* to Cromwell, identifying it as a "very special good thing for your lordship" and suggesting its political use.[42] Henry's propagandist Richard Morison cited Machiavelli's *Discourses* several times in his *A Remedy for Sedition*, his response to the Pilgrimage of Grace.[43] The actual familiarity of Henry himself with Machiavelli's works is more nebulous. Inventories indicate that he did own Machiavelli's *History of Florence*—although this does not prove he actually read it—and Lord

Morley encouraged him to read *The Prince*.[44] Regardless of Henry's actual familiarity with *The Prince*, within the world of *The Tudors*, Meyers' character makes clear his knowledge of the text and its most famous ideas.

The thematic significance of *The Prince* is established early in the first season and remains a constant throughout the entire series. While meeting with More, Henry mentions his interest in the new publication and says that Machiavelli "asked an important question, whether or not it is better for a king to be feared or loved."[45] Poignantly, the characters do not respond to the implied question in their conversation but rather allow the remainder of the series itself to serve as the answer. Henry remains torn on this dividing issue from the very beginning, desiring both the glory of a war against France, even when More warns that it will come at the expense of the welfare of his people, and the delivering of the "treaty of universal and perpetual peace" for Europe.[46] As the series evolves, the question between fear and love is conflated with war and peace, capitalizing on the show's definition of humanism as humanitarianism. With the loss of More as his moral compass, Henry more frequently utilizes war and violence as means to ensure obedience and exact prosperity for himself. He executes Anne, her brother, and her accused lovers without remorse, celebrating their deaths and his new relationship with Jane Seymour with a cooked swan.[47] Henry faces the same Machiavellian dilemma when dealing with the Pilgrimage of Grace, here choosing fear over love. After promising concessions to Robert Aske, who swears that the king's generosity will result in "no more loving and loyal people on the whole of [the] realm than Northern Yorkshire," Henry orders mass executions of the rebels to instill terror and deter against any future revolts.[48] Without More, it seems, Henry begins to lose sight of the real-world application of any humanitarian ideals and instead becomes more convinced that war will always remain an effective means of governance and glory:

Chapuys: The threat of the Turkish invasion has indeed been lifted by the emperor's victory. Peace will follow.
Henry: Ah, would that it followed everywhere.
Chapuys: Yes, pray God. Perhaps one day there will be no more need for war or war's alarms.
Henry: *Laughs*. In the meantime, please convey my love and my congratulations to the emperor. Tell him that ... tell him that of all the princes in the world, I admire him the most.[49]

Henry's arguably caustic laugh in this exchange suggests that he is no longer convinced that such a world could ever exist. War has become a necessary reality and violence—and the fear it inspires—an effective tool for control, security, and advancement.

Despite this thematic attention to humanism's historical goals, later seasons witness a gradual decline in humanist values, both by the show's humanitarian standards and by more accurate Renaissance ones, and the prescription for a peaceful, simple, educated utopia fails on every front. More's *Utopia* demanded a detachment from material possessions, but as the show continues—and distance from More's influence grows—Henry becomes increasingly extravagant. He orders the construction of Nonsuch Palace, which Richard Rich complains is squandering the large fortune gained from the dissolution of monasteries.[50] He spoils Catherine Howard with lavish gifts to keep her affection and bankrupts the kingdom to fund the campaign to capture Boulogne.[51] Cromwell alludes to this turning point when he expresses his goal to make Henry "the most powerful and the richest King in Europe."[52] Shortly before his death, More wistfully admits to Chapuys, "I've been thinking about the past, when I believed the King to be the most enlightened and promising prince in Christendom. I was sure his reign would be a golden age. I had such high hopes." When More dies in the middle of the Season Two, Henry is only just beginning his decline from the humanist standards erected in the early series, but already the effects are identifiable in his realm.[53]

At the same time, the show also deemphasizes education, central to the historical humanist movement, apparent by not only the decline of philosophical discussions but also the show's use of books as props symbolic of knowledge and power. Catherine of Aragon has a book in her lap while confronting the English bishops concerning their failure to adequately represent her case.[54] Cromwell presents Anne with William Tyndale's *The Obedience of the Christian Man*, directing her in her Protestant goals.[55] Even Henry himself participates in the intellectual life of his court through books, mentioning *Utopia* and *The Prince* but also reading Protestant texts that speak directly to his desire to augment monarchial powers over the church.[56] During the divorce trial with Catherine, Henry informs the court that *he* consulted authoritative texts, that *he* conducted the research, placing the agency of scholarship in his hands.[57] Rich visits More in the Tower on Cromwell's orders "to deprive [him] of [his] books and papers and suchlike," symbolizing the final loss of his own power in his situation. He dies an entire 16 minutes later.[58] In sharp contrast, where it was More,

Anne, and Henry often portrayed reading or surrounded by books in the first two seasons, by the end, the association with education has been passed to the next generation and remains conspicuously neglected by Henry and most of his court. The now-teenaged Elizabeth tutors young Edward in Latin grammar, stressing its importance for a strong reign.[59] Edward greets the High Admiral of France in Latin in Episode 4:10.[60] Henry and his advisors are more concerned with the day-to-day grind of war and political–religious intrigues than with any of the philosophical, moral, or academic debates that occasionally shaped the earlier seasons. This removal of scholastic or literary discussion and the symbolic decline of reading for the core characters emphasizes the loss of an intellectual environment in *The Tudors*' later seasons and the failure of humanism's education initiative within the show.

In this diminished intellectual environment and without any depicted association with education, the agency of Henry's wives also starts to decline. In contrast to Anne's direct involvement in matters of state, Henry explicitly orders Jane to stay out of political affairs.[61] She must employ indirect means to achieve her goals: "Women are much put upon in this world. It is my desire as much as I can to promote their interests. I must do it quietly, but I will do it all the same."[62] While Jane exercises some limited political agenda, Anne of Cleves is never even afforded the opportunity—or the voice—to do so. In Episode 3:8, Anne tries to raise some kind of question, possibly about the dismissal of Philip of Bavaria from court or about the legitimacy of their marriage. We can never know for sure because Henry silences her entirely:

Anne: Your Majesty ... I, uh ... I wondered—
Henry: I am sending you away for a while, to my palace at Richmond, for your health and for your pleasure.
Anne: Thank you, Your Majesty.[63]

Catherine Howard, who only displayed a basic competency with letters, is more concerned with fashion and finery than any political purpose.[64] It is not until the very end of Season Four that we see the return of female education, activism, and socio-political agency in Henry's wives with his final wife Catherine Parr. Although her education is never fully detailed, she is portrayed as learned. Henry tells her, "I hear you've been busying yourself with your books," the possessive pronoun making clear the association with intellectualism is no longer shared by Henry.[65] Catherine herself authors *Lamentations of a Sinner*, thematically linking books with her religious cause. With her education symbolically secured, Catherine cleverly asserts her Protestant cause, earning the ire of Bishop Gardiner, who hunts the belongings of her ladies-in-waiting for evidence, notably books.

With More's influence lost and education waning, Henry neglects the final historical example of humanism: he fails Machiavelli's advice concerning fear and love, and his oscillation between the two conflicting methods accelerates until effectiveness is lost. Machiavelli made clear in *The Prince* that "it is desirable to be both loved and feared, but … it is difficult to achieve both."[66] Henry's war between being feared and loved is a constant struggle. Henry chooses tolerance when he rescinds Wolsey's imprisonment and allows him to keep the bishopric of York. He is quite pleased with himself, bragging to More, "You see what kind of monster I am?"[67] But even in this same conversation, he begins his rapid switching between love and fear, threatening More when he initially refuses the position as chancellor. Henry's moderate advisors like More routinely need to rein him in, to keep him from seeming "easily changeable, shallow, intemperate, incapable of keeping his word,"[68] and without their influence, Henry's vacillation becomes more public and frequent. He orders mass executions for rebels participating in the Pilgrimage of Grace but later pardons them, proclaiming, "And since we have seen how much you love us, and seen all your tokens and signs of loyalty, with a free heart, we forgive you."[69] He pardons 500 men imprisoned on suspicion of heresy,[70] even though he later orders the arrest of presumed heretics living in his household.[71] Just as Machiavelli predicted, this has a negative effect on Henry's command. The Earl of Surrey begins maneuvering against the royal line, plotting to take control of young Edward after Henry's death and perhaps press his own Plantagenet claims to the throne. Even Charles Brandon becomes increasingly resentful toward Henry's change of heart, removing himself from court for long periods of time. Although he never betrays his old friend, there is clear tension and Brandon's silent dissatisfaction with Henry's wavering policies. Ultimately, what *The Tudors*' Henry proves is that Machiavelli was correct in his analysis of effective kingship: to command over a successful and stable reign, a prince can be feared or he can be loved but he cannot easily be both.

Piece by piece, as attention to *Utopia*'s simplicity, education, and Machiavelli's princely prescription declines, *The Tudors* ultimately fails even its own definition of humanism as the advancement and security of human life. Already by Season Two, humanism has altogether become a past-tense movement. Henry laments, "We used to call it humanism—Wolsey, More, and me. We were all humanists. Most people think I've changed, but I haven't. At heart, I'm still a humanist."[72] Despite his claim to still be a humanist, the show's interest in humanism vanishes after the deaths of Wolsey and More, and after this final reference in Episode 2:6, humanism is never again mentioned in the show. Even without humanism as the catchword, it takes the rest of the series to finally eliminate the humanitarian ideal presented in the opening episodes. Violence escalates in scale over the course of the later seasons: what was a peace treaty and jousting for sport in Season One becomes the Pilgrimage of Grace in Season Three, and ultimately outright war on several fronts by the end of the series. Furthermore, Henry desires the violence: when he is informed of peace in Europe, Henry remarks, "Something inside me is disappointed. It hungers for war."[73] He has become Hythlodaeus' glory-obsessed warrior-king and no longer prioritizes the welfare of his subjects, refusing to weaken his blockade to transport sick soldiers back to England, commanding that "they will either fight or I will hang them by the wayside!"[74] In a poignant bookend to the peace talks with the French and European treaty of the first season, he pledges a new treaty, one committing English troops, and the final episodes end in war against France, the same enemy with whom he had avoided war in the opening episode. Humanism has disappeared from Henry's world: More's moral philosophy could not redeem England into becoming a utopia; attention to humanism's intellectualism has declined in his court; he neglected to fully heed Machiavelli's advice for leadership; and he no longer prioritizes the preservation of human life. Humanism has become exactly what the fool Will Somers predicted of Nonsuch Palace, "a vacancy, a nullity," another memory and ghost of the past, like the ruins of ancient Rome itself.[75]

Notes

1. David Sandler Berkowitz, *Humanist Scholarship and Public Order* (Washington: Folger Books, 1984), 63.
2. Aysha Pollnitz, "Humanism and Court Culture in the Education of Tudor Royal Children," in *Tudor Court Culture* (Selinsgrove: Susquehanna University Press, 2010), 50.

3. Maria Dowling, *Humanism in the Age of Henry VIII* (London: Croom Helm, 1986), 16.
4. *The Tudors*, Episode 1:1.
5. Ibid.
6. *The Tudors*, Episode 1:6.
7. *The Tudors*, Episode 3:3.
8. *The Tudors*, Episode 3:4.
9. *The Tudors*, Episode 1:2.
10. More, *Utopia* (Oxford: Oxford University Press, 1999), 16.
11. *The Tudors*, Episode 1:1
12. More, *Utopia*, 42.
13. *The Tudors*, Episode 2:4
14. *The Tudors*, Episode 1:10.
15. *The Tudors*, Episode 1:9.
16. Quoted in Dowling, *Humanism*, 220.
17. Dowling, *Humanism*, 219.
18. Antonia McLean, *Humanism and the Rise of Science in Tudor England* (New York: Neale Watson Academic Publications, Inc., 1972), 44.
19. McLean, *Humanism*, 44–45.
20. McLean, *Humanism*, 45.
21. Quoted in McLean, *Humanism*, 46.
22. Bruni, "On the Study of Literature," in *The Humanism of Leonardo Bruni* (Binghamton: Medieval and Renaissance Texts & Studies, 1987), 244.
23. Dowling, *Humanism*, 220.
24. *The Tudors*, Episode 1:9
25. *The Tudors*, Episode 1:2
26. *The Tudors*, Episode 3:3
27. *The Tudors*, Episode 1:10
28. *The Tudors*, Episode 1:8
29. *The Tudors*, Episode 1:6
30. The accurate portrayal of Anne's command over French, thanks to her time in the French court, is evident in her conversation with Francis in Episode 2:2. She also translates, to Catherine of Aragon's surprise, the insult "puta de lujo" in Episode 1:6.
31. *The Tudors*, Episode 2:3.
32. *The Tudors*, Episode 2:7.
33. *The Tudors*, Episode 1:6.
34. *The Tudors*, Episode 4:10.
35. *The Tudors*, Episode 2:7.
36. *The Tudors*, Episode 1:1

37. *The Tudors*, Episode 1:6.
38. *The Tudors*, Episode 1:9.
39. *The Tudors*, Episode 1:6.
40. *The Tudors*, Episode 2:7.
41. *The Tudors*, Episode 2:10.
42. Quoted in Dowling, *Humanism*, 200.
43. Berkowitz, *Humanist Scholarship*, 67.
44. Jasper Ridley, *Henry VIII* (New York: Viking, 1985), 415.
45. *The Tudors*, Episode 1:2.
46. *The Tudors*, Episode 1:1.
47. *The Tudors*, Episode 2:10.
48. *The Tudors*, Episode 3:3.
49. *The Tudors*, Episode 2:8.
50. *The Tudors*, Episode 3:5.
51. *The Tudors*, Episode 4:8.
52. *The Tudors*, Episode 2:7.
53. The belief that humanism in England declined after More's death has highly contested academic roots that unfortunately cannot be explored in the space allotted here. For an analysis of the debate see Alistair Fox, "Fact and Fallacies: Interpreting English Humanism," *Reassessing the Henrician Age: Humanism, Politics, and Reform, 1500–1550* (New York: Basic Blackwell, 1986).
54. *The Tudors*, Episode 1:8.
55. *The Tudors*, Episode 1:8.
56. *The Tudors*, Episode 1.10.
57. *The Tudors*, Episode 1:8.
58. *The Tudors*, Episode 2:5.
59. *The Tudors*, Episode 3:4.
60. *The Tudors*, Episode 4.10.
61. *The Tudors*, Episode 3:2.
62. *The Tudors*, Episode 3:1.
63. *The Tudors*, Episode 3:8.
64. The examples for Howard's lavishness are bountiful, but an excellent point of comparison is between the swearing-in of her ladies-in-waiting and Anne's is Episode 4:1.
65. *The Tudors*, Episode 4:9.
66. Machiavelli, *The Prince*, ed. Quentin Skinner and Russell Price (Cambridge: Cambridge University Press, 1988), 59.
67. *The Tudors*, Episode 1:9.
68. *The Tudors*, Episode 1:2.
69. *The Tudors*, Episode 4:3.

70. *The Tudors*, Episode 4:1.
71. *The Tudors*, Episode 4:6.
72. *The Tudors*, Episode 2:6.
73. *The Tudors*, Episode 4:1.
74. *The Tudors*, Episode 4:8.
75. *The Tudors*, Episode 3:5.

CHAPTER 17

All That Glitters is (Fool's) Gold: Depictions of Court Entertainment in *The Tudors*

Carlie Pendleton

The objective of any television show is first and foremost to entertain, to transport viewers to another time and place where they can escape the drudgeries of their daily lives. It is, therefore, fortunate for Michael Hirst and his historical soap opera *The Tudors* that such was also the primary objective of Henry VIII in entertaining his court. Unlike nearly every other facet of *The Tudors*, court entertainments enhance rather than detract from what audiences are likely to consider good television. Still the real-life decadence of Henry's court, in Hirst's opinion, is not sufficient to satiate the voracious appetite of Tudor enthusiasts. Thus, depictions of court entertainment are not immune from the dramatizations, embellishments, and fabrications commonplace throughout *The Tudors*.

"Court entertainments" is a broad term encompassing many categories, including—but not limited to—music, drama, dancing, feasts, marriages,

C. Pendleton (✉)
Department of History, Oxford University, Oxford, UK

© The Editor(s) (if applicable) and The Author(s) 2016
W.B. Robison (ed.), *History, Fiction, and* The Tudors,
Queenship and Power, DOI 10.1057/978-1-137-43883-6_17

coronations, holiday celebrations, reception of foreign dignitaries, and various tournaments and sporting events. It is difficult to discuss each separately, as—more often than not—they overlapped and enhanced one another. Thus, it is appropriate both chronologically and thematically that the first event discussed here included many forms of entertainment and is the epitome of Henrician court spectacle—the Field of the Cloth of Gold, a quasi-political summit held June 7–24, 1520, in Calais (part of English-occupied France) that the king's chief minister, Cardinal Thomas Wolsey, organized to celebrate Henry and Francis I's agreement to maintain peace. It stemmed from a "wider Universal Peace" Europe's major powers agreed upon in the Treaty of London of October 1518.[1]

Henry and Wolsey got the lion's share of credit for that treaty, thanks to the cardinal's sharp political maneuvering, though it was Pope Leo X who originally had the idea for both a "European-wide peace and a crusade against the Ottoman Turks."[2] The treaty began to unravel in 1519, when Henry, Francis, and Charles I of Spain competed for election as Holy Roman Emperor, and fell apart completely with the Habsburg–Valois War of 1521–1526. Meanwhile, though, in 1520 Wolsey attempted to maintain England's position as the apparent arbiter of Europe by arranging separate meetings with Charles and Francis. With regard to France, Henry's daughter was to be betrothed to the Dauphin Henri-Philippe, Henry was to return the French city of Tournai, and Francis was to pay him a substantial annual pension. Wolsey meant to ensure that others viewed Henry as "the architect of the modern world" and that in a sea of warring princes, Henry would stand above all as one who would deliver his kingdom not through the exercise of arms but by laying them down.[3]

Episode 1:1 of *The Tudors* credits Wolsey with presenting the idea of universal peace to Henry and Thomas More, though it conflates the events of 1518 and 1520. It also alludes to the king's upcoming meeting with Francis. Episode 1:2 depicts the Field of the Cloth of Gold in all its splendor and excess. It also inaccurately portrays the young Princess Mary as attending her formal betrothal to the dauphin; in fact, she did not accompany her parents. More generally, it is here that Hirst first establishes the trademark aspect of Henry's personality that is a dominating theme throughout the series: the king's search for immortality. Henry was constantly aware of and haunted by death, hence his unwavering obsession with having a male child in order to secure the future of the Tudor dynasty. There are numerous instances in *The Tudors* of Henry experiencing existential crises as he grows older, and Hirst uses the king's ever-present angst to fuel his decadence. Like sex, court revels loom large among his distractions from his mortality.

The depiction of the Field of Cloth of Gold, while accurate in many aspects, is a vehicle for furthering this interpretation of Henry. Arriving in Val D'Or, the Valley of Gold, Henry and his retinue are greeted from a distance by Francis and his retinue. "On pain of death," Henry commands them to stay put as he rides down alone to meet Francis.[4] While it is true that Henry and Francis did greet each other this way, the simplicity with which it is shown is not accurate. They did not encounter each other alone merely as two men on horseback; rather, their meeting was choreographed with all the pageantry and magnificence befitting such a royal meeting. According to Edward Hall's *Chronicle* or *The Union of the Two Noble and Illustre Families of Lancastre and Yorke*, the definitive eyewitness account for most events under Henry VIII, Henry and Francis' assembly was preceded by the blowing of "Trumpettes, Sagbuttes, and Clarions, and all other Minstrelles" as they rode down to greet each other. They then embraced each other and with "benyng and curteous maner [and] swete goodly wordes of gretyng" retreated into the tent of cloth of gold that had been constructed for this very purpose.[5]

Despite this atmosphere of amity and amiability, what ensued was each monarch trying to outdo the other with acts of "generosity" and "friendship." Against the backdrop of glittering tents, precious jewels, musicians, acrobats, dances, and feasts, a darker narrative of backstabbing, plotting, and political intrigue takes place. Thus, one must view any gift or act of generosity both as a sign of friendship and as creating challenge and obligation to reciprocate.[6] For example, there is a scene during a feast one night where Francis presents Henry with a gift of fine jewels. While forced to accept them as a good king in good faith, Henry is noticeably chagrined and agitated at their brilliance.[7] Henry then attempts to upstage Francis by gifting him with a pastry that is filled with live birds. While delighted at the spectacle, it is obvious and implied that Francis feels the same irritation as Henry when the latter matches his spectacle. The aptly named "Palace of Illusion" they are dining in earns its moniker well.

While Hirst does not include it, the most prominent example of one-upmanship between Henry and Francis during the Field of Cloth of Gold was Francis "gifting" himself to Henry. On the morning of Sunday, June 17, 1520, ten days into the summit, Francis unexpectedly rode from his lodgings at Ardres to Henry's castle at Guînes and "declared himself to be Henry's prisoner and assured him of good faith." He then proceeded to help Henry dress after which the English king gifted him with a "collar of great value." Naturally, Francis is then said to have returned the favor with "either his own collar or jeweled bracelets." While Francis' spontaneous visit must have seemed unorthodox and a bit mad, it was the ultimate act of good faith and served to distinguish Francis as a monarch of chivalric trust and love.[8] Hirst does include a somewhat lower key example of such generosity by recounting Henry's decision to grow a beard as a symbol of his love for his "brother" Francis.[9]

More dubiously, Hirst also uses the Field of Cloth of Gold to introduce Henry's relationship with Mary Boleyn into the series. Exactly when Henry first met Mary and they began an affair are unknown, but it probably was early in 1522. Mary did attend the Field of Cloth of Gold as an attendant to Queen Catherine; however, there is no evidence to suggest that her affair with Henry began here.[10] Hirst also has Francis bragging to Henry about Mary's sexual prowess, referring to her as his "English mare."[11] While it is known that Mary did have an affair with Francis while at the French court, there is no evidence that Francis "warmly recommended" her to Henry.[12]

Hirst does a much better job portraying the famous wrestling match between Henry and Francis. While this event might seem improbable to modern viewers—and perhaps seemed so to contemporaries—it did happen and was in keeping with the spontaneity of both kings. As in history, on the show Henry suddenly challenges Francis to the match. What exactly triggered this challenge is unknown; however, on the show it is the result of Francis' incessant bragging about French superiority in all things—art, music, women—over the English.[13] The encounter was brief, with Francis quickly throwing Henry with a hip-throw maneuver known as the "tour de Bretayne."[14] Reportedly Henry lunged at the French king after his defeat; however, Queens Catherine and Claude pulled them apart to avoid a "serious diplomatic incident."[15] On the show Henry's reaction is similar, screaming for a rematch and refusing to sign the treaty until Jeremy Northam's skillfully portrayed Thomas More calms his youthful intemperance.[16] Henry then begrudgingly signs the treaty before destroying his quarters in a rage and departing France with a bruised ego. Also, the scene in which Henry tells Mary to leave his bed implies that his reason for discarding her is her association with his humiliation at Val D'Or.[17] Henry, despite his legendary corpulence, was an accomplished athlete in his youth—depictions of him as a fit, capable tennis player, archer, and hunter are accurate—and he was accustomed to victory.[18]

Curiously, Hirst omits tournaments from his version of the Field of Cloth of Gold. While there is a brief scene depicting a fencing tournament, there are no other examples of this lavish spectacle. The celebration of any alliance treaty customarily included a tournament as "peace was thereby invigorated, rejuvenated, heroicised, and thus made acceptable to the chivalric right of both nations."[19] Put simply, tournaments made swallowing the pill of peace more palatable by coating it with the game of battle. Understandably, as television faces strenuous time constraints, abridgement of certain major events is necessary in order to effectively convey the more general themes and plotlines to the viewer. However, Hirst makes up for this glaring exclusion by depicting various forms of tournaments, sports, and games throughout the series.

Tournaments were arguably the most popular form of entertainment in sixteenth-century England, for the "money lavished upon [them] far surpassed that spent on disguisings, pageants, masques, and plays." In addition, the public nature of and access to tournaments made them the perfect events for displaying "royal magnificence, the ideals of courtly virtue, and the unity of the body politic."[20] The main feature of any tournament was the joust—easy to judge, chivalric in nature, and the ultimate spotlight for exhibiting athletic prowess. Throughout the series, Hirst uses the joust not only as a blood sport in the absence of war but also to showcase underlying tensions between characters. For example, Episode 1:1 introduces viewers to Edward Stafford, 3rd Duke of Buckingham, and his resentment at Henry being on the throne. Steven Waddington portrays the fictionalized duke as bitter and treasonous, cursing the fact that despite his being a "direct descendant of Edward II" he is relegated to subject under the young Tudor king. Hirst uses the joust to let this animosity play out.[21]

The first part of the pertinent scene involves Charles Brandon, Henry's best friend and soon-to-be Duke of Suffolk, asking to wear the favors of Buckingham's daughter, whom he is attempting to seduce as the result of a bet with the king. This manifestation of courtly love was commonplace at tournaments; however, it usually was a platonic expression of affection rather than of the raging, lustful intentions in Hirst's universe. Here Brandon is seen jousting with a fictitious "Lord Hallam" *à plaisance*, meaning a peaceful joust of display not aggression. Next, it is Buckingham's turn as he faces the invented Earl of Newcastle. Despite the joust being *à plaisance*, Buckingham unnecessarily strikes a hard blow to his opponent's head. Henry, aware of Buckingham's growing resentment and viewing this as a provocation, enters the lists and challenges the Duke *á la guerre*, the joust of war. Henry, wearing Catherine of Aragon's favors, defeats Buckingham, which heightens his rage against the arrogant, young usurper. In Episode 1:2 Buckingham is arrested, tried, and executed for treason due to his assertion that he has a superior claim to the throne and his implications that he would like to hasten Henry's departure from it. His execution occurs after the Field of Cloth of Gold, which corresponds to the historical timeline as the real Buckingham was executed in 1521.[22]

The series also uses the joust to celebrate Henry's elation at Charles V defeating and capturing Francis I at the Battle of Pavia in February 1525. However, since this scene follows Pope Leo X's appointment of Henry as Defender of the Faith, which took place in 1521, it entails some time compression. During the tournament, the focus is not the sport of the joust but rather the sport of court intrigue. The reaction to Queen Catherine's arrival shows how much the people love her, a detail that More highlights verbally. Given that this scene takes place just as Henry's fixation on Anne Boleyn is getting under way, it foreshadows the difficulty Henry will have with public opinion when eschewing his first wife. Catherine—whom Maria Doyle Kennedy portrays in a manner both heartbreaking and inspirational—secretly gives a letter to an envoy of her nephew, the Holy Roman Emperor, pleading to know of his loyalty as she senses Henry's growing dissatisfaction with their marriage.[23]

The main feature of this jousting scene is Henry's accidental injury at the hands of his friend and courtier, Anthony Knivert. Henry fails to put down his visor, and before Knivert can stop, he strikes Henry in the head. Despite this hard blow, Henry—in a fit of testosterone-laden madness—insists on jousting again, proclaiming, "People of England, your king is unharmed!" Knivert and Henry joust again, and with some deference on Knivert's part, Henry strikes and unhorses his opponent, who is then seen bleeding from his visor on the ground. Knivert is based on Sir Thomas Knyvett, a close friend and frequent jousting companion of Henry who died in 1512, long before the plotline of *The Tudors* begins. Hence, his mere presence, let alone his being injured, at a tournament in 1525 is imaginary. Once again, though, this scene serves to acquaint Henry with his mortality and his lack of a legitimate male heir to carry on the Tudor dynasty. Thus, at the conclusion of the episode, Henry informs Wolsey that he wants a divorce and that the cardinal must get him one.[24]

As noted previously, tournaments played a key part in international relations and the cementing of new alliances. The Anglo-Imperial alliance of 1521–1522 was no exception. When Charles V arrived in England on May 25, 1522, to formally sign the treaty, Henry treated him to nearly two weeks of revel and entertainment. While Hirst only briefly depicts a joust during the imperial visit, both Henry and Charles personally participated in the tournament on June 4–5.[25] Of course, as acknowledged before, the time constraints imposed on hour-long programs necessitate both omission and compression.

However, while the Anglo-Imperial tournament does not garner much airtime, another key element of the emperor's reception does—the staging of *Schatew Vert*, a pageant to entertain Charles' Spanish envoys Mendoza and Chapuys. The masked play involves eight ladies, "The Graces," being kept prisoner in a tower by another group of eight masked women, while eight lords, led by "Ardent Desire," try to rescue them. Those who portray "the Graces" (Beauty, Honor, Perseverance, Kindness, Constancy, Bounty, Mercy, and Pity), their captors (Danger, Disdain, Jealousy, Unkindness, Scorn, Strangeness, and Malebouche, and one unnamed), and the lords (Amorous, Nobleness, Youth, Attendance, Loyalty, Pleasure, Gentleness, and Liberty) include the king and various noblemen and noblewomen, including Anne Boleyn. It is unknown which parts Henry and Anne played, but the show depicts Henry playing "Honesty"—perhaps a more modern take on Nobleness—and Anne "Perseverance." While we know Henry did not portray "Ardent Desire," as Hall records him being "chief of this compaignie" of eight lords, Hall's phrasing suggests that he might have been "Amorous" or "Loyalty," as this fits "Henry's discretion." In reality, Henry's younger sister Mary was among "the Graces"; however, she does not appear on the show, probably to avoid the audience confusing her with Henry's daughter Mary. Rather, Henry's older sister Margaret is an amalgamation of both women and appears in the pageant in place of Mary, cast as "Truth," though what part Mary played is unknown.[26]

While Hirst uses ladies of the English court to depict the captors of the Graces, it was actually the Children of the Chapel Royal who did so. Understandably, the use of children in Hirst's hyperbolically sexualized version of *Schatew Vert*—which leads to Henry and Anne's first encounter—most likely would have made viewers uncomfortable. Though Anne and Henry took part in the production, there is no evidence that Henry took any special notice of her. The character of "Ardent Desire" is portrayed by William Cornish, Master of the Children of the Chapel Royal and the man usually responsible for all pageants and revelries for entertaining foreign dignitaries and diplomats. Once again, whether or not

Mr. Cornish, played by Mark Lambert, actually portrayed "Ardent Desire" is unknown. Hirst makes him the facilitator of Anne and Henry's first meeting, in a scene that shows Anne's father, Thomas Boleyn, paying him a bribe for putting her in the path of the king.[27]

Another court musician who is featured heavily in Season One of *The Tudors* is Thomas Tallis. While both youthfully and capably portrayed by Joe Van Moyland, Tallis' mere presence at the English court during the 1520s is a total anachronism, as Tallis did not enter the Chapel Royal until the early 1540s. Considered the "Father of English Music," Tallis distinguished both himself and the Chapel Royal with his skill and genius during his more than four-decade tenure of royal service. However, Hirst appropriates him as a boyishly shy newcomer to court in 1518. He timidly presents a letter of recommendation from the Dean of Canterbury Cathedral to Richard Pace, Wolsey's secretary. Tallis did, in fact, serve as a clerk at Canterbury Cathedral in the early 1540s. As a novice, Tallis is the perfect vehicle for introducing the viewer to the complexities of court life and etiquette. Everything must be explained to Tallis and, therefore, is explained to the viewer as well. Tallis is present at several high-profile events such as the Field of Cloth of Gold and the production of *Schatew Vert*. Henry, while symbolically having his beard shaved, is deeply entranced by Tallis' singing prowess and pays him a sovereign for his song.[28] This does somewhat represent the respect Henry had—much later—for Tallis' unmatched ability, especially since Henry was an accomplished musician himself.

Henry's musical proficiency is one of the most curious omissions from Hirst's creation. A skilled singer with a "clear, high tenor voice" capable of playing a multitude of instruments—the lute and virginals chief among them—Henry possessed musical aptitude was far beyond his predecessors. Admittedly, it makes sense, given Hirst's vision of Henry, not to spend too much time on him as a musician. In any case, the only true glimpse the viewer gets of this side of Henry's character is a brief scene of him strumming the lute, composing what would become the popular song "Greensleeves," which court musicians play in the background of the next scene. Despite the legend that Henry composed this song for Anne Boleyn, he did not write it. The tune is most likely Elizabethan in origin and is "based on an Italian style of composition that did not reach England" until after Henry's death. Furthermore, there is no record of Henry performing his music in public, as this would be too common for a gentleman, let alone a king.[29] Therefore, Hirst places the majority of music making on Thomas Tallis for Season One of *The Tudors*. Another component of Tallis' onscreen character is his fictionalized romantic relationship with William Compton, one of Henry's most prominent courtiers. Compton initiates their first exchange in Episode 1:5, while watching and listening to Tallis playing the organ. They later kiss, are briefly shown in bed together, and spend time at Compton's estate in Warwickshire. There is no evidence that either was bisexual, and both were married. In addition, it is virtually impossible that Compton and Tallis ever met, since Tallis did not arrive at court until the early 1540s and Compton died of sweating sickness in 1528. After Compton's death, Tallis engages in a relationship with a courtier named Joan and, after her death from the sweat, with her twin sister Jane. Then, following the Season One finale, Tallis mysteriously disappears.[30]

Tallis' absence allows for the introduction in Season Two of another dominating figure of court musicianship—Mark Smeaton. Portrayed with just the right amount of smarminess by David Alpay, Smeaton was a favorite musician of the Boleyn circle, making his first appearance at court both historically and on the show in 1532 and eventually serving in Queen Anne's household. Despite his skill and the Boleyn's patronage, Hirst grossly overstates the familiarity with which he addresses Anne. For example, there are several scenes in which Anne confides her fears to Mark as she begins losing favor with Henry, and in one she kisses him on the cheek. When Henry is seriously injured in a jousting tournament and is thought likely to die, Anne looks to Smeaton for comfort and sinks into his arms. Regardless of Smeaton's talents and Anne's fondness of them, she never would have behaved so informally with him due to his low birth as the son of a carpenter and seamstress. By making their relationship overtly affectionate and showing other characters' reactions, Hirst shows the seed of suspicion being planted in others' minds that they are having an affair. Thus, when he is accused of adultery with Anne along with Henry Norris, Thomas Wyatt, William Brereton, and, her own brother, George Boleyn, the viewer can easily see how these interactions have been misconstrued, lending weight to the widely accepted theory that Anne was innocent of these crimes.[31]

Another fictionalized aspect of Smeaton's life is his romantic relationship with Anne's brother, George. Once again, *The Tudors* shows Smeaton being overly familiar as he converses with George about Anne's attributes and beauty and then proclaims that she is "not as beautiful as her brother." George later visits Smeaton's chambers, and it is implied that they consummate their relationship. While it is possible that Smeaton and Boleyn were either homosexual or bisexual, there is no unequivocal evidence that they were. Unfortunately, they shared the same fate, as both were executed on May 17, 1536, for treason and adultery. These embellishments to Smeaton's character convey to viewers the dangers of the royal court. Hirst depicts it as a place of intrigue and scandal where a single glance or gaze can betray one's utmost secrets and most intimate desires, and one moment or whisper of gossip can undo an entire family. Collusion, plotting, scheming are set against a backdrop of fine clothing, glittering jewels, and joie de vivre, when in reality it was snake pit. But of course no matter how violent, how chaotic the realm, there was always time for feasting, dancing, and revelry.[32]

Hence there are innumerable stolen looks and secret conversations among characters as the court dances in uniformity. For example, there is a scene in which Anne and Smeaton dance and gaze at each other intently while Henry watches from the throne, obviously dismayed. Again, when Anne is later accused of adultery with Smeaton, Henry has less trouble believing it. This scene follows Anne's first miscarriage, hastening her fall from Henry's favor. Later in the season, as the Boleyns are aware that their fall is imminent, Anne quite openly insults the French during a court feast in a last ditch effort to gain the Emperor's favor. Amid the celebration and revelry of Henry's marriage to Jane Seymour, Thomas Cromwell discusses with other ministers whether Jane favors the Catholic religion and is a threat to their Reformation.[33]

While such conversations and interactions are fictionalized, they accurately depict the treacherous minefield that was the court. When access and proximity to the king is the key to favor and advancement, social climbing becomes not only an art form but a blood sport. When Wolsey falls from favor, for example, he is depicted as a victim of both his own high-handedness and of those plotting around him, namely, the Boleyns. Juxtaposed with the Cardinal's fictional suicide, the court acclaims a play satirizing his decadence and showing him consorting with demons until he is condemned to hell. This play, "Cardinal Wolsey Going Down to Hell," did not appear until 1531, after Wolsey's death from natural causes. However, the court did not attend a public performance; rather, Thomas Boleyn held a private performance at his London house to entertain Claude la Guische, the French ambassador.[34]

Understandably, as Henry's reign progressed into its later stages, the instances of court revelry and spectacle began to decline. The 1520s witnessed the height of court entertainment under Henry—or any other

English monarch. The fall of Wolsey, Henry's "Great Matter," and Anne's eventual fall as well were all "events that could neither be celebrated nor forgotten with revels."[35] This post-Boleyn decline is reflected in the show as well, although embellishments and inaccuracies are still present.

The most well-known aspect of Henry's reign is that he had six wives. Consequently, there are weddings and coronations that command royal spectacle as well, regardless of where they fall during Henry's reign. As the show begins several years into Henry's reign, his marriage to Catherine, her coronation, and the birth of Mary are already well past. Traditionally, royal marriages were "small, private affairs" as was the case with Henry's secret marriage to Anne on January 25, 1533. Hirst's portrayal of their wedding is true to this standard, as it is a very brief scene with only Charles Brandon, George and Thomas Boleyn, and Thomas Cromwell in attendance. However, the same cannot be said for Hirst's portrayal of Anne's coronation on June 1, 1533. It is true that there was a paucity of spectators and acclaim compared to Catherine's coronation procession in 1509. However, there was no assassination attempt against Anne by anyone, let alone one sanctioned by the pope and carried out by William Brereton, a courtier and Groom of the Privy Chamber later accused and convicted of adultery with Anne.[36]

The Brereton in Hirst's universe embodies the historical Brereton in name only. Brereton was not a Catholic radical commissioned by Pope Paul III to assassinate the *putain*. Clement VII was still pope at the time of her coronation. Brereton's entry into the Jesuit order is anachronistic as well, since the order was not created until 1540. The scene in which Anne is formally crowned is also subject to embellishment. In an effort to show Henry's obsession with centralizing both his temporal and his spiritual authority over the realm, Hirst depicts the king taking the crown from Cranmer and placing it on Anne's head himself. In reality, Cranmer was the one who formally crowned Anne while Henry "watched [the] proceedings at the banquet from a gallery in Westminster Hall," as it was uncommon for monarchs to attend the crowning of their consorts "if performed separately to their own."[37]

Henry's marriage to his third wife, Jane Seymour, took place on May 30, 1536, in the "Queen's closet" at Hampton Court, 11 days after Anne's execution. Despite their wedding being quick and private like Henry's previous marriages, *The Tudors* lends much pomp and spectacle to the ceremony, having a majority of the court attend in the grand Chapel Royal. Symbolically, this depiction makes sense, as Henry and Jane's marriage offered the hope of a new era of peace and prosperity after the bloody turmoil of the past. Jane was never formally crowned as queen and therefore had no coronation, as Henry strategically waited to anoint her until she could prove capable of bearing sons. While she did deliver on her promise by providing Henry with the male heir he so longed for, she tragically died 12 days after Prince Edward's birth from complications associated with her long labor.[38]

Henry's marriage to his fourth wife, Anne of Cleves, took place in a similar fashion at Greenwich on January 6, 1540. Hirst's depiction of the ceremony is more or less accurate in terms of the small attendance as well as with what must have been palpable tension, given Henry's disappointment with his new bride. Like her predecessor, Anne was never formally crowned queen. Plans for her coronation had been under way in the months leading up to the marriage; however, after Henry's legendary displeasure became apparent, these were abandoned. Following the dissolution of his marriage to Anne after just six months, Henry married his fifth wife, Catherine Howard, on July 28, 1540, the same day as Cromwell's execution. This ceremony also took place in secret, this time at Oatlands Palace, with Edmund Bonner, Bishop of London, presiding instead of Archbishop Thomas Cranmer. *The Tudors* only alludes to this wedding, as Season Four opens with rumors that Henry and Catherine are secretly married. Catherine also never had a formal coronation as queen, as once again Henry strategically waited until she proved capable of bearing sons.[39]

One of the most fantastical yet factual relationships of *The Tudors* is the friendship between Anne of Cleves and Catherine Howard. During the New Year's celebration in 1541, Anne not only gifted "two huge and magnificent horses caparisoned in mauve velvet" to Catherine but also addressed Catherine during her formal presentation at court with genuine deference and obeisance befitting her station. As improbable as it may seem, the cordial friendship depicted between Anne and Catherine really did exist; the scene where they dance together after Henry retires to bed due to his infirmity actually did occur. The scene where the three of them happily dine together and exchange more gifts the following evening is true to form as well, with Anne and Catherine once again dancing together after Henry retires to bed.[40]

Christmas and New Year's celebrations at court are depicted several times in *The Tudors*. Holidays are no exception to *The Tudors*' use of court celebrations as a backdrop to the scandal and intrigue within the nobility.

For example, during the Christmas court held in 1520, the formal reception of gifts from the Dukes of Norfolk and Buckingham (although traditionally these gifts were given on New Year's, not Christmas) by Henry and Catherine of Aragon is juxtaposed with Henry's mistress, Elizabeth Blount, giving birth to their son, Henry Fitzroy. While these events did occur, the scene is completely anachronistic, as Henry Fitzroy was born on June 15, 1519. Arguably, the most cheerful Christmas court of Henry's reign took place in 1536. "Je suis en famille!" Henry proudly proclaims as he sits with Jane, Mary, and Elizabeth after she is formally presented to him as a surprise. For a brief moment, there is a happy royal family on the throne again.[41]

However, by the time the show reaches its conclusion with Henry's marriage to Catherine Parr, the joviality and youthfulness that once defined Henry's court is little more than a distant memory. As he had done with Jane Seymour and Anne of Cleves, Henry married Catherine Parr at Hampton Court in the "Queen's closet" on July 12, 1543. However, unlike his previous weddings, the historic ceremony—like the one on the show—was not private, with both Mary and Elizabeth in attendance. As they had both been restored to the succession after Edward and his heirs, their presence was viewed as a "sign of new harmony" with Henry. Catherine, played by Joely Richardson, is noticeably distressed at her obligation to marry Henry, who was by 1543 infinitely more grotesque than Meyers' generous portrayal, but she does her duty well and submits.[42] While the courtiers conduct themselves as they should in celebrating such an event, everyone is aware that the king is dying, including Henry himself. At this point there is no more spectacle, no more hope, just an ill and infirm king passing his time a little easier with one who would care for him as a nursemaid. Like the three queens before her, Catherine received no coronation and was uncrowned at the time of Henry's death on January 28, 1547.[43]

Conclusion

When we compare the present life of man on earth with that time of which we have no knowledge it seems to me like the swift flight of a simple sparrow through a banqueting hall on a winter's day. After a few moments of comfort, he vanishes from sight into the wintry world from which he came.[44]

So says John-Rhys Meyers—quoting Bede's account of St. Paulinus of York and King Edwin of Northumbria—as he sets the stage for Henry's final bow. Life is short, it is cruel, and whatever distraction one may find should be cherished as a rare gem. Hence these "few moments of comfort" are what the various forms of court entertainment embodied. Whether or not Henry VIII was as unceasingly embroiled in an existential crisis as Meyers portrays him can never be known. However, while the actual function of court entertainments may have been more varied and intricate than Hirst's often hedonistic portrayal, the cult of magnificence that was both Henry VIII's pleasure and duty to cultivate often allows for the history rather than the fiction to dominate compared to other aspects of the show. Hence the show itself, in a certain respect, serves the same purpose as those lavish distractions for which Henry's court was famous. For once one is fully acquainted with the realities of this world, what is better than to escape them if only for little while?

Notes

1. Glenn Richardson, *The Field of Cloth of Gold* (New Haven: Yale University Press, 2014), 1.
2. Glenn Richardson, "Personal Gift-Giving at the Field of Cloth of Gold," in Thomas Betteridge and Suzannah Lipscomb, eds., *Henry VIII and the Court: Art, Politics, and Performance* (Surrey: Ashgate, 2013), 48.
3. *The Tudors*, Episode 1:1.
4. *The Tudors*, Episode 1:2.
5. Edward Hall, *Hall's Chronicle: Containing the History of England, During the Reign of Henry the Fourth, and the Succeeding Monarchs, to the End of the Reign of Henry the Eighth, in which are Particularly Described the Manners and Customs of Those Periods* (London: Printed for J. Johnson, 1809), 610. Accessed 3 March 2015, http://babel.hathitrust.org/cgi/pt?id=mdp.49015000231820;view=1up;seq=1.
6. Richardson, "Personal Gift Giving," 59.
7. *The Tudors*, Episode 1:2.
8. Richardson, "Personal Gift-Giving," 60.
9. *The Tudors*, Episode 1:1.
10. Alison Weir, *Mary Boleyn: Mistress of Kings* (New York: Ballantine Books, 2011), 109.
11. *The Tudors*, Episode 1:2.
12. Weir, *Mary Boleyn*, 117.
13. *The Tudors*, Episode 1:2.

14. Richardson, *Field of the Cloth of Gold*, 138.
15. Weir, *Mary Boleyn*, 111.
16. Ibid., 139; *The Tudors*, Episode 1:2.
17. *The Tudors*, Episode 1:2.
18. *The Tudors*, Episodes 1:1–3, 4: 1.
19. Richardson, *Field of the Cloth of Gold*, 120.
20. Alan Young, *Tudor and Jacobean Tournaments* (Dobbs Ferry, NY: Sheridan House, 1987), 7.
21. *The Tudors*, Episode 1:1; C.S.L. Davies, "Stafford, Edward, Third Duke of Buckingham (1478–1521)," *Oxford Dictionary of National Biography* (Oxford University Press, 2004); online edn, January 2008 [http://www.oxforddnb.com/view/article/26202, accessed 31 October 2015].
22. *The Tudors*, Episode 1:1–1:2; Young, *Tudor and Jacobean Tournaments*, 14.
23. *The Tudors*, Episode 1:4.
24. Ibid.; Hall, *Chronicle*, 534; S.J. Gunn, "Knyvet, Sir Thomas (c. 1485–1512)," *ODNB*; online edn, January 2008 [http://www.oxforddnb.com/view/article/15799, accessed 31 October 2015].
25. W.R. Streitberger, *Court Revels: 1485–1559* (Toronto: University of Toronto Press, 1994), 113–114.
26. Ibid., 112–113; *The Tudors*, Episode 1:3; Hall, *Chronicle*, 631; *The Tudors* names only six of the captors, excluding Malebouche, and Hall names only seven.
27. Streitberger, *Court Revels*, 113; *The Tudors*, Episode 1:3.
28. Neville Williams, *Henry VIII and His Court* (New York: The Macmillan Company, 1971), 239; *The Tudors*, Episode 1:1; John Milsom, "Tallis, Thomas (c. 1505–1585)," *ODNB*; online edn, January 2008 [http://www.oxforddnb.com/view/article/26954, accessed 31 October 2015].
29. Alison Weir, *Henry VIII: The King and His Court* (New York: Ballantine Books, 2001), 130–131; *The Tudors*, Episode 1:9.
30. *The Tudors*, Episode 1:5–1:7, 1:10; Carolly Erickson, *Great Harry: The Extravagant Life of Henry VIII* (New York: Summit Books, 1980), 215; G.W. Bernard, "Compton, Sir William (1482?–1528)," *ODNB*; online edn, January 2008 [http://www.oxforddnb.com/view/article/6039, accessed 31 October 2015].
31. Weir, *Henry VIII*, 318; *The Tudors*, Episodes 2:7–2:8.
32. *The Tudors*, Episodes 2:3–2:4; see also Retha Warnicke, *The Rise and Fall of Anne Boleyn* (Cambridge: Cambridge University Press, 1991).
33. *The Tudors*, Episodes 2:5, 2:9, 3:1.
34. *The Tudors*, Episode 1:10; Greg Walker, *Plays of Persuasion: Drama and Politics at the Court of Henry VIII* (Cambridge: Cambridge University Press, 2008), 20.

35. Streitberger, *Court Revels*, 121, 141.
36. Antonia Fraser, *The Wives of Henry VIII* (New York: Alfred A. Knopf, 1993), 187, 194, 248; *The Tudors*, Episode 2:3.
37. *The Tudors*, Episode 2:3; Fraser, *Wives of Henry VIII*, 195.
38. Fraser, *Wives of Henry VIII*, 258; *The Tudors*, Episodes 3:1–3:4.
39. Fraser, *Wives of Henry VIII*, 308; *The Tudors*, Episodes 3:7, 4:1; Weir, *Henry VIII*, 423, 429.
40. Fraser, *Wives of Henry VIII*, 336–7; *The Tudors*, Episode 4:2.
41. *The Tudors*, Episodes 1:2, 3:3; Williams, *Henry VIII and His Court*, 68.
42. *The Tudors*, Season 4, Episode 7.
43. Fraser, *Wives of Henry VIII*, 367; *The Tudors*, Episode 4:7.
44. *The Tudors*, Episode 4:10.

CHAPTER 18

Holbein and the Artistic Mise-en-Scène of *The Tudors*

Tatiana C. String

The Tudors would not be the *Tudors* without the constant presence of the visual arts: paintings, drawings, tapestries, buildings, and artists take on significant roles, both in the plotting and in the mise-en-scène and art direction of the series. From the heavy staging to create period ambience, to the place of portraiture in the building of characters' identities, to the status of the artist at court, *The Tudors* meditates on art in often precise, frequently fanciful but consistently important ways. This chapter will explore the various modes in which *The Tudors* deploys the visual arts to contribute to the sense of place and time, and, importantly, the manner in which specific works of art by Hans Holbein the Younger, and indeed the artist himself, are integral to the series' narrative arc.

The Tudors has an unusually deep engagement with works of art. This seems to proceed in some ways from the presumed knowledge of the period on the part of the anticipated audience: a knowledge grounded in a small number of contemporary works of art that have taken on a major significance in the modern fascination with the Tudors. There are not all that many extant paintings from sixteenth-century England, especially

---

T.C. String (✉)
Art Department, University of North Carolina at Chapel Hill, Chapel Hill, MC, USA

when compared to the survivals from the Continent. But what paintings there are function as well-known touchstones for what this slice of the past is meant to look like, and there is a corresponding sensitivity to popular understandings and perceptions on the part of the makers of the series. So in the very first minutes of Episode 1:1, Henry VIII gives an audience in a room that takes its entire look from the late Henrician painting of his family of Henry VIII, now in the Royal Collection. The ornate foliate columns of the architectural framing of the chair and cloth of estate are here reified in the representation of Henry's seat of power in the television program.[1] Such is the authority of this one familiar image. That the painting is thought to depict an interior within Whitehall Palace, and the opening scene in *The Tudors* is set in the 1510s, is the first of many anachronisms (or fudges) that we encounter. Henry only took possession of Whitehall in 1529 at the fall of Cardinal Wolsey, but most of *The Tudors* takes place in this palace in its post-Wolsey state. Computer-generated imagery of the palace presents it as a completed whole, but this would not have been possible until late in Henry's reign. That said, the painting of the family of Henry VIII is itself full of anachronism: Jane Seymour appears at Henry's side, accompanying her son Edward, whom she did not live to see beyond his first 12 days. Perhaps this type of compression of past and present gave license to the producers and historical consultants of *The Tudors* to play fast and loose with timelines. Ultimately, the painting, despite the impossible family reunion represented, is called forth as a source for the actual place—Whitehall Palace—and such apparent authorities can prove irresistible to those attempting period settings for historical drama such as this.

A second layer of engagement with the arts can be seen in the careful placement of replica Henrician-era portraits and other types of painting in chambers and indoor spaces throughout the series. Framed panel paintings of Henry V, Henry VI, Richard III, and Henry VII are displayed in Henry VIII's chambers; portraits of Prince Arthur and Elizabeth of York hang on the walls of Catherine of Aragon's rooms; portraits of Thomas More, Henry Guildford, and Thomas Howard, 3rd Duke of Norfolk, among others, all hang in the council chamber, which doubles as Cromwell's office. In each case, the choices of portraits to connect with the occupant of the chamber say something relevant about that person: Henry VIII is associated with previous English monarchs, especially Henry V, to comment on his military aspirations and right to rule; Catherine's first husband Arthur (a regular topic of conversation) and her mother-in-law Elizabeth of York are with her, stressing the importance of her marital history as an agon, or source of dynamic tension, within the plot; and Cromwell's chamber is decorated with the images of powerful men of the realm who similarly held positions of great authority. The precision with which this has been done—identifying period portraits from the Royal Collection, National Portrait Gallery, and Society of Antiquaries for reproduction in the series—suggests that this was informed by a good deal of picture research, which one assumes was performed by the series' historical consultant Justin Pollard and his team at Visual Artefact. In keeping with the impulse to provide appropriate imagery that comments upon each main character, Cardinal Wolsey's chambers and Lady Mary's spaces are each adorned with Italian pictures of religious (read: Catholic) subjects. In George Boleyn's privy rooms, in contrast, an image of the *Rape of Ganymede* hangs on the wall, alluding to George's homoerotic interests and lusty tastes.

An unexpected engagement with the arts comes in the form of a gestural restaging of three well-known paintings from the period. The resultant self-highlighting is almost ekphrastic in its interruption of the narrative flow of the story. The first example comes in Episode 1:6, when George Boleyn walks into his chamber to find two seminude women, sisters and ladies in waiting to the queen, to whom he has made promises of favors in exchange for information, posed exactly as the presumed portrait of Gabrielle d'Estrees and her sister, the Duchess of Villars (Louvre, c. 1594), in which one pinches the nipple of the other. This is such an iconic image that few viewers would miss the reference, even if just for its fame as titillating erotica. In this way the flow is interrupted to ask the viewer to stop for a moment and think of the original painting; indeed, all action stops for that moment, despite the fact that the posing of the two women is here used as a playful invitation to George Boleyn to join them in his bed, and things move quickly and energetically to that end.

The second of these deliberate restagings comes as Thomas Wyatt, the sensitive poet and mooning lover, leans on a tree (Episode 2:2, 37:29) in a pose that directly imitates Nicholas Hilliard's romantic miniature of a heartsick nobleman (Victoria & Albert Museum, c. 1585–1595). Wyatt has written a love sonnet to Lady Elizabeth Darrell, a lady-in-waiting to Catherine of Aragon, speaking of his burning desire. The pose he strikes mimics the melancholy heartache affected in the Hilliard miniature, in which the young man presses his hand to his heart in order to communicate his passion. This is another well-chosen, familiar image with which to suggest and frame a specific mood. Interestingly, this source of inspiration is of a piece with much of the mise-en-scène on show throughout all four seasons, in that the second half of the sixteenth century and early seventeenth century are a rich source of inspiration for the visual feel that the program makers aim toward, as if this period were in some way more properly, and more recognizably, "Tudor": Hilliard's paintings, as well as much of the clothing, furniture, weaponry, and other stuff that flesh out the depicted storyworld, are quarried from Elizabeth I's reign rather than from Henry's.

The third such moment is the wholly fabricated staging of Holbein painting the nude portrait of the fictional character Lady Ursula Misseldon, Henry VIII's mistress (Episode 3:3, 4:49–7:44). Holbein has been at work on the portrait for an impatient Henry, who is keen to possess it. The scene as it is played out, in which Holbein's work on the portrait is interrupted by a nosy and irritated nobleman, loosely derives from an anecdote recorded in Karel van Mander's *Life* of Holbein in his *Het Schilder-boeck* (The Book of Painting, 1603–1604),[2] in which an inquisitive courtier sneaks a peek into Holbein's studio, with violent results. But the painting of a nude is certainly not part of the original story. So, when presented with the idea of Holbein painting a nude—which works well in the television series, but which was never part of the historical painter's oeuvre—the artistic direction has to look further afield for a model. It duly alights on Velazquez's mid-seventeenth century *Rokeby Venus* (National Gallery, London). Its signature back view of the goddess admiring herself in a mirror is entirely recognizable here, but is of course wholly anachronistic. And yet, there is an overlay with Titian's more contemporary *Venus of Urbino* (Uffizi, 1538), in that Henry verbalizes his desire for the painting in the same manner in which Guidobaldo II della Rovere, Duke of Urbino, expressed his impatience to acquire the painting.[3] This scene thus encapsulates much of the role of art within the program's overall narrative project: one sees the playful, or simply casual, subordination of historical rigor in the situating of art within the larger diegesis, done in the service of the greater plot dynamics, in this instance Henry's incorrigibly lustful personality; but there is also a gesture toward the possibility of a more precise handling of the artistic material at the program makers' disposal, had they deigned to attempt it.

In addition to inspiring aspects of the setting and being quoted in certain stagey moments, works of art can on occasion work their way into the flow of the plot and into character motivation. This is particularly evident in Episode 2:2, 55:14–57:20, when Henry lovingly strokes a painted representation of the mythological beauty Psyche (in a painting copied from a portion of the large fresco of the Wedding Feast of Cupid and Psyche by Giulio Romano in the Palazzo del Te in Mantua, 1526–158) and very soon thereafter is inspired by its amorous theme both to reproduce his specific stroking gesture—now on the thigh of a naked Anne Boleyn as she draws him to her—and to imitate the general scene taking place on a bed in the painting. The idea that parts of frescoes would be thus "extracted" in framed paintings is absurd; only the date of Giulio's original suggests a scintilla of attention to period accuracy. But the significance of this sequence lies elsewhere. Insofar as life in this scene does not only imitate art but is directly inspired by it, Henry's amorous attention to the image stands for the self-conscious, self-referential posture of the program makers, commenting on the myths and clichés that undergird their own project, and seizing on art as one multifaceted and resonant means to do so.

In the same spirit of self-referential blurrings of sources of inspiration and variable degrees of attention to historical accuracy, the presence of hybrid works of art—newly invented portraits in the manner of a Horenbout or a Holbein painting that bear the faces of the actors—is one of the more endearing features of *The Tudors*. For example, we see a Horenbout-esque portrait miniature of Anne Boleyn (with Natalie Dormer's face) given as a love token to Henry VIII in Episode 1:5; we learn later, in Episode 2:3, that Thomas Wyatt has one as well, thickening the plot device of Anne as more sexually experienced than she and her family dare reveal to Henry. The miniature as love token appears again when a similar Horenbout-inspired miniature, this time of Henry VIII/Jonathan Rhys-Meyers, is given to Jane Seymour, who responds to the gift by saying, "They will find it at my death close to my heart." These examples are well-crafted, relatively convincing imitations of the "real thing" deployed more or less correctly in the contemporary idiom, even if the effect breaks down somewhat with the intrusive modern faces that shade toward photographic rendering. On the other hand, when a miniature portrait of the infant Princess Elizabeth is presented to Henry, it looks as though it *is* a nineteenth-century photograph in a padded case.

A motif that runs through much of the program's engagement with art is genius. Genius is, of course, a loaded and complicated term. But the program makers cut this particular Gordion Knot by insisting on the premise that genius levels the socioeconomic playing field. Thus, when Thomas Tallis is approached, romantically, by William Compton, his first reaction is to remark, "You're a lord, what am I?," while Compton responds, "A genius," thereby establishing an equivalence between the two that would not otherwise have existed. Similarly, Michelangelo is pardoned for being temperamental and using foul language in the Sistine Chapel (Episode 2:5)—his Italian and body language, in fact, amounting to one of the crudest stereotypes in the whole series—when Pope Paul III, played by Peter O'Toole, says (in what can only be a nod to Prince Charles' notorious comment on the nature of love), "We forgive him because he is a genius—whatever that means." This special category of genius, reserved for (male) artists of extraordinary skill, vision, and innovation, is particularly and routinely accorded to Henry VIII's painter, Hans Holbein. Genius might as well be his nickname, given how frequently it is attached to him. For instance, when Anne Boleyn and her sister Mary are poring over Holbein's designs for the pageants in her coronation procession in June 1533 (Episode 2:3)—one such image indeed survives, now in the Staatliche Museen, Berlin—Mary observes, "Mr. Holbein is indeed a genius." And she seems to know exactly what that means: Holbein has the vision to conceive a grand display of imagery that will exactly capture the significance of the occasion. Henry himself endorses this verdict: when Anne Boleyn gives him a large ornamental cup (Episode 2:4), his appreciative reflex remark, when told it was made by Holbein, is, "The man's a genius."

This ability to give the political zeitgeist particularly judicious visual expression, as qualified by one or two misfires that have significance within the plot, is central to Holbein's identity in *The Tudors*. His ability to reify subtle political thought in his visual output is invested in the way his character has been written. Thus, for example, Holbein is commissioned, implausibly and contrary to the historical record, to design a barge similar to the one that the Doge of Venice uses annually in a ritual reaffirmation of his office (Episode 3:4); the English version will be used for Jane Seymour's coronation. And, with somewhat more historical warrant, Holbein is engaged to produce portraits of prospective brides following the death of Jane Seymour. His artistic genius is what ensures that he can be entrusted with this sensitive task: Henry will not consider marriage negotiations until he has seen the candidates rendered as only Holbein can. Holbein is duly shown drawing the likeness of one such candidate, Christina of Denmark. It is well documented that the historical Holbein was given a three-hour audience with the 16-year-old widow of the Duke of Milan, so in the series there is some attention to correct detail when Holbein is shown making the sketch that he will eventually turn into the full-length painting now in the National Gallery in London. (That said, and as so often throughout the series, a gesture toward accuracy is paired with a counterbalancing gauche, or perhaps calculated, misfire—here the fact that, for reasons that are not explained and indeed defy explanation historically speaking, Christina's character is played with a thick Russian accent.) Henry is extremely taken with the drawing, telling Charles Brandon to keep his hands off it/her and thereby suggesting the collapse of the distinction between the real thing and its representation. Yet again, art serves as a shorthand for the program's self-referential ambitions.

Genius is often associated, especially in the modern era, with high levels of creativity and even madness.[4] So, when Henry VIII is shown (in Episode 3:5) drawing architectural motifs in what could only be called a frenzied manner—there are scores, if not hundreds of charcoal drawings pinned up and piled up in his privy chamber—following the death of his beloved wife (and mother of his long-hoped-for male heir), Jane Seymour, he himself is being associated with genius and extraordinary vision. Moreover, what he is drawing is every bit as important to this representation of Henry as inspired genius: his designs are fanciful, deeply creative, and unique, for they anticipate the building of a fantasy palace that would have no rival … Nonsuch. Now, it is true that no artist or architect has been credited with having designed Nonsuch,[5] but the notion that the king was himself the creative force behind its architectural rendering is the fanciful conceit of the series. Genius is such an animating force within the storyworld that, if only temporarily and in a moment of unusual emotional stress, it spills over into the person of Henry himself, again configuring the contribution of so-called geniuses to the visual material that subtends his myth.

That said, the status of the artist is at times ambiguous in the series. Yes, both Holbein and Michelangelo are accorded the title "genius," as we have seen, and they are both accorded high levels of confidence by their respective patrons. But when Pope Paul III wants to commission Michelangelo to paint the Last Judgment in the Sistine Chapel (Episode 2:7), he downplays the expense to be incurred by noting, "We won't have to pay him much; he's only an artist after all." On the other hand, a more appreciative note is struck in the scene (Episode 3:3) in which Holbein is shown painting the nude portrait of Henry's mistress Ursula Misseldon and her offended fiancé bursts into the painter's studio, only to be shoved away angrily. Moments later, when the artist confesses his rough handling of his uninvited noble visitor to his royal master, he is readily forgiven, but when the fiancé, Sir Robert Tavistock, complains of his ill treatment by a common artist, Henry responds, in words lifted verbatim from the anecdote as told in Van Mander's *Schilder-boeck*, by saying that he could create seven earls from seven peasants, but he could not create one Holbein.[6]

It is important that the viewer should be reminded of Holbein's genius at several junctures over the course of the narrative, for the idea that he possessed special qualities is essential to the storyline with which the whole series concludes and which comments on all that has preceded it. (Indeed, it is noteworthy that Holbein is effectively sanitized by what can only be the deliberate omission of any direct reference to the most well-known and persistent myth attaching to his relationship with Henry, that the king was furious with him for misrepresenting the looks of Anne of Cleves in the portrait now in the Louvre. This incident, which actually has no historical basis, is, much like the belief that Henry composed "Greensleaves," one of the few Henrician cliché dogs that do not bark in the series.) In what he realizes are his final days, Henry commissions a portrait from Holbein (Episode 4:10). We see the king sitting in full Whitehall Mural dress, posing for Holbein, who uses his by now familiar drawing device to mark out his subject's major features and the proportions of his face and body. We know that these are Henry's last moments because of a series of hallucinations that begin as the process of depiction takes place: first Catherine of Aragon appears to Henry, chastising him for his treatment of their daughter Mary; later Anne Boleyn and Jane Seymour make similar appearances, browbeating the king for neglecting his children. So, as the portrait is being created, a process of self-reflection is simultaneously taking place, as if there were a causal relationship. But when the portrait is completed and shown to Henry, he is bitterly disappointed: it is too real, too actual to serve the regal purposes the king has in mind. Henry says that he looks old and that the image is "a lie"—and here we are treated to another of the great chronological fudges of the series, as Henry says accusingly that Holbein had painted his father (Henry VII) and had detracted from his majesty by making him look old and ill, whereas, in historical actuality, we know that Holbein was only about 12 when Henry VII died and first came to England some 16 years into the next reign. (For good measure, the whole setup is simply impossible: Holbein predeceased Henry by four years.)

Rather than being simply reproved, however, Holbein is required to redo the portrait, as if Henry has a powerful presentiment that the new, improved version will have a decisive bearing on his posthumous image and reputation. And with this charge begins the climax of the series.

Henry is dying, having visions of Death on a white horse about to strike his fatal blow. But as if to postpone the moment of death, he is awoken by his groom to view Holbein's new portrait. It is not the Whitehall Mural, which is of course the basis of the quintessential Holbein image of Henry, but a 20-foot framed easel painting of the king posing alone in the costume and stance familiar from the Mural—an impossibly large artifact, but one standing in relation to later sixteenth-century copies, such as that now in the Walker Art Gallery in Liverpool—which has helped to make the Mural-based depiction of Henry the canonical image in the popular imagination.[7] When the outsized portrait is revealed to the king with a flourish of unveiling, a clearly moved Henry is confronted with his life in flashback—more specifically the period of his life covered by the series itself, as glimpsed in moments from scenes we have already seen, as if to assert that what is being reviewed and reexperienced is not the "historically whole" Henry that exists behind and beyond the depicted action, but the Henry specifically crafted by the program makers. Two visions of Henry thus collide: that of the historical Holbein and by extension Henry's place in the traditional historical imaginary that Holbein has helped to cement, and that of the series. Which will prevail? Rhys-Meyers seems to hint at the answer himself: as he turns away from the portrait and hobbles agedly out of shot, his last line is, "Master Holbein, it is well done." We stay with the image for some moments as the musical score swells, and a series of intertitles takes the story on from Henry's death up to Elizabeth. After a further moment of dwelling on the image, the screen fades to black, and some 35 hours of viewing are at an end.

This final scene thus throws out one last piece of postmodern playfulness in a series that has thrived on it. For the closing intertitles, which run from Henry's death, through the mid-Tudor crisis, and on to Elizabeth's reign, which is described as a "Golden Age," reinstate a master narrative that the series had frequently gestured toward rewriting. One of its conspicuous revisionist slants, for example, is its greater sympathy toward the Catholic traditionalists than the Protestant cause in the Henrician Reformation—witness in particular the portrayals of Catherine of Aragon and Mary as well as the disproportionate amount of screen time devoted in Season Three to the Pilgrimage of Grace. In stark contrast, the Mary of the intertitles reverts to the traditional "Bloody Mary" of Foxe and Protestant demonology, a failure of a queen whose "short and turbulent" reign was principally characterized by the burning of Protestant martyrs. Only with Elizabeth is the luster of the Tudor line restored: the viewer is plunged back into an old-fashioned narrative of the Tudors that sees Henry and Elizabeth as the only two monarchs that really mattered, and the latter as the realization of the potential for greatness, personal and national, that is anticipated by the former.

The key to the final scene is the studied ambiguity of the referent of "it" in Henry's parting utterance: within the immediate mise-en-scène and story logic of the moment, he is congratulating Holbein on the portrait; but on another level the "it" is an invitation to the viewer to reflect on the achievement of the series itself and its effect, or lack of effect, on the entrenched images attached to Henry and his reign. The intertitles read like Michael Hirst and his team losing their nerve by reverting to the standard Tudor script. Or perhaps it is one last throw of the postmodern dice, a folding of revisionism back on itself. Given the important place that art plays in the whole series' engagements with questions of popular memory and narrativization, as we have seen, it was perhaps inevitable that art would be central to these atypically reflective, considered, and layered final moments of the last episode. The impossibly outsized portrait, in conjunction with the intertitles, functions as a *mise-en-abyme* of the program makers' myth-making enterprise as well as an acknowledgment of their ultimate inability and perhaps unwillingness, for all their revisionist posturing, to dislodge the tried-and-tested Henrician tropes that Holbein's art itself instantiates and perpetuates.[8]

Notes

1. For a careful explanation of the chair of estate and the cloth of estate and the usage of the term "throne" in Henry VIII's England, see Maria Hayward, "Symbols of Majesty: Cloths of Estate at the Court of Henry VIII," *Furniture History* 41 (2005): 1–11.
2. Karel van Mander, *The Lives of the Illustrious Netherlandish and German Painters, from the First Edition of the Schilder-boeck (1603–1604): Preceded by the Lineage, Circumstances and Place of Birth, Life and Works of Karel van Mander, Painter and Poet and Likewise Death and Burial, from the Second Edition of the Schilder-boeck (1616–1618)*, with an introduction and translation, ed. Hessel Miedema, 6 vols. (Doornspijk, 1994), fols. 221v–222r.
3. For a recent interpretation of the duke's remarks, see David Rosand, "So-and-So Reclining on Her Couch," in Rona Goffen, ed., *Titian's "Venus of Urbino"* (Cambridge: Cambridge University Press, 1997), 37–62, especially 42.

4. For the most significant discussion of artistic genius, see Ernst Kris and Otto Kurz, *Legend, Myth, and Magic in the Image of the Artist: A Historical Experiment* (New Haven and London: Yale University Press, 1979, first published in Vienna in 1934 as *Die Legende vom Kunstler: Ein historischer Versuch*); for the representation of artists as creative, but troubled, types, see Griselda Pollock, "Artists' Mythologies and Media Genius: Madness and Art History," in Philip Hayward, ed., *Picture This: Media Representations of Visual Art and Artists* (London, Arts Council, 1988), 101–139; and for the specific attribution of gender to male artists, see Christine Battersby, *Gender and Genius: Towards a Feminist Aesthetics* (Bloomington: Indiana University Press, 1989).
5. For Nonsuch, see Simon Thurley, *The Royal Palaces of Tudor England: Architecture and Court Life* (New Haven and London: Yale University Press, 1993), especially 60–65; Martin Biddle, "Nonsuch—Henry VIII's Mirror for A Prince: Sources and Interpretation," in Cinzia Sicca and Louis A. Waldman, eds., *The Anglo-Florentine Renaissance: Art for the Early Tudors* (New Haven and London: Yale University Press and the Paul Mellon Centre for Studies in British Art, 2012); and John Dent, *The Quest for Nonsuch* (Surrey: Sutton, 1911).
6. For an in-depth discussion of this "artist anecdote" and its place in Holbein's mythology, see Tatiana C. String, "Henry VIII and Holbein: Patterns and Conventions in Early Modern Writing about Artists," in Tom Betteridge and Suzannah Lipscomb, eds., *Henry VIII and the Court: Art, Politics and Performance* (Farnham, UK and Burlington, Vermont: Ashgate, 2013) 131–141, especially 139.
7. For the Holbein portrait of Henry VIII in the popular imagination, see Tatiana C. String, "Myth and Memory in Representations of Henry VIII, 1509–2009," in Tatiana C. String and Marcus Bull, eds., *Tudorism: Historical Imagination and the Appropriation of the Sixteenth Century*. Proceedings of the British Academy, vol. 170 (Oxford: Oxford University Press, 2011), 201–221.
8. For thoughtful analyses of Henry's presentation on screen, see Thomas S. Freeman, "A Tyrant for all Seasons: Henry VIII on Film," in Susan Doran and Thomas S. Freeman, eds., *Tudors and Stuarts on Film* (Houndmills: Palgrave Macmillan, 200), 30–45, and Greg Walker, "'A Great Guy with His Chopper'?: The Sex Life of Henry VIII on Screen and in the Flesh," in String and Bull, *Tudorism*.

CHAPTER 19

Fashionable Fiction: The Significance of Costumes in *The Tudors*

Maria Hayward

INTRODUCTION

Hans Holbein's full-length image of Henry VIII recorded in the Whitehall cartoon presents the modern viewer with an imposing and impressive portrait of the king responsible for the Break with Rome.[1] Sixteenth-century observers, like their more recent counterparts, also would have been confronted by the artist's skillful montage of the assertive pose, the firm gaze, and the sense of physicality created by the size of the king's body and enhanced by his clothes. From his bonnet to his shoes, via the broad shoulders accentuated by the gown, the sumptuous doublet and the prominent codpiece, Henry VIII's clothing, along with the full range of masculine accessories and jewelry, served to stress his place at the top of English society.[2] Tudor clothing, and especially elite male Henrician clothing, was intended to convey numerous messages about the age, status, and wealth of the wearer which contemporaries were well practiced at interpreting. Interpretation is also at the heart of the discussions about all aspects of *The Tudors*, including the prize-winning costumes. Predicated on the premise that there is a fundamental difference between the clothes made and worn

---

I would like to thank Erin Bateson for her help with this chapter.

M. Hayward (✉)
Department of History, University of Southampton, Southampton, UK

© The Editor(s) (if applicable) and The Author(s) 2016
W.B. Robison (ed.), *History, Fiction, and* The Tudors,
Queenship and Power, DOI 10.1057/978-1-137-43883-6_19

in a specific time and costumes made after the fact to convey an idea of the period being recreated, this chapter is divided into two parts, the first exploring the differences between clothes and costumes and the second providing case studies on the king, his wives, and children.

Clothes and Costumes

The main garments for fashionable men throughout the sixteenth century, which roughly equates with the period of Tudor rule (1485–1603), were the doublet, hose, and shirt, and these were worn with a gown until c. 1550 and after with a short cloak. For women, it was the gown and kirtle, and later the gown and forepart, worn over a smock. From the 1540s the shape of the skirt was dictated by the farthingale, starting with the conical Spanish farthingale and then the round, drum farthingale.[3] In addition, both genders wore headwear, gloves, footwear, and jewelry, with ruffs and matching wrist ruffles starting to develop from the 1550s onward. For men, the right to carry weapons was linked to their social status and it was increasingly significant from the 1540s.[4] While the style of fashionable clothing from 1509 to the 1540s and beyond is well established, the costumes for *The Tudors* owe as much to the late sixteenth century as Henry VIII's own lifetime. For director and designer alike, one virtue of opting for the title *The Tudors*, for a program that encompasses all of the Tudor monarchs apart from the first, was the latitude to dress the actors in a combination of sixteenth-century English fashions, not just those from the decades being portrayed.

Creating a Tudor Wardrobe

The differences between pieces of historic clothing worn at a specific point in time and costumes put on for a performance on stage or in front of the camera are numerous, but the most significant usually relate to cost, materials, and construction techniques. Yet it is also possible to overstress the differences. Some of the challenges and constraints faced by costumiers when making a royal wardrobe, livery for a member of the household, or vestments for a member of the clergy now were also present for the royal tailors in the sixteenth century.

First, sixteenth-century clothing was expensive, and as such it represented a significant financial investment. Individuals justified the cost because clothing helped to visually define their place in society. For the social elite, and the king in particular, excessive expenditure on clothes was as problematic as spending too little, and there was a fine line between magnificence and luxury. As a result, the Great Wardrobe, the department of the household responsible for clothing the king and his sizable household, had a substantial but set annual budget. Even so, the Master of the Great Wardrobe frequently struggled to meet the level of opulence required at the Tudor court while staying within budget. Although the costume budget for *The Tudors* was significant, the number and type of items required inevitably placed limits upon the number of clothes made for the main characters, so giving them smaller wardrobes than they would have had in reality. More challenging for modern productions is the jewelry required by any well-dressed Tudor, which called for lots of gold, large gemstones, and big pendant pearls.[5] Jewels were also sewn to clothes, for example:

> a doblet of blacke veluete enbrauderd lyned with blacke saten and tufte with lynen cloth cut in panes tyed togeders with CC perles set in gold ouer & aboue.[6]

While none of the costumes in *The Tudors* are quite this opulent, some such as the black doublet embroidered with metal thread and small pearls worn by Jonathan Rhys Meyers in Season Four make a nod in this direction.[7]

Second is the problem of access to suitable materials, which in the sixteenth century included handwoven silks, woolens, and linens, along with mixed fiber cloths such as fustian, which combined linen with wool or cotton. Depending on an individual's access to wealth, these fabrics were colored with natural dyes, bleached to make them white, or left undyed. High-quality silks, including velvets, cloth of gold, and satins, and fine linens were not produced in England, so making them ideal signifiers of status because of their limited availability. Equally, events such as royal funerals and coronations could create a scarcity of black and red cloth in London because the Master of the Great Wardrobe had to provide cloth of the suitable color to secular and ecclesiastical elites, along with the royal household, all of whom were required to process through London.[8] Sourcing suitable fabrics, such as cloth of gold or cloth of tissue, is equally challenging for period productions. In part this explains the fairly limited use of these types of fabric in *The Tudors*.[9] While the series uses a range of silks, including plain weave silks and machine-embroidered silk, there is relatively little heavy silk satin or silk damask with the large, very distinctive pomegranate designs.[10]

Third, making the sixteenth-century royal wardrobe relied on hand sewing using contemporary tailoring techniques for pattern drafting, and cutting, of the type seen in Juan de Alçega's book of patterns.[11] A team of specialist royal craftsmen, and on occasion women, made the king's clothes. During the course of his time on the throne, Henry VIII had four personal tailors who dressed him sequentially. In contrast, John Scut worked for each of Henry VIII's wives, indicating that he could ensure certain features were constant in the consort's wardrobe while reflecting the needs and personality of the individual queens. The king, his queens, and their children wore large numbers of bespoke clothes. One of the challenges for dressing the cast of *The Tudors* was the scale, which resulted in the need to hire costumes and adapt them to suit their needs. The second aspect was the time that creating the king's wardrobe took. In the sixteenth century the solution was to vary the size of workforce and to use candles to allow for night working if necessary. Making all of the costumes by hand can be challenging for television productions. The 2009 session of *The Tudors* needed approximately 150 new costumes with the most significant, in relation to the plot, requiring the most labor. The gown Joss Stone wore as Anne of Cleves for her marriage took over 90 hours to make.[12]

As a consequence of these three factors, clothes were recycled in the sixteenth century and in modern productions. Henry VIII's clothes were passed on to friends, visitors to court, and members of his household, and the same happened with the clothes of Henry's wives. This use of clothes as perquisites ensured a trickle down of goods. Reuse of garments happened more frequently in *The Tudors*. In some cases it followed a similar pattern to that at Henry VIII's court as in the case of a jeweled headdress worn by Annabel Wallis as Jane Seymour, Tamzin Merchant as Catherine Howard, and Joely Richardson as Catherine Parr. This reflected how the queen's jewels were passed from one wife to the next, while others reflect the needs of the costume department, such as a dark red gown worn by Natalie Dormer as Anne Boleyn, Sarah Bolger as Mary Tudor, and Emma Hamilton as Anne Stanhope (a grouping that would have been most unlikely to share garments in the sixteenth century).[13] As this discussion has demonstrated there were many points of similarity between the clothes worn by Henry VIII and the costumes worn by Jonathan Rhys Meyers.

Purpose and Function

One of the most important theories underlying how a late medieval and early modern king expressed his authority was the concept of *magnificence*. Magnificence made clear the link between clothing and status, and for a monarch to be seen as magnificent he needed to be dressed in a way that asserted his position at the top of society. Certain fabrics and furs epitomized royal status. The first of these was cloth of gold, which Henry VIII used to good effect at his meeting with Francis I in 1520.[14] Francis was dressed in blue cloth of gold for his first appearance in *The Tudors*.[15] Second was the color purple, or more specifically, purple silk. Its use was restricted to key religious feast days and ceremonies associated with royal authority, such as the coronation in order to keep it exclusive or for significant occasions. As such, Jonathan Rhys Meyers' choice of purple for the departure of his sister Margaret for her marriage to the king of Portugal is appropriate even if the event is fiction.[16] Third was sable, the most desirable fur of the period. Henry VIII owned a number of sable-lined gowns and nightgowns, but it plays a less important role in Jonathan Rhys Meyers' wardrobe.

Linked to this idea and reinforced by the king's sumptuary law or acts of apparel was the close correlation between status, as linked to the landed hierarchy, and the clothing an individual might wear.[17] The law placed emphasis on the men of the landed hierarchy such as Edward Stafford, 3rd Duke of Buckingham, who was well known for his love of flamboyant dress. Other hierarchies, such as the ecclesiastical, were exempt. Yet it is one that *The Tudors* presents very clearly, ranging from Thomas Wolsey, Cardinal Campeggio, and Reginald Pole in their scarlet cardinal's robes, linked and echoing the robes of Pope Paul III, to the black robes of Thomas Cranmer, which draw out one of the visual implications of the Reformation/Break with Rome.[18]

Very few contemporaries witnessed the private life of the king, yet this is what *The Tudors* frequently presents to viewers. As a result, most Tudor sources discussed royal clothes and accessories rather than nudity and partial dress (which is discussed more fully in Chap. 19 by Megan Hickerson). Wardrobe accounts indicate that Henry VIII often wore a nightgown in private such as "a night gowne of russet veluete furred with sabullus—xl^{li}."[19] However, partial clothing was frequently associated with shame, degradation, and punishment. This was demonstrated most notably with executions of the elite of which there are many in *The Tudors*.[20]

Equally, partial dress was unusual, so it was rare to see the king in just his shirt, which explains why the ambassadors noted when he played tennis in his shirt and hose, as we see Jonathan Rhys Meyers do with Brandon, Compton, and Knivert.[21]

Sixteenth-century audiences for the king's clothes and those of his family and household consisted of the court, the ambassadors, the wider population of London, and the suburbs of Westminster and Greenwich. They would have seen set pieces of Tudor ceremony and pageantry. Ceremony played an essential role at defining moments of Henry VIII's reign, including Anne Boleyn's coronation, Elizabeth's baptism, and Henry's wedding to Jane—both in reality and in *The Tudors*.[22] The same was true for religious ceremonies, as indicated by Maria Doyle Kennedy's observance on Good Friday as Catherine of Aragon.[23] The use of best-quality material and craftsmen for ephemeral events was a distinctive feature of Henry VIII's court.[24] The revels were organized by William Cornish, who often participated, as he does in *The Tudors* when he takes the role of Ardent Desire and oversees events when Henry, as Honesty, first meets Anne Boleyn, who represents Perseverance.[25] Dressed in scarlet decorated with gold flames, Cornish's costume contrasts with the white worn by the eight young women who represent the Graces, the black of the women who guard them representing Danger, Jealousy, Disdain and others, and the gold for the eight men who free the Graces, including Youth, Devotion, and Loyalty.[26]

Clothes or Costumes

Henry VIII and his court have inspired many films and television programs that have been described as "costume dramas" or "costume pictures."[27] For directors and producers wanting to suggest "historical accuracy," demonstrably authentic costumes play a key role in evoking the period in question, as in the case of Deborah Lynn Scott's designs for James Cameron's *Titanic*.[28] In contrast, Joan Bergin, the costume designer for *The Tudors*, is well known for stating, "I'm forever searching to interpret with a modern sensibility but still keep 70 percent of what's correct for Tudor time."[29] This is a very different approach, yet arguably a successful one, because *The Tudors* won Emmy Awards for Costumes for a Series in 2007, 2008, and 2010 and Best Costume Design in 2008, 2009, and 2011.

While historians, and in this context dress historians, are often singled out as those who will be critical when television and film stray away from authenticity, there is a significant and knowledgeable body of reenactors who are very discerning about historic clothing as well as an interested viewing public.[30] The reason why authenticity is an issue in *The Tudors* is the decision to favor Elizabethan as opposed to Henrician clothing as the inspiration for the clothing, especially for men and in particular the king. While the core garments were the same during both reigns, the cut of the doublet and hose were markedly different, and in the Elizabethan period the short cloaks replaced the gown. The slim fitting doublet with short skirts and a slight, downward pointing waistline worn with close fitting hose gave the wearer a well-defined waist and emphasized the upper body and the length and shape of their legs. Elizabeth I's reign also saw a shift in color palate with a much broader spectrum of colors being worn by the second half of the century, with more pastel and muted shades.

The role of costumes in *The Tudors* is to create the oeuvre or ambience of the court. As such, linked to the concept of mise-en-scène, the costume should be seen as an extension of character.[31] In *The Tudors* this works well for many of the male figures around the king. Thomas Cromwell's distinctive black gown and Cardinal Wolsey's scarlet cassock, drawn from their portraits, act as shorthand for the serious bureaucrat and the flamboyant churchman.[32] In a similar vein, the costumes made for Robert Aske and the participants in the Pilgrimage of Grace are very effective at providing a point of contrast with the court and indicating the range of colors and fabrics worn by the wider Tudor population.

However, as Jean Hunnisett proved with her designs for Glenda Jackson in *Elizabeth R* (1971), authenticity is an option when dressing actors. Viewed in tandem with the plot and the acting, the result was widespread acclaim.[33] The distinction between costumes and clothes blurred further when Jenny Tiramani made the move to handmade clothes for the actors at the Globe.[34] These clothes were made using traditional sixteenth-century techniques, materials as close as possible to those available to the Tudors, and based on extant garments.[35] Made with the correct stiffenings and fastenings and worn with the appropriate underpinnings and footwear, these clothes influenced how actors moved and held their bodies. As these examples indicate, authenticity based on historic clothing is a valid option for costume designers but one that was not chosen as the underlying principle for *The Tudors*.

Case Studies

There are many aspects of the costumes in *The Tudors* and the clothing to which they compare at the Henrician court that could be considered in more detail. Three brief case studies are presented here. Valid in their own right, they also link with themes emphasized elsewhere in the book—namely, the nature of kingship, queenship, and the significance of family.

Henry VIII: Clothes and Kingship

Clothing plays an important part in creating Henry VIII's image. As noted above, color and fabric type are significant in combination with surface decoration in the form of slashing, pinking, embroidery, and applied guards. Woven patterns are also seen, but they are usually self-colored on damasks, or two-colored in the case of a red cloth of gold or a blue cloth of silver. Some of the costumes made for Jonathan Rhys Meyers have rather flamboyant patterns that would not have been seen in the sixteenth century. Equally, his costumes lack the prominent codpiece that was an integral part of men's hose during the reigns of Henry VIII and Elizabeth I.[36] It was an expression of masculinity, and it was designed to attract the gaze of others. Another way of expressing masculinity, wealth, and status was wearing high-quality armor made by skilled, continental craftsmen. This is conveyed well in *The Tudors* with the armor worn by Henry VIII, Charles Brandon, and Sir William Compton, although some is not as decorative as it would have been.[37]

Henry VIII was keen to manage his image and clothes helped to make him the focal point of his court. They stressed his height and physical size (ranging from his lean physique when young to his fuller figure by the 1540s), and this was something he relied on when going in disguise with Charles Brandon in the early years of his reign. He was aware that his appearance was commented upon and sought to restrict negative comments. Signs of Henry VIII's aging included a receding hairline, his changing body shape, and the slightly myopic stare of someone who is shortsighted. As his body shape changed in the 1540s, he and his tailor had to address that, and they opted for the full gown, long-skirted doublet or jerkin, and the cassock. If Henry VIII had remained slim he too could, and probably would, have dressed as the portraits of a Man in Red or the more figure-hugging style favored by Henry Howard, Earl of Surrey.[38] Jonathan Rhys Meyers is not the only character in *The Tudors* not to age.

However, while Henry Cavill remains useful as Charles Brandon, he quite often does wear the fur-lined, fur-guarded gown that was associated with the mature man in the 1530s and 1540s.

Arguably, the most important Tudor male accessory was the bonnet. It played a key role in the display of social etiquette by conveying ideas of deference and reinforcing the social hierarchy. Jeweled hat badges could reveal a man's religious and intellectual interests, as well as his wealth and taste. Yet in *The Tudors*, though Jonathan Rhys Meyers does wear a bonnet, he does not do so as often as Henry VIII did, and some of the other hats he wears are of an unusual shape, as is the black hat worn by Sir Francis Bryan.

Queenship: The Significance of Being the King's Consort

Henry VIII's complex marital history meant that the role of queen consort gained significance during his reign if for no other reason than that it had six different occupants. Each wife sought to assert her right to the role and to mark herself out as distinctive from her predecessors. Clothes played a significant part in the life of the queens consort—partly through asserting the queen's right to the role on a daily basis by setting her above all other women and partly through her participation in the ceremonies which conferred this status on her, namely, marriage, coronation (or the promise of it), the actuality or potential of motherhood, and acting as a stepmother. All of these occasions are depicted in *The Tudors*, as is the importance of making the king's shirts, which was a wifely duty.[39]

Of Henry VIII's European brides, Catherine of Aragon actively used her clothing to stress her Spanish identity on such occasions as when her nephew Charles V came to England.[40] She also tried to dress Henry in the Spanish style as indicated by "a Spaynisshe cloke of Blak Frisado with a Border of Goldesmythis worke geven by the Quenes grace to the king," listed an inventory of 1521.[41] Maria Doyle Kennedy as Catherine of Aragon wears a lot of black, a color increasingly associated with Spain as the sixteenth century progressed. The ambassadors Henry sent to Cleves thought the clothes were distinctively different to those worn in England, and the costumes created for Anne of Cleves certainly convey this. Here the headdress is used to good effect, in that Anne wore one and it was very different from the gable hood worn in England. Anne marked her transition into English society by adopting English dress. It was much harder for Henry's English brides to create a distinctive identity through clothes. Anne Boleyn, with her knowledge of French fashions, was the most successful. Certainly Natalie Dormer's Anne Boleyn is dressed in a more sensual style than Henry's other English queens, which may be an allusion to her French taste.

Women, especially married women, were expected to keep their heads and, by association, their hair covered. The English gable hood worn by Elizabeth of York was unfashionable compared to the smaller, neater, French hood that left the front of the wearer's hair uncovered. Not surprisingly, the distinctive if unflattering gable hood rarely features in *The Tudors*. Much more prevalent, if ahistoric, is long female hair, something which only would have been seen in private. The little hats, including the round fur hats worn by Anne and Jane or the small headdresses worn by Catherine of Aragon and Jane Seymour's ladies-in-waiting, are inventive. However, the queens' enthusiastic use of crowns of various shapes and sizes and of tiaras is most distracting.

Royal Heirs—The Significance of Family

Henry VIII's wish for a son and his complex relationship with his daughters is well known, and not surprisingly the theme of family is a strong one in *The Tudors*. Ranging from the preparations for childbirth and the specific clothing worn by young children, furnishings and clothing are central in stressing family members' significance at court.[42] Clothes are very effective at stressing change in their lives. For his creation as Duke of Richmond, Henry Fitzroy wears a doublet and hose under his robes.[43] What is not shown is his being breeched and making the transition from youthful coats to the adult doublet and hose. Mary's clothes are used to stress her growing up and the changing nature of her relationship of Henry VIII, such as when she leaves with Lady Salisbury.[44] Equally with Elizabeth, *The Tudors* demonstrates her precarious position after the death of her mother by the reference to the request for clothes for her made by Lady Bryan.[45] Clothes are also used to create a sense of the royal family by having them all dress alike. For example, Catherine Parr ordered clothes of cloth of silver for herself and the king's children.[46] *The Tudors* presents a variant of this in the scene showing Jane, Mary, and Elizabeth all dressed in the same color, and wearing the same floral headdresses to celebrate Christmas in 1536.[47]

Conclusions

The costumes for *The Tudors* were never intended to be an authentic depiction of what was worn at Henry VIII's court. Rather, Joan Bergin aimed to create costumes that conveyed a sense of the court while also appealing to modern audiences. Judged within this framework they are very successful as reflected by the awards that they won and much favorable popular comment. As noted above, the costumes have a number of strengths, including the social range covered from male courtiers to rebels to the ecclesiastical hierarchy, and in creating a sense of Tudor pageantry and revels. Less convincing are the king's clothes and almost all of the bonnets, hoods, tiaras, and coronets. The set designers demonstrate how significant textiles were at Henry VIII's court, ranging from cloths of estate, beds, and their hangings and banners. For all their strengths and weaknesses, the costumes should be compared with those designed by Joanna Eatwell for *Wolf Hall*. These costumes evoke the sumptuous nature of Henry VIII's wardrobe very well by combining traditional cut and construction techniques with an appreciation of the nature of men's clothes in the first half of the sixteenth century that accentuates the shoulders and chest of Damien Lewis as Henry VIII.[48] Ultimately all of the discussion of the costumes made for *The Tudors* demonstrates the significance of "rich apparel" at the court of Henry VIII, both real and imagined.

Notes

1. King Henry VIII and Henry VII (known as the Whitehall Cartoon), by Hans Holbein the younger, ink and watercolor, c. 1536–37, NPG 4027.
2. For the significance of clothing in this period see Anne Rosalind Jones and Peter Stallybrass, *Renaissance Clothing and the Materials of Memory* (Cambridge: Cambridge University Press, 2000).
3. C. Willet Cunnington and Phillis Cunnington, *Handbook of English Costume in the Sixteenth Century* (London: Faber and Faber, 1954); Jane Ashelford, *Dress in the Age of Elizabeth I* (London: B.T. Batsford Ltd., 1988); M.A. Hayward, *Dress at the Court of King Henry VIII* (Leeds: Maney, 2007).
4. Tobias Capwell, *The Noble Art of the Sword: Fashion and Fencing in Renaissance Europe 1520–1630* (London: Wallace Collection, 2012), 82–111.
5. See Diana Scarisbrick, *Tudor and Jacobean Jewellery* (London: Tate Publishing, 1995).

6. BL Harley MS 4217, f. 6v.
7. For a sample of this fabric, see Breygent costume card C–11 (48 of 65).
8. See Ian Archer, "City and Court Connected: The Material Dimensions of Royal Ceremonial," *Huntingdon Library Quarterly* 71 (1) (2008): 157–179.
9. For an example of a synthetic fabric incorporating metal threads for a long-skirted jerkin worn by Jonathan Rhys Meyers as Henry VIII, see Breygent costume card KHNC (132 of 200).
10. For plain silks of this type see the gold-colored gown worn by Sarah Bolger as Mary Tudor, Breygent costume card MJBD (87 of 200) and the pale gray sleeves of a doublet worn by Jonathan Rhys Meyers, C–8 (128 of 155) and embroidered silks, see the sleeves of the green gown worn by Natalie Dormer as Anne Boleyn, ABGD (101 of 200) and her green and yellow gown, ABBD (113 of 200). For a very lightweight damask, see the orange and green gown worn by Annabelle Wallis as Jane Seymour, JSGD (158 of 200).
11. Juan de Alçega and J.L. Nevinson, *Tailor's Pattern Book, 1589/Libro de Geometria, Practica y Traca* (Marlborough, Wiltshire: Ruth Bean Publishers, 1999).
12. Margy Rochlin, "Joan Bergin: The Tudors," *The New York Times*, 5 June 2009, http://www.nytimes.com/2009/06/07/arts/television/07berg.html?_r=0.
13. For the headdress see *The Tudors*, Episodes 3:2, 4:2, and 4 7. The red dress can be seen in Episodes 1:10, 3:3 and 4:2. For many other examples, accessed 15 June 2015, http://www.thetudorswiki.com/page/Re-used+Costumes+on+The+Tudors.
14. Episode 1:2; J.G. Russell, *The Field of Cloth of Gold: Men and Manners in 1520* (London, 1969); Glenn Richardson, *The Field of Cloth of Gold* (New Haven and London: Yale University Press, 2013).
15. *The Tudors*, Episode 1:2.
16. *The Tudors*, Episode 1:4.
17. For a detailed discussion of clothing in relation to the law, see M.A. Hayward, *Rich Apparel: Clothing and the Law in Henry VIII's England* (Aldershot: Ashgate, 2009).
18. In spite of their differing views on religion, Pope Paul III (in Season Two) and Thomas Cranmer (in promotional images of him) both wore the same cross in *The Tudors*.
19. BL Harley MS 4217, f. 2r.
20. For example, the executions of Edward Stafford, 3rd Duke of Buckingham, Sir Thomas More and Thomas Cromwell, Earl of Essex.
21. *The Tudors*, Episode 1:1.
22. *The Tudors*, Episodes 2:3–2:4, 3:1.

23. *The Tudors*, Episode 1:5; Jennifer Loach, "The Function of Ceremonial in the Reign of Henry VIII," *Past and Present* 142 (1994): 43–68.
24. Sydney Anglo, *Spectacle, Pageantry and Early Tudor Policy* (Oxford: Clarendon Press, 1997) and *The Great Tournament Roll of Westminster* (Oxford: Clarendon Press, 1968); W.R. Streitberger, *Court Revels 1485–1559* (Toronto, Buffalo and London, 1994).
25. *The Tudors*, Episode 1:3.
26. This can be compared with the revel that mocked Wolsey in Episode 1:10. While this specific event may not have taken place, anti-clerical events at court were not unheard of; see Sydney Anglo, "An Early Tudor Programme for Plays and Other Demonstrations Against the Pope," *Journal of the Warburg and Courtauld Institutes* 20 (1957): 176–179.
27. Thomas Freeman, "A Tyrant for All Seasons: Henry VIII on Film," in Susan Doran and Thomas Freeman eds., *Tudors and Stuarts on Film: Historical Perspectives* (Basingstoke: Palgrave Macmillan, 2009), 30–45.
28. Doran and Freeman, *Tudors and Stuarts on Film*, 15; E.W. Marsh, *James Cameron's Titanic* (London and Basingstoke: Boxtree Ltd., 1998), 40–41. Deborah Lynn Scott won the Academy Award for Best Costume Design in 1997.
29. Compare with the work of Jacqueline Durran, who won the award for best Costume Design at the 85th Academy Awards and the 66th British Academy Film Awards for *Anna Karenina* based on the novel by Leo Tolstoy. The 2012 film was directed by Joe Wright and starred Keira Knightly as Anna Arkadievna Karenina. The costumes echoed the 1870s silhouette in tandem with the elegance of 1950s couture to evoke the fashions contemporary with the novel in a way that was sumptuous while keeping frills and decoration to a minimum.
30. See Elizabeth Friendship, *Creating Historical Clothes: Pattern Cutting from Tudor to Victorian Times* (London: Batsford, 2013) and J. Malcolm Davies and N. Mikhaila, *The Tudor Tailor: Reconstructing Sixteenth Century Dress* (London: Batsford Ltd., 2006).
31. Allan Rowe, "Film Form and Narrative," in Jill Nelmes ed., *An Introduction to Film Studies* (London: Routledge, 1996), 93–101.
32. See, for example, the miniature of Thomas Cromwell, attributed to Hans Holbein the younger, watercolor and bodycolor on vellum, c. 1532–33, NPG 6310 and Thomas Wolsey, unknown artist, c. 1520, NPG 32.
33. Jean Hunnisett, *Period Costume for Stage and Screen: 1500–1800: Patterns for Women's Dress (Practical Period Costume)* (London: Harper Collins Publishers Ltd., 1986). Also see Janet Arnold, *Patterns of Fashion: The Cut and Construction of Clothes for Men and Women, c. 1560–1620* (London and Basingstoke: Macmillan, 1985), 126, figs. 380–381.
34. Since leaving The Globe, Jenny Tiramani has won Best Costume Design in 2014 for a Play (*Twelfth Night*) at the 68th annual Tony Awards.

35. The thinking behind creating clothes in this spirit is evident in the garments made by Jenny Tiramani in 2011 to recreate the clothes worn by Matthäus Schwarz in 1530 when he attended the Imperial Diet in Augsburg, see Jenny Tiramani, "Reconstructing a Schwarz outfit," in Ulinka Rublack and Maria Hayward eds., *The First Book of Fashion: The Book of Clothes of Matthaeus and Veit Konrad Schwarz of Augsburg* (London: Bloomsbury Academic, 2015), 369–398.
36. Tatiana C. String, "Projecting Masculinity: Henry VIII's Codpiece," in Mark Rankin, Christopher Highley, and John N. King eds., *Henry VIII and His Afterlives: Literature, Politics and Art* (Cambridge: Cambridge University Press, 2009), 143–159. This was also the case in *Wolf Hall*, see http://www.dailymail.co.uk/news/article-3063705/Codpieces-seen-hit-BBC-drama-Wolf-Hall-twice-small-wouldn-t-offend-American-audience-says-expert.html#ixzz3Z6JovuN8.
37. For example, the silver and engraved armor for horse and man at the Tower of London, see Claude Blair, "The Emperor Maximilian's Gift of Armour to King Henry VIII and the Silver and Engraved Armour at the Tower of London," *Archaeologia* 99 (1965): 1–52. Equally as the Breygent costume cards reveal, the mail worn by Jonathan Rhys Meyers as Henry VIII and David O'Hara as Henry Howard in Season Four was made from a coarse paper-wrapped yarn which had been knitted and sprayed with metallic paint—C-3 (82 of 155) and C-7 (39 of 155).
38. Portrait of a man in red, unknown artist, 1540s, RCIN 405752 and Henry Howard, Earl of Surrey, attributed to William Scrots, 1546, oil on canvas, NPG 5291, on display at Arundel Castle, West Sussex.
39. *The Tudors*, Episode 2:1.
40. *The Tudors*, Episode 1:3.
41. BL Harley MS 4217, f. 4v.
42. For the birth of Edward, see Episode 3:4. Compare with *Britain's Tudor Treasure: A Night at Hampton Court* by Lucy Worsley and David Starkey and shown on BBC2 on February 7, 2015.
43. *The Tudors*, Episode 1:5. The doublet and hose worn by Zac Jenciragic as Henry Fitzroy on this occasion are later worn by Eoin Murtagh as Prince Edward in Episode 3:8.
44. *The Tudors*, Episode 1:5.
45. *The Tudors*, Episode 3:1.
46. TNA E101/423/12, unfoliated.
47. *The Tudors*, Episode 3:3.
48. Made by the BBC and shown in the UK between January 21 and February 25, 2015. According to Sam Wollaston in a review in *The Guardian* on January 22, 2015, *Wolf Hall* was "event television: sumptuous, intelligent and serious," http://www.theguardian.com/tv-and-radio/2015/jan/22/wolf-hall-review-slabs-of-guilt-lifted-triumphantly-from-the-bookshelf.

CHAPTER 20

Putting Women in Their Place: Gender, Sex, and Rape in *The Tudors*

Megan L. Hickerson

In a troubling scene from *The Tudors: King Takes Queen* (2008), a novel of Season Two of Showtime's *The Tudors* written by the series' creator and writer, Michael Hirst, and Elizabeth Massie, Sir Thomas Wyatt, poet and courtier, seeks to seduce a devoutly Catholic lady-in-waiting to Catherine of Aragon, Lady Elizabeth Darrell. As Lady Elizabeth attempts to refuse Wyatt's advances, insisting that she has done nothing to provoke his desire, he begins, nevertheless, both to tell her that she has indeed provoked it and physically to act on her provocation:

> "My lady ... Your hair, your eyes, your lips. All are causes of my desire." [Wyatt] put his index finger to her cheek, then drew it to her lips. She inhaled sharply, a mixture of desire and trepidation in her eyes. Holding her shoulders, he pressed his lips against hers.

Quickly, as Hirst describes, Elizabeth begins to feel desire for Wyatt—her desire artfully set against a reminder of her religious commitment: as a church bell begins to ring, Elizabeth pushes Wyatt away saying, "Please don't. I must go to Mass." In answer to this, rather than let her go, Wyatt

M.L. Hickerson ()
Department of Social Sciences, Henderson State University,
Arkadelphia, AR, USA

© The Editor(s) (if applicable) and The Author(s) 2016
W.B. Robison (ed.), *History, Fiction, and* The Tudors,
Queenship and Power, DOI 10.1057/978-1-137-43883-6_20

307

begins stroking her neck saying, "Yes, I know. You must. Just stay an instant." He then begins to undress her:

> He ... kissed her softly, then slid his fingers to the ribbons at her shoulder, untying them, allowing him to pull the sleeve free. The white skin of her naked arm stood against the chill of the air.
> Elizabeth gasped as Wyatt removed the second sleeve. "What are you doing?"
> "Giving you a chance to be penitent, my beautiful, pious lady."
> She glanced in the direction of the tolling bell. "Please, don't!"

Wyatt now unlaces Lady Elizabeth's bodice and opens it to expose her "small, virginal breasts." His seduction becomes urgent:

> He kissed them roughly, pushing her body against the scabby trunk of the tree. Elizabeth squeezed her eyes shut and began to recite bits of Mass in Latin, her words quivering with fear and Wyatt's increasingly powerful, rhythmic groping.
> And the bell continued to toll.[1]

Lady Elizabeth Darrell, the object of Thomas Wyatt's violent passion in this scene, was a real lady-in-waiting to Catherine of Aragon: one of Catherine's retainers who refused to take the Oath of Succession. However, while her loyalty to Catherine plays true in Hirst's book (and Showtime series), her story, nevertheless, is dramatically fictionalized in both book and series. The real Elizabeth, destitute after Catherine of Aragon's death in 1536, became Wyatt's mistress the next year. She remained with him until his death in 1542, bearing him at least three children.[2] In *The Tudors*, however, Elizabeth does not survive the year 1536. The story of her relationship with Wyatt is both telescoped and retold with an agenda: to romanticize male sexual conquest, in the process blurring the line between seduction and rape.

Elizabeth Darrell, played by Krystin Pellerin, enters *The Tudors* in Episode 2:2. She serves at The More, Catherine of Aragon's stripped-down residence, where Wyatt (Jamie Thomas King) comes to demand Catherine's return of the queen's jewels. Finding Catherine at prayer, Wyatt approaches the young woman—whom he knows but the audience has not yet met—saying in a breathy tone, "Lady Elizabeth." She responds, "What do you want?" He replies, "You know what I want." At this Elizabeth makes herself clear: "Mr Wyatt, I have no intention of becoming your mistress, nor anyone else's for that matter. I shall be a virgin when I marry, but I doubt I shall marry at all. I would rather be a bride of Christ." "A nun," Wyatt says mockingly, "I don't think so. Check your pocket." When he leaves Elizabeth pulls a paper from her pocket; it is a declaration of desire in verse: "Would God thou knewest the depth of my desire/Then might I hope, though nought I can deserve/some drops of grace would quench my scorching fire."

If Wyatt thinks this is enough to seduce Elizabeth, he is apparently correct. The next interaction between the two, later in the same episode, takes place at a tree on a hill—and the scene as from the book (as quoted above) proceeds with slight revision. Wyatt stands leaning against the tree, his eyes calculating as he watches Elizabeth approach. When he greets her, she tells him she wishes to return his poem. "You cannot give a poem back, or a kiss, or a thought," he tells her—she gasps lightly and looks down in what appears to be shame. She looks up: "I'm sorry that you are unhappy … burning as you say. I'm sure I've done nothing to cause it." He responds, as she appears increasingly nervous: "My lady you are full of causes. Your hair, your eyes, your lips, all are causes of my desire," he says, leaning in to kiss her. She instantly drops the poem and gasps—she is alarmed but smiling: "I must go to Mass!" She turns to leave, but he holds her back: "I know you must," he says, "I know. Stay a moment." He pulls her toward the tree and begins kissing her—within seconds he unties the ribbons securing her dress. She stares at him with big eyes, panting—soon he has turned her so that her breasts are fully exposed to the audience as he kisses her shoulders. Once he has her dress fully off she says, "What are you doing?" He answers, "Giving you a chance to be penitent, my beautiful, pious lady." One minute into the seduction scene, she turns and kisses him, now pulling him toward her, her leg raised as she begins to straddle him against the tree. She is overcome with desire—her desire created of his. Sadly, when we next see Wyatt, he is gazing with desire at his former lover, Anne Boleyn—now lost to him in her relationship with Henry VIII: "I've tried to run from the fire that burns me. But when I look around, there the fire still is." The verse, given *to* Elizabeth, was not *for* her.

Wyatt confirms his indifference to Elizabeth in their next scene together in Episode 2:3. Catherine has been informed of the king's marriage to Anne Boleyn; henceforth Catherine will be known as the Princess Dowager of Wales, and Henry will no longer pay her expenses. Devastated for her mistress, Elizabeth visits Wyatt to ask for his help. She mentions that Henry, in his cruelty, has "pretend[ed] to marry that harlot." That gets Wyatt's attention—shocked, he asks in a whining tone, "What can I do?" When Elizabeth asks him to use his influence as both privy councilor and one of Thomas Cromwell's clients, he demurs, pointing out that Cromwell is "the least likely man to sympathize with your mistress." Elizabeth counters: "But what about you? If you still had feelings for me, you would speak up for her." "I'm sorry," he says. She leaves, still unaware—as the audience knows—that Wyatt has actually never cared for her. Upset (but not over Elizabeth's trouble), he gazes at a picture of Anne Boleyn that he keeps in a locket on his desk.

Elizabeth now disappears from the series until the scenes depicting Catherine of Aragon's final days in Episode 2:7. In the first of these, Wyatt finds her scrubbing a floor; he asks why she does not return to court rather than suffer such hardships. She tells him of her love for "the Queen," as she still calls Catherine. Then, as Wyatt attempts to approach her, she says, "I am a Catholic. I believe in my faith. Perhaps you poets don't believe in anything." "In love perhaps?" he replies. After a lingering kiss, Wyatt leaves, never to see Elizabeth alive again. For after Catherine's heart-wrenching death, her loyal lady-in-waiting kills herself. Wyatt discovers her hanging body.

The story of Thomas Wyatt and Elizabeth Darrell as played in *The Tudors* is paradoxical. On the one hand there is a half-hearted attempt to cast it as a love story; thus, the players' interactions are accompanied by beautiful and romantic string music that rises as they approach physical contact. Also to this end, Wyatt both seems concerned for Elizabeth as Catherine's poverty increases and looks for her after her mistress's death. However, the effort to create romance of this story fails because it falls secondary to the series' higher priorities: to both negate women's right to sexual autonomy and valorize men's sexual aggression. The storyline peaks in Wyatt's easy seduction of a young woman who has declared herself unwilling to give up her virginity. Her protestations are made laughable by the ease with which she succumbs to Wyatt. No means yes.

While in the story's television depiction Elizabeth feels quickly overcome by desire for Wyatt, Hirst's book carries a rare departure from the televised version. As written, Wyatt's conquest of Elizabeth engages with modern discourses of rape, both posing against each other such constructs as "legitimate" and "illegitimate" rape and either explicitly denouncing women's right to say "no" or bringing into question the word's real meaning. Elizabeth says "Please don't" twice in the text version of the scene, but these words (alone of the written scene) do not make it to the screen.

However, the text also carefully describes her experiencing a mixture of trepidation *and desire*; she gives in for a minute but then pushes away. And so, presumably led there, Wyatt roughly kisses her breasts, pushes her body against a tree and gropes her, powerfully, as she shuts her eyes and attempts to distract herself by reciting the Mass. Indeed, not only is this a rape scene, it could describe the rape of a child—an impression sharpened by the writer's reference to Elizabeth's "small, virginal breasts." The scene is horrifying, but Hirst intends to titillate and even earn the reader's approval: Wyatt has been betrayed, and because of his love—the only thing in which he believes—he exists in a state of perpetual burning; he writes beautiful poetry expressing that he is passionate, romantic, a poet—how could she not want him?

Wyatt's rape of Elizabeth, as written, celebrates the sexual enforcement of a gender hierarchy (echoed in the power status of these two courtiers) achieved through sexual aggression: in effect, the rape is acceptable. On the one hand, its depiction engages, among others in *The Tudors*' television and book series, with some modern claims about male nature, according to which men are biologically hardwired to rape women: men are incapable of going without sex and have been programmed by evolution to take sex when it suits them.[3] On the other hand, the scene serves to celebrate the idea that a woman's "No" really means "Yes"—a frequent claim and defense against "date rape" accusations: "How many of you guys, in your own experience with women, have learned that no means yes if you know how to spot it?" Rush Limbaugh recently asked his radio audience, objecting to efforts to clarify the issue of consent at Ohio State University.[4] Both sets of ideas—that men are hardwired to rape and that "No" means "Yes"—carry with them the idea that women's abstinence from sex, certainly as a lifestyle choice, either defies nature or just cannot be expected to stand. And so Wyatt reacts to Elizabeth's choice with disdain: "A nun? I don't think so," he says, the decider. Elizabeth's very choice is negated; her natural role is as a vessel for penetration. In addition, her "no" is also linked to her adherence to superstition and papal tyranny: "Please don't. I must go to Mass."

While the written scene at the tree casts Elizabeth's "noes" as "yesses," departures in the scene's televised version implicate Elizabeth even further in the loss of what she perceives to be her principal virtue. In short, while the written version depicts the beginning of what reads as an *acceptable* rape, the televised version depicts a scene in which Wyatt cannot be held accountable for moving aggressively against Elizabeth's expressed desire, even as it also serves to offer confirmation of a particular view of women's nature: whatever women claim, they cannot conquer their natural desire for penetration. Thus, while Elizabeth has made it clear to Wyatt that she prefers to remain a virgin and even become a nun, this scene's audience is free, first to agree with Wyatt's dismissal of her protestations and then to enjoy watching his violation of her. In this we see a careful calculation: Wyatt's penetration of the boundaries Elizabeth has clearly set for herself engages the viewers as collaborators in the series' approval of male sexual aggression. In this sense, this version of the scene is even more disturbing than the one in Hirst's book. While now wholly responsible for what happens, Elizabeth has no agency. She cannot control her own desire despite her clearly stated intentions. She actually wants Wyatt even as he operates against her adored mistress and mocks everything precious to her: her faith, her church, her virginity. Sadly, as she comes to discover—dramatically having chosen Wyatt's body over the Body of Christ—it is not actually even she for whom Wyatt burns. Finally, with all that matters stolen from her—her queen, her faith, her virginity, the future she has chosen for herself—she kills herself, losing her salvation.

Elizabeth is the victim of her own expectations—her wrongheaded belief in her self-determination and sexual autonomy. As such she exemplifies—in her destruction—*The Tudors*' ideal of gender power relationships. While Ramona Wray argues that "with a few important exceptions, female roles [in *The Tudors*] are filled out, maximized and treated sympathetically," Natalie Dormer—who plays Anne Boleyn in the series—has suggested that Hirst unconsciously wrote its female characters (particularly, as she is discussing them, the characters of Henry VIII's first two queens) according to traditional stereotypes: "Men still have trouble recognizing," she told Susan Bordo (as Bordo reports in her recent study of representations of Anne Boleyn), "that a woman can be complex, can have ambition, good looks, sexuality, erudition, and common sense … and yet men, in literature and in drama, seem to need to simplify women, to polarize us as either the whore or the angel … I think it's something innate that just happens and he [Hirst] doesn't realize it."[5] These are quite generous views. Indeed, *The Tudors* forcefully presents Henry's court (Henry himself embodies this) as a masculine idyll in which triumphant, hetero-normative masculine power so successfully asserts itself as to obliterate both autonomous femaleness on the one hand and effeminate maleness on the other.

Basil Glynn has recently argued (engaging with the work of John Beynon) that *The Tudors* asserts a "'hegemonic masculinity' (that reinforces dominant gender ideology)" over "'subordinate variants' (that oppose and challenge it)."[6] Both in its service to what Adrienne Rich calls "the bias of compulsory heterosexuality"—embodied both in Henry VIII's "forceful virility" and in the series' shockingly negative portrayal of gay (if not homosocial) relationships—and in its celebration of "white, Western heroic qualities," Glynn suggests that *The Tudors* "reasserts WASP masculinity for a wide variety of Western audiences."[7] Glynn contextualizes this agenda in pan-Western anxieties about the "threatened present in which Western countries have been drawn into questionable military expeditions abroad and heightened security at home." I argue that in its depiction of women and their sexual relationships with men, the series also reacts to contemporary Western anxieties regarding male domestic and sexual power. The series thus participates in the deployment of a post-feminist "enlightened sexism" (the word "enlightened" is intended ironically), working hand in glove with the "beauty myth," recently noted of feminist scholars as following (and much more insidious than)—while still driven by its same anxieties—the anti-feminist backlash of the 1980s and 1990s.[8]

Enlightened sexism "insists that women have made plenty of progress because of feminism—indeed, full equality has allegedly been achieved—so now it's OK, even amusing, to resurrect sexist stereotypes of girls and women."[9] As Susan Douglas argues in *The Rise of Enlightened Sexism* (2010), the success of the women's movement has provided "permission" to the modern, post-sexist mediator to "resurrect retrograde images of girls and women as sex objects … still defined by their appearance and their biological destiny."[10] In fact, it is only in a post-sexist world that the kind of extreme sexism found in *The Tudors* could stand: "the extremeness of the sexism is evidence that there's no sexism."[11] In that vein, *The Tudors* conflates women's identities with their sexual desirability (as imposed), basing the latter on physical appearance. Women's bodies are fully commoditized; the series' sexually desirable female characters are objects of art with all their value aesthetic, in line with the idea that women's self-worth rests on men's determination of their identities as premised upon a sexualized "beauty."[12]

This is the "beauty myth" as described by Naomi Wolf (1991): a "backlash against feminism that uses images of female beauty as a political weapon against women's advancement." The link between women's commoditized beauty and women's sexuality, as Wolf argues, undermines women's self-worth with the constant proliferation of images according to which virtuous women are women sexually objectified—virtue thus has nothing to do with qualities bringing women love or respect.[13] In fact, the beauty myth does not teach women to want to be loved, but rather madly and even violently desired for their beauty. In *The Tudors*, partners portrayed as in love either do not appear emotionally intimate in their sexual relationships or do not make love on screen.[14] Increasingly, the success of the beauty myth depends on girls and women's *self*-objectification. As Douglas notes, if value comes from being objects of desire, girls and women must choose to become sex objects. The achievement of the myth is recasting female confidence as woman's sexual *self*-objectification.[15]

The Tudors' success in its deployment of enlightened sexism depends on its portrayal of the womanizing of Henry, Charles Brandon, and others—far from unacceptable—as admirable and titillating. Thus it foregrounds the idea that heterosexual, masculine power houses like Jonathan Rhys Meyers' Henry or Henry Cavill's Brandon are entitled to sex with beautiful, nubile (young, fertile) women (whose very nubility indicates sexual accessibility), and, by this, to negate the idea that sexual exploitation of such women by such men could ever be read as rape. To this end, even in the types of contexts in which women frequently are or have been historically raped, women in *The Tudors* self-objectify and show desire, enabling *The Tudors* to promote a paradigm by which nubile women both exist for and crave male penetration, even if they fail to realize it.[16]

Enlightened sexism hoodwinks by asserting two assumptions: first, by portraying some women as intellectual or moral (existing outside sexual life), mediators "prove" that they are not sexist; and, second, extreme misogynist depictions in the post-feminist world expose themselves as absurd. In other words, cultural mediators can trust their audiences to see misogynist depictions without deriving negative meaning from them—sexist characters should be seen as simply silly. But they are not; this is ensured in *The Tudors* by the clear heroic standing of the characters played by Meyers, Cavill, and others—as Bordo reminds us, Meyers' refusal to wear a "fat suit" in the show was due, as he claimed, to his desire to allow people to embrace "the fantastic monarch [Henry] was … Heroes do not look like Henry VIII. That is just the world we live in."[17] As Glynn notes:

> *The Tudors* presents the king of a Christian country standing firmly against the military aggression of Catholic Spain and the religious intolerance of the Pope in Rome, a position of defiance against a menacing external religion and threatening foreign powers that broad Western audiences familiar with the "war on terror" can easily identify with … Henry founds the Church

of England and becomes, quite literally, the first and most powerful symbol of WASP resistance and power ... England's dynamic nature is presented as bound up with the king's forceful virility and militaristic aggression as he propels his country towards a better future, a reclamation of Western masculinity under threat by weakness on the international stage following events such as the London bombings of 7 July 2005 that directly preceded *The Tudors*.[18]

Henry's heroism derives from more than just his sexual mastery. However, his sexual mastery provides the most important foundation for his heroism. His persona as a "fantastic monarch" or "hero" could not survive without his audience reveling with him in his sexual power, as it is taught to do from Episode 1:1, in which he is seen both vigorously fornicating with his married mistress and appropriating another of his wife's ladies-in-waiting for his pleasure. In the first sexual encounter witnessed by *The Tudors*' audience, between Henry and Lady Elizabeth Blount (Ruta Gedmintas), the audience learns both of the graphic nature of the series' sex scenes and that Meyers' Henry is a sexual dynamo fully up to the task of starring in them. Bessie is bare-chested almost immediately in this scene, which opens with Henry chasing her around the bed in mock aggression while she laughs and tumbles to the bed. Looking down at her, Henry smirks while opening his pants, turns her over and penetrates her from behind; Lady Blount's immediate cries clearly reflect a pain that can only be caused by Henry's size and power. In this encounter the audience catches a glimpse of what will emerge as a standard proof of Henry's sexual prowess—his ability to cause his partners exquisite pain as he (mock-)rapes them.

The audience also quickly learns that Henry considers himself entitled to have sex with any woman he chooses, including other men's wives. Hirst's decision for example, to introduce the subject of Bessie's husband—invented for the purpose (the real Bessie Blount did not marry until her affair with Henry had ended)—into Henry's first conversation with his mistress (the only one he has with her in the series) clearly establishes Henry's sense of entitlement and even his amusement at the idea of his own and her adultery. The same is true of other early scenes in which Henry first inspects and then acquires beautiful women, selecting them off market shelves as commodities: additional ladies-in-waiting to Catherine of Aragon played by Slaine Kelly in Episode 1.1 and Rachel Montague in Episode 1.3. Importantly, even as Henry acquires Kelly's and Montague's characters by winking at his servant, he is redeemed by cleverly written details: the audience learns that Henry is a virile young man tied to a barren, much older wife (while Catherine of Aragon was five years older than Henry, Maria Doyle Kennedy, who plays her in the series, is thirteen years older than Meyers); we are assured that Henry does not take women by force—as he disrobes Kelly's character (having already stroked her belly and exposed her breasts), he whispers, "Do you consent?" She replies, "Yes, Your Majesty," before they begin passionately to kiss; as Montague's character drops her gown before Henry saying, "How like you this?" she objectifies herself on his behalf, establishing her willing participation in his acquisition of her. As a "this." In addition, and importantly, both Kelly's and Montague's characters explicitly want Henry. His virile power—his "hotness"—makes inevitable women's lust. Henry's acquisition of these interchangeable women is not just tolerable *to* them, but also desired *by* them as affirmations of their successful self-objectification: "How like you this?"

The Tudors' celebration of Henry's acquisitional power peaks during Episode 2:5. Anne, having born Henry a daughter, has now had a miscarriage, and Henry is less and less happy with her. Clearly troubled, as he rides through a forest with Brandon, he asks his friend, "Have any of the women you've bedded ever lied about their virginity?" Brandon answers, "I'd say it's the other way around. Did any of them not lie about it?". Soon the men come across a young man, William Webbe (played by Damien Kearney), riding through the forest with his pretty "sweetheart," Bess (played by Katie McGrath) behind him. Henry dismounts his horse, approaches the couple and holds up Bess' chin to get a better look, all the while extravagantly ignoring Webbe in favor of his sweetheart. Bess is a beautiful brunette; she looks up at Henry, who kisses her and says "Come with me"; she follows him to his horse while Charles looks on approvingly, a smirk on his face. Ignoring Webbe's stammering assurances that he has permission to penetrate his king's property, Henry prepares to penetrate Webbe's (as such) without it; in the next scene he is having intercourse with Bess, hard from behind, much to her pleasure.

In these few seconds Henry appropriates both the dignity of a male subject and the body of a female subject, taking the latter from her partner and asserting (and inserting) his rights over her—and this is exactly what is intended for the audience: both to see him and to enjoy seeing him, doing. There is no anger. Both Henry's moral ability to simply "see and take" one of his beautiful subjects and his conviction that he is entitled to do this survive moral censure partly in light of his conversation with Brandon preceding: Henry is devastated by the loss of his child and he is also becoming convinced of the dishonesty of his wife—a woman known to the audience to be guilty of exactly the lie of which Henry suspects her. Wyatt has already told Thomas Tallis—and *The Tudors'* audience—in Episode 1:10, "For what it's worth, I did fuck her."

The scene of Henry's liaison with Bess the peasant girl is based on Alison Weir's description (in *The Six Wives of Henry VIII*) of a complaint made in 1535 by a courtier called William Webbe, according to which the king had encountered Webbe and Bess, in the woods, put Bess on his horse, kissed her, and rode away with her.[19] In *The Tudors* the writers distort the relative status of Henry and Webbe—the man portrayed in the series is of a lower social station than a courtier, as is his "sweetheart," thus underscoring the sense, embedded in the scene, that Henry is committing rape—which he essentially is (and was, according to Webbe's complaint). This sense is also underscored by two subsequent references to the scene. The first, in Episode 2.5, is subtle and easy to miss, as the character Webbe is the first to cry, "God Bless you Cardinal Fisher," at the Bishop of Rochester's piteous execution; this is Webbe's only opportunity to push (albeit impotently) against the king's abusive exercise of power. The second comes as part of the series of reminders in the montage leading to Episode 2.6: as Henry looks down at Bess in the replayed scene, we hear Natalie Dormer as Anne Boleyn say, "He can do whatever he wants now"; as we see Henry penetrating Bess, we hear the same voice say, "He has absolute power." This is powerful—both lines come from a scene in which Anne Boleyn expresses terrible fears to her brother, George. With this, *The Tudors* unabashedly links Henry's accumulation of political power to his exercise of sexual dominance—if Henry can do whatever he wants, does it matter whether Bess agrees? As suggested in the frontispiece and poster for *The Tudors'* Season Three—Henry seated on a throne made of men's and women's naked bodies—it is his sexual dominance on which Henry's power rests. This is how it is exercised, what it achieves.[20]

This power—sexual and political—the audience is supposed to adore. It is by our approval of what we know to be his abuse of power that the audience become Henry's collaborators, complicit in approving of male sexual aggression even beyond the king's own commission of it. Bess eagerly leaves with Henry, complicit in her own (and Webbe's) violation. It is useful to compare her reaction in this scene—and the audience's reaction—to another engagement with the common legend of misuse of seigniorial power with which this scene engages, as it is portrayed in the 1995 movie, *Braveheart*. The eager lasciviousness on the face of Webbe's sweetheart as she is taken away by Henry stands in appalling contrast to the devastation on the face of Morrison's bride (Julie Austin) in *Braveheart* as she is taken away by Lord Bottoms. At issue here is the female characters' responses to strangers' power over their bodies—Webbe's sweetheart's libidinousness as opposed Morrison's bride's horror—and then the former's response to the penetration of that power (pleasure in pain), fully displayed for a titillated audience sympathetic to the man doing the penetrating.

The theme of rape legitimized (and appealing) plays again in Episode 4:8, in which Brandon seduces his French prisoner of war, Brigitte Rousselot, played by Selma Brook. Following a battle in which Brigitte's father is injured, Charles takes her prisoner: "[Y]ou're my prisoner now. Perhaps I'll even get a ransom for you." Once Brigitte's father is healthy, Brandon informs him that he can leave if Brigitte promises not to attempt to escape. First arguing, Monsieur Rousselot finally departs, saying to Brandon, "I believe that you are an honorable enemy. I expect that you will treat my precious daughter with honor and respect." Charles answers him, "I give you my word." The old soldier, comforted by Charles' lie, leaves.

In Brigitte's next scene, she asks Charles why he let her father go. He gives a reasonable answer—"He couldn't tell me anything useful about the town's defenses"—to which she replies with a reasonable question: "And I can? Why are you keeping me here?" Charles leaves without speaking. But now, in the next scene, we see a reversal. Brigitte becomes the agent of her own captivity, ultimately exonerating Charles of culpability for what will be the sexual consummation of his prisoner's imprisonment: she wakes a sleeping Charles, whispering, "I proved my promise. I escaped and then came back"; Charles kisses her; Brigitte puts herself under Charles, her breast exposed; she arches her back, he tears her garment; and finally we see *her* hand on *his* backside, pulling him into her. Once again, in a traditional context for rape, the victim desires her sexual conquest.

The audience should see Brigitte's participation in her own appropriation as at best an instance of Stockholm syndrome. Instead, we are taught to approve of her relationship to Charles: in Episode 4:9 he tells her, "You are worth everything ... *Je t'aime*"; he was "dead" but is now "alive again." The audience believes not only that Brigitte is a good mistress to Charles, but that Charles deserves her affection, because we have also by this time witnessed a storyline about Charles's marriage that makes us agree that he both deserves and needs a good woman's love: his marriage to Catherine Brooke, played by Rebekah Wainwright in Episode 2:1. For most of her portrayal—until Wainwright leaves the series—Catherine is played as virtuous and beautiful. When Brandon marries her, she is his seventeen-year-old ward, a fact that amuses both Anthony Knivert (played by Callum Blue) when he meets Catherine and, later, Henry. The king asks, "You married your ward. Why her?" Charles answers, "I love and admire Miss Brooke, and my young son needs a mother." "How old is she?" asks Henry. "Seventeen," answers Charles. Laughing loudly, Henry says, "Some mother. Poor Catherine. You are incapable of fidelity Charles, you always have been." Charles demurs: "This time it's different ... I just feel it. It's not just that she's beautiful. It's a marriage of true souls."

Catherine begins her married life a child, which she remains in Wainwright's portrayal. Her married relationship is not erotic—an example of the series' unwillingness either to depict sex as loving and intimate or to display a woman portrayed as a moral touchstone engaged in intercourse. In the one scene in Episode 2:1, in which Charles and Catherine are seen in their chamber preparing for bed, Catherine undresses behind a net curtain, back turned, as Charles watches. Her distant posterior nudity is visible to both the audience and her husband, but her breasts are never exposed, and when she approaches the bed she shares with Charles, she wears a demure nightdress. The scene perfectly deploys an archetype of the woman as moral touchstone in the dialogue that follows. Charles has visited Catherine of Aragon at Henry's behest, in a scene with no purpose but to set in train a process by which Charles becomes ennobled by exposure to moral women. Quickly following, the scene between Charles and his own Catherine serves to display this. Having donned her nightdress, Catherine comes to bed and asks Charles, "How was the queen?" He answers, "Mmmm. Beautiful. It was like a thing of the other world to watch her courage." After a series of kisses, Catherine then says to him, "I remember when you once told me you might sometimes have to make me feel sad, even if you didn't mean to. Are you really going to make me sad?" He answers, "No, I swear to all that is holy, all things worthy and good, to you I will always be true, never changing."

Charles becomes a better man both by his relationship with his wife and by what he witnesses of the morally righteous Catherine of Aragon. Importantly, both women, as moral touchstones and gatekeepers, operate outside the sexual business of the series, Catherine of Aragon as postmenopausal and Catherine Brooke as eternally childlike: "Are you really going to make me sad?" she asks, childishly; and then—when despite his protestations of eternal fidelity Charles slips (remarkably easily) into an adulterous tryst with a French visitor in Episode 2:5—she tearfully accuses him (before, with the audience, forgiving him), "You did make me sad after all."

Catherine is the series' most clearly moral character. She is pure, virginal at the time of her marriage, and never expresses sexual desire. She is Charles's keeper of morality, and she is this as a child. For Catherine will only reach maturity when she has fallen out of love with Charles in response to his slaughter of women and children after the Pilgrimage of Grace. Having forgiven his adultery, she cannot forgive him this, and so she withdraws her love from Charles and (as played by Wainwright) disappears from the series. Charles is devastated by the loss of her, a changed man, but his sadness at losing her love, together with his own apparent guilt at his actions during and after the Pilgrimage of Grace, serves to redeem him of his sins, both past—his adultery against not just Catherine but also Margaret Tudor, his first wife (in the series)—and future—his now quite flagrant adulterous affair with his prisoner of war.

Charles and Catherine's marriage could easily cause unease to members of *The Tudors*' audience. Not only is Catherine a teenager, she is also Charles's ward, indicating a significant power imbalance in their relationship as he appropriates her to his purpose (as her ward she would be hard pressed to deny him). The series alleviates part of the problematic attached to the relationship by minor but important fictionalizations: Henry Cavill's Charles Brandon is significantly younger than the forty-nine year old Duke of Suffolk who married his ward in 1533 (Cavill was twenty-five in 2008 but played Charles as around thirty—by this point in the series it has been six years since Henry met Anne Boleyn), and Wainwright, at seventeen, is three years older than Catherine Willoughby, who was fourteen years old when she married Suffolk. (The real Catherine was Charles' fourth wife rather than his second and had been betrothed to his ten-year-old son by Mary Tudor prior to marrying him.) However, even despite the assertion of her age as seventeen—presumably with an eye to ages of consent in most American states—Charles's own, Knivert's, and then Henry's laughter over her age is telling; Brandon, previously married to the fully sexually mature Margaret Tudor, is marrying his seventeen-year-old ward, and it is funny.

Catherine's innocent purity begs Charles's paternal affection, and their relationship is enjoyable to observe. However, the story of Brandon's sexual history participates in a fetishizing of virginity embedded in the series' larger arc. It is likely no accident that Catherine as played by Wainwright (a lovely brunette with dramatically winsome features) superficially resembles the Duke of Buckingham's daughter, Anna, played by Anna Brewster in Episodes 1:1 and 1:2. Anna is Brandon's first sexual conquest in the series. When we first see her, Brandon draws Henry's attention to Anna, whom he admires for her "exquisite virginal face." He announces his intention to seduce her, and thus he embarks, spurred on in his determination by his friend Henry's wager of 100 crowns against his success. Securing Anna's admiration at a tournament—he requests that she tie her favor on his extremely phallic lance (complete with provocatively fashioned head)—Brandon easily seduces her. As the two engage in doggie-style sex in Episode 1:1, Anna's outraged father discovers them:

Buckingham: What's this?
Brandon: It's what it looks like ... Your Grace.
Buckingham: You've violated my daughter!
Brandon: No, no—she begged!
Buckingham: You've taken her honor!
Brandon: I swear to you, Your Grace, someone else was there before me.
(Anna Buckingham laughs.)
Buckingham (his sword at Brandon's throat): You son of a Whore.
Brandon: That is true Your Grace.
Buckingham: I should kill you for this ... Get out.

When Buckingham complains to the king of Brandon's seduction of his daughter, Henry refuses to impose any punishment on his friend.

As he tells Henry, Brandon's first attraction to Anna Buckingham is her "exquisite, virginal face"—a face not unlike, in this respect, the character Catherine Brooke's. However, as Catherine's surely is not, Anna's virginal face is revealed a facade, which Brandon quite enjoys reporting to her enraged father: "She begged ... someone was there before me," he assures Buckingham, as Anna laughs in the corner, the camera close on her face. All traces of the "exquisite virginal face" are gone, as is any respect either Brandon or her father might feel for her. Brandon's words here regarding Anna's lack of honor provide an interesting context, in turn, for his later conversation with Henry about women's virginity: "Did any of them not lie about it?" he asks in Episode 2:3, just before Henry abducts the peasant Bess. We can be sure that Catherine did not.

As with the series' other moral touchstones—Catherine of Aragon and to a lesser extent Catherine Parr—Catherine Brandon's identity depends on her retention of sexual purity (as a child bride, she is a virgin; as a bride who remains a child, she thus remains forever a virgin). And yet, first being set up in the series as its principal location of moral goodness, Catherine loses the audience's sympathy exactly because of her moral principles once she realizes that she cannot overcome her horror at Brandon's slaughter of children in the north. Because Charles is himself haunted by what he believes he *had to do* in the north, the audience forgives him and blames Catherine for causing him further pain in her loss (as she moves into this stage she appears pregnant for the first time—but wishes she were not). Finally, Catherine's abandonment of Charles serves to legitimize his relationship with Brigitte—a much younger woman stolen by Brandon from her father, whom he now replaces as her master—especially once Catherine's disapproval of it is set against its support by Charles's son, who only wants his father to be happy. The mature Duchess of Suffolk (whose face we never see)—no longer a young, innocent ingénue—becomes now every man's fantasy of the bitter, morally demanding, emotionally, and sexually withholding wife, who deserves her husband's infidelity.

In the stories of these two liaisons—Henry's with Bess the peasant girl and Brandon's with Brigitte the prisoner of war—we see two obvious contexts for rape become instead scenes of legitimate seduction. In both cases, sympathy for the male protagonists (who are both also adulterers) finds support in the characters' unhappy personal stories: Anne has lied to Henry and Catherine has abandoned Charles. However, both scenes are also significantly affected by characterizations of women informed in turn by developments in post-feminist misogynist discourse during the years between 1995, when *Braveheart* appeared, and 2007, when *The Tudors*' first season appeared—developments that aid *The Tudors*' writers as they seek to implicate female characters in their own objectification: Bess smiles and squeals as Henry penetrates her; Brigitte places herself under Charles and pulls him into her; Anna Buckingham smiles as Brandon says of her "someone else was there before me"; Montague's nameless lady-in-waiting drops her gown for Henry, saying "How like you this?"

Embedded in such characterizations are celebrations not just of female self-objectification but also of a growing rape culture in Western society, resting on two linked assumptions: men are entitled to sexual intercourse and men are biologically incapable of controlling their sexual urges. *The Tudors* promotes both of these assumptions: embracing her father's teaching—"it is natural for a man, when his wife is big with child and not willing to lie with him, to find some temporary consolation elsewhere"— Anne provides her husband with a mistress in Episode 2.4; unlike appears to have been the case historically, even Henry's love for Jane Seymour cannot push Henry into fidelity; Charles is "incapable of fidelity," says his best friend Henry; despite his love for Catherine and his promises of fidelity to her, Charles strays, even while his marriage is at the height of its happiness; in love with Anne Boleyn, Wyatt is, nevertheless, entitled to quench his thirst with Elizabeth Darrell, even if it drives her to suicide. While the model of the man who cannot control himself serves to justify both infidelity and sexual aggression, it also carries (and promotes) another assumption regarding female sexuality, which is that there is no legitimacy in sexually desirable women denying men sex. No means yes.

Elizabeth Darrell's mistake—leading first to her rape and then to her premature death—is her vow of celibacy, a vow which, if honored, would wholly negate the privileges attached in *The Tudors* to hetero-normative masculine power: powerful men are entitled both to sex and to expressing their masculine power in sexual and personal/political aggression. *The Tudors*' expression of this conflation is most artfully realized in its depiction of Henry's relationship with a character wholly invented for the purpose, Lady Ursula Misseldon, played by Charlotte Salt. Lady Misseldon, Jane Seymour's lady-in-waiting, is highly confident as a sexual object. She expects nothing emotional from her liaisons; she is greedy but not ambitious; she is great in bed. She serves in Episodes 3:1–3.5, first, as mistress to Sir Francis Bryan (Alan van Sprang), and then as Henry's mistress during his third marriage (during which there is no reason to believe he actually was unfaithful). Despite her engagement to Sir Robert Tavistock, she sells herself to Bryan in exchange for a necklace. He then pimps her to Henry, sending her to the king's bedside late at night to treat the wound in his leg.[21] As she treats Henry's wound he flinches, and her response, "Hold still," earns his admiration: "You're very brave … braver I think than my captains … and much more beautiful." She smiles: "I trust Your Majesty is more comfortable. … Does your Majesty wish me to stay?" He stares at her. She takes down her hair, removes the robe over her loosely tied nightgown, and the scene fades as she takes Henry's hand and moves toward him on the bed. From this point, she is Henry's mistress: "Noli me tangere," she says to Bryan when he strokes her hair in a later scene; "You cannot touch me, for Caesar's I am."

Lady Misseldon's character exemplifies *The Tudors*' principal female virtue: not sexual chastity, but sexual accessibility. This is very clear in the two scenes featuring her fiancé, Sir Robert Tavistock. Early in Episode 3:3, Lady Misseldon, lying on a bed, gazes into a mirror with one of her breasts exposed, positioned for a portrait (posterior view including the image in the mirror) that Henry has commissioned from Hans Holbein (Peter Gaynor). As Holbein works, into the room comes Tavistock (Danny Seward): "My God, it's true. I didn't believe it!" he cries. As he and Holbein scuffle, he continues, "She's my fiancé!" Holbein throws him into some shelves and Lady Misseldon calmly asks, "Is he alive?"

The scene is comic, as are the encounters that follow, first between Henry and Holbein and then between Henry and Tavistock. First, when Holbein comes to Henry to report that he has assaulted Tavistock, Henry reassures him and instructs him to finish the painting: "I can't wait," he says. Then, with Holbein returned to his work, Tavistock enters the room. Henry rolls his eyes. As Tavistock reports that he found his fiancé "naked, on a bed ... like some concubine," Bryan, also in the room, snorts in amusement. "Naked!" Henry expostulates, "Tsk, tsk." Tavistock requests Holbein's punishment, and Henry goes dark, cowing Tavistock into submission. "If I had seven peasants I could make seven lords," he whispers, close to Tavistock's ear. "But if I had seven lords I could not make one Holbein! Now, tell me truthfully, do you really want me to punish Master Holbein?" Tavistock, now stammering and frightened (like Webbe in Episode 2.3), says, "No, Your Majesty. I ask your Majesty's pardon. I am Your Majesty's humble and obedient servant." Murmuring, "Mmm hmm ... good lad," Henry sends the poor man away.

Tavistock is emasculated in every possible way: his fiancé betrays him with other, more masculine men; a knight, he is unable to defend himself against an artist; he is made to look ridiculous in his nasally voiced protestations to the king, to whom his fiancé actually is a concubine; his fiancé's former lover witnesses and mocks his humiliation. The purpose of the scene is to make Tavistock appear unattractive and ridiculous—thus valorizing the behavior of those humiliating him. The intended impression—that he is foolish for minding other, more masculine men's enjoyment of his fiancé—carries into Lady Misseldon's next significant scene in Episode 3.5. As she walks with the king and Bryan, Henry asks her about her plans (the dead queen's household is dissolved). When she answers that she will move in with her mother, Henry asks about "the young man" to whom she was engaged. Amused, she states that Tavistock has lost interest in her, to which Bryan says, "He is a fool then." When Henry asks if Tavistock is foolish enough to refuse a peerage and property in return for marrying her, the woman bought and paid for with a necklace replies, "I would think less of him if he needed to accept such gifts in order to love me ... I'm settled in my purpose to go home and see what becomes of me." Henry is enchanted: "You could not have said a more admirable thing"; he states (not as a question), "One more night." She nods. He strokes her face, gazing down at her intently, while Bryan stands a few paces away.

This discussion, establishing both her ex-fiancé's foolishness and Lady Misseldon's ongoing accessibility, segues into a reading of the new Six Articles of religion (these articles are not of parliament). As bishops read the articles, Henry malevolently observes the suffering of his evangelical Lord Privy Seal, Thomas Cromwell. Clearly Henry is in the process of abandoning Cromwell, dashing the latter's hope for evangelical reform. The scene shifts quickly between the reading of the articles—the camera either on Henry's face as he watches Cromwell or on Cromwell's as he experiences growing dismay and fear—to Cardinal Pole's performance of a Mass, to Henry with Lady Misseldon. As Bishop Gardiner reads the article affirming the doctrine of transubstantiation, Pole begins the Mass. During the reading of the second article, we see Henry in bed, waiting; Lady Misseldon walks in; Henry tears her nightdress, exposing her breasts, as we hear Pole beginning the Latin service. As the third article, on clerical celibacy, is read, Henry and Lady Misseldon kiss; Henry watches Cromwell; Henry kisses Lady Misseldon's breasts as she instantly begins writhing in ecstasy; Henry turns her over and stares down at her as he tears open his pants, moving into her from behind as they both cry out in delight. The reading of the fourth article, on chastity, accompanies a shift in the lovers' position—Henry is now on top of Ursula, the two of them face-to-face, as Pole chants, "hoc est corpus meum." As we hear the fifth article on private masses, Ursula is now on top of Henry; Pole distributes the wafer. As Pole says, "sanguinus Christi," we hear the article on confession; Cromwell is now utterly defeated, and Henry smiles, watching him, as the terrible punishment for treason is announced against any who defy these articles. Then Henry dips his wick, again, to sign the articles, but first adds his final amendment, the doxology: "For thine is the kingdom, the power and the glory, Amen." This is about him—the man on the throne made of naked bodies. Henry, lost temporarily to his grief over Jane's death, is back— which he has demonstrated in dramatic, erotic fashion by conquests sexual, personal, and political. As he passionately and repeatedly penetrates his mistress, he begins the destruction of his loyal servant, finding and enjoying his power in both. The scenes of his conquest are fully conflated:

the graphic sex scene and Henry's malicious attack on Cromwell are one, and they are satisfying, concluding with Henry lying in bed—alert and ready to move on—his sated, nude mistress resting by his side. We will never see her again—she has served her purpose.

Notes

1. Michael Hirst and Elizabeth Massie, *The Tudors: King Takes Queen* (Gallery Books, 2008).
2. See Susan Brigden, *Thomas Wyatt: The Heart's Forest* (London: Faber and Faber, 2012), 1–17.
3. Michael S. Kimmel, *Manhood in America: A Cultural History*, 2nd ed. (Oxford: Oxford University Press, 2006), 233–236.
4. Jenny Kutner, "Rush Limbaugh's New Definition of Consent: 'No Means Yes If You Know How to Spot It,'" *Salon*, accessed 15 September 2014, http://www.salon.com/2014/09/15/rush_limbaughs_new_definition_of_sexual_consent_no_means_yes_if_you_know_how_to_spot_it/ (visited 1 February 2015). The "No Means Yes" mantra is common on American university campuses: from Yale University, whose Delta Kappa Epsilon chapter was disciplined in 2011 for organizing a chant of "No means Yes"; to Texas Tech University, whose Phi Delta Theta chapter lost its charter in 2014 after posting a banner reading "No means Yes, Yes means Anal"; to Louisiana State University, where "No means Yes, Yes means Anal" was written on the wall of the Kappa Sigma fraternity house in 2014. See Tara Culp-Ressler, "Fraternity Loses Its Charter After Displaying 'No Means Yes' Banner At A Party," Think Progress (8 October 2014), http://thinkprogress.org/health/2014/10/08/3577243/texas-tech-fraternity-banner/ (visited 1 February 2015). Meanwhile, reported rapes on American college campuses have increased by 50 % between 2001 and 2011, according to federal statistics (Valerie Bauerlein and Douglas Belkin, "UVA to Tackle Sexual Assaults After Alleged Gang Rape," *Wall Street Journal* [24 November 2014], http://www.wsj.com/articles/uva-to-tackle-sexual-assaults-after-alleged-gang-rape-1416874964 [visited 1 February 2015]). Such problems are not limited to American universities. See Laura Bates, "Ten Things that Female Students shouldn't have to go through at University," *The Guardian* (online edition, 10 October 2014), http://www.theguardian.com/lifeandstyle/womens-blog/2014/oct/10/10-things-female-students-face-university-misogyny-banter (visited 2 February 2015).
5. Ramona Wray, "The Network King: Re-creating Henry VIII for a Global Television Audience," in Mark Thornton Burnett and Adrian Streete, eds.,

Filming and Performing Renaissance History (Houndmills, Basingstoke: Palgrave Macmillan, 2011), 24; Susan Bordo, *The Creation of Anne Boleyn: A New Look at England's Most Notorious Queen* (New York: Houghton Mifflin Harcourt, 2013), 214–215.

6. Basil Glynn, "The Conquests of Henry VIII: Masculinity, Sex and the National Past in *The Tudors*," in Basil Glynn, James Aston, and Beth Johnson, eds., *Television, Sex and Society: Analyzing Contemporary Representations* (New York and London: Continuum, 2012), 166. Glynn draws on analyses by John Beynon, *Masculinities and Culture* (Buckingham: Open University Press, 2002), 16.
7. Glynn, "Conquests of Henry VIII," 166. Glynn is drawing on Adrienne Rich's terminology in "Compulsory Heterosexuality and Lesbian Existence," *Signs* 5 (4) (1980): 632.
8. Susan B. Douglas, *The Rise of Enlightened Sexism: How Pop Culture Took Us from Girl Power to Girls Gone Wild* (New York: St Martin's Griffin, 2010); Naomi Wolf, *The Beauty Myth: How Images of Beauty are Used Against Women* (New York: William Morrow and Company, 1991).
9. Douglas, *The Rise of Enlightened Sexism*, 9.
10. Ibid., 9–10.
11. Ibid., 13. Douglas is quoting Rosalind Gill, *Gender in the Media* (Cambridge: Polity Press, 2007), 267.
12. Wolf, *The Beauty Myth*, 11–12, 171.
13. Ibid., 10–11.
14. Ibid., 171.
15. Douglas, *The Rise of Enlightened Sexism*, 156.
16. Two unacceptable rapes occur in *The Tudors*. One is George Boleyn's anal rape of his wife on their wedding night in Episode 2:6. Boleyn (Padraic Delaney) is established as gay and in love with Mark Smeaton (David Alpay). Glynn suggests that his rape of his wife serves to allow Boleyn's character an acting out of desire in a series unwilling to depict gay sex; unlike Thomas Tallis (Joe Van Moyland), as Glynn also notes, Boleyn is unable fully to abandon his gayness (Glynn, "Conquests of Henry VIII," 167). The other is Thomas Culpepper's (Torrance Coombs) rape of a farmer's wife in Episode 4:1, preceding the storyline of his love for Catherine Howard. This rape takes place off camera; Culpepper is not a pleasant character, but perhaps as importantly the woman he rapes is plain and middle-aged. This rape, along with Culpepper's subsequent murder of the woman's husband, also serves to increase sympathy for Henry as Culpepper contrives to seduce the king's wife.
17. Bordo, *The Creation of Anne Boleyn*, 202.
18. Glynn, "Conquests of Henry VIII," 169.
19. Alison Weir, *The Six Wives of Henry VIII* (New York: Grove Press, 1991), 274.

20. As Jerome de Groot also notes, the frontispiece/poster for Season Two "Combines Rape Fantasy, Domination, and Unpleasant Associations of Happily Passive Women," "Slashing History: *The Tudors*," in Tatiana C. String and Marcus Bull, eds., *Tudorism: Historical Imagination and the Appropriation of the Sixteenth Century* (Oxford: Oxford University Press, 2011), 251.
21. Soon before this scene, following one of Henry's tantrums about the rebellion in the North, Bryan says to him, "Can I get Your Majesty Anything for Your Pain?" Henry responds, thoughtfully, "Yes I Believe You Can." While not explicit, this scene provides the only platform for Ursula's appearance at Henry's bedside.

CHAPTER 21

Incomplete Prescription: Maladies and Medicine in *The Tudors*

Elizabeth Lane Furdell

Issues of health and well-being factor frequently in Showtime's series about the Tudors or, more correctly, about Henry VIII. As written by Michael Hirst with historical consultation from Justin Pollard, blood, gore, and pestilence dominate several episodes in the four seasons of *The Tudors*, but there are as many sins of omission in the medical narrative as sins of commission. The real Henry—played onscreen by Jonathan Rhys Meyers—performed an active role in establishing a regulated profession of healers, encompassing both elite doctors and barber-surgeons, thereby influencing the course of medicine in the kingdom for generations to come. The king used the services of several university-trained physicians, some of whom figured prominently in his administration, and generally followed their advice. At the same time, the monarch relied on the ancient belief in a "royal touch": to bolster his own authenticity as God's chosen ruler and—like many who worried about sickness incapacitating them and their families—he self-prescribed from a cabinet full of folk medicines.[1]

Thomas Linacre, a physician featured in *The Tudors* (played by Clive Geraghty), enjoyed a strong connection to the dynasty. A scholar of classical languages at Oxford, Linacre obtained his medical education in Padua, among the most prestigious institutions of higher learning in Europe.

E.L. Furdell (✉)
Department of History, University of North Florida, Jacksonville, FL, USA

Appalled by the poor quality of iatric schooling in England, Linacre undertook to restore the classical teachings of Hippocrates and of his interpreter Galen, doctor to Marcus Aurelius. In 1501 Henry VII appointed Linacre to be the tutor and physician of Prince Arthur, and though the prince died not long after, Linacre maintained his standing among elite patients like Erasmus and Thomas More. He became court physician to Henry VIII upon the king's accession in 1509 and began to promote the creation of a professional organization that could police the practice of medicine. In 1512 parliament passed the Medical Act, the first legislative enactment concerned with medical affairs. In order to combat incompetence and fraud among hacks selling bogus cures throughout the realm, the statute required that practitioners within seven miles of the capital who did not hold a university degree from Cambridge or Oxford must pass a compulsory examination by the Bishop of London to be supervised by accredited physicians and surgeons. Outside of the metropolis the bishop of the appropriate diocese would examine all applicants with expert help.[2] Competency testing was important to the king, as he wished to raise medical standards in his domain, but at this stage of his reign he still trusted ecclesiastical authorities in the countryside to administer iatric appraisals.

However, Linacre had not yet achieved his own goal of elevating the quality of English medicine, and—perhaps in response to an outbreak of plague that drove the court from London—he persuaded the king to found the College of Physicians in September 1518, modeling its charter after comparable institutions in Italian cities and abrogating the licensing power of the bishop in the capital. In 1523 the College jurisdiction extended to all of England, although the absence of any enforcement machinery made national control nebulous. The College's Fellows enacted professional decrees and legal enhancements themselves, exempting members from civic responsibilities like serving as constables in order to concentrate on their important patients. They also embraced classical medicine as their exclusive guide to patient care, disdaining less academic approaches to healing. Physicians in Henrician England almost universally subscribed to the humoral theory of wellness, the Galenic teaching that the four humors of the human body—blood, phlegm, yellow bile, and black bile—must be kept in balance for health to be maintained. A surfeit or deficit of any of the humors resulted in illness, so the healer's job was to restore the balance by bleeding and purging or by stipulating a hodgepodge of drugs targeting the humoral imbalance. Moreover, physicians also considered the stars in their medical analyses, melding astrology with zodiacal magic and patient symptoms. For example, an astrologer-physician in *The Tudors* predicts that Anne Boleyn (Natalie Dormer) will give birth to a boy because she craves apples during her pregnancy. Likewise, Jane Seymour (Annabelle Wallis) must be expecting when she eats quail eggs. University-educated doctors like Linacre, schooled in the liberal arts, dealt with the theoretical side of medicine, working out the individualized diagnoses of sick people while leaving the actual treatment of patients to their surgeons and apothecaries. Though Henry VIII enjoyed reasonably good health throughout his youth, his physicians, who regularly examined his urine, stool, and sputum, had him bled and cupped in accordance with the phases of the moon. Linacre became the College's first president and served until his death.[3]

Which brings us back to *The Tudors* and Linacre's part in it. He is on the scene in Episode 1:4, when the king is injured in a joust sometime after the Battle of Pavia (1525), and he is there again later that year when Henry nearly drowns vaulting a ditch while hunting. Consistent with treatment at the time, in the latter vignette physicians bleed the king "to drain away the bile." They use a leather tie and basin, standard equipment in venesection, but they give no indication how many ounces the king should be bled. Linacre is also the doctor on call in Episode 1:7, when sweating sickness swept the land in 1528. William Compton (Kristen Holden-Ried), Henry's Groom of the Stole, got sick from "the sweat." Once again, the cinematic Linacre prescribes bleeding to draw out the toxins, using a sort of hammer and nail to lance the patient's back.[4] Linacre precociously orders that the man's bedding and clothing be burned to avoid contagion but warns that mental disturbances, fear itself, can cause the sweat. Despite his scientific prowess and medical professionalism, fearing contamination, Linacre treats his patients' letters with incense, just to be on the safe side. When Anne Boleyn falls ill from sweating sickness at Hever Castle, the cinematic Henry sends Linacre to minister to her, but in reality he dispatched Dr. William Butts to Anne's bedside.[5] Admirable as this all may seem, in reality Linacre's service to Henry did not extend to these incidents, any of them, as the physician had died four years earlier. The king makes his own medications for the sweat and gives them to his friends; he especially promotes an infusion of marigold, sorrel, ivory scrapings, and sugar, mixed with linseed vinegar. Henry also prays and exercises since (the dead) Linacre told him that natural sweat blocks the pernicious version of the disease.

But Henry did not end his medical reformation with the College of Physicians. He also chartered the Company of Barber-Surgeons in 1540.

Surgeons did the "hands on" work of healing: they set bones, pulled teeth, administered enemas, treated syphilis, and performed other noxious tasks, while apothecaries made the prescriptions ordered by the physicians. Medical jurisdictions and tasks should be scrupulously discrete, at least as far as the College Fellows contended. A Barbers' Company including surgeons preceded *The Tudors* by three generations, but barbers were more numerous and senior to the surgeons in their civic guild. Nonetheless, surgeons acquired sophisticated new techniques on the countless battlefields of the fifteenth century, raising their expert reputations and value to the crown. Just as Henry let Linacre guide him in establishing the College of Physicians, so too was he led to further attentiveness to the medical profession by an outstanding surgical practitioner and visionary, Thomas Vicary. Sergeant surgeon to the king from 1530 but unnamed in *The Tudors*, Vicary may have been among the group of barber-surgeons (among them actor Dennis Quilligan) summoned to lance the king's leg ulcer in Episode 3:6, but it is Thomas Cromwell (James Frain), the king's secretary, who is shown preparing "bills for parliament on the medical profession" in Episode 3:8. The Act of Union in 1540 created a super guild, the Barber-Surgeons, with full parliamentary authority and clearly defined roles for each member occupation. Surgeons could not shave or barber clients and barbers (despite those red and white poles) could no longer bleed or operate on patients; there could be no more blending of their separate callings. Moreover, to encourage surgical education, each year the Company was allocated the bodies of four executed felons to dissect.[6] Vicary himself benefitted from this privilege, publishing in 1548 the first English anatomy printed in the vernacular. Hans Holbein (Peter Gaynor) executed a famous if fanciful cartoon of the granting of the new Barber-Surgeons' Company charter with the king handing the document to Vicary; a grateful Henry also bestowed on Vicary the lease to Boxley Abbey in Kent along with the right to its tithes.

Two years after the chartering of the Company, motivated by concern for the poor, the king required that a new statute protect traditional male and female healers, who ministered to their neighbors out of charity, from harassment by mercenary medicos. Henry himself sponsored altruistic medicine, and in August 1543 he sent the Lord Mayor of London a remedy against plague to be disseminated to the people for their protection. This recipe, preserved in the Corporation of London Record Office, calls for herbs, elder and briar leaves, and ginger, mixed with white wine and drunk for nine days.[7] *The Tudors* often shows scenes of the king taking medicines from his personal pharmaceutical cabinet and dosing himself or others at court. By his creation of a college for the physicians and a united company of barber-surgeons, as well as through his own amateur pharmacy, Henry demonstrated serious royal patronage and interest in medicine.

Apothecaries constituted the third leg of the official medical pyramid in Tudor times. Tasked with making the medicaments prescribed by physicians, apothecaries initially resided within the company of grocers, spicers, and pepperers. Henry appointed Richard Babham his apothecary for life and then outlived both Babham and his successor, Cuthbert Blackeden. Babham supplied the entire court with medicines for which he received bouche, an allowance of food and drink at court, and a quarterly allotment. Blackeden got about £60 annually for medical materials and extra money for perfuming gloves, gowns, and other clothes. Henry's last and best known apothecary, Thomas Alsop, made various medicaments for the king, potpourri, and gilt reading glasses. Alsop was rewarded handsomely for his service and benefitted from the dissolution of the monasteries, buying several properties in London, Deptford, and Greenwich.[8] The Society of Apothecaries evolved from the Grocers' Company in 1617, having sought autonomy for many years and continued for a century more to challenge the monopoly held by the College of Physicians to practice medicine in London.

Besides the jurisdictional split among medical practitioners in Tudor times, differences arose about medical philosophy. Although new theories developed on the continent and were taught in foreign universities during the reign of Henry VIII, especially the chemical medicine of the sixteenth-century Swiss maverick Paracelsus, only a few English doctors, mainly those educated abroad, espoused them. Between the 1520s and his death in 1541, Paracelsus argued directly against Galenism with its humoral imbalances, instead insisting that disease came from outside the body as a material entity that could be made apparent and detectable. He advocated chemical experimentation to find specific cures for specific ailments and became famous for his reliance on urine testing ("water-casting") of patients. By attacking classical medicine, Paracelsus undercut the authority of Galenic doctors, and although the College remained steadfastly traditional throughout the Tudor era, he is credited with encouraging "the subject classes of the medical profession, the surgeons and apothecaries, to claim rights above their station."[9] Additionally, the growing availability of medical texts in the vernacular further affected the coming jurisdictional struggle within the profession. *The Tudors* makes a slight allusion to this phenomenon in Episode 4:3, when Catherine Parr (Joely Richardson) reads a book on midwifery by Richard Jonas, but many English-language tomes promulgating cures for ailments were printed in Henry's reign. One early sixteenth-century medico, the king's nurse-surgeon, William Bullein, published a therapeutic herbal and a book on the sweating sickness epidemic of 1517. Andrew Boorde, an irregular or unlicensed doctor to the king and a friend of Thomas Cromwell, penned several works of self-help remedies and preventives in the 1540s, some with woodcut illustrations. Ever more vernacular texts undercut the exclusive power of the elite physicians.[10]

Viewers see some of the king's interest in curatives beyond his fascination with special remedies when he performs the "royal touch." In Episode 4:3, Henry lays hands on the sick poor who cluster in pathetic groups outside his castles. He also presents them with gold coins called "angels" and commands the ill to be healed. The royal touch gave authenticity to monarchs and buttressed their claim to have been chosen by God to lead their people. The healing power of English sovereigns was believed to be particularly efficacious for scrofula, tubercular lesions in the neck. Henry and his successors used faith in this capacity to make their subjects well for their own benefit, even if it meant being in close proximity to the suppurating sores of the sick. Both Mary I and Elizabeth I touched, clearly to reinforce their legitimacy as queens, but usually resorted to blessing the gold "angels" and having them distributed, rather than laying hands on tubercular lesions. Henry, something of a hypochondriac himself, nonetheless, tries to heal his friend Charles Brandon (Henry Cavill) in Episode 4:10 with the royal touch; Brandon dies anyway.[11]

The Tudors is filled with dreadful disease and contagion, none more frightening than the sweating sickness, a mysterious infection associated with the royal house itself. Beginning in 1485, the sweat was thought by many to be God's punishment for Henry VII usurping the throne from Richard III. Others blamed foul air or general sinfulness. An epidemic raged through London and its environs in 1517, striking its victims with "a great sweating and stinking, with redness of the face and of all the body, and a continual thirst with a great heat and headache."[12] The sickness terrified with its swiftness; a pimply rash led to collapse and death, often with no time to make a will or call a priest. Tens of thousands succumbed that summer as survivors whispered prayers and downed preventive medicines. Henry sent his own recipe to friends and relatives, but despite his concoctions the king's household did not escape contamination. After several secretaries and pages perished, Henry fled to the countryside, stopping at several palaces, each further away from the capital. In the spring of 1518 the scourge resurfaced, even more virulent than before. Those who lived in houses visited by the disease had to carry white rods to announce their proximity to infection. Epidemics of the sweat occurred at least five times between 1485 and 1551, after which the malady seems to have mutated and disappeared.

So what was sweating sickness? The disease continues to be one of the great puzzles of historical epidemiology because no modern malaise corresponds exactly to its principal clinical features. Contemporaries recognized that the disease differed from plague and malaria and that it did not affect infants much at all. They noticed that it struck the rich more often than poorer populations, which seemed to rule out the suggestion from the continent that a lack of English cleanliness alone caused the contagion. They did believe the disease was communicable, and *The Tudors* depicts that conviction when in Episode 1:4 Linacre orders the linen of the dead William Compton burned to avoid spreading the scourge further and Compton buried immediately. Moreover, when servants steal some of Compton's furniture, they die, too. The king, self-dosing with pills and plasters, warns Charles Brandon and Anthony Knivert (Callum Blue) about the sweat and gives them cough medications and foul-tasting infusions against the sickness. Significantly, no medical commentary from the Tudor era mentions scabs on victims, a characteristic of tick and lice-borne diseases. Perhaps the sweat was an unknown hantavirus, and although these are not usually spread human to human, they can be. Among the more popular recent theories is that hantavirus pulmonary syndrome, like the 1993 outbreak in the American southwest, arose from dusty rodent droppings; maybe hygiene factored in this terrifying mystery after all.[13]

Even more frightening than the sweat, bubonic plague troubled the kingdom throughout the Tudor century and beyond. Outbreaks of plague were recorded in 1498, 1509–1510, throughout the 1530s, and 1543. The Showtime series does not cover the 1531 outbreak of plague in England, but its virulence forced the king to take refuge in Hampton Court in November of that year when an estimated 300–400 citizens succumbed to the disease. Active again the following autumn, the malady struck London's Fleet Street and the Temple particularly hard, causing real fear and panic among parishioners there. Likewise, plague was prevalent in Kent and Oxford. Carried and spread by infected black rat fleas, bubonic plague manifested itself with hemorrhaging lymph nodes or buboes as well as fever, headache, chills, and weakness. The bacteria multiply and result in death to 80 % of those infected. Reports throughout the 1530s indicate the ebb and flow of an epidemic; however, not all accounts make clear that it was bubonic plague that struck the kingdom and not some other epidemic. *The Tudors* does represent the plague in 1536, when its recurrence postponed the coronation of Jane Seymour as Henry's third queen. However, the historical Duke of Norfolk, busy suppressing the Northern Rebellion, thought the weather was too cold for plague fleas to survive and presumed another epidemic fever was present (Henry Czerny, the onscreen Norfolk, disappears at the end of Season One).[14]

Malaria or ague bedeviled Englishmen of all ranks. A febrile disease, it arises as a reaction of the body to invasion by parasitic protozoa of the genus *Plasmodium* brought in the bite of an infected female insect and exhibits a circular transmission as waves of parasites are released in fever paroxysms. These organisms can remain entrenched in the liver and within eight to ten months reenter the bloodstream, beginning the febrific cycle anew. Two species of parasites infect humans: untreated *plasmodiumvivax* has a lower rate of mortality (5%) than *plasmodium falciparum* (25%), but displays the classic relapse pattern. Besides high body temperature, secondary symptoms include headache, chills, sweating, loss of appetite, nausea, various pains, and respiratory weakness.[15] Though usually associated with more tropical climates, malarial fevers frequently occur in colder zones due to the prolonged incubation period of the disease. The southeast of England persisted as a malarial trouble spot throughout the early modern period despite some improvements in public sanitation and the drainage of swamps. Given such environmental conditions as proximity to shallow lagoons in the marshy ground upstream from the city's western perimeter, ague figured constantly in London life. Summer and autumnal infections caused outbreaks each spring, and the resultant fever, or ague as contemporaries called it, could be debilitating, recurrent, and even fatal.[16] Tudor doctors categorized fevers according to their seasonal outbreaks: a quotidian fever revealed itself in winter; a tertian appeared in spring or summer; and quartan arrived in the fall. They tried to determine the sort of ague from which their patients suffered by timing febrile recurrence, by gauging the color of the patient's skin, and by administering special remedies. Relying largely on Galenic theory, for quotidian agues they recommended vomits and plasters; for tertian, emetics, diaphoretics, and topicals to the wrist and feet; and for quartan, all of the above plus splenetics.[17] One preferred ague cure in Henrician times, taken twice daily, was a decoction of snails, boiled in milk sweetened with sugar and candied eryngo, to which cut-up earthworms were added. Many ague prescriptions called for spiders' webs or pellets of opium poppy juice.[18] In *The Tudors*, Episode 4:4, Henry worries about a "tertiary fever" that Prince Edward manifests.

War is hell in so many ways, not the least of which arises from the diseases it inflicts on participants and civilians alike. During the English attack on Boulogne in 1544, as depicted in *The Tudors*, venereal disease ("the pox"), blamed on French whores, lays the king's soldiers low.[19] Sufferers experienced abscesses and sores as well as unbearable nocturnal bone pains. Syphilis was often fatal in Tudor times, more deadly than today, with hideous disfigurement rewarding those who outlasted its ravages. Treatment with ingested mercury, an initial therapy, killed many who might have survived, and led to mercury inunctions, rubbed on several times a day, and suffumigations of the metal in hot rooms to produce sweat. But even these "lighter" applications caused neuropathy, kidney failure, mouth sores, and tooth loss in victims. Connecting the pox with sexual activity subsequently led Henrician authorities to close the brothels and communal bathhouses of London in 1546. And in that cinematic camp at Boulogne the "bloody flux," or dysentery as the king refers to it, kills 2000 and sickens another 3000 troops. The king's "master-surgeon" reports to his majesty that the cause of the flux is unknown and that there is no way to cure it, but in reality medical recommendations did exist. A Doctor Hector's recipe for dysenteric flux included a dram of opium dissolved in honey, sprinkled on a clean cloth and placed upon the cleansed penis. Inducing sleep, according to claim, it stills the flux.[20]

As Henry VIII's reign came to a close, the king suffered from a variety of painful ailments, none more problematic than the recurrent ulcers on his leg. Although in *The Tudors* Henry insists that he could find his own remedies for the infected injury, surgeons lance the excruciating wound but to no avail. In Episode 3:7, Henry's fourth wife, Anne of Cleves (Joss Stone), complains that the king's putrid leg stinks, oozing pus and blood. Doctors later in the episode want to drain the ulcer again and royal doctor William Butts (uncredited as such in the cast) informs Catherine Parr that the king's ulcer has burst. Butts and others would have prescribed for the ulcer a decoction of guaiacum, made from the bark of an ornamental evergreen, which appeared in the king's medical expenses. Some modern historians attribute the persistence of Henry's leg wound to chronic osteomyelitis, brought on by his jousting accident in 1536 and exacerbated by obesity, which would account for the rotting condition of the leg bone.

Much has been written about Henry's obsession with having a legitimate male heir and with the changes in the king's body and temperament over time. Diagnostic suggestions have included type II diabetes, scurvy, syphilis, hypothyroidism, and Huntington's disease. One recent explanation for the frequent miscarriages borne by his first two queens centers on blood group incompatibility of the Kell antigen. Infertility is not the result of a Kell-positive father and a Kell-negative mother, but fetal mortality is. Additionally, if the king also suffered from McLeod syndrome, a genetic disorder specific to the Kell group, his transformation from an athletic man to one with massive weight problems exacerbated his leg ailments.[21] In his later years, weighing nearly 400 pounds, Henry had to be carried about on a litter, unlike the star of *The Tudors*, who remains relatively slight and mobile to the end. The king's obsession with an heir inevitably raises questions about obstetrics and gynecology in the sixteenth century. Miscarriages were not uncommon, breastfeeding among the upper classes was deemed inappropriate when wetnurses were available, caesarian sections and childbed fever were fatal. Midwives, the only medicos who attended births in Tudor times, did not wash their hands for deliveries, thereby spreading germs to mothers. In Episode 3:4, when Jane Seymour experiences a prolonged birthing, the palace doctors get out their scalpels while the king mulls over the precedence of a living mother or a living child. Jane's son lived, but she did not. When Jane tells Henry that she has childbed fever, he replies that his mother succumbed to the same affliction.

Henry died in January 1547 to be succeeded by his nine-year-old son Edward VI, who in turn was followed to the throne by his older half-sisters Mary I and Elizabeth I, all progeny of the man who feared leaving his realm without an heir. The royal apothecary, Thomas Alsop, made perfumes and potpourri for the king's coffin and funeral. He was left 100 marks in the king's will to which he was a subscribing witness. Like most of the iatric personnel who attended Henry in his final years, Alsop continued his services to the crown under the Tudors. So, too, can one find continuity in medical theories and practices throughout the rest of the tumultuous sixteenth century.

NOTES

1. Excellent biographies of Henry VIII include J. J. Scarisbrick, *Henry VIII* (Berkeley: University of California Press, 1970); Lacey Baldwin Smith, *Henry VIII: The Mask of Royalty* (Chicago: Academy Publications, 2005); David Starkey, *The Reign of Henry VIII* (London: Vintage, 2002) and *Henry: Virtuous Prince* (Harper, 2009). See also the exhibition catalog for the 500th anniversary of Henry's accession, Vivat Rex! by Arthur Schwartz, John Guy, Dale Hoak, et al., published by the Grolier Club of London, 2009. Justin Pollard, the historical consultant for the series, has worked on a number of feature films and television programs.
2. George Clark, *A History of the Royal College of Physicians of London*, 2 vols. (Oxford: Clarendon Press, 1964), 1: 54–55. For the foundation of the College of Physicians and the kerfuffle that followed, see Harold Cook, *The Decline of the Old Medical Regime in Stuart London* (Ithaca: Cornell University Press, 1990) and Margaret Pelling, *Medical Conflicts in Early Modern London* (Oxford: Clarendon Press, 2003). To learn more about popular remedies, see Louise Hill Curth, *English Almanacs, Astrology and Popular Medicine 1550–1700* (Manchester: Manchester University Press, 2007).
3. He died in 1524. For more on Linacre and his impact, see Francis Maddison, Margaret Pelling, and Charles Webster, *Essays on the Life and Work of Thomas Linacre* (Oxford: Clarendon Press, 1977). No other early royal physician for Henry VIII is acknowledged in the series script, although other well-known doctors figured prominently in the king's life. John Chambre, for instance, cared for Anne Boleyn in her confinement and delivery of Princess Elizabeth; presided over the disastrous labor of Henry's third wife, Jane Seymour; and attested to the non-consummation bulletin prepared for the king's divorce from wife number four, Anne of Cleves.Jack Dewhurst, *Royal Confinements: A Gynaecological History of Britain's Royal Family* (New York: St. Martin's Press, 1980), 7. For more on Henry VIII's physicians, see Elizabeth Lane Furdell, *The Royal Doctors: Medical Personnel at the Tudor and Stuart Courts* (Rochester: University of Rochester Press, 2001), 17–43.
4. Compton did die of the sweat in 1528, but the series does not always get the cause of death right; for instance, Cardinal Thomas Wolsey (Sam Neill) did not commit suicide and reformer Simon Fish did not die at the stake but of plague.
5. In reality the king dispatched William Butts, the only Henrician royal doctor to be knighted, to Anne's bedside and paid him £100 annually after that, Furdell, *Royal Doctors*, 26–27.
6. Two separate corporations were established in 1745. For more on the guild, see R. Theodore Beck, *The Cutting Edge: The Early History of the*

Surgeons of London (London: Lund Humphries 1974) and Cecil Wall, *History of the Surgeons' Company* (London: Oxford University Press, 1937).
7. Blaxland Stubbs, "Royal Recipes for Plasters, Ointments and Other Medicaments,"*Chemist and Druggist* 114 (1931): 794.
8. Furdell, *Royal Doctors*, 36–37.
9. Hugh Trevor Roper, *Renaissance Essays* (Chicago: University of Chicago Press, 1985), 159. Though some College Fellows flirted with the New Medicine in the 1580s, English Paracelsianism reached its height after 1650.
10. See William Bullein, *Bulwark of Defense Against All Sicknes, Soreness and Wounds* (London: John Kyngston, 1579); Andrew Boorde, *Introduction and Dyetary*, ed. F.J. Furnivall (London: Trubner, 1870). For more on the connection between medicine and publishing, see Elizabeth Lane Furdell, *Publishing and Medicine in Early Modern England* (Rochester: University of Rochester Press, 2003) and *Textual Healing: Essays on Medieval and Early Modern Medicine* (Leiden: Brill, 2005),119–194.
11. For more on monarchical healing, see Marc Bloch, *The Royal Touch* (London: Routledge, 1973).
12. John Caius, quoted in Carolly Erickson, *Bloody Mary* (Garden City, NY: Doubleday, 1978), 24.
13. Jon Arrizabalaga, "Problematizing Retrospective Diagnosis in the History of Disease,"*Asclepio* 54 (2002): 62–67. See also Eric Bridson, "The English Sweate,"*British Journal of Biomedical Science* 58 (2001): 1–6. Cases of human transmission of Hantavirus pulmonary syndrome have been proven for the Andes virus in 1995.
14. J.F.D. Shrewsbury, *A History of Bubonic Plague in the British Isles* (London: Cambridge University Press, 1970), 168–171. See also Paul Slack, *The Impact of Plague in Tudor and Stuart England* (Oxford: Oxford University Press, 1991). Pneumonic plague and septicemic plague, even more lethal forms, affect the lungs and blood.
15. Darrett B. Rutman and Anita Rutman, "Of Agues and Fevers," in *The Biological Consequences of European Expansion, 1450–1800* (Burlington, VT: Ashgate, 1997), 205–208. Of course, malaria remains a scourge into our own times. Within malarial species there are still an unknown number of strains, complicating treatment.
16. L.W. Hackett, *Malaria in Europe* (London: 1937), 31, 88, 161. See also Mary Dobson, "Marsh Fever," *Journal of Historical Geography* 6 (1980): 357–389. Dale C. Smith separates ague into three classes of fevers: continued, periodic, and eruptive. He has further subdivided periodic fevers into intermittent, remittent, and malignant types. Intermittent fevers rarely killed in any of their forms, but remittent fevers were much more severe, with higher levels of fatality than simple ague. Malignant fevers, however,

were fiercest, registering many deaths following delirium and coma. See Dale C. Smith, "Quinine and Fever," *Journal of the History of Medicine* 31 (1976): 344–345.

17. Robert Talbor, *Pyretologia: A Rational Account of the Causes and Cures of Agues* (London: R. Clavel, 1672), 27. Talbor enjoyed a monopoly in England, granted by Charles II, of a New World cure for recurrent fevers. Called Jesuits' Bark or cinchona, the material did work to mitigate the worst symptoms of malaria.
18. For some antimalarial recipes, see W.S.C. Copeman, *Doctors and Disease in Tudor Times* (London: Dawson's, 1960), 132.
19. Kevin Siena, *Venereal Disease, Hospitals and the Urban Poor* (Rochester, NY: University of Rochester Press, 2004). The standard cure in Tudor times for syphilis was a six-week regimen of applied mercury, but none of Henry's doctors record treating the king with mercury. However, doctors also used guaiacum, which does appear in his medical expenses, for venereal disease. See also John Frith, *JMVH* 20 (4) (2012): 49–58 and Henry Ansgar Kelly, "Bishop, Prioress and Bawd in the Stews of Southwark," *Speculum* 75 (2) (2000): 342–388.
20. Bodleian Library, MS Ashmole 1441, 357.
21. Catrina Banks Whitley and Kyra Kramer, "A New Explanation for the Reproductive Woes and Midlife Decline of Henry VIII," *Historical Journal* 53 (2010): 827.

INDEX

A
Adams, John (d. 1546) heretic, 243
Adams, Jonathan (b. 1931) actor:
  Henry VIII in *It Could Happen to You* (1977), 53
Agincourt, Battle of (1415), 29, 187, 251
Agony, film (1981), 53
Agricola, Rodolphus (1443–85) humanist, 249
Ahnert, Ruth (n.a.) historian, 201
Alberti, Leon Battista (1404–72) humanist, 139
  On the Family (c. 1432 and after), 139
Alçega, Juan de (fl. 1580s) tailor, 296
Allington Castle, Kent, 159
Alpay, David (b. 1980) actor: Mark Smeaton, 147, 273, 327
Alsop, Thomas (d. 1558) apothecary, 333, 338
Altazin, Keith (n.a.) historian, v, xi, 17, 223–34

Ambassador, 4, 11, 29, 34, 39, 43, 47, 65, 67, 80, 99, 100–02, 120, 129, 143–44, 146, 157–59, 161, 200–01, 212, 215, 224, 226, 255, 274, 298, 301
Embassy, 46, 107, 142, 158, 161, 163
Envoy, 34, 39–40, 129, 160, 270–71
Amiel, Jon (b. 1948) director, 25
Ampudia, Pascal de (1442–1512) friar, 61
Anderson, Maxwell (1888–1959) playwright, 31, 53, 61, 85, *see also Anne of the Thousand Days*
Anglican Church. *See* Church of England
Anglo-French relations, 32, 47, 129, 163
Anglo-Imperial relations, 34, 39, 47, 158, 270, 271
Anna Bolena, opera (1830), 54
Anna Boleyn, film (1920), 30, 73, 85
Anna Karenina, film (2012), 305

© The Editor(s) (if applicable) and The Author(s) 2016
W.B. Robison (ed.), *History, Fiction, and The Tudors*,
Queenship and Power, DOI 10.1057/978-1-137-43883-6

Anne Boleyn, film (1911), 52, 73
Anne Boleyn, film (1912), 52, 73
Anne de Boleyn, film (1913), 52, 73
Anne of Cleves (1515–57) Queen of England and fourth wife of Henry VIII [Joss Stone], 4, 6, 10, 21–2, 45, 51–2, 54, 97, 100–04, 110, 119, 122–23, 158, 259, 276–77, 288, 296, 301, 337, 339
Anne of Lavenne, potential bride (n.a.), 43
Anne of the Thousand Days, play (1948), 31, 53, film (1969), 9, 31, 53, 59–62, 71, 80, 84–5, 185, 191, *see also* Anderson, Maxwell
  Film (1969), 9, 31, 53, 59–62, 71, 80, 84–5, 185, 191
Anne of York (1475–1511) daughter of Edward IV, 129
Antiquaries, Society of, 283
Anwar, Gabrielle (b.1970) actress: Margaret Tudor, 33, 130–31
Aquitaine, France, 47
Ardres, France, 47, 267
Aristotle (384–322 BC) Greek philosopher, 180
Armbruster, Caroline (n.a.) historian, v, xi, 16, 209–22
Armesto, Sebastian (b. 1982) actor: Charles V, 5, 14, 60
Army, 17, 29, 33, 48, 65
  Commander, 47, 164
  Marshal of, 47–8
  Soldiers, 23, 48, 147, 261, 318, 337
  Troops, 65, 160, 163–64, 261, 337
Art, 6, 20, 30–1, 100, 186, 190, 252, 268, 281–92, 313, 324
  and Clothing 281–206
  and the Field of the Cloth of Gold, 143, 183, 186, 188, 267–70, 272

Architecture, 186, 282, 287
Cartoons, 293, 332
Drawings, 232, 281, 287
Frescoes, 285
Miniatures, 283, 285, 305
Murals, 20–1, 32, 49, 190, 204, 288–89
Painting, 6, 20–1, 28, 32, 43, 49, 68, 82, 100, 134, 136, 186, 190, 205, 281–92, 324
Portraiture, 6, 20–1, 28, 32, 34–5, 43, 49, 54, 71, 98, 100, 103, 190, 281–92, 293, 299–300, 324
Tapestry, 281
Art and Clothing, 281–306
Arthur, Prince of Wales (1486–1502) brother of Henry VIII, 9, 62–3, 66, 68, 162, 282, 330
Arts and Field of the Cloth of Gold, 143, 183, 186, 188, 267–70, 272
Arundel Castle, Sussex, 306
Arundell, Sir Thomas (c. 1502–1552) courtier, 112
Ascham, Roger (1515–68) humanist and teacher, 108, 110
Ashton–Griffiths, Roger (b. 1957) actor: John Hutton, 43
Aske, Robert (1500–1537) rebel [Gerald McSorley], 17, 41, 204, 216–17, 228–30, 241, 257, 299
Askew, Anne (1521–46) martyr [Emma Stansfield], 6, 16, 47, 108, 218, 243–44
Audley, Sir Thomas (1487/8–1544) courtier, 46
Austen, Jane (1775–1817) novelist, 189
Austin, Julie (n.a.) actress: Mrs. Morrison in *Braveheart* (1995), 318

B

Babham, Richard (d. 1527) apothecary, 333
Bale, John (1495–1563) author, 37, 243
  King John, play (1538), 37
Bana, Eric (b. 1968) actor: Henry VIII in *The Other Boleyn Girl* (2008), 31
Barlow, William, Bishop of Chichester (d. 1568), 9
Barron, Keith (b. 1934) actor: Henry VIII in *God's Outlaw* (1986), 53
Bates, Alan (1934–2003) actor: Henry VIII in *The Prince and the Pauper* (2000), 53
Beard, Richard (fl. 1540) courtier [Wesley Beard], 43–4, 100, 103
Beaufort, Margaret, Countess of Richmond and Derby (1443–1509) mother of Henry VII, 252
Beaulieu Palace, Essex, 186
Beauty and the Beast: Masques, television show (1987), 53
Becket, St. Thomas (c. 1119–70), Archbishop of Canterbury Shrine of, 104
Beddington, Surrey, 100
Bede, The Venerable (673/4–735) historian, 49, 278
Belenian, Nicholas (d. 1546) heretic, 243
Bellafante, Ginia (b. 1965) critic, 7, 170–72
Bend It Like Beckham, film (2002), 28
Bergin, Joan (n.a.) costumer, 21, 28, 298, 303
Bernard, George (n.a.) historian, 86, 91
Beroard, Jean–David (n.a.) actor: Lord Talleyrand, 42

Betteridge, Thomas (n.a.) literary scholar, v, xi, 15, 169–70, 195–208
Bewitched: 'How Not to Lose Your Head to Henry VIII,' television episode (1971), 53
Beynon, John (n.a.) literary scholar, 12, 327
Bible, 9, 37, 81, 86–8, 108, 210, 213, 215, 253
  Gospel, 108, 109
  Leviticus, 63
  New Testament, 87, 110
  Psalms, 225
  Psalter, 108
  Scripture, 9, 81, 211
Bill, William (d. 1561) Dean of Westminster, 9
Blackeden, Cuthbert (d. 1540) apothecary, 333
Blackfriars, *see* London
Blessed, Brian (b. 1936) actor: Henry VIII in *The Complete and Utter History of Everything* (1999) Henry VIII in *Henry 8.0* (2009), 53, 54
Bletchingley, Surrey, 102–03
Bloom, Claire (b. 1931) actress: Catherine of Aragon in Shakespeare's *Henry VIII* (1979), 61
Blount, Elizabeth 'Bessie' (c. 1500–1539/41) royal mistress, 5, 11, 32, 34, 66, 116, 120, 128–29, 133, 190, 277, 315
Blount, William, 4th Baron Montjoy (c. 1478–1534) courtier, 252
Blue, Callum (b. 1977) actor: Anthony Knivert, 154, 225, 319, 335
Bluteau, Lothaire (b.1957) actor: Charles de Marillac, 47

Boleyn, Anne, Marquess of Pembroke (c. 1500–1536) Queen of England and second wife of Henry VIII [Natalie Dormer], 4–6, 8–10, 12–13, 15, 17–20, 24, 27–8, 30–1, 34–40, 49–50, 52, 53, 59–71, 77–92, 98–100, 116–18, 121–25, 130, 132, 134–35, 140–46, 153, 155–58, 160, 163, 168, 172, 184–85, 187, 191, 196–97, 200–03, 205–06, 212, 214–15, 219, 223, 225–28, 232, 241, 252–59, 262, 263, 270–75, 285–86, 288, 296, 298, 302, 304, 309–10, 312, 316–17, 320, 322–23, 331, 339

Boleyn, Elizabeth, Countess of Wiltshire and Ormond (née Howard d. 1538) wife of Thomas Boleyn and mother of Queen Anne, 92

Boleyn, George, Viscount Rochford (c. 1504–36), brother of Queen Anne [Padraic Delaney], 12, 36–9, 141, 144–47, 151, 255, 273, 275, 283, 317, 327

Boleyn, Jane, Viscountess Rochford (née Parker, d. 1542) wife of George Boleyn [Joanne King], 38, 46, 49, 104–07, 144

Boleyn, Mary (later Carey, Stafford, c. 1499–1543) royal mistress and sister of Queen Anne [Perdita Weeks], 11, 33–4, 65–6, 134, 190, 268

Boleyn, Thomas, Earl of Wiltshire and Ormond (1476/7–1539) father of Queen Anne [Nick Dunning], 4, 12, 29, 33, 36–8, 69–70, 132, 142–44, 146, 213, 224–25, 255, 272, 274–75

Bolger, Sarah (b. 1991) actress: Princess Mary, 10, 60, 99, 117, 215, 296, 304

Bolt, Robert (1924–95) playwright, 31, 53, 60, 73, 77–8, 92, *see also Man for All Seasons, A*

Bonner, Edmund (d. 1569) Bishop of London, 158–59, 276

Bonnivet, Bishop, fictional prelate [Barry McGovern], 172, 220

Book Revue, cartoon (1946), 52

Books of Hours, 210

Boorde, Andrew (c. 1490–1549) physician, 334

Border Warfare, film (1990), 53

Bordo, Susan (b. 1947) philosopher, v, xi, 9, 70, 77–96, 312, 314

Borough, Sir Edward (c. 1508–33) first husband of Catherine Parr, 109

Bos, Monique Rood (n.a.) actress: Catherine of Aragon in *H VIII: The Male Heir* (2015), 74

Bosworth, Battle of (1485), 140, 155, 162

Bottoms, Lord, fictional character in *Braveheart* [Rupert Vansittart], 318

Boulogne, Siege of (1544), 6, 23, 29, 48, 65, 110, 164, 181, 187, 258, 337

Bourchier, Arthur (1836–1927) actor: Henry VIII in *Henry VIII* (1911), 52

Bowes, Robert (c. 1492–1555) lawyer, 229

Boxley Abbey, Kent, 332

Bradley, David (b. 1942) actor: Will Somers, 6

Brandon, Catherine (née Willoughby, 1519–80) wife of Charles Brandon, 163, 320, 321

Brandon, Charles 3rd Duke of Suffolk (1537/8–1551) son of 1st Duke [David Browne for unnamed son], 164

Brandon, Charles, 1st Duke of Suffolk
(c. 1484–1545) courtier
[Henry Cavill], 4–7, 11, 13,
16–17, 29, 33, 36, 38–9, 41–2,
44–9, 69–71, 97–8, 101, 105,
130–33, 140–41, 143, 146,
149, 154, 157, 161–65,
184–85, 187–88, 198–99, 205,
224, 228–32, 237, 243, 260,
269, 275, 287, 298, 300–01,
314, 316, 318–22, 334–35
Brandon, Henry, 2nd Duke of Suffolk
1535–51) son of 1st Duke
[Michael Winder], 164
Brandon, Sir Thomas (d. 1510)
courtier, 162
Braveheart, film (1995), 317–18, 322
Bray, Edmund, 1st Baron (c. 1484–1539)
courtier, 45
Brennan, Barbara (n.a.) actress: Agnes
Howard, Dowager Duchess of
Norfolk, 12, 44–5, 104
Brennan, Jane (n.a.) actress: Lady
Margaret Bryan, 101
Brennan, Stephen (n.a.) actor: Sir
John Seymour, 98, 147
Brereton, Sir William
(c. 1487/90–1536) courtier
[James Gilbert], 17, 37–8, 215,
222, 226, 273, 275
Brewster, Anna (b. 1986) actress:
Anna Stafford a/k/a
Buckingham, 33, 321
Bride of Frankenstein, The, film
(1935), 52
Briem, Anita (b. 1982) actress: Jane
Seymour, 4, 10, 38, 97, 99,
142, 214
Broderick, Robert (1864–1921) actor:
Henry VIII in *The Prince and
the Pauper,* 52
Brooke, Catherine, fictional wife of
Charles Brandon [Rebekah
Wainwright] 317–19, 321

Brooke, Elizabeth, *see* Carew, Elizabeth
Brooke, Thomas, 8th Baron Cobham
(d. 1529), 157
Brook, Selma (n.a.) actress: Brigitte
Rousselot, 6, 46, 318
Brophy, Anthony (n.a.) actor: Eustace
Chapuys, 4, 29, 65, 99, 215,
226
Brough, Antonia (n.a.) actress:
Catherine of Aragon in *The
Tudor Touch* (1937), 73
Brower, Robert (1850–1934) actor:
Henry VIII in *A Tudor Princess*
(1913), 52
Brown, Max (b. 1981) actor: Sir Edward
Seymour, 4, 98, 147–48, 217
Bruni, Leonardo (c. 1370–1444)
humanist, 249, 252, 256
Brussels, 102
Bryan, A.S. (n.a.) actor: Little King in
The Bride of Frankenstein, 52
Bryan, Lady Margaret (née Bourchier,
c. 1468–c. 1551/2) royal
governess, 44–5, 101, 103,
122, 159, 166, 302
Bryan, Sir Francis (d. 1550) courtier
[Alan Van Sprang], 4, 6, 10,
12–13, 18–19, 29, 40–2, 44,
46, 104, 118, 148–49, 155,
159–61, 165, 175, 204, 231,
301, 323–25, 328
Vicar of Hell, 159
Bryan, Sir Thomas (d. 1518)
courtier, 159
Buckingham, Anne, *see*
Stafford, Anne
Bujold, Genevieve (b. 1942) actress:
Anne Boleyn in *Anne of the
Thousand Days* (1969), 31, 62,
85, 90, 191
Bullein, William (c. 1515–76)
surgeon, 334
Bull, Marcus (n.a.) historian, 3, 24,
51, 128

Bullwinkle Show, The: 'Mr. Peabody's Improbable History' cartoon (1962), 53
Bulmer, Joan (née Acworth, 1519–90) friend of Catherine Howard [Catherine Steadman], 45, 104, 106, 225
Burnet, Gilbert (1643–1715) Bishop of Salisbury and historian, 44, 103
Burton, Richard (1925–84) actor: Henry VIII in *Anne of the Thousand Days*, 28, 31, 62
Butler, Joan (née Fitzgerald, later Bryan, n.a.) Dowager Countess of Ormond, 161
Butterfield, Herbert (1900–79) historian, 168–69
Butts, Sir William (c. 1485–1545) physician, 331, 337, 339
Byrne, Adrienne (b. 1955) actress: Catherine of Aragon in *The Shadow of the Tower* (1972), 73

C

Calais, France, 43, 101, 103, 129, 266
Callaghan, Sorcha (b. 1983) actress: Germaine Chabot, 39
Calvo, Rafael Luis (1911–88) actor: Henry VIII in *Catalina de Inglaterra* (1951), 52
Cambridge University, 9, 61, 84, 330
 St. John's College, 156
Cameron, James (b. 1954) director of *Titanic* (1997), 298
Campbell, Douglas (1922–2009) actor: Henry VIII in *The Prince and the Pauper* (1957), 53
Campeggio, Cardinal Lorenzo (1474–1539), papal legate [Marne Maitland], 14, 35–6, 62–3, 68, 160, 172, 215, 226, 297

Canterbury Cathedral, 272
Capon, Naomi (1921–87) director of *Six Wives of Henry VIII* (1970), 31
Cardano, Gerolamo (1501–76) astrologer, 247
Cardinal Wolsey, film (1912), 52, 73
Cardinal Wolsey Going Down to Hell, play (1531), 274
Carew, Elizabeth (née Bryan, c. 1500–46) wife of Sir Nicholas Carew, 133, 157, 159
Carew, Sir Nicholas c. 1496–1539) courtier, 18, 42, 159, 231
Carey, Catherine (later Knollys, c. 1523–69), daughter of Mary Boleyn, 11, 134
Carey, Henry, 1st Baron Hunsdon (1526–96) son of Mary Boleyn, 11, 134
Carey, William (c. 1496–1528) courtier, husband of Mary Boleyn, 11, 134
Carleton, Guy (n.a.) actor: Chamberlain, 16
Carley, James (n.a.) historian, 87, 113
Carlisle Castle, Cumbria, 228–30
Carlyle, Thomas (1759–1881) historian, 13
Caroz, Don Luis (fl. early 16th century) Spanish ambassador, 65, 224
Carry On Henry, film (1971), 19, 53
Cartago, Valentina (n.a.) actress: Catherine of Aragon in *Fires of Faith* (2012), 74
Carter, Helena Bonham (b. 1966) actress: Anne Boleyn in *Henry VIII* (2003), 86
Castiglione, Baldassare (1478–1529) author, 181
 Book of the Courtier (1528), 181

Castillon, Louis de Perreau (1489?–1547/9) French ambassador, 43
Catalina de Inglaterra, film (1951), 52, 73
Catherine of Aragon (1485–1536) Queen of England and first wife of Henry VIII [Maria Doyle Kennedy], 4–5, 8–10, 12, 16, 19, 24, 27–8, 30. 33–40, 49, 59–74, 81, 83–5, 99, 116–17, 119, 121, 125, 128, 132–35, 140, 144, 146–47, 157–59, 162, 168, 182–83, 185, 205, 210, 215, 226–27, 249, 252–56, 258, 262, 268, 270, 275, 277, 282, 288–89, 298, 301–02, 307–10, 315–16, 319, 321
Catholicism, 4–5, 8–10, 16–17, 39, 47, 60, 64, 78, 81, 84, 97, 99, 103, 117, 119–21, 168, 173, 209–20, 226, 254–55, 274–75, 283, 289, 307, 310, 314
Cavendish, George (1494–1562?) biographer, 81, 212
Cavill, Henry (b. 1983) actor: Charles Brandon, 4, 13, 29, 57, 69, 97, 140, 154, 161, 184, 198, 224, 301, 314, 320, 334
Cellier, Frank (1884–1948) actor: Henry VIII in *Tudor Rose* (1936), 52
Cervantes, Stephanie (n.a.) actress: Catherine of Aragon in *Love Across Time* (2010), 74
Chabot, Germaine (n.a.) fictional niece of Philippe Chabot, 39
Chabot, Philippe (c. 1492–1543) Admiral of France [Philippe de Grossouvre], 39
Chamberlain, Martin (n.a.) actor: Henry VIII in *A Man for All Seasons* (1988), 31

Chamber, Royal, 98, 108, 134–35, 182, 292
Chambers, R.W. (1874–1942) literary scholar, 53
Chambre, John (1470–1549) physician, 339
Chapuys, Eustace (1490/2–1556) Imperial ambassador [Anthony Brophy], 4, 9, 16, 29, 34, 36, 39, 41–3, 45, 47–8, 65, 69–70, 80–1, 92, 99–100, 106, 119–20, 125, 129, 135, 200, 215, 226–28, 257–58, 271
Charles, Duke of Angouleme (1522–45), 39
Charles I and V (b. 1500, r. Spain 1516–56, r. H.R.E. 1519–56, d. 1558) King of Spain and Holy Roman Emperor [Sebastian Armesto], 5, 14–15, 20, 29, 32, 34–6, 38–9, 41–4, 47–8, 49, 60, 66–9, 80, 101, 103, 117, 129, 157–58, 161, 175, 187, 215, 227, 255, 257, 266, 270–71, 274, 301, 323
Charles, 4th Duke of Alençon (1489–1525), 135
Chauteau Vert, 144, *see also Schatew Vert*.
Christianity, 49, 173, 209–20, *see also* Catholicism; Church; Clergy; Humanism; Lutherans; Protestantism
Almsgiving, 67, 88, 211, 251
Christendom, 173, 219, 226, 258
Christian education, 61, 180, 252
Christian humanism, 19, 61, 64, 173
Christian monarchy, 180, 211, 314
Heresy, 4, 10, 14, 16, 18, 36, 41, 47, 50, 68, 78, 81, 108, 117, 119–20, 173, 177, 210, 215–19, 222, 236, 241–42, 260
Lord's Prayer, 28, 41, 211

Christianity (*cont.*)
  Piety, 61, 185, 210, 213, 215–16, 219
  Pilgrimage, 61, 219
  Polemic, 9, 16, 19, 81, 86, 167, 216
  Prayer, 34–5, 37, 42, 61, 63, 66–9, 85, 100, 110, 118, 124, 133, 161, 173, 182, 185–86, 210, 212–13, 215–16, 257, 308, 331, 334
  Ritual, 210
  Ten Commandments, 28, 41, 211
  Theology, 9, 28, 36, 42, 86, 100, 210, 215, 217, 258
  Women, 61, 252
Christina of Denmark, Duchess of Milan (1521–90) potential bride for Henry VIII [Sonya Cassidy], 43–4, 100, 158, 286–87
Christine de Pizan (1364–c. 1430) author, 91
Christ, Jesus, 37, 85, 145
  Blood of, 325
  Body of, 312
  Bride of, 309
  Five Wounds of, 18, 41, 42, 231
  Law of, 37
  Passion of, 216
Church, 36, 40, 46, 69, 82, 86, 102, 108, 168, 180, 186, 213, 238, 241, 258, 307
  Anglican (Church of England), 86, 118, 170, 172, 186, 211, 214, 314
  Legislation, 16
  Roman Catholic, 5, 60, 61, 64, 121, 144, 168, 173, 210, 213, 215, 254, 312
  Supreme Head of, 37, 109, 118, 186
Cicero, Marcus Tullius (106–43 BC) Roman philosopher, 180
Cinema, *see* Film

Clansey, Dorothy (1512–?) daughter of Thomas Wolsey and nun, 220
Class, 21, 31, 195, 338
  Bourgeoisie, 200
  Gentry, 155, 162, 164, 180, 224
  Nobility, 150, 165, 168, 170, 224, 239, 276
  Peasants, 288, 317, 321–22, 324
Claude (1499–1524) Queen of France [Gabriella Wright], 33, 66, 143, 268
Clement VII, Pope (Giulio di Giuliano de' Medici, b. 1478, r. 1523–34) [Ian McElhinney], 34–6, 69, 134, 160, 226, 275
Clergy, 16, 28, 37, 209–20, 239, 294
  Archbishops, 4, 36, 213–14, 217, 276
  Bishops, 5, 36, 39, 42, 44, 47, 78, 99, 103, 108, 110, 120, 144, 146, 172, 210, 215, 217, 220, 225–26, 236, 241, 247, 252, 258, 260, 276, 317, 325, 330
  Cardinals, 14, 34–6, 39, 42, 55, 59, 62–3, 69, 93, 142, 144, 160–61, 170, 172, 175, 181–83, 210–12, 215–16, 219, 224, 226–27, 231, 266, 270, 274, 282–83, 297, 299, 317, 325, 339
  Carthusians, 225
  Churchmen, 14, 299
  Dominicans, 61
  Jesuits, 215, 226, 275
  Monks, 16
  Nuns, 10, 35, 63, 68, 309, 311–12
  Papacy, 16, 34, 48, 62, 186–87, 215–17, 221
  Papal legate, 35, 42, 172, 212
  Popes, 5, 16–17, 34–39, 42–3, 62, 67–8, 81, 108, 134, 160, 210–11, 215, 226, 266, 270, 275, 286–87, 297, 304, 314
  Priests, 40, 81, 168, 219, 238, 334

Cleves, Amelia of (1517–86) sister of Anne of Cleves [Roxana Klein], 43
Cleves, John III the Peaceful, Duke of (1490–1539), 102
Cleves, William, Duke of (1516–92) brother of Anne [Paul Ronan], 100
Clifford, Eleanor (née Brandon), Countess of Cumberland (1519–47), 132
Clothing, 21, 23, 28, 62, 83, 98, 112, 171, 274, 284, 293–306, 331
Cluny, France, 132
Coda, Michelle (n.a.) actress: Catherine of Aragon in *The Six Wives of Henry VIII* (2013), 74
Colet, John (1467–1519) Dean of St. Paul's, 19
Collinson, Patrick (1929–2011) historian, 171
Common law, *see* Courts of Law
Complete and Utter History of Britain, The, film (1969), 53
Complete and Utter History of Everything, The film (1999), 53
Compton, Sir William (c. 1482–1528) courtier [Kris Holden-Ried], 13, 23, 154–55, 165, 183, 224, 273, 285, 298, 300, 331, 335, 339
Compton, Spencer, 7th Marquess of Northampton (b. 1946), descendant of Sir William Compton, 154
Compton Wynates, Warwickshire, 154
Conisbrough Castle, South Yorkshire, 158
Conlon, Declan (b. 1975) actor: Mendoza, 34, 67

Conover, Theresa Maxwell (1884–1968) actress in *When Knighthood Was in Flower* (1922), 73
Conspiracy, 17–18, 42, 70, 110, 132, 159, 175, 177, 215, 223–34
Conspiracy, and Rebellion, 223–48
Constables, 330
Constable, Sir John (1479–1537) rebel [Robert Doyle], 17, 18, 228–30
Constable, Sir Robert (1478–1537) rebel, 228–30
Convocation, 37, 102, 144, 237
Cooke, Alastair (1908–2004) broadcaster, 31, *see also Omnibus*
Coombs, Torrance (b. 1983) actor: Sir Thomas Culpeper, 4, 45, 104, 327
Copp, Karis (b. 1989) actress: Catherine of Aragon in *The Six Wives of Henry VIII* (2001), 74
Court
Cleves, 43, 100
England, 3, 5, 13, 15–16, 20–1, 28, 34, 38, 46, 52, 55, 60, 79, 80–1, 83, 88, 91, 99–100, 102, 104–05, 107–08, 110, 116, 118, 122, 124, 128, 130, 132–33, 143–44, 147–48, 150, 153–65, 175, 181–92, 195–208, 212, 215, 217–19, 222, 224, 227, 235, 249, 250–51, 255–56, 258–61, 265–80, 281, 295–96, 298–300, 302–03, 305, 310, 312, 330, 333, 667–0
France, 9, 79, 82, 83, 129, 160, 183, 252, 268
Holy Roman Empire, 161
Netherlands, 143, 256

352 INDEX

Court and Court Entertainments, 195–208, 265–80
Courtenay, Henry, Marquess of Exeter (1498/9–1538) courtier, 18, 42, 231
Court entertainments, 3, 15, 19–20, 37, 41, 52, 60, 64, 66, 99, 102, 104, 144, 155, 156, 162, 189, 195–208, 212, 265–80, 298, 305, *see also* Art
Archery, 188, 268
Card playing, 44, 52, 101, 102, 103, 107, 131
Ceremony, 67, 182, 197, 206, 212, 275–77, 298
Christmas, 20, 37–8, 40–1, 46, 70, 107, 109–10, 122, 156, 276–77, 302
Courtly love, 15, 20, 269
Dancing, 19–20, 28, 38, 64, 67, 83, 102, 104, 105, 117, 123, 133, 135, 183, 188–89, 253, 265, 267, 274, 276
Disguisings, 103, 104, 269, 300
Drama, 19, 265
Drinking, 102, 159, 161, 333
Feasting, 20, 40, 204, 265, 267, 274, 285, 297
Gambling, 159, 161, 183
Gift giving, 20, 21, 33, 35, 70, 98–101, 103, 106, 109, 124, 186, 237, 253, 258, 267–68, 276–77, 285, 324
Good Friday, 298
Hunting, 29, 160, 183, 188, 268, 331
Jousting, 15, 19, 20, 29, 33, 37, 38, 67, 79, 155, 159, 162, 183, 193, 261, 269, 270, 271, 273, 331, 338
Literature, 15, 19, 180, 181, 255, 259
Masques, 20, 129, 130, 269, 271

Maundy Thursday, 200
May Day, 155
Music, 12, 15, 19, 20, 23, 28, 83, 103, 106, 147, 186, 189, 218, 253, 265, 267, 268, 272–73, 289, 310
New Year's Day, 20, 33, 101–03, 276–77
Pageants, 3, 5, 15, 20, 32, 34, 66, 144, 256, 267, 269, 271, 286, 298, 303
Plays, 20, 37, 167, 212, 269, 274
Poetry, 13, 15, 19, 45, 156–59, 196, 201, 204, 283, 307, 310, 311
Ritual, 182, 183, 186, 204, 286
Tennis, 188, 268, 298
Tournaments, 98, 162, 188–89, 266, 269–71, 273, 321
Weddings, 20, 40, 44, 46, 52, 63, 68, 99, 100, 106, 146, 162, 275–77, 298
Wrestling, 27, 33, 66, 184, 188, 268
Courtiers, 12, 15, 16, 19, 30, 67, 83, 140, 142, 145, 147, 148, 150, 154, 159, 181, 182, 183, 187, 202, 224, 270, 273, 275, 277, 284, 303, 307, 311, 317
Courtship, 12, 34, 44, 45, 46, 97, 99, 107, 109, 111, 117, 202
Courts of law, 18–19, 153, 181, 237–43, *see also* Crime
Common law, 18–19, 23, 240, 243
Common law courts: Common Pleas, Exchequer, King's Bench, 18
Conciliar courts: Chancery, Requests, Star Chamber, 18, 225
Court trial, 31, 33, 46, 140–41, 146–47, 150, 175, 182, 202, 212, 215, 225, 240, 241
Ecclesiastical courts, 18, 35
Justice, 14, 18, 33, 68, 180, 238–39
Lawyers, 181, 253

Legatine court, 36, 62–3, 68
Oyer and terminer, commission of, 38
Property, 16, 163, 189, 222, 237, 239, 316, 324
Rights, 32, 100, 180, 187, 189, 239, 316, 333
Cramer, Richard (1889–1960) actor: Henry VIII in *Don't Play Bridge with Your Wife*, 52
Cranmer, Margarete (d. c. 1575) wife of Thomas Cranmer misidentified in the credits for *The Tudors* as Katharina Prue [Julie Wakeham], 221, 254
Cranmer, Thomas (1489–1556) Archbishop of Canterbury [Hans Matheson], 4–5, 8–9, 16, 36–7, 40–1, 46, 107, 141, 155, 212–14, 217, 254, 275–76, 297, 304
Crawford, Katherine (n.a.) historian, 189
Crime, 18–19, 160, 172, 203, 226, 235–49, 273, *see also* Courts of Law
  Assassination, 1, 6, 11, 13, 18, 32, 37, 127, 129, 148, 161, 215, 225, 226, 232, 235, 275
  Attainder, 46, 107
  Benefit of clergy, 239
  Breach of the peace, 239
  Buggery, 238
  Felony, 237, 239, 241
  Forfeiture of property, 237, 239
  Misdemeanor, 238
  Murder, 6, 11, 14, 17–18, 33, 39, 60, 81, 129, 131–33, 147, 175, 184, 187, 226, 237, 241, 327
  Pardon, 41, 46–7, 142, 156, 228–29, 238–39, 242, 260
  Petty treason, 241
  Poison, 5, 12, 121, 144, 158, 225–26, 241

Rape, 18, 21–2, 105, 146, 189, 283, 307–28
Sanctuary, 136, 238
Suicide, 5, 36, 69, 182, 274, 323, 339
Theft, 38, 146
Treason, 12, 14, 18, 37, 41, 46, 107, 140, 144, 147, 150, 156, 159, 175, 212, 224, 225, 230–31, 237–39, 241–42, 269–70, 274, 325
Witchcraft, 38, 81, 84, 103, 121, 238, 241
Cromwell, Thomas, Earl of Essex (c. 1485–1540) minister [James Frain], 4–6, 8, 12–14, 16, 29, 35–41, 43–46, 60, 68–9, 71, 77–80, 86–8, 91, 101–04, 119, 136, 141, 145–46, 153, 155–59, 161, 164, 168, 170–71, 174–75, 177, 181, 191, 200–01, 212–17, 223, 226–28, 230, 232, 242, 253–56, 258, 274–76, 282–83, 299, 304–05, 310, 325, 332, 334
Crosbie, Annette (b. 1934) actress: Catherine of Aragon in *The Six Wives of Henry VIII* (1970), 59, 63, 71, 72
Crossed Swords, film (1977), 53
Crutchley, Rosalie (1920–97) actress: Catherine of Aragon in *The Sword and the Rose* (1953), 73
Cuka, Frances (b. 1936) actress: Catherine of Aragon in *Henry VIII and His Six Wives* (1972), 61
Culpeper, Thomas (c. 1514–1541) courtier [Torrance Coombs], 4, 6, 18, 22, 45–6, 104–07, 110

Cumbria, 230
Czerny, Henry (b. 1959) actor: Thomas Howard, Duke of Norfolk, 4, 12, 29, 69, 140–43, 224, 336

D

Dacre, Lord (Thomas Fiennes), 45, 230
Dacre, Sir Christopher (?1470–1440 or after) northern official, 230
Daniell, David (b. 1929) literary scholar, 86
Darcy, Thomas, Baron Darcy (in or before 1467–1537) rebel [Colm Wilkinson as Lord Darcey], 13, 228–30
Darrell, Elizabeth (c. 1513–c. 1556) mistress of Thomas Wyatt [Krystin Pellerin], 70, 157, 159, 283, 308, 310, 323
Deadwood, television series, (2004–06), 7
Delaney, Padraic (b. 1977) actor: George Boleyn, Viscount Rochford, 36, 146–47
Della Rovere, Guidobaldo II, Duke of Urbino (1514–74), 284
Dereham, Francis 1513–41) courtier [Allan Leech], 6, 45, 104–07
Derrida, Jacques, (1930–2004) philosopher, 13
Desmeules, Philip (n.a.) actor: Edward Foxe, 35
D'Estrees, Gabrielle, Duchess of Beaufort and Verneuil (1573–99), 283
D'Etaples, Jacques Lefevre (c. 1455–1536) humanist, 87
Devereux, Robert, 2nd Earl of Essex (1565–1601) courtier, 154
Discourse, 15, 170, 174, 202, 206, 310, 322

Disease, 22, 35–6, 70, 107, 110, 133, 154, 212, 219, 329–42
and Medicine, 329–42
Ague (malaria), 336–37, 340–41
Contagion, 23, 35, 331, 334–35
Diabetes, 338
Dysentery, 23, 182, 337
Epidemic, 35, 48, 164, 334–36
Fevers, 99, 336–38, 340–41
Hantavirus, 335, 340
Huntingdon's Disease, 338
Hyperthyroidism, 338
Infection, 23, 334–36
McLeod Syndrome, 338
Osteomyelitis, 337
Plague, 131, 177, 216, 236, 330, 332, 335, 339;
  Bubonic, 335–36;
  Pneumonic, 340;
  Septicemic, 340
Scrofula, 334
Scurvy, 338
Sweating Sickness, 13, 23, 35, 68, 120, 154, 164, 219, 273
Ulcers, 22–3, 44, 48, 97–8, 102, 104, 108, 332, 337
Venereal disease (pox), 337;
  Syphilis, 332, 337, 338, 341
Diseases and Medicine, 329–42
Donizetti, Gaetano (1797–1848) composer, 54
Don Luis of Portugal, Duke of Beja (1506–55), 43
Donnelly, Ciaran (b. 1984) director, 3, 240
Don't Play Bridge With Your Wife, film (1933), 52
Doran, Susan (n.a.) historian, v
Dormer, Natalie (b. 1982) actress: Anne Boleyn, 4, 9, 27, 36, 40, 59, 64–5, 70–1, 79–91, 142, 202, 214–15, 285, 296, 302, 304, 312, 317, 331

INDEX   355

Douglas, Archibald, 6th Earl of Angus (c. 1489–1557), second husband of Margaret Tudor, 11, 33, 130, 131, 184
Douglas, Susan (n.a.) feminist critic, 313
Dover, Kent, 108
Dowler, Annabelle (b. 1973) actress: Catherine of Aragon in *The Six Wives of Henry VIII* (2001), 74
Dowling, Tim (b. 1963) journalist, 7
Downton Abbey, television (series 2010–15), 182
Doyle, Robert (n.a.) actor: Sir John Constable, 228
Dublin, Ireland, 89
Dudley, John, Duke of Northumberland (1504–53) courtier, 47, 116
Dudley, Robert, 1st Earl of Leicester (1532/3–88) courtier, 123
Duffy, Eamon (b. 1947) historian, 17
Duggan, Kate (n.a.) actress: Princess Elizabeth, 11
Dunning, Nick (b. 1959) actor: Thomas Boleyn Earl of Wiltshire, 4, 12, 29, 69, 144–46, 224
Durham, England, 242
Durran, Jacqueline (n.a.) costumer for *Anna Karenina* (2012), 305

E

Eatwell, Joanna (n.a.) costumer for *Wolf Hall* (2015), 303
Edinburgh, Scotland, 132
Education, 9, 19, 38, 60–2, 110, 122, 143, 180, 185, 210, 215, 217–18, 227, 249–56, 258–60, 329, 332
  Quadrivium (arithmetic, geometry, music, astronomy), 23
  Trivium (grammar, logic, rhetoric), 23

Edward II, King of England (b. 1284, r. 1307–27), 224, 269
Edward IV, King of England (b. 1442, r. 1461–70, 1471–83), 11
Edward the Confessor (b. 1003, r. 1042–66), 150
Edward VI a/k/a Prince Edward (b. 1537, r. 1547–53) son of Henry VIII and Jane Seymour [Jake Hathaway, Eoin Murtagh], 5, 10–11, 29, 40, 45–6, 48–9, 100, 104, 106, 108, 110, 116, 119–20, 122–25, 130, 146, 148, 150, 190, 218, 259, 260, 276–77, 282, 306, 337
Edwin of Northumbria (b. 586, r. 616–33), 49, 278
Elizabeth, film (1998), 3, 7, 170
Elizabeth I a/k/a Princess Elizabeth (b. 1533, r. 1558–1603) daughter of Henry VIII and Anne Boleyn [Kate Duggan, Claire Macaulay, Laoise Murray], 5, 10–11, 17, 30, 37–40, 45–6, 64, 82, 85, 87, 90, 102, 104, 108, 110, 116–19, 121–25, 130, 135, 148, 154, 168, 171, 202, 206, 218, 242–44, 250, 253, 259, 277, 284–85, 289–90, 298–300, 302, 334, 338–39
Elizabeth of York, Queen of England (1466–1503), mother of Henry VIII, 11, 20, 32, 129, 190, 282, 302
Elizabeth R, television mini-series (1971), 21, 299
Elizabeth: The Golden Age, film (2007), 3, 7
Ellerker, Sir Ralph (in or before 1489–1546) soldier [David Wilmot], 229

Ellis, Martyn (b. 1960] actor: Henry VIII in *Julia Jekyll and Harriet Hyde* (1998), 53
Elton, Geoffrey (1921–94) historian, 15, 174
Elwyn, Michael (b. 1942) actor: John Neville, 3rd Baron Latimer, 107
England, 2, 8–9, 22, 29, 34–5, 39, 42, 44–7, 50, 52, 61–3, 65–6, 69, 72, 81, 84–7, 101–02, 115, 119–20, 129–30, 132, 141, 150, 158, 160, 164–65, 167–69, 172, 181, 186–87, 189–90, 210–12, 214–17, 219–20, 224, 226, 236, 238, 241–42, 249, 252–55, 261, 263, 266, 269, 270–72, 281, 288, 295, 301, 330, 335–36
Erasmus, Desiderius (1466–1536) humanist, 19, 61, 64, 108, 110, 119, 180, 249, 252, 330
Education of a Christian Prince, The, 180
Paraphrases on the New Testament, 110
Erskine, Margery Bonney (1864–1949) actress: Catherine of Aragon in *A Tudor Princess* (1913), 73
Essex, 186
Exchequer, 18, 153
Execution, 6, 18, 22, 30, 39, 40, 42, 45–6, 50, 66, 81, 85–6, 89–90, 107, 116, 121, 140–41, 145, 148–49, 156, 158, 161, 175, 177, 184, 187, 204, 212, 217, 225–28, 230–31, 237, 240–44, 257, 260, 270, 275–76, 297, 304, 317
  Beheading, 6, 18, 86, 107, 156, 161, 225, 228, 230, 232, 241–42
  Boiling, 5, 14, 18, 226, 237, 241–42
  Burning, 4, 14, 18, 36, 41, 47, 50, 117, 119, 120, 173, 177, 216, 218, 236, 240, 241–43, 289
  Gallows, 225–26, 238, 241
  Hanging, 41, 204, 238, 240, 241
  Hanging, drawing, and quartering, 41, 156, 241–42
  Hanging in chains, 241
  Statistics, 242–43
Execution of Mary, Queen of Scots, The, film (1895), 30
Exeter Conspiracy (1538), 18, 42, 223, 231–32

F
Ferdinand II of Aragon (b. 1452, r. 1479–1516), father of Catherine of Aragon, 8, 61, 65
Field of the Cloth of Gold (1520), 15, 20, 32, 65–6, 129, 143, 154, 183, 186, 188, 266–69, 270, 272, 297
Fiennes, Thomas, 9th Baron Dacre, *see* Dacre, Lord
Fife, Jack (1923–75) actor: Henry VIII in *I Dream of Jeannie* (1966), 53
Film (cinema, movies), 3–4, 7–12, 17, 21, 28, 30–2, 40, 51, 54, 57, 60–2, 71, 72, 73, 74, 77, 79–82, 85–6, 89, 115, 121, 130, 150, 167, 169–70, 177, 185, 192, 197–98, 200, 210, 235, 298–99, 305, 317, 331, 337, 339
Filmer, Henry (d. 1543) martyr, 47
Fisher, John, Bishop of Rochester (1469–1535) martyr [Bosco Hogan], 5, 12, 18, 36, 37, 39, 50, 110, 144, 215, 225–26, 236, 241, 252, 253, 317
Fish, Simon (1500–31) Protestant reformer [Martin Murphy], 9, 14, 36, 87, 177, 216, 236, 240
Supplication of the Beggars, 9, 216, 339

Fitzwilliam, William, Earl
of Southampton (1490–1542),
courtier, 17, 42, 44, 46,
103, 184
Flandes, Juan de (c. 1460–by 1519)
Spanish painter, 71
Fletcher, John (1579–1625)
playwright, 30, 32
Flodden, Battle of (1513), 29, 33, 65,
140, 143, 184
Florence, Italy, 189, 256
Folger Shakespeare Library,
Washington D.C., v, 24
"Reassessing Henry VIII," v, 24
Forward, Susan (n.a.) psychotherapist, 37
Foucault, Michel (1926–84)
philosopher, 170
Foxe, Edward, Bishop of Hereford
(c. 1496–1538) courtier [Philip
Desmeules], 9, 35, 36
Foxe, John (1516/7–87) historian,
110, 218, 243–44, 247, 289
*Book of Martyrs (Acts and
Monuments)*, 218
Frain, James (b. 1978) actor: Thomas
Cromwell, Earl of Essex, 4,
13–14, 68, 100, 170, 212–14,
332
France, 1, 5, 9, 11, 15, 20, 29, 33–5,
37–40, 42–4, 47–8, 65, 108,
129, 131, 133–34, 143–44,
149–50, 156, 161–64, 183–84,
187, 190, 252, 255, 257, 259,
261, 266, 268
Francis I, film (1937), 52
Francis I, King of France (b. 1494, r.
1515–47) [Emmanuel Leconte],
5, 11, 14, 15, 27, 29, 32–3,
34–6, 39, 42–4, 47, 49, 66–7,
79, 83, 101, 117, 129, 132, 135,
143–44, 154–56, 158, 160–61,
163, 175, 183, 187–88, 190,
253, 262, 266–68, 270, 297

Franco–Imperial relations, 36, 102, 161
Fraser, Antonia (b. 1932) historian and
actress: Catherine of Aragon in
Whatever Next? (1969), 73
Freeman, Thomas (n.a.) historian,
v, 31, 47, 53, 198, 206
French ambassador (unnamed), 39, 43,
47, 274
Fresno, Maruchi (1916–2003) actress:
Catherine of Aragon in *Catalin
de Inglaterra* (1951), 73
Friedmann, Paul (n.a.) biographer, 9
Furdell, Elizabeth (n.a.) historian, v, xii,
22, 329–42

G
Galen (129–200/16) physician, 300,
see also Disease; Medicine
Galenic theory, 333, 336
Game of Thrones, television series
(2011-present), 167, 207
Garcia, Nerea, (n.a.) actress: Catherine
of Aragon in *Mad Love (Juana
de Loca,* 2001) 74
Gardiner, Stephen, Bishop of
Winchester (c. 1483–1555),
courtier [Simon Ward], 4, 6, 12,
16, 19, 29, 35–6, 40–1, 46, 47,
49, 99, 105, 107, 108, 110, 120,
164, 217–18, 222, 260. 325
Gaynor, Peter (n.a.) actor: Hans
Holbein the Younger, 6, 100,
324, 332
Gedmintas, Ruta (b. 1983) actress:
Elizabeth Blount, 5, 32,
133, 315
Gender, 21–2, 57, 90–1, 119, 205,
252, 254, 291, 294, 307–28
and Sexuality, 307–28
Enlightened sexism, 313–14
Feminism, 62, 78, 90–1, 191,
313–14, 322

Gender (*cont.*)
  Masculinity, 185–86, 188–89. 195. 197–99, 203–5, 293, 300, 312–15, 323–24
  Rape culture, 311, 326
Gender and Sexuality, 307–28
Geraghty, Clive (n.a.) actor: Thomas Linacre, 35, 329
Gerladini, Alessandro (1455–1524) humanist, 61
Gerladini, Antonio (n.a.) humanist, 61
Ghosts, 6, 13, 20, 46, 49, 71, 125, 146, 205, 261
Gilbert, Gerard (n.a.) journalist, 90
Gilbert, James (b. 1982) actor: William Brereton, 226
Gilbert, Robert (n.a.) servant to Buckingham, 225
Glenister, John (b. 1932) director of *The Six Wives of Henry VIII* (1970), 31
Globe Theatre, London, 299, 305
Glynn, Basil (n.a.) film scholar, 312
God's Outlaw, film (1986), 53
Goffe, Rusty (b. 1948) actor: Henry VIII in *U.F.O.* (1993), 53
Golden Age, The, film (1967), 53
Gómez de Fuensalida, Don Gutierre (c. 1450–c. 1535) Spanish ambassador, 65
Goodrich, Thomas, Bishop of Ely (1494–1554) courtier, 9, 42
Gordon, Julia Swayne (1878–1933) actress: Catherine of Aragon in *Cardinal Wolsey* (1912), 73
Granada Television, 31, 61
Greenblatt, Robert (b. 1960) Showtime official, 168
Greensleeves, song, 28, 186, 272
Greenwich, 101, 110, 121, 132, 155, 276, 298, 333

Greenwich, Treaty of (1543), 48
Gregory, Philippa (b. 1954) author, 9, 54, 80, *see also Other Boleyn Girl, The*
Grey, Catherine (1540–68), granddaughter of Charles Brandon and Mary Tudor, 33, 132
Grey, Francis (née Brandon), Duchess of Suffolk (1517–59) daughter of Charles Brandon and Mary Tudor, 132
Grey, Jane (1536/7–1554) granddaughter of Charles Brandon and Mary Tudor and Queen of England, 10, 22, 33, 117, 132–33
Grey, Mary (1545–78) granddaughter of Charles Brandon and Mary Tudor, 33, 117, 132
Grocers, Company of, 333
Grootenboer, Lisa (b. 1961) video editor, 3
Groot, Jerome de (n.a.) film scholar, 7, 136, 327
Grossouvre, Philippe de (n.a.) actor: Philippe Chabot, Admiral of France, 39
Guelders, Netherlands, 103
Guildford, Sir Henry (1489–1532) courtier, 282
Guînes, France, 267
Guische, Claude la (d. 1553) French ambassador, 274
Guns, 48
Gunpowder, 244

H

Hackett, Francis (1883–1962) historian and novelist, 53, 85
Haigh, Christopher (n.a.) historian, 17

Hailes Abbey, Gloucestershire, 37
Hallam, Lord, fictional jouster [uncredited], 269
Hall, Edward (1497–1547) historian, 267
  Chronicle or The Union of the Two Noble and Illustre Families of Lancastre and Yorke, 267
Hallett, Rod (n.a.) actor: Sir Richard Rich, 4, 105
Hamilton, Emma (b. 1984) actress: Anne Stanhope, 4, 148, 218, 296
Hamilton, James, 2nd Earl of Arran (c. 1517–1575) illegitimate son of James V, 48
Hampton Court Palace, 36, 46, 98, 100, 109, 175, 186, 275, 277, 335
Hampton Court Palace (1926), 52
Harding, Lyn (18670–1952) actor: Henry VIII in *When Knighthood was in Flower* (1922), 52
Harman, Edmund (c. 1509–77) barber [Paul Connaughton], 47
Harris, Jared (b. 1961) actor: Henry VIII in *The Other Boleyn Girl* (2003), 31
Harrison, Rex (1908–90) actor: Henry VIII in *The Trial of Anne Boleyn*, 53
Hastings, Anne (née Stafford, n.a.) mistress of William Compton [Rachel Kavanagh], 23
Hayward, Maria (n.a.) historian, v, xii, 21, 293–306
Hector, Doctor (n.a.) physician, 337
Henri II, King of France (b. 1519, r. 1547–59), 47
  As Dauphin, 266
Henri II, King of Navarre (1503–55), 15, 135
Henry, Duke of Cornwall (1511), 63, 64

Henry Fitzroy, Earl of Nottingham, Duke of Richmond and Somerset (1519–36) illegitimate son of Henry VIII and Elizabeth Blount [Zak Jenciragic], 5, 11, 34, 35, 64, 66, 67, 116, 120–21, 124, 128, 134, 149, 277, 302, 306
Henry 8.0, online series (2009), 54
Henry V, King of England (b. 1386, r. 1413–22), 29, 187, 251
Henry VII, King of England (b. 1457, r. 1485–1509), father of Henry VIII, 20–1, 32, 49, 129, 190
Henry VIII and Catherine Howard, film (1910), 52
Henry VIII and His Six Wives, television movie (1972), 31, 61
Henry VIII, film (2003), 31, 61
Henry VIII in *Henry VIII and His Six Wives* (1972), 31, 86
Henry VIII in *The Prince and the Pauper* (1996), 31
Henry VIII in *The Six Wives of Henry VIII* (1970), 31, 46, 62
Henry VIII, King of England (b. 1491, r. 1509–47) [Jonathan Rhys Meyers], *see also* Art and Clothing; Catholicism; Christianity; Clergy; Conspiracy and Rebellion; Court and Court Entertainments; Courts of Law; Crime; Diseases and Medicine; Gender and Sexuality; Humanism and Renaissance; Kingship; Lutheranism; Protestantism and Reformation)
Henry and His Children;
  Edward, 5, 10–11, 29, 40, 5–6, 48–9, 100, 104, 106, 108, 110, 116, 119–20, 22–25, 130, 146, 148, 150, 190, 218, 259, 260, 276–77, 282, 306, 337;

Henry VIII in *The Six Wives of Henry VIII* (1970) (*cont.*)
    Elizabeth, 5, 10–11, 17, 30, 37–40, 45–6, 64, 82, 85, 87, 90, 102, 104, 108, 110, 116–19, 121–25, 130, 135, 148, 154, 168, 171, 202, 206, 218, 242–44, 250, 253, 259, 277, 284–85, 289–90, 298–300, 302, 334, 338–39;
    Henry Fitzroy, 5, 11, 34, 35, 64, 66, 67, 116, 120–21, 124, 128, 134, 149, 277, 302, 306;
    Mary, 4–6, 10–11, 31, 34–44, 46–7, 49, 60, 62, 64, 66–71, 81, 98–100, 104, 106–10, 112, 116–25, 129–32, 134, 144, 148, 156–58, 162–63, 204, 215, 232, 253, 255–56, 266, 271, 275, 277, 283, 288–89, 296, 302, 304, 334, 338

Henry and His Friends and Ministers;
    Anthony Knivert (based on Thomas Knyvett), 4, 13, 154, 224–25, 270, 298, 319–20, 335;
    Charles Brandon, 4–7, 11, 13, 16–17, 29, 33, 36, 38–9, 41–2, 44–9, 69–71, 97–8, 101, 105, 130–33, 140–41, 143, 146, 149, 154, 157, 161–65, 184–85, 187–88, 198–99, 205, 224, 228–32, 237, 243, 260, 269, 275, 287, 298, 300–01, 314, 316, 318–22, 334–35;
    Francis Bryan, 4, 6, 10, 12–13, 18–19, 29, 40–2, 44, 46, 104, 118, 148–49, 155, 159–61, 165, 175, 204, 231, 301, 323–25, 328;
    Henry Norris, 13, 38, 154–56, 165, 202, 273;
    Stephen Gardiner, 4, 6, 12, 16, 19, 29, 35–6, 40–1, 46, 47, 49, 99, 105, 107, 108, 110, 120, 164, 217–18, 222, 260. 325;
    Thomas Cranmer, 4–5, 8–9, 16, 36–7, 40–1, 46, 107, 141, 155, 212–14, 217, 254, 275–76, 297, 304;
    Thomas Cromwell, 4–6, 8, 12–14, 16, 29, 35–41, 43–46, 60, 68–9, 71, 77–80, 86–8, 91, 101–04, 119, 136, 141, 145–46, 153, 155–59, 161, 164, 168, 170–71, 174–75, 177, 181, 191, 200–01, 212–17, 223, 226–28, 230, 232, 242, 253–56, 258, 274–76, 282–83, 299, 304–05, 310, 325, 332, 334;
    Thomas More, 1, 4–5, 7, 13–14, 16, 18–19, 27, 29, 31–2, 36, 38–9, 50, 60–5, 67, 69–70, 77–8, 82, 91–2, 168, 170–75, 177, 180, 201, 209, 215–16, 219, 236, 237, 249–53, 257–58, 260–61, 266, 268, 270, 282, 304, 330;
    Thomas Wolsey, 1, 4–5, 8, 13–14, 16–17. 19, 27, 29, 32–6, 59, 62–3, 65–9, 81–2, 93, 132, 134–5, 142–45, 160, 170–75, 180–86, 191, 201, 209, 211–12, 216, 219, 224–25, 227, 250, 252–55, 260–61, 266, 270, 272, 274–75, 282–83, 297, 299, 305, 339;
    Thomas Wyatt, 13, 15, 19, 29, 38, 61, 70, 156–59, 161, 165, 196, 201–04, 224, 273, 283, 295, 307–12, 317, 323;
    William Compton, 13, 23, 154–55, 165, 183, 224, 273, 285, 298, 300, 331, 335, 339

INDEX 361

Henry and His In-Laws;
  Boleyns, 4, 12, 29, 33, 36–9, 46, 49, 69–70, 132, 141–47, 151, 213, 224–25, 255, 272–75, 317–27;
  Cleves, 43, 100, 102; Ferdinand of Aragon and Isabella of Castile, 8, 34, 61, 65;
  Howards, 4, 6, 12–13, 17, 19, 29, 33–4, 40–1, 44–8, 65, 69, 100, 104, 118, 125, 129, 132, 140–44, 148–50, 155, 164, 184, 217, 224–25, 228–30, 237, 255, 277, 282, 336;
  Parr, 108; Seymours, 6, 11, 17–18, 42, 45–9, 105, 107, 109, 147–49, 160–61, 175, 204, 217–18, 231–32, 243
Henry and His Mistresses;
  Elizabeth Blount, 5, 11, 32, 34, 66, 116, 120, 128–29, 133, 190, 277, 315;
  Elizabeth Luke (fictional), 37, 135;
  Madge Shelton, 5, 11, 13, 38, 135, 155;
  Marguerite of Navarre (fictionalized), 15, 19, 34, 67, 79, 87, 91, 135, 252;
  Mary Boleyn, 11, 33–4, 65–6, 134, 190, 268;
  Ursula Misseldon (fictional), 6, 28, 40, 71, 127, 160, 284, 287, 323–25
Henry and His Queens;
  Anne Boleyn, 4–6, 8–10, 12–13, 15, 17–20, 24, 27–8, 30–1, 34–40, 49–50, 52, 53, 59–71, 77–92, 98–100, 116–18, 121–25, 130, 132, 134–35, 140–46, 153, 155–58, 160, 163, 168, 172, 184–85, 187, 191, 196–97, 200–03, 205–06, 212, 214–15, 219, 223, 225–28, 232, 241, 252–59, 262, 263, 270–75, 285–86, 288, 296, 298, 302, 304, 309–10, 312, 316–17, 320, 322–23, 331, 339;
  Anne of Cleves, 4, 6, 10, 21–2, 45, 51–2, 54, 97, 100–04, 110, 119, 122–23, 158, 259, 276–77, 288, 296, 301, 337, 339;
  Catherine Howard, 4, 6, 10, 12, 18, 22, 45, 47, 50, 97, 102, 104–07, 118–19, 123–24, 140–41, 149, 160, 206, 237, 258–59, 276, 296, 327;
  Catherine of Aragon, 4–5, 8–10, 12, 16, 19, 24, 27–8, 30. 33–40, 49, 59–74, 81, 83–5, 99, 116–17, 119, 121, 125, 128, 132–35, 140, 144, 146–47, 157–59, 162, 168, 182–83, 185, 205, 210, 215, 226–27, 249, 252–56, 258, 262, 268, 270, 275, 277, 282, 288–89, 298, 301–02, 307–10, 315–16, 319, 321;
  Catherine Parr, 4, 6, 10, 16, 19, 45–7, 49, 54, 65, 97, 107–11, 112, 119–20, 123–24, 148, 217–18, 254, 259, 277, 296, 302, 321, 334, 337; Jane Seymour, 4–5, 10, 13, 20, 32, 38, 97–100, 110, 118, 123, 125, 135, 141–42, 145–46, 158, 164, 190, 200, 214, 227, 257, 274–75, 277, 282, 285–88, 296, 302, 304, 323, 331, 336, 338, 339
Henry and His Rivals;
  Charles V, 5, 14–15, 20, 29, 32, 34–6, 38–9, 41–4, 47–8, 49, 60, 66–9, 80, 101, 103, 117, 129, 157–58, 161, 175, 187, 215, 227, 255, 257, 266, 270–71, 274, 301, 323;

Henry VIII in *The Six Wives of Henry VIII* (1970) (*cont.*)
  Clement VII, 34–6, 69, 134, 160, 226, 275;
  Francis I, 5, 11, 14, 15, 27, 29, 32–3, 34–6, 39, 42–4, 47, 49, 66–7, 79, 83, 101, 117, 129, 132, 135, 143–44, 154–56, 158, 160–61, 163, 175, 183, 187–88, 190, 253, 262, 266–68, 270, 297;
  Martin Luther, 5, 14, 28, 35–6, 44, 47, 81, 102, 112, 119, 173, 213, 216, 219;
  Martin Luther: In Defence of the Seven Sacraments a/k/a Assertio Septem Sacramentorum (1521), 28, 211;
  Paul III, 5, 17, 37, 39, 215, 226, 275, 286, 287, 297, 304;
  Reginald Pole, 6, 13, 19, 42, 159, 204, 215, 231, 297, 325
Henry and His Sisters;
  Margaret Modified, 5–6, 11, 13–14, 18, 33, 43, 130–33, 162, 184, 271, 297, 320;
  Mary Missing, 7, 11, 13, 33, 162–63, 184, 271, 320
Henry and His Uncles;
  Fictitious Uncle, 1, 11, 18, 32, 127, 129, 133, 187, 235;
  Jasper Tudor, 11, 129
Henry, Michael Hirst, and Jonathan Rhys Meyers;
  Acting and characterization, 4, 7–8, 27, 150, 179, 186, 190–91, 201–02, 205, 211–12, 219, 257, 278, 329;
  Aging and body, 3, 27–8, 32, 45, 50, 64, 128, 190, 201, 206, 277, 314;
  Archetypal Henries, 1, 28, 32, 49–50, 128, 289;
  Casting, 13–15, 27–8, 65–6, 140, 149–50, 197–98;
  Costuming and comportment, 21, 28, 179, 295–98, 300–01, 306;
  Humanizing elements, 46, 89, 128; Sex and voyeurism, 49, 57, 65–6, 82–3, 93, 128, 140, 143, 191, 199, 314–16;
  Warrior or playboy, 27–50
Henry VIII, Shakespeare's, film (1979), 53, 61, film (1991), 53
Herbert, Anne, Countess of Pembroke (née Parr) sister of Catherine Parr [Suzy Lawlor], 108
Hermann, Robin (n.a.) historian, v, xii, 13, 167–78
Heston, Charlton (1923–2008), actor: Henry VIII in *Crossed Swords* (1977), 53
  Director and actor: Thomas More in *A Man for All Seasons* (1988), 31
Hever Castle, Kent, 35, 68, 102, 103, 219, 331
Hewlett, Siobhan (b. 1984) actress: Catherine of Aragon in *Henry VIII: Mind of a Tyrant* (2009), 74
Hickerson, Megan (n.a.) historian, v, xii, 21, 297, 307–28
Highley, Christopher (n.a.) literary scholar, 167
Hildreth, Mark (b. 1978) actor: Cardinal Reginald Pole, 6, 42
Hilliard, Nicholas (c. 1547–1619) English artist, 283–84
Hippocrates, (460–370 BC) physician, 330, *see also* Disease; Medicine

Hirst, Michael(b. 1952) screenwriter, 2–3, 6–14, 16–17, 22–3, 27–8, 33–4, 40–1, 48, 50, 59, 66, 70–1, 78, 82–84, 87–9, 91, 93, 97, 99, 100, 106, 110–11, 116, 118, 120–21, 123, 127–33, 135–36, 139, 141, 143, 146–47, 149, 150, 154–55, 168–75, 210, 212–19, 223–26, 228–32, 265–69, 271–78, 290, 307–08, 310–12, 315, 323, 329, *see also* Tudors, The
Hogan, Bosco (b. 1949) actor: Bishop John Fisher, 5, 36, 215
Hogan, Stephen (n.a.) actor: Sir Henry Norris, 38, 154
Holbein, Hans the Younger (c. 1497–1543) German painter [Peter Gaynor], 6, 20–1, 28, 30–2, 40, 43, 49, 54, 100, 103, 136, 186, 190, 204–05, 281, 283–91, 293, 305, 324, 332, *see also* Art
Holden-Ried, Kris (b. 1973) actor: Sir William Compton, 154, 331
Holfland, Michael (n.a.) actor: Henry VIII in *Relic Hunter: The Royal Ring* (2001), 53
Hollywood, 167
Holy Roman Empire, 39, 44, 255
Horenbout, 186, 285
Household, Royal, 16, 162, 182–83, 238, 260, 294–96, 298, 335
 Anne Boleyn, 98, 99, 215, 226, 273
 Catherine Howard, 104–06
 Catherine of Aragon, 99
 Catherine Parr, 218
 Henry Fitzroy, 120, 149
 Jane Seymour, 324
 Mary, 67, 117
Howard, Agnes, Dowager Duchess of Norfolk (née Tilney, in or before 1477–1545) grandmother of

Catherine Howard [Barbara Brennan], 44, 104
Howard, Catherine, Queen of England (1518/24–42) fifth wife of Henry VIII [Tamzin Merchant], 4, 6, 10, 12, 18, 22, 45, 47, 50, 97, 102, 104–07, 118–19, 123–24, 140–41, 149, 160, 206, 237, 258–59, 276, 296, 327
Howard, Henry, Earl of Surrey (1516/17–1547) courtier (David O'Hara), 4, 6, 12, 19, 29, 45–8, 140–41, 148–50, 155, 161, 240, 250, 260, 300, 306
Howard, Jane, fictional royal mistress [Slaine Howard], 13
Howard, John, 1st Duke of Norfolk (c. 1425–85), 140
Howard, Lord Edmund (c. 1478–1539), father of Catherine Howard, 45
Howard, Thomas, 2nd Duke of Norfolk (1443–1524), character amalgamated with 3rd Duke, 4, 140
Howard, Thomas, 3rd Duke of Norfolk (1473–1554) courtier [Henry Czerny], 4, 6, 12–13, 17, 29, 33–4, 40–1, 44–6, 65, 69, 100, 118, 125, 129, 132, 140–44, 149–50, 155, 164, 184, 217, 224–25, 228–30, 237, 255, 277, 282, 336
Hull, 17, 228, 230, 242
Humanism, 8, 15, 19, 28, 60–1, 64, 156, 173, 177, 180, 249–61, 262, 263
 and the Renaissance, 249–64
 Antiquity, 185, 249
 Classical ideal, 249–50
 Genius, 272, 285–88
 Greek (language), 147, 249, 252, 253

Humanism (*cont.*)
  Heroism, 10, 29, 71, 78, 80, 82, 85, 92, 187, 189, 191, 197, 201–02, 205, 216, 269, 313–15
  Latin, 42, 110, 124, 125, 185, 203, 216, 249, 251–53, 259, 308, 325
  New Learning, 146
  Studia humanitatis, 180
Humanism and Renaissance, 249–64
Humanitarianism, 19, 249–61
Hume, Martin (a/k/a Martin Sharp, 1843–1910) historian, 53
Hunnisett, Jean (n.a.) costumer for *Elizabeth* R (1971), 299
Hurst, Harry, fictional soldier at siege of Boulogne [Jody Latham], 48
Hutton, Sir John (n.a.) diplomat, based on Hutton and Sir Nicholas Wotton (1497–1567) [Roger Ashton–Griffiths], 43, 44, 100, 102
Hyrde, Richard (d. 1528) humanist, 252

I
I Dream of Jeannie: 'The Girl Who Never Had a Birthday'(1966), 53
Imperial Election (1519), 32
Ireland, 7, 22, 161
Isabella I, Queen of Castille (b. 1451, r. 1474–1504), mother of Catherine of Aragon, 34
Isabel of Portugal (1503–39), wife of Charles, V
Isleworth, Surrey, 249
Italy, 42, 187
It Could Happen to You (film 1977), 53
Ives, Eric (1931–2012) historian, 15, 86, 91, 227

J
Jackson, Glenda (b. 1938) actress: Elizabeth I in *Elizabeth R* (1971), 299
James IV, King of Scotland (b. 1473, r. 1488–1513), 11, 33, 65, 130, 162, 184
Jameson, Fredric (n.a.)literary scholar (b. 1934), 170
James, Sara (n.a.) actress: Marguerite of Navarre, 34
James, Sid (1913–76), actor: Henry VIII in *Carry On, Henry* (1971)
James, Susan (n.a.) historian, 110, 112
James IV, King of Scotland (b. 1473, r. 1488–1513), 11, 33, 65, 130, 162, 184
James V, King of Scotland (b. 1512, r. 1513–42), 43, 48, 105, 130
James VI and I, King of Scotland and England (b. 1566, r. Scotland 1567–1625, England 1603–25), 130, 133, 168
James V, King of Scotland (b. 1512, r. 1513–42), 43, 48, 105, 130
Jannings, Emil (1884–1950) actor: Henry VIII in *Anna Boleyn* (1920), 28, 30
Jarrott, Charles (1927–2011) director of *Anne of the Thousand Days* (1969), 31, 61
Jenciragic, Zak (n.a.) actor: Henry Fitzroy, 5, 11, 35, 64, 134, 306
Jenkins, Philip (b. 1952) historian, 242
Jenney, Christopher (by 1489–1542) judge, 242
Joanna the Mad, Queen of Castile and Aragon (b. 1479, nominal r. Castile 1504–1555, Aragon 1516–55), 140

INDEX   365

João III the Pious, King of Portugal (b. 1502, r. 1521–57), 131
Johnson, Nöel (1916–99) actor: Henry VIII in *A Man for All Seasons* (1957), 53
Johnson, Tefft (1883–1956) actor: Henry VIII in *Cardinal Wolsey* (1912), 52
Jonas, Richard (n.a.) physician, 104, 334
Jones, Terry (b.1942) actor: Henry VIII in *The Complete and Utter History of Britain* (1969), 53
Jousting, *see* Court Entertainments
Julia Jekyll and Harriett Hyde, film (1998), 53
Justice, James (1907–75) actor: Henry VIII in *The Sword and the Rose* (1953), 52–3

K

Kapur, Shekhar (b. 1945) director of *Elizabeth* (1998) and *Elizabeth: The Golden Age* (2007), 3
Kavanagh, John (n.a.) actor: Cardinal Campeggio, 35
Kearney, Damien (n.a.) actor: William Webbe, 37, 316
Kelly, Joseph (n.a.) actor: King of Portugal, 11, 33
Kelly, Slaine (b. 1952) actress: Jane Howard, 315
Kempis, Thomas a, author (c. 1380–1471), 110
  The Imitation of Christ, 110
Kemp, Shep (n.a.) actor: Henry VIII in *Hampton Court Palace* (1926), 52
Kennedy, Maria Doyle (b.1964) actress: Catherine of Aragon, 4, 9, 27, 59, 62–5, 71, 72, 215, 270, 298, 301, 316

Kent, 103, 157, 158, 332, 335
Kesselring, Krista (n.a.) historian, v, xii, 18, 235–48
Kilmainham Jail, Dublin, Ireland, 89
King and Women, film (1967), 53
King, Jamie Thomas (b. 1981) actor: Sir Thomas Wyatt, 29, 70, 308
King, Joanne (b. 1983) actress: Jane Boleyn (née Parker), Viscountess Rochford, 38, 104
King, John N. (n.a.) literary scholar, 167
King's Great Matter, 35, 60, 81, 91, 160, 210–11, 236, 252, 275
Kingship, 14, 64, 179–92, 179–94, 249, 256, 260, 300, *see also* War
  Chapel Royal, 40, 47, 271–72, 275
  Chivalry, 45, 66, 100, 251, 268–69
  Coronation (crowning), 20, 37, 45, 140, 157, 266, 275–77, 286, 295, 297, 298, 301, 336
  Counsel, 142, 181
  Crown (the headgear), 104, 120, 179–80, 187, 302
  Crown (the institution), 99, 103, 145, 150, 174, 181, 237, 255, 332, 338
  Defender of the Faith, 270
  Discipline, 238
  Garter, Order of the, 45, 162
  Imperium, 174
  Jewels, Royal, 34, 37, 69, 70, 104, 109, 156, 157, 163, 186, 267, 274, 295, 296, 308
  Magnificence, 185–87, 267, 269, 278, 295, 297
  Majesty, 15, 20, 184, 185, 288
  Patronage, 9, 15, 28, 61, 62, 86, 155, 158, 180. 186, 215, 218, 252, 273, 287, 333
  Royal Supremacy, 41, 146, 174, 213
  Royal Touch, 211, 329, 334

Kingship (*cont.*)
  Throne, 5–6, 32, 46, 82, 90, 115, 117, 124, 130, 132–33, 150, 156, 158, 167, 223–24, 232, 260, 269–70, 274, 277, 290, 296, 317, 325, 334, 338
  Tyranny, 8, 82, 128, 189, 197, 198, 311
Kirk, Brian (b. 1983) director, 3
Klein, Roxana (n.a.) actress: Amelia of Cleves, 43, 100
Knighthood, 187, 230, 324, 339
Knight, William, Bishop of Bath and Wells (1475/6–1547) courtier [Brian de Salvo], 35, 253
Knivert, Sir Anthony, fictional courtier based on Thomas Knyvett [Callum Blue], 4, 224–25, 270, 298, 319–20, 335
Knyvett, Charles (n.a.) servant of Buckingham, 225
Knyvett, Sir Thomas, courtier (c. 1485–1512), 13, 154, 224–25, 270
Korda, Alexander 1890–1956) director of *The Private Life of Henry VIII* (2003), 3, 24, 78–9, 85
Krueger, Freddy, fictional character, *Nightmare on Elm Street series* (1984–2010), 82

L

La jument du roi, film (1973), 53
Lambert, John (d. 1538) heretic [Ben Price], 41, 240
Lambert, Mark (n.a.) actor: William Cornish, 272
Lambeth Palace, Surrey, 45, 67
Larke, Joan (c. 1490–after 1529) mistress of Thomas Wolsey [Lorna Doyle], 220
Lascelles, John (d. 1546) heretic, 243

La segunda señora Tudor, film (1977), 53
Latimer, Hugh, Bishop of Worcester (c. 1485–1555) deposed prelate [Jack Sandle], 9–10, 47, 108, 110, 216
Laughlin, Laura Jane (n.a.) actress: Madge Shelton as Sheldon, 5, 135
Laughton, Charles (1899–1962) actor: Henry VIII in *The Private Life of Henry VIII* (1933), 28, 30–1, 49–50, 52, 78
Law courts, *see* Courts of law
Lawlor, Suzy (b. 1984) actress: Anne Herbert as Anne Parr, 108
League of Nations, 1, 173
Leconte, Emmanuel (b. 1982) actor: Francis I, 5, 14, 27, 66, 188
Leech, Allen (b. 1981) actor: Francis Dereham, 6, 45, 104
Leland, John, (c. 1503–52) antiquary [Tony Flynn], 61
Leland, Richard, fictional soldier at siege of Boulogne [Moe Dunford], 48
Lempereur, Martin a/k/a Martin de Keyser (d. 1536) French publisher in Antwerp, 87
Leo X, Pope (Giovanni di Lorenzo de' Medici, b. 1475, r. 1513–21), 266, 270
Levin, Carole (n.a.) historian, v, xii, 10, 64, 115–26
Lewis, Damian (b. 1971) actor: Henry VIII in *Wolf Hall* (2015), 49
Lima, Maria de (n.a.) actress: Catherine of Aragon in *I Am Henry* (2015), 74
Limbaugh, Rush (b. 1951) broadcaster, 311
Linacre, Thomas (c. 1460–1524) physician [Clive Geraghty], 23, 35, 61, 329–32, 335, 339

Lincoln, 105
Lincolnshire, 163, 164
Lincolnshire Rising, 41, 228–29, 231
Lipscomb, Suzannah (b. 1978) historian, 121, 227
Lisbon, Portugal, 131
Lisle, Lord, *see* Plantagenet, Arthur
Loades, David (1934–2016) historian, 15, 91
London, 69, 110, 156, 182, 212, 228–30, 241, 249, 274, 276, 284, 286, 295, 298, 315, 330, 332–37
  Aldgate, 241
  Bishopsgate, 242
  Blackfriars, 36, 68, 186
  Charing Cross, 241
  Cheapside, 241
  Corporation of London Record Office, 332
  Fleet Street, 335
  Gracechurch Street, 241
  Leadenhall Street, 242
  Lord Mayor, 332
  Smithfield, 241
  Tyburn, 230, 241
  Wapping Docks, 241
London, Tower of, 6, 14, 18, 21, 40, 42, 45, 47, 80, 85, 89, 106, 141, 145, 150, 157, 159, 231, 232, 241, 258
  Lieutenant, 244
London, Treaty of (1518), 14, 22, 129, 172–73, 266
Long, Ronald (1911–86) actor: Henry VIII in *Bewitched*, 53
Looney Tunes, 52
Lorraine, Antoine the Good, Duke of (1489–1544), 43, 101
Lorraine, Francis, Duke of (1517–45), 43, 101, 103

Louis XII, King of France (b. 1462,r. 1498–1515), 11, 33, 65, 131–32, 162, 184, 187
Louth, Lincolnshire, 230
Louvre, Paris, 283, 288
Love Across Time, film (2010)
Love, Montague (1877–1943) actor: Henry VIII in *The Prince and the Pauper* (1937), 52
Loyola, Javier (n.a.) actor: Henry VIII in *La segunda señora Tudor* (1977), 53
Lubitsch, Ernst (1892–1942) director of *Anna Boleyn* (1920), 85
Ludlow, Wales, 14, 35, 67–8
Luke, Eleanor, fictional royal mistress [Andrea Lowe], 37, 135
Lutherans, 5, 14, 35, 36, 44, 47, 81, 102, 112, 119, 173, 213, 219
Luther, Martin (1483–1546) Protestant reformer, 5, 28, 36, 216
Luxembourg, 48

M

Macaulay, Claire (n.a.) actress: Princess Elizabeth, 11, 102
MacCulloch, Diarmaid (b. 1951) historian, 227
Machiavelli, Niccolo 469–1527) humanist, 14, 19, 174, 180, 249, 256–57, 260–61
  Discourses on Livy (written 1517, published 1531), 256
  History of Florence (written 1520–26, published 1532), 256
  *The Prince (*written 1513, published 1532), 19, 174, 180, 249, 251, 256–58, 260
Maclean, Alison (b. 1958) director, 3

Maitland, Marne (1920–92) actor: Cardinal Campeggio in *Anne of the Thousand Days* (1969), 62
Man for All Seasons, A, 14, 60, 77–8, 168, 173, 177, *see also* Bolt, Robert
  Australian television (1964), 53
  BBC television (1957), 53
  Film (1966), 4, 31, 62–3, 191
  Original BBC radio play (1954), 31, 53
  TNT television (1988), 31
Man in Red, anonymous painting, 300, 306
Manoel I the Fortunate, King of Portugal (b. 1469, r. 1495–1521), 131
Manox, Henry (fl. 1530s–early 1540s) paramour of Catherine Howard, 45, 105–07
Mantel, Hillary (b. 1952) novelist, 9, 77–80, 86–7, 91, 168
  Bring Up the Bodies (novel 2012), 9, 77–8, 80
  Wolf Hall (novel 2009), 9, 77–8, 80, 168
  Wolf Hall (television miniseries 2015), 30, 49, 59, 61, 71, 72, 78–80, 306
Mantua, Italy, 285
Mapp, Walter (d. 1209/10) author and royal clerk, 181
Maps, 186
Marbeck, John (c. 1505–1585?) composer [Fergal Titley], 47
Marcus Aurelius (b. 121, r. 161–80) Roman Emperor and philosopher, 330
Margaret of Austria, Duchess of Savoy (1480–1530), 131, 143, 256

Margaret Tudor, Queen of Scotland (1489–1541) sister of Henry VIII [Gabrielle Anwar], 5–6, 11, 13–14, 18, 33, 43, 130–33, 162, 184, 271, 297, 320
Marguerite, Queen of Navarre (1492–1549) sister of Francis I and humanist [Sara James], 15, 19, 34, 67, 79, 87, 91, 135, 252
  Mirror of the Soul (Miroir de l'ame perch-ersee), 87
Marie de Guise, Queen of Scotland (1515–60) wife of James V and mother of Mary, Queen of Scots, 43, 48
Marie de Vendome, of Luxembourg, Countess of Vendôme (d. 1547) potential bride for Henry VIII, 43
Marie Tudor, film (1966), 53
Marillac, Charles de (1510–60) French ambassador [Lothaire Bluteau], 47–8
Marin, Georgeta (n.a.) actress: Catherine of Aragon in *The Madness of Henry VIII* (2006), 74
Marshall, Peter (n.a.) historian, 197
Marsh, Jean (b. 1934) actress: Catherine of Aragon in *Monarch* (2000), 73
Martial (Marcus Valerius Martialis, 38/41–102/104), Roman poet, 250
  Ad Seipsum, 250
Martin, Jake (n.a.) journalist, 15
Martin, Wendy Hallam (n.a.) editor, 3
Martyrs, 14, 39, 60, 82, 92, 215–16, 218, 247, 289

INDEX 369

Marx, Karl (1818–83) philosopher, 36
  Marxist theory, 170, 195, 201
Mary, Princess a/k/a Mary I
  (1516–58) daughter of Henry
  VIII and Catherine of Aragon
  [Bláthnaid McKeown, Sarah
  Bolger], 4–6, 10–11, 31,
  34–44, 46–7, 49, 60, 62, 64,
  66–71, 81, 98–100, 104,
  106–10, 112, 116–25,
  129–32, 134, 144, 148,
  156–58, 162–63, 204, 215,
  232, 253, 255–56, 266, 271,
  275, 277, 283, 288–89, 296,
  302, 304, 334, 338
Mary, Queen of Scots (1542–87),
  29, 30, 48, 130, 133
Mary Rose, ship, 34, 187
Mary Tudor, Queen of France
  (1496–1533) sister of Henry
  VIII, wife of Louis XII and
  Charles Brandon, 7, 11, 13, 33,
  162–63, 184, 271, 320
Maskall, Jake (b. 1971) actor: Sir
  Henry Pole, 42
Massie, Elizabeth (n.a.) co–author with
  Michael Hirst of *The Tudors:
  King Takes Queen* (novel 2008),
  307
Matheson, Hans (b. 1975) actor:
  Archbishop Thomas Cranmer,
  4, 142, 213–14
Maxudian, Max (1881–1976) actor:
  Henry VIII in *Anne de Boleyn*
  (1913), 52
May, Jodhi (b. 1975) actress: Anne
  Boleyn in *The Other Boleyn Girl*
  (2003), 31, 86
McCarthy, Colm b. 1973) director, 3
McCarty, Nick (n.a.) screenwriter for
  The Six Wives of Henry VIII
  (1970), 85

McCusker, Frank (b. 1967) actor:
  Thomas Wriothesley as Risley,
  4, 46
McDougall, Charles (n.a.) director, 3
McElhinney, Ian (b. 1948) actor: Pope
  Clement VII, 35
McGrath, Katie (b. 1983) actress: Bess
  Webbe, 37, 316
McKeown, Bláthnaid (n.a.) actress:
  Princess Mary, 10, 117
McNair, Andrew (b. 1979) actor:
  Sir Thomas Seymour, 4, 42,
  105, 148
McSheffrey, Shannon (n.a.) historian, 136
McSorley, Gerard (b. 1950) actor:
  Robert Aske, 216–17, 228
Medici, Alessandro de, Duke of Medici
  (1511/12–37), 189
Medici, Catherine de, Queen of France
  (1519–89), 47
Medici, Cosimo I de, Duke of Medici
  (1519–74), 189
Medicine, 22–3, 329–42, *see also*
  Disease
  Apothecaries, 23, 331–33; Society
    of (founded 1617 from
    Grocer's Company), 333
  Barber–Surgeons, 23, 329, 331–33;
    Company of (founded 1540),
    331–32
  Hygiene, 335
  Midwives, 104, 107, 334, 338
  New Medicine, 340
  Physicians, 23, 219, 227, 329–34;
    College of (founded 1518),
    330–31
  Surgeons, 330–34, 337
Mendoza y Zúñiga, Íñigo López de
  (1476–1535) Spanish
  ambassador, 34, 42, 54, 67–8,
  129, 255, 271
Merchants, 180, 241

370 INDEX

Merchant, Tamzin (b. 1987) actress: Catherine Howard, 4, 10, 45, 97, 106, 296
Meyers, Jonathan Rhys (b. 1977) actor: Henry VIII, 1, 3, 7–8, 13–15, 21, 27–8, 32, 45–6, 49–50, 57, 64–6, 82, 89, 93, 128, 140, 143, 149–50, 179, 186, 190–91, 197–90, 201, 205–06, 211–12, 219, 257, 277–78, 289, 295–98, 300–01, 306, 314–16, 329
Michelangelo di Lodovico Buonarroti Simoni (1475–1564) Italian artist [James McHale], 286–87
Michell, Keith (1926–2015) actor: Henry VIII in *Six Wives of Henry VIII* (1970), *Henry VIII and His Six Wives* (1972), *The Prince and the Pauper* (1996), 28
Milan, Francis II Sforza, Duke of (1495–1535), 286
Minions, 40, 129, 159–60
  Boon companions, 13
  Expulsion of, 129, 160
Misseldon, Ursula, fictional royal mistress [Charlotte Salt], 6, 28, 40, 71, 127, 160, 284, 287, 323–25
Molina, Mélida (n.a.) actress: Catherine of Aragon in *Carlos, Rey Emperador* (2015), 74
Monasteries, 9, 86, 88, 99–100, 249
  Dissolution of, 16, 18, 41, 145, 174, 214, 217, 227, 238, 253, 258, 333
Montague, Rachel (b. 1987) unnamed character who sleeps with Henry VIII, 134, 315
Montoya, Iñigo, fictional character in *The Princess Bride* [Mandy Patinkin], 14

Montreuil, France, 48
More, Sir Thomas (1478–1535) courtier, humanist, and martyr [Jeremy Northam], 1, 4–5, 7, 13–14, 16, 18–19, 27, 29, 31–2, 36, 38–9, 50, 60–5, 67, 69–70, 77–8, 82, 91–2, 168, 170–75, 177, 180, 201, 209, 215–16, 219, 236, 237, 249–53, 257–58, 260–61, 266, 268, 270, 282, 304, 330, *see also* Roper, Margaret
  Supplication of Souls, A (1529), 173
  Utopia (1516), 19, 173, 249, 251–52, 258, 260
More, The (Hertfordshire), 37, 69–70, 157, 308
Morison, Richard, humanist (c. 1513–56), 249, 256
  A Remedy for Sedition, 256
Morrison, fictional character in *Braveheart* [Tommy Flanagan], 318
Morris, Trevor (b. 1970) composer, 3
Moses, 108
Movies, *see* Film
Mr. Peabody's Improbable History (1962), 53
Murphy, Gary (n.a.) actor: Richard Rouse, 5, 12
Murphy, Wesley (n.a.) actor: Richard Beard, 43, 100
Murray, Laoise (b. 1996) actress: Princess Elizabeth, 11, 104
Murtagh, Eoin (n.a.): actor Prince Edward, 11, 104, 123, 306
Music, *see* Court Entertainments
Myth, 78, 81, 167, 189, 235, 284–85, 287–88, 290, 291, 313–14
  Psyche, 284–85

N

Nabakov, Vladimir (1899–1977), 10 *Lolita* (1955), 10
Nabakov, Vladimir
  Lolita (1955), 10
Nabakov, Vladimir
  (1899–1977), 10
Najera, Antonio Manrique de Lara, Duke of (d. 1535) Spanish soldier [Fabio Tassone], 48
National Gallery, London, 284, 286
National Portrait Gallery, London, 283
Navy, 29
  Admiral of England, 47, 143
  Admiral of France, 39, 124, 259
  Fleet of France, 187
  Fleet of the Holy Roman Empire, 43
Neill, Sam (b. 1947) actor: Cardinal Thomas Wolsey, 4, 13, 27, 65, 93, 170, 209, 211–12, 224, 339
Nepotism, 215
Netherfield, Mayor of, fictional character in *Pride and Prejudice*, 189
Netherlands, 42, 46, 131, 143
Neville, John, 3rd Baron Latimer (1493–1543) courtier [Michael Elwyn], 6, 45–6, 107–10
Neville, Margaret, daughter of Baron Latimer (1495–?), 112
Newcastle, Earl of, fictional jouster [uncredited], 20, 269
New Men, 150, 224
New World, 251
Nielsen Ratings, 89
Nightmare on Elm Street films (1984–2010), 82
Nobrega, Manoel de (n.a.) actor: Henry VIII in *The Prince and the Pauper* (1972), 53
Nonsuch Palace, 258, 261, 287

Norfolk House, 106
Norris, Sir Henry (before 1500–1536) courtier [Stephen Hogan], 13, 38, 154–56, 165, 202, 273
Northam, Jeremy (b. 1961) actor: Sir Thomas More, 4, 13–14, 27, 65, 170, 173, 209, 215–16, 251, 268

O

Oath of Allegiance, 5
Oatlands Palace, Surrey, 276
Oberon, Merle (1911–79) actress: Anne Boleyn in *The Private Life of Henry VIII* (1933), 85
Observant Franciscans, 61
O'Donoghue, Collin (b. 1981) actor: Philip of Bavaria, 6, 44
Ogle, Charles (1865–1940) actor: Henry VIII in *The Prince and the Pauper* (1909), 52
O'Hara, David (b. 1965) actor: Henry Howard, Earl of Surrey, 4, 29, 149, 306
Omnibus, television series, 31, 53
Orvieto, Italy, 35
Osiander, Andreas (1498–1552) Lutheran theologian, 221
Other Boleyn Girl, The, 34, 54, 84, *see also* Gregory, Philippa
  Film (2008), 31, 61, 115
  Novel (2001), 9, 80
  Television movie (2003), 31, 61, 86
O'Toole, Kate (b. 1960) actress: Lady Margaret Pole, Countess of Salisbury, 42
O'Toole, Peter (1932–2013) actor: Pope Paul III, 5, 37, 215, 226, 286
Oxford University, 61

P

Pace, Richard 1483?–1536) courtier [Matt Ryan], 14, 19, 61, 249, 272
Padua, Italy, 329
Page, Richard (d. 1548) courtier, 38
Pagett, Nicola (b. 1945) actress: Princess Mary in *Anne of the Thousand Days* (1969), 62
Palazzo del Te, Mantua, Italy, 285
Palmer, Lily (1914–86) actress: Anne Boleyn in *The Trial of Anne Boleyn* (1952), 53
Papas, Alkis (b. 1922) actor, 72
Papas, Irene (née Lelekou b. 1926), actress: Catherine of Aragon in *Anne of the Thousand Days* (1969), 59, 62–3, 71, 72
Paracelsus a/k/a Philippus Aureolus Theophrastus Bombastus von Hohenheim (1493–1541), physician, 333, *see also* Disease; Medicine
Paranque, Estelle (n.a.) historian, vi, xiii, 10, 64, 115–26
Pardon of the Clergy (1531), 37
Paris, 103, 160–62, 209. 255
Parker, Henry, 10th Baron Morley (1476/81–1553/56) courtier [Alan Stanford], 256–57
Parker, Matthew, Archbishop of Parker (1504–75), 9
Parliament, 15, 28, 36–7, 41, 46, 102, 107, 134, 144, 153, 181, 213, 219, 237–38, 325, 330, 332, *see also* Statutes
House of Lords, 240
Parr, Catherine, Queen of England (1512–48) sixth wife of Henry VIII [Joely Richardson], 4, 6, 10, 16, 19, 45–7, 49, 54, 65, 97, 107–11, 112, 119–20, 123–24, 148, 217–18, 254, 259, 277, 296, 302, 321, 334, 337

Lamentations of a Sinner, 260
Prayers and Meditations, 110
Parrill, Sue, literary scholar, v
Paso, Encarna (b. 1931) actress: Catherine of Aragon in *Mujeres insólitas* (1977), 73
Pasquagliano, 128
Patinkin, Mandy (b. 1952) actor: Iñigo Montoya in *The Princess Bride* (1987), 14
Patric, Michael (n.a.) actor: Anthony Willoughby, 68
Patton, Frank (n.a.) actor: Henry VIII in *Beauty and the Beast: Masques* (1987), 53
Paul, Anthony (n.a.) actor: Henry VIII in *The Golden Age* (1967), 53
Paulet, William, 1st Marquess of Winchester (1483/5–72), 46
Paul III, Pope (Alessandro Farnese, b. 1468, r. 1534–49) [Peter O'Toole], 5, 17, 37, 39, 215, 226, 275, 286, 287, 297, 304
Paulinus, Bishop of York (d. 644), 49, 278
Pauly–Winterstein, Hedwig (1866–1965) actress: Catherine of Aragon in *Anna Boleyn* (1920), 73
Pavia, Battle of (1525), 34, 67, 270, 331
Peasants Revolt, German (1524–25), 36
Peerson, Anthony (n.a.) chorister, 47
Peiró, Victoria (n.a.) actress: Catherine of Aragon in *The Twisted Tale of Bloody Mary* (2008), 74
Pellerin, Krysten (b. 1983) actress: Elizabeth Darrell, 70, 157, 308
Pendleton, Carlie (n.a.) historian, vi, xiii, 19, 265–80
Pepe le Pew, cartoon character, 14
Perez, Samantha (n.a.) historian, v, xiii, 19, 64, 249–64
Pertwee, Sean (b. 1964) Henry's (nonexistent) uncle, 11, 129

Pharaoh, 108
Philip of Bavaria the Contentious, Duke of Palatinate–Neuberg (1503–48) [Colin O'Donoghue], 6, 44, 119, 259
Philip, Prince of Spain, later Philip II (b. 1527, r. 1556–98), 117
Philosophy, 180, 249, 251–52, 255, 261, 333
  Neo–Platonism, 180
Pickford, Mary (1892–1979) actress, 85
Pilgrimage of Grace (1536–37), 5–6, 13, 17–18, 29, 41, 54, 107, 109, 143, 163–64, 181, 204, 211, 216–17, 223, 228–32
  Doncaster Agreement, 228–29
Plantagenet, Arthur, Viscount Lisle (pre–1472–1542) diplomat, 45
Plantagenets, 18, 33, 42, 179, 232, 260
Plato (424/423–348/347 BC) Greek philosopher, 180
Platonic love, 20, 79, 269
Podeswa, Jeremy (b. 1962) director, 3
Pole, Cardinal Reginald (1500–58) [Mark Hildreth], 6, 13, 19, 42, 159, 204, 215, 231, 297, 325
  Defence of the Unity of the Church (Pro ecclesiasticae unitatis defensione), 42
Pole Conspiracy, 17–18, 163, 231–32
Pole, Henry [Daniel Rhattigan–Walsh], 231–32
Pole, Henry, Lord Montague (1492–1539) alleged conspirator [Jake Maskall], 231–32
Pole, Margaret, Countess of Salisbury (1473–1541) alleged conspirator [Kate O'Toole], 17, 160–61, 231
Pole, Sir Geoffrey (d. 1558) alleged conspirator, 231
Pollard, A.F. (1869–1948) historian, 34

Pollard, Justin (b. 1968) historian and consultant, 283, 329, 339
Pontefract, Yorkshire, 105, 229
Poovey, Mary (n.a.) literary scholar, 200, 202
Popincourt, Jane (n.a.) royal mistress?, 134
Popular culture, 24, 49, 84, 167
Portman, Natalie (b.1981) actress: Anne Boleyn in *The Other Boleyn Girl* (2008), 31
Portugal, 5–6, 11, 14, 33–4, 43, 67, 130–31, 184, 297
Poulain, Jean Le (1924–88) actor: Henry VIII in *La jument du roi* (1973), 53
Presley, Elvis (1935–77) singer, 150
Prince and the Pauper, The, novel (1881), 11, 30
  Films (1909, 1915, *Prinz und Bettelknabe* /1920, 1937), 52
  Films (1957, 1962, 1972, 1976, *Crossed Swords* 1977), 53
  Film (1996), 31
  Film (2000), 53
Princess, Bride, The (1987), 14
Printing press, 146
Private Life of Henry VIII, The, film (1933), 4, 30, 40, 44, 51, 52, 60, 78–9, 85, 115
Privy Chamber, 15–16, 99, 108, 154, 155, 160, 183, 190, 226, 275, 287
Privy Council, 16, 106, 164, 171, 181, 243, 310
Protestantism, 6, 10, 14, 16, 17, 32, 43, 60, 61, 65, 82, 84, 87, 101, 102, 135, 174, 209–20, 243, 254, 255, 258, 260, 289
  and the Reformation, 209–22
Protestantism, and Reformation, 209–22
Protestant League, 43, 100

Prue, Katharina (n.a.), 214, 221
Pryce, Jonathan (b. 1947) actor: Cardinal Thomas Wolsey in *Wolf Hall* (2015), 60

Q

Quayle, Anthony (1913–89) actor: Cardinal Thomas Wolsey in *Anne of the Thousand Days* (1969), 62
Queen's Closet, 40, 46, 109, 275, 277
Quilligan, Dennis (n.a.) actor: unnamed physician, 332

R

Radcliffe, Robert, 1st Earl of Sussex (c. 1483–1542), 125
Radd, Ronald (1929–76) actor: Henry VIII in *The Prince and the Pauper* (1976), 53
Rampling, Charlotte (b. 1946) actress: Anne Boleyn in *Henry VIII and His Six Wives* (1972), 86
Rankin, Mark (n.a.) literary scholar, 167
Rape of Ganymede, painting, 283
Rawi, Ousama (b. 1931) cinematographer, 3
Reeves, Gemma (b. 1982) actress: Margaret Roper as Margaret Moore, 36
Reform, 5, 9, 16, 36, 41, 46, 61, 86–8, 91, 108, 146, 159, 164, 173, 209–20, 221, 226, 243–44, 254, 325, 331, 339
Reformation, 2, 8, 17, 36–7, 47, 54, 60, 82, 84, 99, 128, 134, 141, 174, 209–20, 226, 238, 254, 274, 289, 297
Regent, 9, 48, 108, 109, 111, 150, 225
Relic Hunter: The Royal Ring, television episode (2001), 53

Ré, Michel de (1925–79) actor: Henry VIII in *Marie Tudor* (1966), 53
Renaissance, 7, 8, 19, 28, 131, 173, 180, 185, 249–52, 256, 258
Renaissance man, 15, 28, 50, 54, 61, 128
Renaissance monarchy, 180, 199
Rhattigan–Walsh, David (n.a.) actor: Henry Pole, 42
Rich, Adrienne (1929–2012) feminist, 313, 327
Richard III, King of England (b. 1452, r. 1483–85), 140, 162, 225, 282, 334
Richardson, Glenn (n.a.) historian, vi, xiii, 14, 64, 179–94
Richardson, Joely (b. 1965) actress: Catherine Parr, 4, 10, 45, 65. 97, 218, 227, 296, 334
Richmond Palace, Surrey, 101, 102, 103, 259
Rich, Richard, 1st Baron Rich (1496/7–1567) courtier [Rob Hallett], 4, 14, 105, 175, 258
Riddoch, Billy (n.a.) actor: Henry VIII in *Border Warfare* (1990), 53
Rignault, Alexandre (1901–85) actor: Henry VIII in *Francis I* (1937), 52
Ripon, North Yorkshire, 230
Risley (Wriothesley, Thomas), 1st Earl of Southampton (1505–50) courtier [Frank McCusker], 4, 14, 46–7, 105, 108, 109
Robison, William (b. 1954) historian, xiii, 1–76, 144, 169
Rochester Castle, Kent, 101
Rodríguez, Natalia (b. 1992) actress: Catherine of Aragon in *Isabel* (2014), 74
Rogers, Paul (1917–2013) actor: Henry VIII in *The White Falcon* (1956), 53

Rohan, Eamon (n.a.) actor: Archbishop William Warham, 36
Rollett, Ramond (1907–61) actor: Henry VIII in *The Trial of Andy Fothergill* (1951), 52
Romano, Giulio (c. 1499–1546) Italian painter, 285
Wedding Feast of Cupid and Psyche, 285
Romantics, 82
Rome, 8, 36, 64, 68, 117, 156, 160, 212, 256, 261, 314
  Break with, 8, 29, 39, 41, 87, 118, 121, 172, 173, 174, 226, 231, 293, 297
  Sack of, 34
Rome, television series (2005–07), 7
Ronan, Paul (b. 1965) actor: William, Duke of Cleves, 43, 100
Roper, Margaret (née More, 1505–44) daughter of Thomas More [Gemma Reeves], 36
Rosenstone, Robert (n.a.) film historian, 191
Rose Without a Thorn, The films (1947, 1952), 52
Rouen, Treaty (1517), 129
Rough Wooing (1543–51), 29, 130
Rouillon, Philippe (n.a.) actor: Henry VIII in Shakespeare's *Henry VIII* (1991), 53
Rouse, Richard (d. 1531) cook and poisoner [Gary Murphy], 5, 12, 14, 18, 144
Rousselot, Brigitte, fictional mistress of Brandon [Selma Brooke], 6, 46, 71, 205, 318, 322
Rousselot, Monsieur, fictional father of Brigitte [Owen Aaronovitch], 38
Royal Collection (Art), 282–83

Royal Officials and Servants
Carver, 183
Chamberlain (character), 16
Cupbearer, 197
Esquire of the Body, 162
Gentleman of the Privy Chamber, 155, 160
Groom of the Privy Chamber, 275
Groom of the Stool, 154, 155, 183
Knight of the Body, 159
Lord Chamberlain of the Household, 16
Lord Chancellor, 36, 37, 252, 255, 260
Lord Great Chamberlain, 16
Lord High Admiral, 47, 143, 259
Lord High Steward, 240
Lord President of the Privy Council, 164
Lord Privy Seal, 36–7, 325
Lord Protector, 37, 49
Lord Treasurer, 143
Marshal of the Royal Household, 162
Master of the Children of the Chapel Royal, 271
Master of the Great Wardrobe, 295
Master of the Horse, 162
Master of the King's Jewels, 156
Master of the Revels, 144
Sewer, 183
Sheriff, 158
Rumor, 41, 98, 99–100, 104, 120, 127, 131, 133, 135, 161, 187, 214, 227, 276
Ryan, Jonathan (n.a.) actor: unnamed French ambassador, 39
Ryan, Matt (b. 1981) actor: Richard Pace, 14
Rylance, Mark (b. 1960) actor: Thomas Cromwell in *Wolf Hall* (2015), 60

S

Sacraments, 16, 28, 36, 210–11
   Baptism, 298
   Christening, 146, 156
   Confession, 41, 66, 68, 186, 215, 217, 219, 325
   Eucharist, 218
   Extreme Unction, 219
   Marriage, 5–6, 9–13, 21, 29–35, 39–41, 43–4, 48, 60–4, 67–8, 83, 85, 97–8, 102–05, 107, 117–19, 129–32, 134–35, 139, 142–45, 148–49, 155, 157–58, 162–64, 181, 183–85, 210, 215, 259, 265, 270, 274–77, 286, 296–97, 301, 309, 318–20, 323
   Mass, 67, 183, 210–12, 217, 219, 307–09, 311, 325
   Transubstantiation, 217–18, 325
Saint–Denis, France, 48
Salt, Charlotte (b. 1985) actress: Ursula Misseldon, 6, 40, 136, 323
Salvo, Brian de (n.a.) actor: William Knight, 35
Sander, Nicholas (c. 1530–81) Catholic polemicist, 9, 81, 99
Sandle, Jack (n.a.) actor: Bishop Hugh Latimer, 108
Saville, Nan, fictional servant of Anne Boleyn [Serena Brabazon], 122
Savonarola, Girolamo (1452–98) friar and reformer, 108
Scarisbrick, J.J. (b. 1928) historian, 227
Schama, Simon (b. 1945) historian, 78
Schatew Vert (Chateau Vert), 144, 271–72
Schmalkaldic League, 43
Schneider, Ron (b. 1963) actor: Henry VIII in *Love Across Time* (2010), 54
Schreiber, Albert (n.a.) actor: Henry VIII in *Prinz und Bettelknabe* (1920), 52
Schulz, Eva Katharina (1922–2007) actress: Catherine of Aragon in *Heinrich VIII und seine Frauen* (1968), 73
Science and pseudo-science, 23, *see also* Medicine
   Alchemy, 23
   Astrology, 23, 330–31
   Elements (earth, air, fire, water), 23
   Humoral theory, 23, 330, 333
   Magic, 23, 330
Scofield, Paul (1922–2008) actor: Sir Thomas More in *A Man for All Seasons* (1966), 31
Scotland, 29, 33, 43, 48, 65, 72, 129–30, 162, 184, 241
Scott, Deborah Lynn (b. 1954) costumer for *Titanic* (1997), 298, 305
Scott, Margareta (1912–2005) actress: Catherine of Aragon in *The White Falcon* (1956), 73
Scrots, William (fl. 1537–53) Dutch painter, 306
Scut (Skut), John (fl. 1519–47) mathematician and tailor, 296
Seneca the Younger (Lucius Annaeus Seneca, 4 BC–65 AD), philosopher, 180
Serna, Assumpta (b. 1957) actress: Catherine of Aragon in *Henry VIII* (2003), 61
Seward, Danny (n.a.) actor: Sir Robert Tavistock, 40, 324
Sex, 1–2, 5–6, 8–10, 13, 15, 18–19, 21–2, 28, 32, 34, 36–8, 40, 42, 44–5, 49, 60, 65–8, 70–1, 79, 82–4, 88, 90, 93, 97, 101, 104–07, 115, 124–25, 127–28,

131–32, 134, 136, 143, 146–48, 159, 172, 177, 182–84, 186, 189–91, 198–99, 203–04, 206, 214, 226, 236, 239, 244, 247, 267–68, 271, 285, 307–25, 326, 327, 337, *see also* Crime
 Adultery, 5, 12, 38, 53, 83, 98, 105, 135, 145, 148, 156, 206, 215, 273–75, 315, 320
 Brothels, 12, 43, 45, 337
 Celibacy, 93, 217, 323, 325
 Chastity, 201, 217, 323, 325
 Eroticism, 7, 16, 188, 198, 199, 203, 204, 210, 236, 283, 319, 325
 Homosexuality, 12, 13, 20, 22, 28, 146, 151, 154, 198, 224, 273–74, 283, 313, 327
 Nudity, 4, 7, 22, 28, 45–6, 83, 90, 104, 106, 121, 135–36, 256, 283–85, 287, 297, 308, 317, 319, 324–25
 Pornography, 2, 4, 22, 31, 115, 119
 Virginity, 44, 101, 308–12, 316, 320–22
Seymour family, 6, 12, 139, 141, 147, 161
Seymour, Edward, Duke of Somerset (c. 1500–1552), uncle of Prince Edward [Max Brown], 17–18, 42, 45–6, 48–9, 147–49, 160, 204, 217–18, 231–32, 243
Seymour family, 6, 12, 139, 141, 147, 161
Seymour, Jane, Queen of England (1508/9–1537) third wife of Henry VIII [Anita Briem, Annabelle Wallis], 4–5, 10, 13, 20, 32, 38, 97–100, 110, 118, 123, 125, 135, 141–42, 145–46, 158, 164, 190, 200, 214, 227, 257, 274–75, 277, 282, 285–88, 296, 302, 304, 323, 331, 336, 338, 339

Seymour, Sir John (1474–1537) father of Queen Jane [Stephen Brennan], 147
Seymour, Thomas, 1st Baron Seymour of Sudeley (in or before 1509–1549), uncle of Prince Edward [Andrew McNair], 6, 11, 42, 46–7, 105, 107, 109, 148, 161, 175
Shadow of the Tower, television series (1972), 21, 73
Shakespeare in Love, film (1998), 7
Shakespeare, William (1564–1616) playwright, 28, 30–2, 49, 61, 168, 187
 Famous History of the Life of King Henry the Eight, The, 30, 32
 Henry V, 187
 Merchant of Venice, The, 185
 Twelfth Night, 305
Sharpe, James (n.a.) historian, 238
Sharp, Jason (n.a.), actor: Henry VIII in *The Twisted Tale of Bloody Mary* (2008), 32
Sharrock, Ken (1950–2005) actor: Henry VIII in *Agony* (1981), 53
Shaw, Robert (1927–78) actor: Henry VIII in *A Man for All Seasons* (1966), 28, 31, 191
Shaxton, Nicholas, Bishop of Salisbury (c. 1485–1556), 9
Shelton, Madge (1510/15–70/71) royal mistress? [Laura Jane Laughlin], 5, 11, 13, 38, 135, 155
Shelton, Mary (1510/15–70/71) royal mistress?, 135
Shill, Steve (n.a.) director, 3
Simpsons, The: 'Margical History Tour' (2004), 45
Sisson, Rosemary (b. 1923) television writer for *The Six Wives of Henry VIII* (1970), 85

Sistine Chapel, 286–87
Last Judgment, 287
Sittow, Michael (c. 1469–1525) Estonian painter, 71
Sixteenth Century Society and Conference, v
Six Wives of Henry VIII, The, television miniseries (1970), 9, 21, 31, 59, 62, 79, 85
Skelton, John (c. 1463–1529) poet, 196–97
Bowge of Court, The, 196–97
Smeaton, Mark (c. 1512–36) musician [David Alpay], 12, 20, 38, 70, 83, 146–47, 273–74
Snitow, Ann (n.a.) literary scholar, 199
Solway Moss, Battle of (1542), 29, 48
Somers, Will (d. 1559) court fool [David Bradley], 6, 13, 261
Soprano, Tony, fictional character in *The Sopranos* (1999–2007), 31
Spain, 32, 43, 68, 81, 156, 266, 301, 314
Spurs, Battle of (Guinegate 1513), 29, 65
Staatliche Museen, Berlin, 286
Stafford, Anna (n.a.) daughter of the Duke of Buckingham, misnamed Anne Buckingham [Anna Brewster], 133, 198, 224, 321–22
Stafford, Edward, 3rd Duke of Buckingham (1478–1521), courtier [Steve Waddington], 5, 12, 17, 33, 66, 140, 143–44, 154, 175, 182–84, 197–98, 223–25, 232, 240, 269–70, 277, 297, 304, 321–22
Stanhope (Seymour), Anne, Duchess of Somerset (c. 1510–87) wife of Edward Seymour [Emma Hamilton], 4, 6, 12, 22, 46. 71, 148, 160, 204, 218, 296

Stansfield, Emma (b. 1978) actress: Anne Askew, 6, 108, 218
Starkey, David b. 1945) historian, 9, 15, 78, 80, 87, 112, 148, 227
Starkey, Thomas (c. 1495–1538) humanist, 249
Stater, Victor (n.a.) historian, vi, xiii, 13, 153–66
Statutes, 99, 174, 238, 332, *see also* Parliament
Annates (1532), 37
Medical Act (1512), 330
Praemunire (1353), 36, 213
Restraint of Appeals (1533), 37, 174, 213
Six Articles (1539), 41, 217, 238, 325
Submission of the Clergy (1533), 37
Succession (1534), 37, 213; Oath, 308
Sumptuary law, 21, 297
Supremacy (1534), 37, 175, 213; Oath, 70, 118
Ten Articles (1536), 41
Treason (1534), 37, 238
Union (1540), 332
St. Casilda of Toledo (d. c. 1050), 61
St. Crispin's Day (25 October, feast day of Crispin and Crispinian, martyred c. 286), 187
Steadman, Catherine (n.a.) actress: Joan Bulmer, 45, 104
Sterne, Gordon (b. 1923) actor: Bishop Cuthbert Tunstall, 36
St. Etienne, France, 149
Stewart, Henry, 1st Lord Methven (c. 1495–1553/5), third husband of Margaret Tudor, 11, 33, 130
St. George (275/81–303), 40, 187
St. John, 108, 110
Stockholm Syndrome, 318
Stone, Joss (b. 1987) actor: Anne of Cleves, 4, 16, 43–4, 296, 337
St. Paul's Churchyard, 241

Strickland, Agnes (1796–1874) historian, 84
Strickland, Elizabeth (1794–1875) historian, 84
Stride, John (b. 1936) actor: Henry VIII in Shakespeare's *Henry VIII* (1979), 53
String, Tatiana C. (n.a.) art historian, vi, xiii, 3, 20, 24, 51, 97, 102, 128, 204, 281–92
Strype, John (1643–1737) historian, 252
Stuart, Henry, Lord Darnley (1545–67) second husband of Mary, Queen of Scots, 33, 130
Sword and the Rose, The, film (1953), 73
Sydney, Basil (1894–1968) actor: Henry VIII in *The Rose Without a Thorn* (1952), 52
Syon Monastery, 249

T
Tacitus, Publius Cornelius (c. 56–117) Roman historian, 123, 250, 253
Tailboys, Elizabeth (c. 1520–c. 1563) daughter of Elizabeth Blount, 134
Tailboys, Gilbert, 1st Baron Tailboys of Kyme (1497/8–1530), husband of Elizabeth Blount, 134
Talleyrand, Lord, fictional French official [Jean-David Beroard], 42
Tallis, Thomas (1503–85) musician and composer [Joe Van Moyland], 13, 20, 28, 154, 183, 272–73, 285, 317, 327
Jane and Joan, fictional twins associated with Tallis, 273
Tassone, Fabio (n.a.) actor: Duke of Najera, 48
Tattershall College, Lincolnshire, 164

Tavistock, Robert, fictional courtier [Danny Seward], 21, 40, 287, 323–24
Teems, David (n.a.) biographer, 86
Television, 1–3, 7–8, 30–1, 51, 53, 61, 71, 72, 73, 77, 79–82, 86, 97, 115, 139–40, 150, 156, 159, 171, 173, 179, 197–98, 200–01, 203, 206, 210, 235, 240, 265, 269, 282, 284, 296, 298–99, 306, 310–11, 339
Temple, 335
Terrible Tudors, The (Horrible Histories), television, 54
Testwood, Robert (c. 1490–1543) musician and martyr [Lee Williams], 47, 218, 222
Thames River, 241
Therouanne, France, 29, 65
Throckmorton, Anne (n.a.) historian, vi, xiii, 12, 139–52
Tiramani, Jenny (n.a.) costumer for the Globe Theatre, 299, 305
Titanic, film (1997), 298
Titian (Tiziano Vecellio, c. 1488/90–1576) Italian painter, 284
Venus of Urbino, 284
Toledo, 129
Toledo, Eleonora di (1522–62) wife of Cosimo I de' Medici, 189–90
Toledo, Treaty of (1539), 43
Torrent, Ana (b. 1966) actress: Catherine of Aragon in *The Other Boleyn Girl* (2008), 61
Torture, 18, 47, 78, 105, 174, 218, 230, 243–44
Tournai, France, 29, 65, 266
Towns, 180
Travis, Pete (n.a.) director of *Henry VIII* (2003), 31
Treaty, 14, 19, 32, 43, 47, 48, 49, 129, 158, 172, 173, 250, 257, 261, 266, 268, 269, 271

Treviso, Girolamo de (1508–44) Italian painter [Daniel Caltagirone], 48
Trial of Andy Fothergill, The, film (1951), 52
Trial of Anne Boleyn, The, television episode from *Omnibus1* (952), 31
Tropes, 8, 12, 30, 44, 51, 52, 290
Tudor Despotism, 237
Tudorism, 3, 24, 31, 51, 128
Tudor, Jasper, Duke of Bedford (c. 1431–95), uncle of Henry VII, 11, 129
Tudor Princess, film (1913), 52, 73
Tudor Rose, animated short (2008), 54, 74
Tudor Rose, film (1936), 52
Tudors and Stuarts on Film, Historical Perspectives, v
Tudors: King Takes Queen, The, novel (2008), 307, *see also* Hirst, Michael and Massie, Elizabeth
Tudors on Film and Television, The, v
Tudors, The (2007–10):, 6, 20, 27, 72, 102, 191, 197, 299, 327, *see also* Hirst, Michael
 Anachronism, 1, 5, 20, 64, 66, 68, 171–72, 180, 197, 201, 210, 213–14, 249–50, 272, 275, 277, 282, 284
 Awards, 2, 31, 61–2, 191, 303;
  Academy, 305;
  BAFTA, 72, 305;
  Emmy, 21, 150, 298;
  Gemini, 72;
  Golden Globe, 150;
  IFTA, 72;
  Tony, 305;
  The Tudors complete list, 24

Characterization, 9, 27, 63, 86, 115, 170, 172–73, 191, 197, 322
Chauvinism, 40
Cinematography, 3
Costuming, 3, 7, 21, 28, 190–91, 289, 293–306
Dialogue, 6, 10, 21, 79, 171, 202–03, 319
Ethics, 203, 236, 244
Gaze, 196, 201, 300
Gesture, 284, 287, 289
Historical drama, 2, 6, 7, 28, 32, 66, 78, 82, 84, 115, 116, 121, 127, 140, 147, 162, 164, 167, 168, 169, 171, 191, 192, 195, 210, 219, 235, 236, 239, 240, 245, 265, 282, 298, 312;
 Historicism, 196, 244
History, Burden of, 196, 199, 205
Mise-en-abyme, 290
Mise-en-scène, 20, 281–90, 299
Misogyny, 22, 34, 50, 66, 87, 172, 199, 314, 322
Narrative, 10, 63, 71, 78–81, 110, 141, 167, 169, 172–73, 187–88, 196–97, 200–04, 206, 211, 237, 244, 267, 281, 283–84, 288–90, 329
Networks (BBC2 United Kingdom, CBC Television Canada, TV3 Ireland), 2
Plot, 2–3, 11, 22, 29, 33, 34, 48, 49, 54, 86, 130, 133, 134, 135, 136, 141, 191, 205, 223, 226, 228, 231, 236, 269, 270, 281, 283, 284, 285, 286, 296, 299
Postmodernism, 7, 13, 59, 71, 167–75, 197, 250, 289–90
Presentism, 14, 128, 168, 172
Publicity, 22, 90, 192, 236, 317, 327

Scenery, 191
Screenplay, 3, 62, 102
Seasons (all), 1, 4, 24, 71, 97, 125, 171, 210, 219, 232–33, 284, 329; One, 2, 4–5, 9, 12–13, 22, 29, 32, 36, 59, 82–3, 87–9, 117, 128, 133, 140–44, 146, 148–50, 154, 156, 172, 177, 181, 183–84, 190, 197–98, 209, 212–13, 223, 228, 236, 250, 257, 259, 261, 272–73, 322, 336; Two, 2, 4–5, 7, 10, 13, 16, 27, 29, 36, 39, 40, 59, 69, 70, 83, 87, 88–9, 97, 117, 128, 135, 141, 143–47, 150, 174, 184, 190–91, 212–15, 225, 226, 236, 258–59, 261, 273, 304, 307, 327; Three, 2, 4–5, 10, 13, 28–9, 40–1, 44–6, 70, 90, 97, 99, 116–18, 127, 136, 141, 149, 160, 174–75, 204–05, 213, 215–17, 228, 231, 258, 259, 261, 289, 317; Four, 2, 4, 6, 12, 27–9, 45–6, 65, 70, 90, 116–19, 146, 148–49, 164, 215–17, 240, 250, 258–59, 261, 276, 295, 306
Showtime, 2, 25, 59, 84, 97, 104, 107, 109–10, 115, 162, 169, 307–08, 329, 335
Soap opera, 7, 8, 28, 37, 50, 127, 130, 148, 265
Sony Pictures Television International, 2
Space, 3, 90, 127, 153, 183, 195–96, 198–202, 204, 206, 240, 241, 282, 283
Staging, 28, 195, 271, 281, 283, 284
Voyeurism, 52, 199
Tunis, 39

Tunstall, Cuthbert, Bishop of Durham (1474–1559) courtier [Gordon Sterne], 36, 68
Turks, 44, 47, 257, 266
Tutin, Dorothy (1930–2001) actress: Anne Boleyn in *The Six Wives of Henry VIII* (1970), 85
Twain, Mark, author (1835–1910), 31, *see also Prince and the Pauper, The*
Twisted Tale of Bloody Mary, The, film (2008), 31, 74
Tyndale, William, Biblical translator (c. 1494–1536), 9, 258
Obedience of the Christian Man (1528), 9, 258

U
Uffizi, 284
U.F.O., film (1993), 53
Undercover Scandals of Henry VIII, The, a/k/a Royal Flesh, film (1970), 53–4
United Nations, 173
Urbino, Italy, 11, 32, 129, 284

V
Val D'Or, France, 33, 267–68
Valor Ecclesiasticus, 27, 144, 210, 324
Vanbrugh, Violet (1867–1942) actress: Catherine of Aragon in *Henry VIII* (1911), 73
Van Mander, Karel (1548–1606) Flemish painter, 284, 288
Het Schilder-boeck (The Book of Painting, 1603–1604), 284
Van Moyland, Joe (b. 1983) actor: Thomas Tallis, 272, 327

Van Sprang, Alan (b. 1971) actor: Sir Francis Bryan, 4, 29, 40, 104, 159, 323
Van Sprundel, Tamara (n.a.) actress: Catherine of Aragon in *A Royal Love* (2016), 74
Vazquez, Yolanda (n.a.) actress: Catherine of Aragon in *The Other Boleyn Girl* (2003), 61
Velázquez, Diego Rodríguez de Silva (1599–1660) Spanish painter, 284
Rokeby Venus, 284
Venice, Italy, 185, 286
Doge, 185, 286
Vicary, Thomas (c. 1490–1561) physician, 332
Vice(s), 34, 196
Vicegerent for Ecclesiastical Affairs, 37
Victoria & Albert Museum, London, 283
Victorians, 82, 84, 85
Villars, Duchess of, sister of Gabrielle d'Estrees, 283
Violence, 2, 18–19, 105, 107, 115–18, 125, 215, 235–48, 257–58, 261
Virgin Mary, 40, 185, 215
Virtue(s), 34, 98, 185, 211, 269, 294, 311, 313, 323
Visual Artefact (company), 283
Vives, Jean Luis (c. 1493–1540) humanist, 61
Education of Christian Women, The (De institutione foeminae Christianae), 61
Volny, August (n.a.) actor: Henry VIII in *Anne Boleyn* (1911), 52
Von Sydow, Max (b. 1929) actor: Cardinal Von Waldburg, 42
Von Waldburg, Cardinal Otto Truchsess (1514–73) [Max Von Sydow], 42

W
Waddington, Stephen (b. 1968), actor: Duke of Buckingham, 5, 33, 66, 197–98, 223, 269
Wainwright, Rebekah (b. 1988) actress: Catherine Brooke, 318–21
Wakeham, Julia (n.a.) actress: Margarete Cranmer misidentified as Katharina Prue, 214, 221
Wales, 186
Prince of, 68, 309
Princess Dowager of, 70
Welsh Marches, 144
Walker Art Gallery, Liverpool, 289
Walker, Greg (n.a.) literary scholar, 227
Wallis, Annabelle (b. 1984) actress: Jane Seymour, 4, 10, 40, 97, 99, 142, 296, 304, 331
Walsh, Dearbhla (n.a.) director, 3
Walsingham, Our Lady of, 61, 66, 219
Walton, Kristen (n.a.) historian, vi, xiii, 11, 127–38
War, 7, 8, 15, 29, 32, 65, 99, 173, 174, 179, 180, 181, 187, 188, 229, 230, 250–52, 257–59, 261, 269, 270, 318, 320, 322, 337
with France, 1, 5, 15, 32, 48, 108, 129, 133, 171, 187, 257, 261
Habsburg–Valois War (1521–26), 266
with the Holy Roman Empire, 5
Hundred Years War, 188
Martial Arts, 165, 188
War on terror, 314
Wars of the Roses, 179
World War II, 168
Ward, Simon (1941–2012) actor: Bishop Stephen Gardiner, 4, 29, 99, 217–18

Warham, William, Archbishop of Canterbury (c. 1450–1532) [Eamon Rohan], 36, 37, 68
Warnicke, Retha (n.a.) historian, vi, xiii, 10, 56, 97–114, 151
Warwickshire, 154, 273
WASP, 313, 315
Waterford, Ireland, 161
Webbe, Bess (n.a.) royal mistress or victim [Katie McGrath], 37, 135–36, 316–18
Webbe, William (n.a.) husband of Bess [Damien Kearney], 37, 135–36, 316–18, 324
Weeks, Perdita, (b. 1985) actress: Mary Boleyn, 11, 34, 65, 134
Weir, Alison (b. 1951) historian, 136, 227, 317
Werich, Jan (1905–80) actor: Henry VIII in *King and Women* (1967), 53
Westminster, 110, 298
  Old Palace Yard, 241
  Tothill, 241
  Westminster Hall, 275
  Westminster sanctuary, 136
Weston, Sir Francis (1511–36) courtier, 38
Whalley, Joanne (b.1964) actress: Catherine of Aragon in *Wolf Hall* (2015), 59, 72
Wharton, Thomas, 1st Baron Wharton (1495–1568), 48
When Knighthood Was in Flower, film (1922), 53, 73
White Falcon, The, television episode (1956), 53, 73
Whitehall Palace, London, 32, 282, *see also* York Place
  Whitehall Mural, 20, 21, 32, 49, 190, 204, 288, 289, 292, 332
Whitelock, Anne (n.a.) historian, 235
White Rose Faction, 231

Willoughby, Anthony (fl. 1500–20s) courtier [Michael Patric], 68
Wilson, Woodrow (1856–1924) American president, 14
Windsor Castle, 164
  St. George's Chapel, 164
Wingfield, Sir Richard (in or before 1469–1525) diplomat, 129
Winstone, Ray (b. 1957) actor: Henry VIII in *Henry VIII* (2003), 28, 31, 46, 86
Wolfe, Alice, criminal, 241
Wolfe, John, criminal, 241
Wolf Hall, Wiltshire, 33, 40, 98, 100
Wolf, Naomi, author (b. 1962), 313
Wolsey, Cardinal Thomas (1473–1530), minister [Sam Neill], 1, 4–5, 8, 13–14, 16–17. 19, 27, 29, 32–6, 59, 62–3, 65–9, 81–2, 93, 132, 134–5, 142–45, 160, 170–75, 180–86, 191, 201, 209, 211–12, 216, 219, 224–25, 227, 250, 252–55, 260–61, 266, 270, 272, 274–75, 282–83, 297, 299, 305, 339
Women, 5, 7, 13, 18, 21–2, 34, 37–8, 40, 57, 61, 72–3, 79, 83–4, 89–91, 127, 130, 142, 148, 181–82, 188–90, 203–05, 214, 230, 236, 240–41, 244, 247, 249, 252–56, 259, 268, 271, 283, 294, 296, 298, 301–02, 307–25
  Amazons, 256
  As commodities, 313, 315
Wooding, Lucy (n.a.) historian, 150, 151
Wotton, Nicholas, Dean of Canterbury and York (c. 1497–1567), 102–03, 144
Wriothesley, Charles (1508–62) chronicler, 24

Wriothesley, Thomas. *see* Risley
Wyatt, Elizabeth (née Brooke 1503–60), 157
Wyatt, Sir Henry 1460–1536) courtier and cat fancier, 156
Wyatt, Sir Thomas (c. 1503–42) courtier and poet, 13, 15, 19, 29, 38, 61, 70, 156–59, 161, 165, 196, 201–04, 224, 273, 283, 295, 307–12, 317, 323
  Circa Regna Tonat, 202
  They Flee from Me, 203–04
Wyatt's Rebellion (1554), 117
Wynter, Thomas, Archdeacon of Norfolk (c. 1510–c. 1543) son of Thomas Wolsey, 220

Y
York, 41, 105, 204, 242–43, 260
York Place, London, 99, 100, *see also* Whitehall
Yorkshire, 41, 164, 228, 229–30, 257
Young, Arthur (1898–1959) actor: Henry VIII in *The Rose Without a Thorn* (1947), 52
Young Bess, film (1953), 30

Z
Zinneman, Fred (1907–97) director of *A Man for All Seasons* (1966), 31, 61
Žižek, Slavoj (b. 1949) philosopher, 195, 205

Printed in the United States
By Bookmasters